Charles Eugene Knox

A Year with St. Paul

Fifty-Two Lessons for the Sundays of the Year

Charles Eugene Knox

A Year with St. Paul
Fifty-Two Lessons for the Sundays of the Year

ISBN/EAN: 9783744744522

Printed in Europe, USA, Canada, Australia, Japan

Cover: Foto ©Thomas Meinert / pixelio.de

More available books at **www.hansebooks.com**

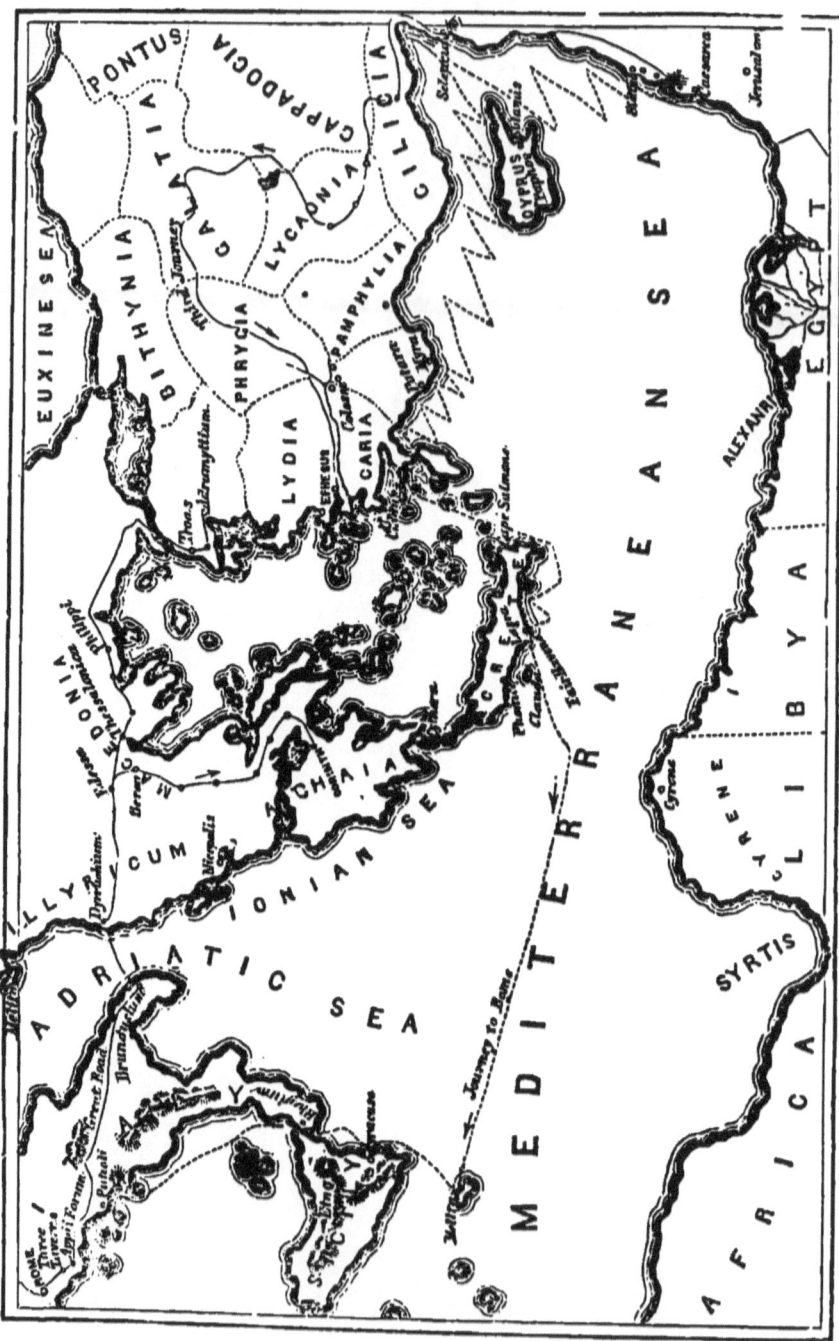

A YEAR WITH ST. PAUL;

OR

FIFTY-TWO LESSONS

FOR THE

SUNDAYS OF THE YEAR

BY

CHARLES E. KNOX.

NEW-YORK:
ANSON D. F. RANDOLPH & CO., 770 BROADWAY,
CORNER OF NINTH STREET.
1869.

JOHN A. GRAY,
Printer, Stereotyper, and Binder,
FRANKFORT AND JACOB STREETS,
Fire-Proof Buildings.

Introduction.

IT is my desire and my hope to interest young people who are beginning to study the Scriptures by subjects rather than by the regular, measured lesson of verses. This "Year with St. Paul" is designed to give variety to the course of Biblical Instruction in the Church, the Family and the School; and especially to open, if possible, a new and attractive department of study to those just ready to advance from seven-verse lessons to something more general and more continuous, and who, in the transition from childhood to youth, are growing impatient of the ordinary unvarying recitation and questioning of verse by verse. The subjects have been stated with the hope of exciting and fixing the attention. The questions are intended to bring out both the text of the Scripture-lesson and the descriptions which follow, and to be *suggestive* to those who find such questions a help in teaching.

The descriptions of the Apostle's life, as it is illustrated by civil history and geographical scenery, are taken substantially from "Conybeare and Howson's Life and Epistles of St. Paul." The attempt is simply to sketch the outline of that 'living picture.' Quotations will be found frequent; and even where there are no quotations, the spirit of many a paragraph or sentence is almost literally preserved. If the Scripture, thus illustrated by the life of the age in which it was written, shall produce in the minds of young people an impression, in some measure like that which was awakened in the mind of the early oriental reader of the book of Acts, the object will be secured. It is believed those external helps will aid the young to form a conception of the Apostle's life, as it appeared to one who, at Jerusalem or at Rome, in the first century, read the last half of the Acts of the Apostles; and therefore will aid to exalt in their minds the heroism, the courage, the zeal, the faith, which the religion of Jesus wrought in the life of Paul.

These lessons have been confined within the limit of a year, in the conviction that young persons at the age alluded to generally tire of a study protracted beyond that length of time. Why should we do that in teaching the Bible, which we never do in our secular schools? Why should we protract the one same study, year after year, till the mind is wearied with the sameness? A series of yearly subjects, adapted and graduated to the advancement of the scholar, would widen the range of Biblical teaching, would, without harm, meet the fondness of all young people for marked points of progress, and give them a more general knowledge of the Bible. Such a system the author has had in mind in the preparation of the present work; and should these lessons on the Life of St. Paul be received with favor, another volume may supply lessons for another year.

Table of Contents.

CONTENTS.

CONTENTS.

CONTENTS.

A YEAR WITH ST. PAUL.

THE INFANCY AND CHILDHOOD OF PAUL.

LESSON.

Acts xxi. 39; xxii. 3; xxiii. 6, 8, 16; xxvi. 5; Phil. iii. 5;
I. Sam. x. 21, 24; Acts xvi. 37, 38, and xxii. 26–28.

WE need some knowledge of the province and the city in which Paul passed his infancy and childhood, to have a correct idea of Paul's life.

CILICIA was a province of the Roman Empire, and at the time when Paul lived was divided into two nearly equal portions. The *western part* was filled with bold, rough mountains from the great chain of Mount Taurus to the sea. On the Mediterranean they form the high, wild coast of broken cliffs, in the centre of the curve from the Bay of Issus to the Sea of Pamphylia. The whole region was therefore called *Rough* Cilicia. The people who lived in all this district were notorious robbers. They formed innumerable strongholds in the mountains. The name of *Isauria*, in the interior, represented to the Romans all that was bold and cruel in robbery. The forests and many cliffs, the little bays and creeks on the sea, made an easy escape and refuge for pirates. These *Isaurians* were so resolute and in dependent in their rough country, that the Romans, after many attempts, gave up subduing them on land. They then became more bold on the sea, until they dis-

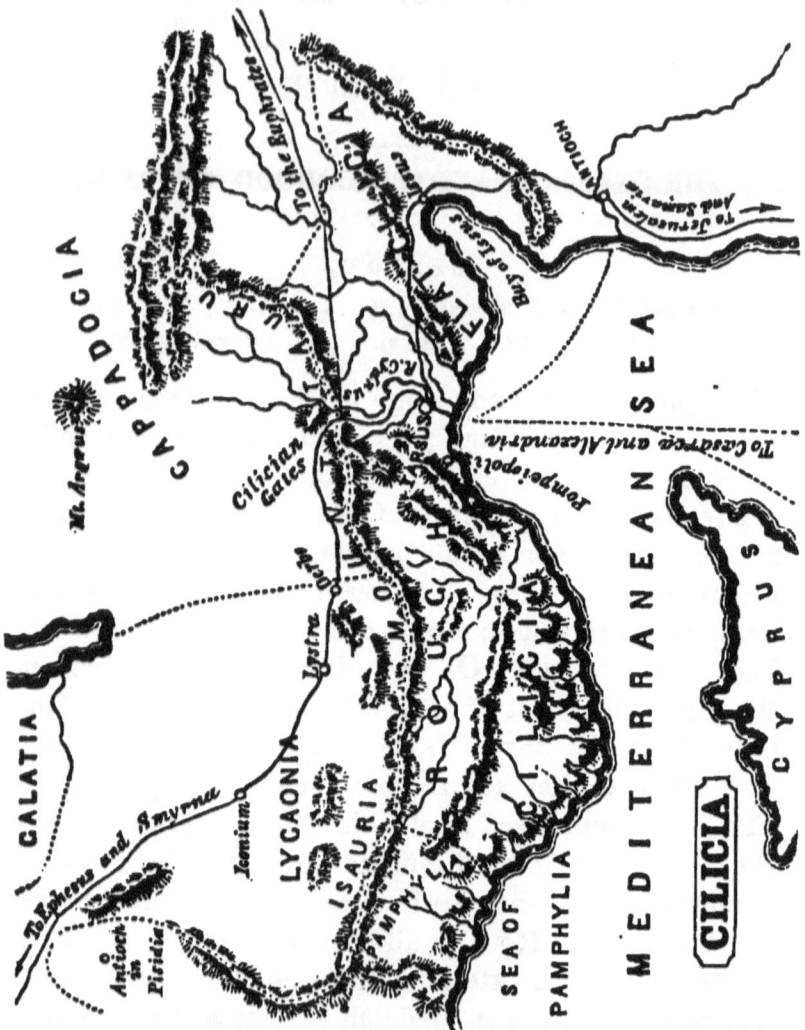

turbed the whole commerce of the Mediterranean; "their fleets seemed innumerable; they were connected with other desperate men, far beyond their own coasts; and they began to arouse attention at Rome. A vast expedition was fitted out under the command of Pompey the Great; thousands of piratic vessels were burnt on the coast of Cilicia, and the inhabitants dispersed; and the Mediterranean was made safe for the voyages of merchants and apostles. A city on the borders of the two divisions of Cilicia was named, in honor of the conqueror of the pirates, Pompeiopolis," (city of Pompey.)

The *eastern part* of Cilicia was called *Flat* Cilicia. It was a rich and extensive plain, and was esteemed valuable on account of its rich fertility, and because its fruitful valleys were so well protected. The long range of mountains on the north and west rose like a wall all the way from Pompeiopolis to the very centre of Asia Minor, and formed a safe defence for all travellers up the valleys, while there was another road of travel around the corner of the sea, and southwards through the mountains towards Antioch and Syria. Flat Cilicia was, therefore, the natural high-road for caravans and armies. It was the route of some of the greatest generals of antiquity. Cyrus led his army over this plain, on his way from the western part of Asia Minor to attack his brother, King of Persia. Alexander the Great and his army, on his career of victory from Macedonia, was met here by the five hundred thousand men of Darius, and just above the gulf of Issus won the victory which made him master of the Persian empire. The hosts of the Crusaders, too, passed along this plain. It was here, not more than half a century before Paul was born, that Cicero the orator was Governor or Pro-Consul of Cilicia. While here, he wrote many letters to his friends, which give a good general idea of the way in which the Roman Empire governed the province. He travelled over the same country, and through the same places, through which Paul travelled. He probably regarded the Jews with much contempt, and would be likely to treat them with great injustice.

TARSUS was the capital of the whole province of both Rough and Flat Cilicia. A clear and cold river flowed from the snows of the steep mountains of Taurus through the city, and spread out into a harbor below the town. Alexander the Great nearly lost his life in bathing in the cold and rapid waters of the Cydnus. Tarsus was an ancient and great city. About the time of Paul, it is said, that "in all that relates to philosophy and general education, it was even more illustrious than Athens or Alexandria." It was therefore a learned city: there "the Greek language was spoken, and Greek literature studiously cultivated." "The people of Tarsus were celebrated for their mental power, their readiness in repartee, and their fondness for the study of philosophy." In general, we may infer that, commercially, Tarsus was the principal port in the eastern part of the Mediterranean, and that, in cultivation, it was "a city where the language of refinement was spoken and written in the midst of a ruder population, who use a different language and possess no literature of their own."

This was the city in which the parents of Paul lived, when Saul was born. We know that both father and mother were Hebrews, for Paul himself says that he is 'a Hebrew *of* Hebrews,' (or *from* Hebrews,) which means that he was a *pure* Hebrew, and that neither father nor mother was at first a proselyte from any other nation to the Jews. They spoke, no doubt, their native tongue, and yet Saul, in his early years in Tarsus, would as often hear the Greek. He must have learned both the Hebrew and the Greek almost as soon as he learned to talk. At home, however, the family were strictly Hebrews. His parents were Pharisees: they taught him the rigid observance of all the rites and traditions of his sect. They were of the tribe of

Benjamin, and they gave their son the name of the first King of Israel taken from the same favored tribe. It may be that the great Apostle had both names, Saul and Paul, from his infancy. Although in the book of Acts he is called Paul only after the conversion of Sergius *Paulus* in Cyprus, as we shall hereafter see, yet "it is most probable that he had both names in childhood:" that in his Hebrew home he was called by the ancient Hebrew name of Saul, and that the Gentiles (the Romans especially) gave it the Roman form of Paulus. It may possibly be, too, that from motives of interest and policy, he was called sometimes, among his friends and by the family, the Roman name, Paul, as we know he mentions, in his epistle to the Romans, two "kinsmen," Junia[1] and Lucius[1], whose names are Roman.

Saul's father was also a Roman citizen. How did he gain this privilege? It was not because he was a native of the city. "It had been given him, or had descended to him, as his own right; he might have purchased it for a large sum of money[2], but it is more probable that some influential Roman had obtained it for him as a reward for services rendered during the civil wars." And hence, as this citizenship, procured by money, or by valuable service, belonged to the family, Saul was 'free-born,' and could afterwards rely upon his citizenship as a defence in the time of trouble.

We cannot decide whether Saul's parents were wealthy or poor. If his father *purchased* the Roman citizenship, it would have required large expense; but on the other hand, when it was bestowed by the government for services done to the army or to the state, it would have been given to the poor as well as to the

---

[1] Romans xvi. 7, 21.   [2] See Acts xxii. 28.

rich. Saul learned a trade. He was a tent-maker, as we learn from his occupation when he came to Corinth,[2] but this does not prove that either he or his parents were reduced to necessary labor for a livelihood. " It was the custom among the Jews that all boys should learn a trade. Rabbi Judah saith, 'He that teacheth not his son a trade, does the same as if he taught him to be a thief,' and Rabban Gamaliel saith : 'He that hath a trade in his hand, to what is he like ? he is like a vineyard that is fenced.'" Tent-making was a profitable occupation at Tarsus. The goats of his native province furnished hair, from which was woven hair-cloth, sold in the markets for the tent-covering. It is perhaps well to think that Saul's father was in moderate circumstances and position, occupied, like many of the Jews, in the traffic of the land-merchants, or of the sea-commerce, and that he gave his son a trade which would be of use to him wherever his lot might be cast, and however he might be reduced from a learned or a professional life to dependence on common labor for a living.

Did Saul have brothers and sisters ? We read of one sister at Jerusalem, whose son saved his life. Some of Saul's kindred became Christians before Saul himself, as is clear from the Epistle to the Romans, where Andronicus and Junia are said to have been in Christ before himself.

Here Saul was born, in this flourishing city of Tarsus. Here, as a boy, he played perhaps by the side of the clear, cold river, building his little ships to sail upon the water, and sometimes losing them on account of the swiftness of the current which came rushing down from the mountain-sides to the sea. He saw

[2] xviii. 8.

the fertile plains, and the high mountains beyond. He saw the water-falls pouring over the rocks in full flood, when the snow melted. He saw in the streets, and on the wharves, men of various languages and costumes: the Cyprian from the island opposite; the Syrian from Antioch; the rough, wild, mountain-ranger from Rough Cilicia or from Isauria, half-suspected as a very robber; the hardy Cappadocian from the interior; the handsome Greek from the famous land beyond the Archipelago; the Roman trafficker and the Roman soldier from the seven-hilled city; and now and then the swarthy Egyptian and the wandering Arab; while his own nation never lacked representatives. He saw the eastern caravan, with its long train, start off up the valley for the head-waters of the Euphrates, and the company of traders on the route around the Bay of Issus, composed of its smaller parties, on their way to Antioch, to Cæsarea, to Samaria, or even to Damascus or to Jerusalem. He saw ships from Cyprus and from Cæsarea, from Alexandria and from the western seas, in the harbor; and the toil-worn throng of men and animals which had just arrived through the wild Cilician gates, from the Ephesus and Smyrna road, bringing their strange stories from the ruder regions of the interior. Eager and quick to observe, Saul the boy was now making the acquaintance of these various nations and their people, whom afterwards he was so much to influence.

QUESTIONS.

WHERE was Paul born?
> Where in the Scriptures do you find the place of Paul's
> birth?
> Does more than one person speak of it?
> Who speaks the greater number of times of Paul's early
> life?
> Where was he when he spoke of it?
> In which place does he speak most of it?

What was Cilicia?
> What was the name of the western part?
> What kind of people lived there?
> What famous robbers lived near?
> What drove the pirates from the sea?
> What has the driving of pirates from the sea to do with
> Paul's life?

What was the name of the eastern part?
> How did it differ from the western part?
> What were the principal roads out of it?
> What travelled on these roads?
> What great generals have passed over these roads?
> What great armies have marched here?

What famous Roman was once Governor of this province?
> Was it before or after Paul's birth?
> Why doesn't he notice the Jews in his letters to his
> friends?

Was Tarsus a place of much consequence in the province?
> In what respects was it 'no mean city'?
> With what cities did it rank in learning at *that time?*
> What were the people especially celebrated for?
> What language was spoken there?
> Did all the people probably use one language?
> With what great cities did Tarsus probably have trade?

Of what nation was Paul?
> Were his father and mother *both* of the same nation?
> How do you know?

How many brothers and sisters had Paul?

Did Paul have any relatives not Jews?

What language was spoken in the house?

Did Paul learn any other language?

What tribe did his parents belong to?

Can you find more than one place where Paul speaks of his tribe?

Whose name, in their tribe, did they give to their son?

How is it that we have two names?

Would his own family be likely to call him by the Roman name?

Had he any relatives with Roman names?

What sect of his nation did Saul's parents belong to?

When Saul grew up, did he prefer his father's sect, or some other?

In how many places does Paul speak of this sect? To whom?

Was Saul's father connected in any way with any other nation?

In what two ways might he have become a Roman citizen?

Was this of any consequence to Saul?

What does he mean, when he says he is 'free-born'?

Did he ever make use of this right of his birth?

Can you tell whether Saul's parents were wealthy or poor?

What does their sending Saul to Jerusalem to be educated seem to show?

Were the other Apostles wealthy or poor?

What trade did Saul learn when young?

Does this show whether his parents were wealthy or poor?

What two maxims of the Rabbis, in respect to trade, are given?

What were tents made from?

What people did Saul the boy see in the streets of Tarsus?

What difference did it make with Saul in after life?

Was Saul taught to read the Scriptures and to pray?

(2)

Second Sunday.

SAUL AT SCHOOL.

LESSON.

Acts xxii. 3; xxvi. 4, 5; xxiii. 6–8. Galatians i. 14.

TARSUS was a place of learning, but the learning was under the control and teaching of the Greeks. The Hebrews looked at the Greeks as 'strangers' and 'aliens;' and the strict Pharisees no doubt held these schools in abhorrence. If there were Greek schools for children, it is not probable that Saul the boy would be permitted to attend them. 'He received his education, therefore, at home rather than at school;' or, if he went to a school, it was not to a Greek school, but rather to "some room connected with a synagogue, where a noisy class of Jewish children were seated on the ground with their teacher, after the manner of Mohammedan children in the East, who may be seen at their lessons near the mosque." At such a place, it may be, he learned to read and write, going to school and returning, as was the custom, with a servant. Perhaps he thought of his own boyish school-days, and of the servant who took him to school and brought him home, when he afterwards wrote to the Galatians that the Law is a servant who leads us to the school of Christ.[1] As he grew older, he gained his religious knowledge

---

[1] Galatians iii. 24. The word translated 'schoolmaster,' in this passage, means literally, *boy-leader*, the servant who *led* boys *to* school, not the master who taught them *after* they were there.

"from hearing the Scriptures read in the synagogue, from listening to the arguments and discussions of learned doctors, and from that habit of questioning and answering which was permitted even to children among the Jews." It is not at all improbable that, when a boy, Saul, with his mind wide-awake to all the life of his busy city, and sharpened by what he heard and saw, carefully trained by his Pharisaic parents, quick to ask and to answer questions at the synagogue, was known as a child of more than usual promise, and as "one likely to uphold," when he should become a man, "the honor of the Scriptures against the half-infidel teaching of the day." His parents and friends would wish therefore that he should have a more careful training than he could obtain in a heathen city; and that at the capital city of Jerusalem itself, he should learn more perfectly the law of his fathers.

There are three opinions in respect to the *time* when he went to Jerusalem. The first opinion is, that he was sent by his parents, "between the ages of ten and thirteen," since if he went at a later age, "he could not have said that he had been '*brought up* in Jerusalem.' It is thought, too, that as Paul before Agrippa said, 'My manner of life *from my youth*, which was *at the first* among mine own nation *at Jerusalem*, know all the Jews, which knew me *from the beginning*,' it implies that he came from Tarsus at an early age." The second opinion is, that "in his youth he was brought up in the schools of Tarsus, fully instructed in all the arts and sciences, before he went to study the law under Gamaliel." The third opinion is, that "though as a Jew and a Pharisee, he would not be educated in the heathen schools of Tarsus, he did not go to Jerusalem to be trained under Gamaliel till about the age of thirty, and after the ascension of Christ." It seems more correct to suppose that Saul went to Jerusalem when he was young. Perhaps he went to live with that sister who seems to have lived afterwards in Jerusalem.[2] And we may suppose he was taken first, as the Saviour himself was at about this very time and at twelve years of age, by his parents when they ' went up ' to attend one of the great festivals of the Hebrew nation. About the time of the Hebrew Thanksgiving, (Feast of Tabernacles,) or of the Feast of Passover, when all the men journeyed in companies to the great and holy city, the Jews of Cilicia and of the surrounding region would begin to gather in Tarsus, either to make up the caravan which would move around the corner of the sea to Antioch, and so down the sea-coast toward Palestine, or to go aboard the swifter ships, which would take them across to Cæsarea, and then to make the shorter caravan-journey through Judea to the capital. Think of the wonder and delight with which the Hebrew boy would long for the day when he would sail out of the clear, cold river, out of the harbor, on the great Mediterranean, away and across toward the beautiful mountains where Abraham and Jacob and Joshua once lived, among which David once led his flocks of sheep, to the city and to the very temple in which the holy child Samuel answered the voice of the Lord in the night. How many pleasant thoughts would crowd into his mind, all along the way.

As he sailed toward the high Mount Carmel, where Elijah sent his servant to look off upon the sea for clouds rising to give rain, as he rode high on the back of a camel through the ancient land of his forefathers, from the sea-coast up towards the interior, how quickly he would catch the conversation of his fellow-travellers,

[2] xxiii. 16.

and remember all he had learned in the synagogue. As he left Cæsarea, his father would point out to him, away off on one side, the distant hills of Mount Gilboa, near

MOUNT CARMEL.

which his great namesake, King Saul, and his three sons and his armor-bearer died.[3] As he came to the borders of his own tribe of Benjamin, he would look for the village of Gibeah, Saul's home, when Samuel anointed him to be king,[4] and would know that on the further border was Jerusalem, with all its glory. Climbing over the range of hills, he saw the temple glittering with gold; the pile of sacred buildings around the shining centre; he saw the whole ancient and honored and holy city surrounded by its wall, and beyond, the Mount of Olives; and, when the caravan-train wound its way under the arch of the gates into the very streets, more than ever before would he thank God he was a Jew 'of the tribe of Benjamin,' and 'a Hebrew of the Hebrews.' Here he is to finish his education. Here he is to learn and to know more of the history and prophecy and poetry of his honored nation. Here he will min-

[3] I. Samuel xxxi. 1–6.   [4] I. Samuel x. 26; xv. 34.

gle in the worship of the very temple. Here he will see and hear the greatest doctors of the world. Here, thinks the Hebrew boy, will I study with zeal what I now more than ever love, and will prove that I am worthy of my tribe and family, and diligently will I serve my God!

Alas! in Jerusalem itself, Saul sees Roman soldiers, just as he has seen them in Tarsus and in all the places along the route, reminding him that his country, once free under God, is now ruled by foreign power. Indeed, when he first landed from the sea, he had paid his travelling-fee in Roman coin, and on all the coin he had taken in Judea, he had seen the "image and superscription" of the Roman emperors; he had heard Roman words used in the common conversation of the Jews; there were Roman buildings in the towns through which he passed; and did not the very first city in which he set foot in his native land, (Cæsarea,) bear the name of a cruel tyrant of Rome? How the patriotism of the Hebrew boy would rise, quick and warm within him, when he thought how shamefully his country was oppressed by the great empire which now stretched from the distant islands of Britain to the Euphrates! and especially as he thought how the governors appointed to rule over this 'promised' land had sometimes set up and put down the high-priests, just as they liked, and how perhaps even the schools of the famous teachers, to which he had come, might be all interrupted and broken up if any successor of the impious Herod should wish.

The great schools at Jerusalem were of course religious schools. Two among them were greatest of all, and were rivals, as they had been from the days of Hillel and Shammai, their founders. Both these schools taught the traditions as well as the law of Moses; both taught the doctrines of the Pharisees: but the school of Hillel said tradition was better than the law, and above it, while the school of Shammai said the law was the better and the greater. The disputes between these schools were so violent, that it grew into a proverb, "that even Elijah the Tishbite would not be able to reconcile the disciples of Hillel and Shammai."

Hillel was grandfather of Gamaliel. When, therefore, Saul entered *Gamaliel's* school, and became an earnest student of tradition and of law, (putting tradition first, according to the school of Hillel,) he soon learned to be "exceedingly zealous of the traditions of his fathers." [*] Except his teaching that tradition had more authority than the law of Moses, (which our Saviour so sharply rebuked,[*]) Gamaliel was perhaps the very best teacher Saul could have had, other than the Saviour himself, to fit him for his future life. "His learning was so eminent and his character so revered, that he is one of the seven who alone among Jewish doctors have been honored with the title of 'Rabban.'"[7] He was not so bigoted as many of the Pharisees. Candid and wise as he shows himself to be when he afterwards gives advice to the high-priest and the Sadducees, when Peter and the other Apostles are brought before them for preaching,[*] he is said to have been 'in reputation with all the people,' and it is added that 'to him they agreed.' Unlike many of the Pharisees, he made no objection to studying the learning of the Greeks.[*] This shows no small degree

[*] Galatians i. 14.

[*] Matt. xv. 1–6. Mark vii. 3–13.

[7] Rab, *master ;* Rabbi, *my master ;* Rabban or Rabboni, (John xx. 16.) *my great master*.

[*] Acts v. 17, 29, 34–40.

[*] And it may be thought, from the fact that Saul was placed under Gamaliel, that his parents did not object to his attending the Greek schools of Tarsus.

of intelligent judgment and independence in Gamaliel, for even the Greek *language* had at one time been forbidden to be taught to the Hebrew youth. How important it was that Saul should know both the Greek language and be familiar with the Greek writings, we now know, who have seen how he was able to preach at Athens and at Corinth, to dispute with Epicureans and Stoics, [10] and to quote their own authors to the Greeks.[11]

We should think of Saul, now growing to be a young man, as one of the younger speakers in the assemblies of the Rabbis of Jerusalem, in the midst of whom was Gamaliel. All are seated, as was the custom, according to their rank and advancement and wisdom. The principal subjects of discussion are the tradition, the law, the prophets and the psalms, the power to interpret which was " the one thing most prized by his countrymen." Some one, perhaps Gamaliel himself, reads a passage out of the Hebrew Bible, or gives out in Hebrew some topic of discussion, which is translated into the common language, then interpreted in various ways by various persons, illustrated by maxims and allegories, compared with the opinions of ancient Rabbis, and last of all, perhaps expounded by Gamaliel himself. The younger students were present to listen and to inquire, " both hearing them and asking them questions,' as our Saviour did ; [12] for it was a peculiarity of the Jewish schools that the *pupil* was encouraged to *catechise the teacher,* and contradictory opinions were expressed with the utmost freedom." Among the many Hebrew youth gathered in Jerusalem from distant cities and foreign

[10] xvii. 18.

[11] xvii. 28. I. Corinth. xv. 33. " Evil communications," etc., is a quotation from a Greek Comedy. Titus i. 12.

[12] Luke ii. 46.

lands, young Saul was certainly one of the most active and most promising students; for he himself said afterwards: "More zealous of the traditions of my fathers, I *pushed forwards* in the study of the Jews' religion, *above many of my school-fellows* of my nation."[13]

Saul is now just coming to manhood, and we can think of the *result* of his education. That result, we suppose, was something like this: He was candid and honest in judgment; he was willing to study and to use the books and the language of the Greeks; he was intensely zealous for the traditions and for the law of Moses. He had learned to dispute keenly, clearly, and learnedly, and to quote the Scriptures quickly and aptly. He had filled his memory with the traditions, with the difficult points of Jewish controversy, and with the opinions of the great teachers. Born a Pharisee, educated at home a Pharisee, trained in Jerusalem by the very chief of the Pharisees, he was now, in his strong, matured judgment, heartily an advocate of the very strictest school of the Pharisees, which taught tradition to be superior to Moses' commandments; and he was most rigid in his conscientious practice of washings and prayers and fastings, and all the other ceremonies.

[13] Galatians i. 14. I *profited* (the Greek word means literally 'to drive forward,' not unlike the English 'to push forward,') in the Jews' religion above many my equals (literally equals in age or fellow-equals) in mine own nation, being more exceedingly zealous, etc.

QUESTIONS.

WHAT kind of learning was there in Tarsus?

How would the Jews think of it?

Do you think Saul attended a Greek school?

What kind of a school was his?

What did he mean, afterwards, when he said, " The law is our schoolmaster to bring us to Christ"?

Where was he taught in religious things? and how?

Do you think Saul would be well known at the synagogue?

Why should he go to Jerusalem?

What are the three opinions in respect to the time when he went to Jerusalem?

What do 'brought up in this city,' and 'from my youth . . . at Jerusalem,' seem to show?

At what age do you think he went?

What relative of his probably lived in Jerusalem afterwards?

With whom would he go to Jerusalem?

What would he see and think of on the way?

What would he think of, if he sailed past Mount Carmel?

What hills would he see on the way from Cæsarea?

What village would he look for, as he came to the tribe of Benjamin?

What would Saul think of, as he entered Jerusalem?

Is it a good thing to make high resolutions at such a time?

What proofs of Roman authority did Saul see at Jerusalem, and on his way?

What did the very name of Cæsarea show?

How might the schools of Jerusalem be interrupted?

What kind of schools were the great schools of Jerusalem?

What two were greatest of all?

Did they both belong to one or to different sects?

Did they belong to Pharisee or Sadducee?

(3)

What were the doctrines of the Pharisees?

What the doctrines of the Sadducees?

What was the one principal doctrine on which they dif-
fered?

What was the difference between the two schools?

What was the proverb about their bitter disputing?

When our Saviour rebuked traditions, which one of
these schools did he especially rebuke?

Who was Saul's teacher?

What was the name of his grandfather?

What was Saul taught 'at the feet of Gamaliel'?

Did Saul like traditions?

What does 'zealous towards God' mean?

Was Gamaliel a good teacher for Saul?

What kind of a man was he?

Where else is he mentioned in the Bible

What was his advice in respect to the Apostles at that
time?

How did he differ from many Pharisees?

Why was it important for Saul to know Greek?

Can you mention any instances of his quoting from
Greek authors?

What was the manner of teaching?

What was most prized?

Did the teacher question the scholar?

Was Saul equal to his school-fellows?

How do you know?

What does 'profited' mean in that passage?

How many things can you mention as the result of Saul's
education?

Was he more or less a Pharisee than before?

What kind of a life did Saul lead in Jerusalem?

Did he like tradition more or less than before?

Is it right to put any thing *before* the commandments of the
Bible?

Can you think of any things which men do put before these
commands?

SAUL AND STEPHEN.

LESSON.

I. CORINTHIANS xv. 9; ACTS xxii. 20; vii. 54–60; viii. 1–4.

A NUMBER of years must have passed, after Saul came up to Jerusalem, before the persecution of Stephen took place. If Saul came to Jerusalem at about twelve years of age, there must have been nearly, if not quite, eighteen years before he makes his appearance at the stoning of the first martyr; for soon after Stephen's death he preached at Damascus, and it is not probable that he would commence public preaching before the usual priestly age of thirty. We may suppose that Saul visited his home frequently during these eighteen years. It may be that he spent much of his time at home, especially as he grew older, returning now to the schools of his native town to study the Greek language and literature, so that he might be fully prepared to meet the arguments of the heathen infidels. During these years, other children were becoming men. Years before, there had been a child born in the hill-country of Judah, not far away, who was now receiving his rough training in the wilderness and in the deserts, where he grew, 'waxing strong in spirit, till the day of his showing unto Israel,' when he preached 'the baptism of repentance.' Along the shore of the Lake of Galilee were boys mending their fathers' nets, who were growing hardy and strong for their future work, and who, even before they had grown to be men, were no doubt thinking of, and watchful for, the Messiah. The GREAT TEACHER, born in Bethlehem, now nearly ready to fulfil the prophetic words of John the Baptist, was at Nazareth, waiting for the time when his great work should call him into public life. He, too, at twelve years of age, had heard and asked questions of the doctors in the temple. He would soon be as old as the priests, who at thirty entered on their office, when he would preach, and teach the whole world the most important of all doctrines. How is it that Saul never meets any of these persons? How is it that, while he believed with his nation that it was the time for the Messiah to appear, and Jesus was claiming to be the Messiah, and all the wonderful works of the Saviour were occurring through all the country, and the condemnation and the crucifixion were taking place, he seems not to know of any of these events by personal presence and sight? In none of his epistles or speeches, after his conversion, does he allude to the fact of having seen the Saviour, or of having known the disciples, though they all visited the temple, and were conspicuous to all men at the great festivals of the capital. We must think that Saul was at this time absent from the city, and probably at Tarsus, just as after his conversion he returns again for a short time to Tarsus.[1] If he were absent only three years, it will be sufficient to show why he did not meet Jesus or any of his disciples. It is more creditable to Saul's candor and wisdom and conscientiousness to believe that he was busy with the Greek scholars of Tarsus, and heard of the great events occurring in Judea only from a distance: that he thought of the miracles of Jesus only as the work of some extraordinary and skilful magi-

[1] Acts ix. 30.

cian, and of his disciples as a band of honest and credulous and deluded men. In all the confessions of his sins afterwards, he never speaks of the trial and crucifixion of his Lord, as he would have done had he been one of the persecutors then. It was not till after the resurrection of Jesus that Saul came back to Jerusalem. He then found in Jerusalem quite a number of these men, who had been followers of Jesus the Nazarene, and who believed that he was the Messiah. He would at once think of them as a new sect, who were giving a wrong meaning to the Scriptures, who were trying to make known their pernicious doctrines, and who ought, therefore, to be put down as soon as possible. When we read that 'certain men of *Cilicia* and of Asia' arose' to dispute with Stephen, we may think that Saul, recently returned from Tarsus, was among them, eager to show his zeal for the law of his forefathers, and his power of disputation against the teachers of this new doctrine. Saul no doubt prided himself on his own upright life, his careful observance of all the duties laid down in the traditions and in the law, and that he was faultless in washings and prayers and fastings, in phylacteries and fringes, in sacrifices and charities and good works. He would be bitterly provoked that any follower of a teacher, (a magician, perhaps,) who had condemned so earnestly the keeping of the tradition, should be teaching in the temple, and that the disciples of Jesus were increasing in Jerusalem[3]; that great wonders and miracles were done among the people[4]; and that many even of the priests[3] were turning to this pretended Messiah. With all the earnestness of his nature

[2] Acts vi. 9. Proselytes of *Africa*, (from Cyrene and Alexandria,) of Asia Minor, (from Cilicia and Asia,) of Rome, (Libertines, probably freed-men from Rome.)
[3] vi. 7. [4] vi. 8.

and the power of his mind, he would join with the Pharisees in crushing out this new sect. Hence it is, we suppose, that we have Saul introduced to us in the Acts just at this point, when not only the miracles of the Pentecost had been 'noised abroad;'[5] when not only the healing of the lame man at the gate of the temple by Peter and John was well known; when not only the strange death of Ananias had caused excitement among the people; when the resolute Peter and John were braving the threats of the chief council, preaching, in spite of it, in the temple; but when, also, a new member of the sect, said to possess more than usual wisdom,[6] was attracting the attention of the learned men of the different synagogues. Stephen was 'full of faith and power.' He met the disputers from Africa and Asia Minor and Rome[6] boldly, and 'they were not able to resist the wisdom and the spirit by which he spake.'

The fact that they had been defeated in fair argument, stirred the fury of men bad at heart and determined to uphold their school and sect and law by whatever means. Murder was in their hearts, and it soon came out in words of falsehood and crime. When we read that they 'suborned men,' (hired men to perjure themselves,) and hear also afterward from Paul's own lips, 'I have lived in all good conscience before God unto this day,'[7] we cannot suppose that Saul deliberately helped to bribe a false witness to perjure himself for the purpose of taking life. It is by no means probable that all of the Jews consented to this most wicked act of perjury; but when the witnesses appeared, Saul no doubt took little pains to inquire into their character, and was glad of any pretext by which this pestilent

---

⁵ Chap. ii: 6. ⁶ vi. 10. ⁷ xxiii. 1.

Stephen could be got out of the way. In the midst of all this excitement, when 'they stirred up all the people and the elders and scribes,' and caught Stephen, and brought him to the council, Saul must have watched every event with the most eager eye; and he must have hoped that Stephen would be brought to silence, if not to punishment and to death. It was in this very trial of Stephen, no doubt, that Saul's bitterness became more and more inflamed. He was one who looked on that face, like 'the face of an angel,' while the high-priest put the customary charge: 'Are these things so?' And that pure and shining countenance did not win his heart, but rather fired his persecuting spirit. He heard Stephen's speech before the council.[*] At first he approved of it, and prided himself in his righteousness perhaps, while Stephen was giving the history of the race; but when the honest, faithful man called all the council stiff-necked, uncircumcised, resisters of God's Spirit, persecutors, betrayers, murderers,[*] all the haughty pride of his Pharisaic nature, and all the power of his education, rose in a moment, and fixed his purpose to condemn him. 'Cut to the heart,' 'gnashing on him with his teeth,' he, like the rest, was only provoked the more by the calm serenity of the culprit; and now, when their passion was overflowing, it needed but those other words of Stephen, 'I see the Son of Man at the right hand of God,' to let loose all restraint. Blind and unreasoning, stirred to the depths of their sensitive pride, boiling with rage, all was over. Now there was only a violent, relentless, cruel mob. They cried out with a loud voice; they rent their clothes; they ran upon him with one accord; they cast him out of their city. And now Saul, a maddened bigot against the truth, kept the garments which the witnesses had

[*] vii. 2-53.　　[*] vii. 51, 52.

laid off that they might stone him. While the angelic Stephen, with the light of heaven on his face, and the prayer of Jesus on his lips, received the blows of his brutal murderers, Saul kept their garments, that they might the more easily do their murderous deed. He consented, or *approved* of it, as the word means. We are therefore fully prepared for what follows. Once permitting his wicked passion and pride to master him, thinking his rage and prejudice were religion, he entered into the persecution with all his heart. While devout men carried Stephen to his burial, Saul 'made havoc of the church, entering into every house, and haling men and women, committed them to prison.' How much he was doing for the very religion he aimed to destroy! He scattered the disciples of Jesus; and filled with the Holy Ghost, they went everywhere preaching the word.

QUESTIONS.

HOW many years were there between Saul's coming to Jerusalem and the stoning of Stephen?

How do you know?

Was Saul in Jerusalem all these years?

What other persons were there in other parts of the land?

How is it that Saul meets none of these persons?

Why may we think Saul was *not* in Jerusalem during our Saviour's public ministry?

When did he probably return to Jerusalem?

What did he now find?

What would he think of these persons?

Why may we suppose that Saul was one of those who disputed with Stephen?

Repeat the verse.

How do you show that there were representatives from Europe, Asia and Africa?

What would touch his pride, as belonging to that school which held the supremacy of tradition?

What events had recently occurred in Jerusalem?

What new member of the new sect now appears?

What kind of a man is he?

Which is the better, faith or wisdom? Why?

Is a man who has faith ever entirely destitute of wisdom?

Whom did he meet in dispute?

Who had the better argument?

What was the result?

What is meant by 'suborn'?

Do you think Saul 'suborned' men?

What did he have to do with the 'suborned men'?

What would Saul hope?

What effect did Stephen's speech have on Saul's mind?

What did he probably think when Stephen began?

What especially cut him to the heart?

What good thing will 'cut people to the heart' now?

What added most of all to Saul's rage?

What does 'gnashed on him with their teeth' show?

Do you think Stephen had a vision of heaven?

Whom did Stephen see in heaven?

Which person of the Trinity gave Stephen power to see Jesus?

Who gives power to see spiritual things?

If we ever see Jesus in heaven, whose guidance will lead us there?

Why did they stop their ears?

Did Stephen have a regular trial?

What did Saul have to do with the witnesses?

Did Saul help stone Stephen?

Whose dying prayer did Stephen use?

To 'fall asleep' like Stephen, at the last, what must we have?

Did Saul like the death of Stephen?

When he 'consented,' did he only give permission?

What act shows that he publicly consented?

What did Saul mistake for religion?

Can you think of anything in men themselves which they sometimes mistake for religion?

Do you suppose Saul forgot the death of Stephen?

What effect might Stephen's prayer have had on him?

Who buried Stephen?

Is it right to lament over friends?

Is it right to grieve for friends who, we are satisfied, are in heaven?

What was Saul now doing?

Did he overthrow the new sect?

What did he do?

What is the better way to treat any despised cause, when it is first advocated?

Who were left in Jerusalem?

What did Paul think of his own conduct afterwards?

Did he ever condemn his feelings against Stephen?

Fourth Sunday.

THE CONVERSION.

LESSON.

Acts viii. 3; ix. 1–18; xxii. 4–16; xxiii. 1; xxvi. 9–15.

"THERE are strong grounds for believing that if Saul was not a member of the Sanhedrim at the time of Stephen's death, he was elected into that powerful Senate soon after: possibly as a reward for his zeal against the heretic, for he himself says that when the Christians were put to death, 'I gave my *vote* against them.'"[1] If he were a member of this national council, he must have been married, for it is said one of the qualifications for the office was, that the person should be both husband and father. Whether he was or was not a member of the Sanhedrim, he was trusted by them as one who would execute their plans for rooting out the new sect. He was chief man in the persecution, and his persecution grew more and more bitter and violent. He made havoc of the Church; he went into every house; he *haled* men and women, (the old English word for *haul*, to drag;') he bound them; he shut them up in prison; in every synagogue he punished them; and though he had succeeded in driving the

[1] xxvi. 10. The word *voice* means strictly a pebble used for voting, and so a *vote* or voice.

[2] As in Spenser's *Fairy Queen:*

'Him sternly grypt and *hailing* to and fro,
To overthrow him strongly did assay.'

most of the disciples from the city, he was still breathing *in* (as the word may be translated) threatening and slaughter. He dragged forth even the women, although, in the East, the women are kept so secluded. He shut them up in prison. He gave his voice against the disciples to the death; and, the worst of all, he tried to make them blaspheme the name of their Lord. His name as a persecutor had become notorious in the distant city of Damascus. Many had brought to Ananias[3] the report of his horrible injustice, and far and near, he was the terror of all believers. His own sorrow afterwards, shows how malignant was his spirit, for it was in his own speeches afterwards in Jerusalem,[4] and at Cæsarea,[5] that he confessed with shame these crimes; and in his letters, too, he laments how he 'persecuted beyond measure the Church of God and laid it waste,'[6] how he was 'a blasphemer and a persecutor, and injurious';[7] how he felt that he was not fit to be 'called an Apostle because he persecuted the Church of God.'[8]

It may be that Saul seized also Samaritans and Gentiles. More cities than Damascus felt the power of his fierce hate. Perhaps the Samaritans, in whose city there had been great joy that Philip had preached to them as well as to Jews, and the many Samaritan villages[9] in which Peter and John preached, had proof of Saul's double spite against them as Samaritans and Christians.

Mad with fury and blind bigotry, Saul tried to carry is persecutions to the beautiful city of Damascus. We do not suppose the chief priests had any *civil* authority over Damascus, but only an *ecclesiastical* authority, as the Pope of Rome claims ecclesiastical power over distant and foreign countries. What was the route he

[3] ix. 13. [4] xxii. [5] xxvi. 10, 11. [6] Galatians i. 13. [7] I. Tim. i. 13.
[8] I. Corinth. xv. 9. [9] Acts viii. 5, 8, 25.

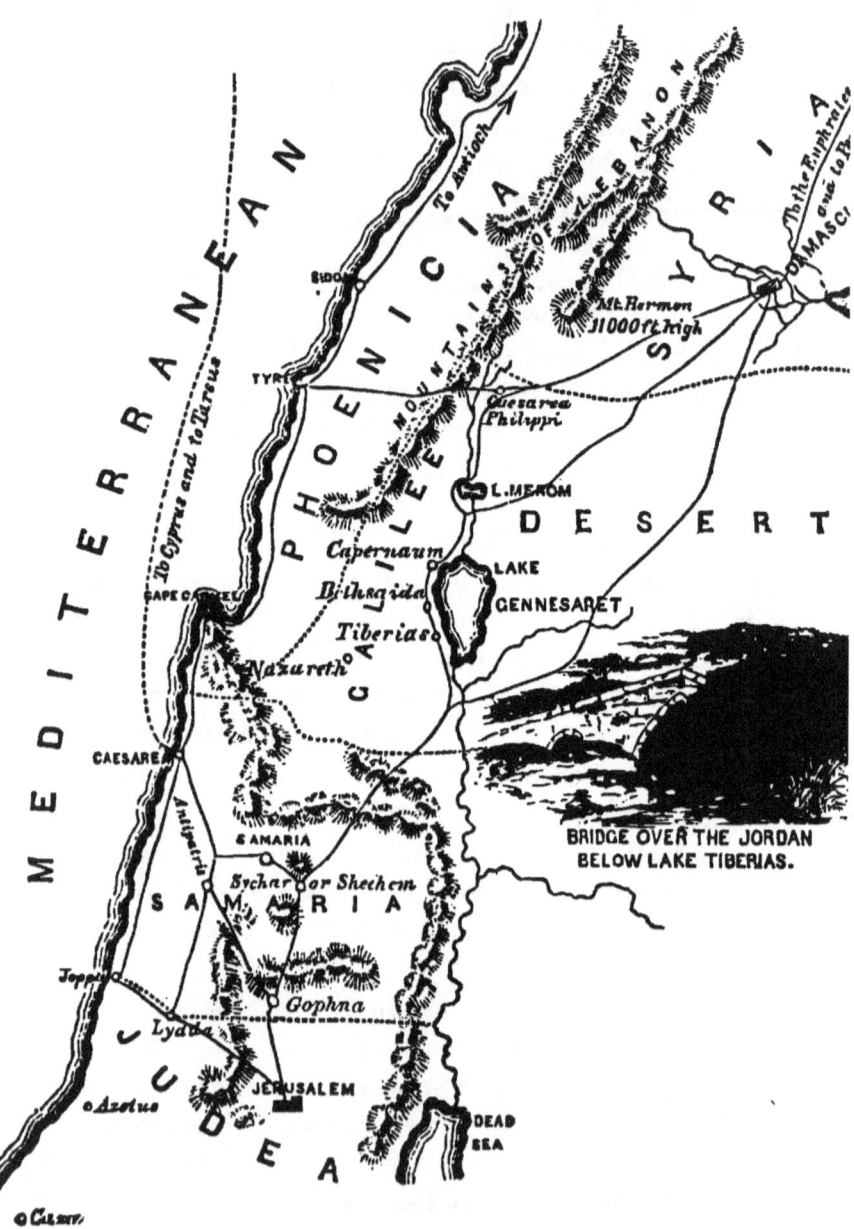

BRIDGE OVER THE JORDAN
BELOW LAKE TIBERIAS.

took we do not know. He would first go north, through
that Samaria and that Galilee in which lay so many
scenes of our Saviour's life, persecuting, perhaps, as he

went, all he found 'of that way.' He might then follow
the road up the Jordan, around the Sea of Galilee, and
cross the river just below the little Lake Merom, or still
following the small streams of the upper Jordan, strike
the road from Tyre to Damascus somewhere near Cæsarea Philippi; but he would more probably take the
most direct course, and cross the Jordan *below* the Sea
of Galilee. As he rode along the tops of the hills in
Samaria, he would get occasional glimpses of the Mediterranean. Further on he would look down on the blue
waters of Gennesaret, now perhaps hateful in his glaring
eye, as the place where the Nazarene wrought his magic
wonders; and in the far distance he would see the
glistening snow of Mount Hermon, near Damascus itself. After he had crossed the Jordan, he would take
his tedious journey through one vast desert plain. "All
around are stony hills, through which the withered
stems of the scanty vegetation hardly penetrate. Over
this desert, under the burning sky, full of fiery zeal, the
impetuous Saul holds his course. When some eminence
is gained, the vast horizon is seen stretching on all sides,
except where the steep sides of Lebanon interrupt it,
like the ocean without a boundary. Damascus, at
length anxiously looked for, is seen from afar, resting
in the green enclosure of its beautiful gardens, like an
island of Paradise in the desert." Wearied with his
long journey, no sight can be more refreshing; for the
view is one of the most celebrated, and the city is one
of the most illustrious in the world. Damascus is one
of the two oldest cities in the world. It was already
built in the time of Abraham.[10] David fortified it with

---

[10] Genesis xiv. 15; xv. 2. 'Josephus makes it even older than
Abraham.' Hebron is *mentioned* first, but it may not have been
older. Genesis xiii. 18.

a garrison, when it was a part of his kingdom." It
made trouble to Solomon." Naaman, the Syrian General, proudly told Elisha that the sweet, fresh waters
of Damascus were "better than all the waters of Israel." Its merchants, and the merchants of Syria,
over which it was capital, brought to the fairs of the
rich city of Tyre, emeralds, purple embroidery, fine
linen, coral, and agates. They expended a 'multitude
of riches,' and bore away from Tyre a 'multitude of
wares.' To the time of Saul it continued to be a rich,
a powerful, a beautiful emporium of trade, between the
countries on the Mediterranean and the distant Persia
and India, as to this very day the costly merchandise
of the distant West and the distant East meet in its
streets. About thirty or forty years before Saul's birth,
Pompey the Great "received at Damascus ambassadors
and presents from the neighboring kings, and the next
year all Syria became a Roman province." The life
of Damascus is its rivers and fountains and lakes. The
streams which rise in the mountains of Lebanon, become
one 'deep, broad, rushing' river, as they flow eastward
towards the city; and at length the river "is drawn
out again into watercourses and spread in all directions.
For miles around, is a wilderness of gardens, with roses
in the tangled shrubbery, and with fruit on the branches
overhead. Everywhere among the trees the murmur
of unseen rivulets is heard. Every dwelling has its
fountain; and at night, when the sun has set behind
Mount Lebanon, the lights of the city are seen flashing
on the waters." "Without the waters of this river,

[11] II. Sam. viii. 6.   [12] I. Kings xi. 24, 25.   [13] II. Kings v. 12.
[14] Ezekiel, xxvii. 16, 18.

[15] While Saul was at Damascus, the city was under the temporary
rule of Aretas, King of Arabia Petræa, (II. Corinth. xi. 32, 33,) but
it soon became subject again to the Romans.

the splendid plain would be a desert; with them, it is an earthly paradise, luxuriating with fields of the heaviest grain, as also with groves and orchards of the finest fruit. Damascus is still a gem, 'the eye of the whole East.'" "All travellers in all ages have paused to feast the eyes with this prospect, on which Saul looked; and the prospect has always been the same."

On his wicked and awful errand, the bold man approaches this ancient and beautiful city. Here, under the glow and heat of an Eastern sun at mid-day, just as he expects to reach the city of rest and comfort, he is struck down, blinded and astonished by that Flashing Light, more brilliant than the noon-day brightness. All his attendants are terrified, bewildered, and dumb.[16]

And there appeared to Saul in the light, One whom he now saw was Jesus the Despised. From him came a voice of authority: 'Why persecutest thou ME?'

It was then the awaked man saw what an awful crime he had been committing, and that Jesus of Nazareth was the Messiah. "I am *Jesus whom thou persecutest*." "He does not say, 'I am the Son of God — the Eternal Word—the Lord of men and of angels,' but, 'I am Jesus, Jesus of Nazareth, who was mocked and crucified, who was buried and who rose from the dead, and

---

[16] In Acts ix. 7, it is said that Saul's companions '*stood* speechless, and in xxvi. 14, that *all fell* to the earth. There is no contradiction. In the xxvi. chapter, they fall *before* the voice speaks; in the ix., it is *after* the voice speaks, and Saul answers, the voice speaks again, and Saul answers again, and the voice speaks the *third* time, that the men with Saul *stood*. All but Saul had risen. There had been abundant time, after the first awful surprise, for them to rise.—In ix. 7, the men are said to stand, '*hearing a voice;*' in xxii. 9, it is said they ' heard *not* the voice.' There is no contradiction, if we suppose that in one case it is meant that they *heard* the *sound* of the voice, as we say we hear the *voice* of thunder, and in the other that they *heard not* the *words* of the voice.

who now appears to thee that thou mayest know the truth of my resurrection, that I may convince thee of thy sin and call thee to be my Apostle.'" Submitting to that call, he is directed what to do; and, arising and opening his eyes, dark and blind, he is led into Damascus; not now to persecute, but, in the agony of his deep contrition and shame, to be separate from all men. There he is left *alone*. No disciple of Jesus would come to him to give him sympathy, for they were all terrified at his coming to Damascus; and he would shrink with horror from the Jews who still reviled the true Messiah. He is alone; alone to think of his former life; alone to think of his raging wickedness, of his proud hatred and blind prejudice against Jesus the Son of Joseph; alone to think that same Jesus had proved, by the especial favor of a miracle, that He was the Messiah; alone to confess all his wickedness; alone, fasting and praying and receiving pardon from Jesus his Lord and his Christ. And now he prayed as he had never prayed before. Now he saw that all his prayers which, as a Pharisee, he had repeated from a child, were idle and vain repetitions. Now, as he gave up all his ambitious plans for life, his thought of being a great scholar and Doctor among the Rabbis of Jerusalem; now, as he made that other greater sacrifice of his opinion and his will, he humbly prayed to Jesus, his former enemy, his glorious Lord, for pardon and for some place in his service. The same Jesus sent his messenger to open his eyes by a miracle, and to teach him that he must himself suffer and be persecuted, and preach the name of the Son of Joseph ' to Gentiles and to kings and to the children of Israel.'

QUESTIONS.

WHAT reason is there to suppose that Saul was a member of the Sanhedrim ?

What does ' I gave my *voice* against them,' mean ?

Name as many distinct acts of his persecution in Jerusalem as you can.

What is the meaning of ' haling ' ?

How may the words ' breathing *out* ' be translated ?

What was the worst act of all ?

Can you prove that Saul's reputation as a persecutor had extended beyond Jerusalem ?

How do you certainly know that his spirit was malignant ?

Did Saul think in his heart that he was right ?

May a man be conscientiously cruel ? conscientiously wicked ?

Did Saul ever regret his *conscientious* persecution afterwards ?

Is it a duty to have a *right* conscience ?

While Saul is persecuting at Jerusalem, where are Philip and Peter and John ?

Did Saul go to more than one strange city ?

What authority would a priest in Jerusalem have in Damascus ?

What parts of the land, in which our Saviour had especially been, would he pass through ?

What would he be likely to think of, when he saw Lake Gennesaret ?

Where do you think he crossed the Jordan ?

What kind of country is he in after crossing the Jordan ?

What kind of a city is Damascus ?

What events in its history can you state ?

In what kind of scenery is the city ?

How many separate accounts are there of Saul's conversion ?

Where are they, and which is the most complete ?

(7)

Does the same person give them all?

At what time of day did the miracle take place?

What do you think of Saul's being deceived at such a time and in such a place?

Could this be lightning?

What was the effect on the men with him?

How do you reconcile '*stood* speechless,' (ix. 7,) and 'all *fallen* to the earth' (xxvi. 14)?

How do you reconcile '*hearing* a *voice*,' (ix. 7,) and 'heard *not* a voice' (xxii. 9)?

How was Saul persecuting Jesus himself?

What is it to 'kick against the pricks'?

What meaning is there in the answer, 'I am *Jesus of Nazareth*'?

Why did he now tremble?

Why should a clear and powerful conception of God or of the Saviour make men tremble?

Did Saul *see* Jesus at the time of the miracle?

Was the conversion now, or when he is said to pray at Damascus?

What does his question show in respect to the surrender of himself?

How long a time is necessary to be converted?

Why was Saul now alone in Damascus?

How did Ananias feel about going to him?

What kind of a man was Ananias?

What reason is given why he *should* go?

What Christian virtues did it require in Ananias to g' to him?

What was Saul doing and thinking before Ananias came

Had Saul been accustomed to pray before?

Was it easy for Saul to become a Christian?

What two great sacrifices did it cost Saul?

How does it cost every one the same two things now, to be a Christian?

Fifth Sunday.

DAMASCUS, ARABIA, AND TARSUS.

LESSON.

Acts ix. 19–30 ; xxii. 15–21 ; xxvi. 16–20 ; Galatians i. 15–23 ; II. Corinthians xi. 32, 33.

THE work of Saul's future life was at once revealed to him at the time of his conversion.[1] Least of all had that proud Pharisee thought that he would ever preach to Gentiles.   But so complete was his surrender of himself to the first command of his Messiah, that, with all the ardor of his strong nature, he accepted the service assigned him. 'A minister and a witness of the things he had seen,' and of those things he was yet to see, he now was to go especially to the Gentiles.[2] And yet he was to preach to the Jews wherever he had opportunity.

No sooner, therefore, had he recovered strength from the exhaustion to which the shock to his physical system and his anguish and fasting had reduced him, than he boldly preached Christ in the synagogues.   The disciples of Jesus had now gathered around him.   And now it was that all his previous training came to the assistance of the cause he had once despised.   He knew the Scriptures ; he knew the teaching of the Rabbis, even those of Jerusalem ; he knew the traditions.   All his accurate learning in their minute investigations was not

[1] I. Corinth. ix. 1 ; xv. 8 ; Acts ix. 17, 27 ; xxii. 14 ; xxvi. 16.
[2] See too I. Timothy ii. 7.

lost, for he knew every form and phase of the argument which any Jew could advance. Out of their own Scriptures, and with unusual power, he could prove that Jesus the Nazarene was the Son of God. The Jews 'that heard him were amazed.' They knew his reputation at Jerusalem : they knew with what fiery Pharisaic zeal and with what authority, he had come to Damascus : they knew what he meant to do when he reached Damascus. And now, instead of 'arresting' and 'haling' and 'imprisoning' and accusing to the death men and women too, and sending them off under safe escort to Jerusalem, he was advocating with all his eminent ability the Nazarene cause, and giving it his warmest sympathy and love.

Saul's preaching was directed to the two points : First, The Messiah, *the Christ, is the Son of God;*[3] he unfolded from the Scriptures the true nature of the Messiah's *spiritual* kingdom ; and, secondly, *This Jesus is that very Messiah,*[4] and has already established his spiritual kingdom in the heart of his disciples. The more he reflected, the more he saw how all the works of Jesus fulfilled the Scriptures. Increasing more in strength therefore, 'he confounded the Jews which dwelt in Damascus.'

Saul was not probably long at Damascus immediately after his conversion. When it is said, 'after *many days* were fulfilled,' his life in Arabia, and his dwelling in Damascus the second time, are doubtless included. "The fury of the Jews must have been excited to the utmost pitch." He must, therefore, leave Damascus. But it would not do to go back at once to Jerusalem. The Jewish fury would be doubled against him there. His life would not be worth a tithe of annis there ; and even if he should escape, the people would be too much

[3] ix. 20.   [4] 22d verse.

enraged now to listen to him candidly. He did not
need the instruction of the other apostles at Jerusalem.
He knew the Scriptures perhaps better than they; the
Divine Spirit had wrought in him the great change, and
Jesus himself had instructed him. He was no doubt
divinely guided to retire into seclusion. He did not,
therefore, go " to Jerusalem to those who were apostles
before him, but he went into Arabia, and returned
again to Damascus."[b]

There is so much difference of meaning in the word
'Arabia,' as it is used by different geographers, that it
cannot be determined with any certainty where Saul

went. The whole northern portion of Arabia is so com posed of endless desert plains stretching to the north and east towards Palestine, Mesopotamia, and Babylonia, that its boundary has never been exactly fixed. Even the three great divisions of Arabia have their boundaries but loosely drawn. · Along down the coast of the Red Sea, and in the south-west corner of the great Arabian peninsula, was Happy Arabia, fruitful and rich, (Arabia Felix.) The great central and northern deserts, stretching across the wilderness and plains towards the Euphrates and Damascus and the Jordan, was Desert Arabia, (Arabia Deserta.) The Great Rocky Wilderness, from the south of Palestine down into the small peninsula between the two heads of the Red Sea, was Rocky Arabia, (Arabia Petræa,) with Petra its capital. It is more probable that Saul retired either into the borders of Desert Arabia, and did not go far from Damascus, or that he went into Rocky Arabia, and it may be trod the hallowed ground of Horeb and of Sinai. It may be that he preached the Gospel in rock-hewn Petra; it may be that he spoke of Jesus to the Arabian Christians who were at Jerusalem during the Pentecost Festival;[*] it may be that to wise men of the East he described the great mission of the Babe of Bethlehem; it may be that for communion with God alone, and for repentance, he sought the solitudes of that wild and silent region, and like Moses, like Elijah, even like Christ himself, was strengthened 'in the wilderness' for his great work by especial divine influences.

Precisely how long he was in Arabia we do not know. But when he left Damascus the second time for Jerusalem, it was at least 'three years after' his conversion. This may mean indeed only parts of three years, as the 'three days' between the crucifixion and resurrection,

[*] Acts ii. 11.

according to the Jewish mode of reckoning, mean
parts of three days, (a part of the first day, the whol
of the second, and a part of the third.) He must hav
been in Arabia more than one year.

Once more he stepped from the borders of the descr
into the gardens of Damascus, prepared now hencefort
to meet persecution at every step of his eventful lif
Even now his life was in double peril, for not only th
Jews, but the governor of the city tried to seize hin
The king's garrison,' as well as those furious men wh
were unable to meet him in argument from the Scriptur
'watched the gates day and night to kill him.' In th
darkness of the night, at an unguarded part of th
city, through the window of a house built in the oute
wall, the great and good and hated Apostle, like th
spies from Jericho,* and like David escaping from Kin
Saul,* was forced to escape, let down in a basket. A
mid-night perhaps, instead of mid-day, he passed th
place on the road to Jerusalem, where the light flashe
about him from heaven. What thoughts were now i
his mind, as he journeyed towards the holy city: th
temple; the sacrifices; the Messiah really come; the pr
phecies fulfilled; his own wicked, blind persecution; th
change in himself; Gamaliel and the Rabbis; the watei
of Galilee, now sacred to him as he passed them, becaus
Jesus had been there; the yearning of his soul with a
fection for every true disciple, as he trod again the hil
of Samaria; the thought of friends in Tarsus, and the
mistaken knowledge of Jesus, as he caught sight of th
Mediterranean from the hill-top—as he came near th
walls of Jerusalem, Calvary and the crucifixion, Stephe
and his murder and *his* vision of Jesus, so unlike hi
own; his familiar places of resort, where he learne
the traditions and the law, and disputed in the syn:

* See note 15, on page 26.   * Joshua ii. 15.   * I. Sam. xix. 12.

gogues. How gladly he would bring the good news he had learned to his old friends and fellow-students, to the teachers and to Gamaliel! Surely some of them will believe on Jesus. How eagerly he will join himself to the disciples of the despised Messiah!

But in the city he soon found that "as the Jews hated him, so the Christians suspected him. They could not believe he was a disciple." The long distance to Damascus, the uncertain roads, the frequent interruption and robberies, the infrequent return of Christians to Jerusalem, the seat of persecution, all might have prevented the disciples from getting knowledge of his conversion, or might have led them to distrust such a strange conversion till it had been tested. 'Barnabas took him and brought him to the apostles.' Why Barnabas? Barnabas was from Cyprus.[10] Cyprus was not far from Tarsus. Barnabas may have been at school at Tarsus. He and Saul may have been acquainted before. There is an ancient tradition that they studied together in the school of Gamaliel. If not acquainted, Barnabas would feel especial interest in a native of a city which was within a few hours' sail of his early home, and in which, no doubt, he had often been. Barnabas was a kind-hearted and generous man, too; for he had sold his land, and had brought the money for the disciples to use.[11]

Barnabas brought Saul to Peter and James, the only two apostles whom Saul at this time saw; and he was with them only fifteen days. How many things were said by these good men, in these few days, of Jesus and his life and work, and of their work! 'And now boldly in the temple he disputed with the Grecians,'[12] and as

[10] Acts iv. 36.   [11] iv. 37.

[12] This word does not mean native Greeks, but foreign *Jews* who spoke Greek

his Rabbinical knowledge served him in Damascus, so did his knowledge of Greek probably serve him here. But as he did to Stephen, so did they to him. 'They went about to kill him.' He must 'make haste to get out of the city.' 'They will not receive thy testimony concerning me,' were the words of his Divine Lord to him, in a trance, while at prayer in the temple. And although Saul seems to have clung fondly to his desire to try to convert his friends and acquaintances, the command is plain and emphatic: 'Depart, for I will send thee far hence to the Gentiles.' So the brethren brought him down to Cæsarea, probably where he first landed years ago, and sent him home to Tarsus. Whether the family at Tarsus mourned over their apostate son, and shut him out of their home, or themselves found the Messiah and Saviour in the Nazarene, we do not know. "We may well imagine that some of his Christian kinsmen,[13] whose names are handed down to us—possibly his sister, the playmate of his childhood, and his sister's son,[14] who afterwards saved his life—were gathered at that time by his exertions into the fold of Christ." Doubtless, too, he disputed in the synagogues of Tarsus, and perhaps in the public schools of the learned Greeks, well furnished now against the heathen philosophers of the place. He would now win them to the Messiah of Gentile as well as of Jew. No doubt he preached in other towns and villages of Cilicia. Certainly there were churches in Cilicia afterwards ;[15] and we love to think that some of its early members were converted by Saul's labors, and that, although the brethren in Judea did not know him by face, they were thankful to God for what he was doing, when they heard, 'That he which persecuted us in times past, now preaches the faith he once destroyed.'

---

[13] Romans xvi. 11, 21.   [14] Acts xxiii. 16.   [15] xv. 23, 41.

QUESTIONS.

WHAT was to be Saul's great work now?

At what two places was his life-work given him?

By what two persons?

What shows the thoroughness of Saul's conversion?

Should people expect to be converted by strange appearances now?

How long was Saul in Damascus now?

What did he do there?

To whom did he preach?

How was he fitted to argue with them?

In what thing did he *not* speak like a Pharisee?

What were the two subjects of his preaching?

What did the people who heard him think?

How much time is included in the 'many days' that 'were fulfilled'?

Were the Jews of Damascus converted when they heard of Saul's conversion?

What one of two effects may be expected in one who knows his friend or companion is converted?

Where did Saul go from Damascus?

Why not go to Jerusalem?

Did he need instruction in order to become an Apostle?

Into what part of Arabia do you think he went?

What did he go there for?

How long was he there?

'After three years I went up to Jerusalem:' three years *after* what?

When Saul came back to Damascus, what put his life in double peril?

Who was King over Damascus now? *Aretas, King ...*

Was it the King, or who was it who tried to arrest Saul?

How did he escape?

What other persons in Scripture escaped in the same manner?

What would Saul think of on the way to Jerusalem ?

For what especial purpose did he now go to Jerusalem ?

How did the disciples at Jerusalem treat him at first ?
Why ?

What motive might they think Saul had ?

Why is it that *Barnabas* brings him to the discip.es ?

What kind of a man was Barnabas ?

What reason did he give why they should receive Saul?

How many of the Apostles did he see ?

How long was he in Jerusalem ?

What did he do in Jerusalem ?

Who were the 'Grecians' ?

Did he, or did he not, wish to stay ? Why ?

What confession does Saul make at this time ?

Was it in Jerusalem, or where was it, that his life-work
was to be ?

Where did he now go ?

How would his own family think of him ?

Were any of his kinsmen converted ?

What would he do in Tarsus ?

Can a person be a Christian and *never* speak of it ?

Do you think Saul went to any other cities of Cilicia ?

How do you know there were churches in Cilicia afterwards ?

Did the disciples in Judea know Saul personally at that
time ?

What did they say of him at this time ?

Did Saul's conversion do good where he had never been ?

Did his persecution do harm where he had never been ?

Is it possible for a man to confine his Christian or unchristian influence to the place where he is?

If it is not Christian, what must it be ?

(10)

Sixth Sunday.

BARNABAS GOES FOR SAUL.

LESSON.

ACTS ix. 30–35; xi. 19–30; xii. 24, 25.

AND now, while Saul is at Tarsus, and the Church from Judea to Galilee had rest, believers are multiplied. Peter preaches at Lydda, and heals a palsied man; at Joppa, and raises Dorcas to life; at Cæsarea, and Cornelius and his kinsmen and friends believe. Others, scattered by the persecution of Stephen, little thinking that the 'young man Saul' was now too a believer, travelled to Phenice, (Phenicia,) and to Cyprus and to Antioch. Some of these men from Cyprus and from Cyrene,[1] who could therefore speak Greek, and who knew the manners and the character of the Greeks better than the others, preached to the Greeks[2] at Antioch; and a great number of the Greeks believed. The story now gathers around the two places, Cæsarea and Antioch, in which the Gospel is preached to the Gentiles, and where are now gathered into the Church representatives of the two great nations of Greece and Rome.

And now, no doubt Saul, under the direction of the Holy Spirit, was waiting for the door to the Gentiles to be fully opened before he should enter directly on his

---

[1] Cyrene is directly south of Greece, in Africa, six hundred miles farther west than the map extends. See Map in frontispiece.

[2] Possibly these may have been Greek-speaking Jews, but more likely Greeks.

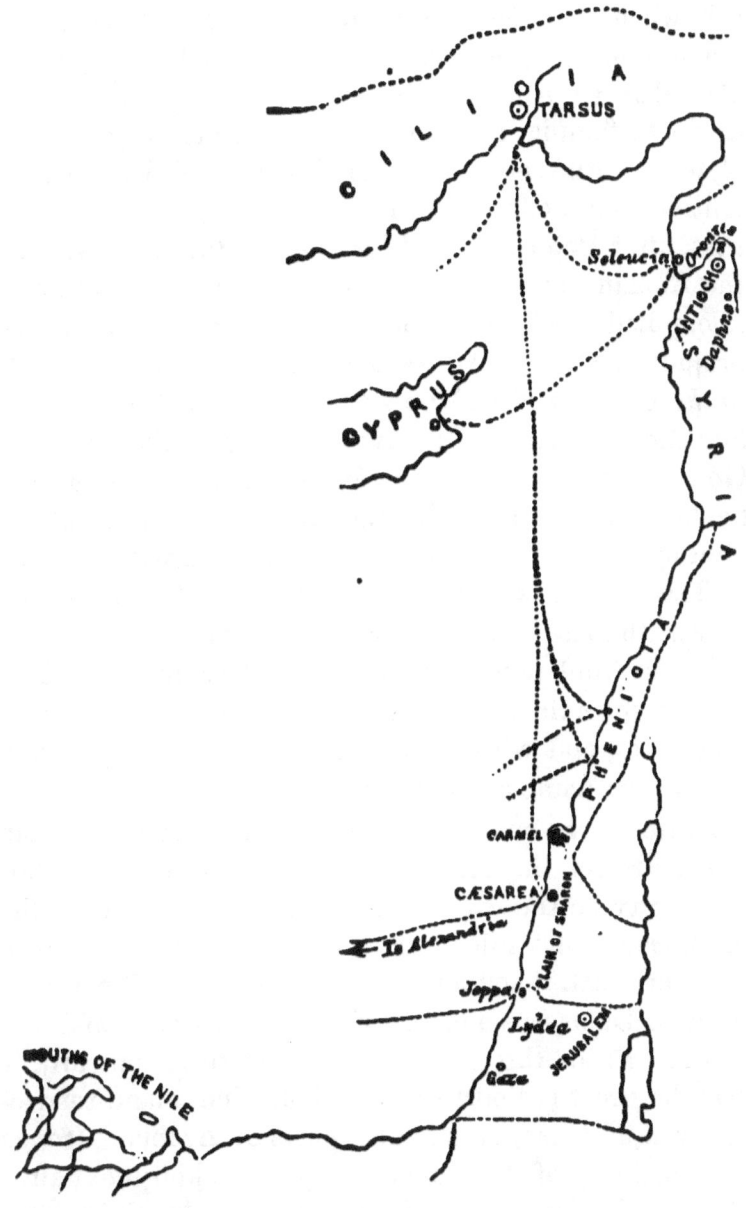

great life-work. Here he had been two or three years,
and was now ready for further direction, when he was
sent for by his Christian brethren. It is Barnabas who
comes to introduce him to his work. It was natu-

ral, when the disciples of Jerusalem heard what was being done in Antioch, that they should send down Barnabas to Antioch, for with that city he was no doubt as familiar as with Tarsus, from his early home in Cyprus. And now that the Greeks and Romans, at Antioch and at Cæsarea, are receiving the Gospel; now that, after Peter had told his story of the conversion of the Roman centurion Cornelius, the Apostles at Jerusalem had boldly said, in opposition to all the Jewish prejudice, 'Then hath God given repentance unto life *to the Gentiles* also;' now that the Apostles had sent him down to Antioch; now that he saw the Spirit of God was working mightily in Antioch; and now that he knew Saul was to be the Apostle to the Gentiles, 'full of the Holy Ghost and of faith,' Barnabas set off to Tarsus to seek Saul. To Antioch Saul returns, and here with Barnabas labors a whole year.

Let us think now what kind of a place this is in which these two eminent Christian teachers pass a year of their lives, and with such success that the disciples first receive the name of 'Christians.'

Antioch was one of the ancient cities of the Syrian coast. From the river Orontes, and from the harbor of the city on the sea, its ships sailed to all parts of the Mediterranean, while along the valley of the Orontes to the south-east, it communicated with the great caravan-trade of Damascus and the East, of Jerusalem and the South. From this time, and two centuries onward, it was the great sea-port of the whole rich inland territory, even of Mesopotamia and parts of Arabia. It was the third city of the Roman Empire, ranking next after Rome and Alexandria. It was adorned by the emperors as the capital of the Syrian provinces. A long, level and broad street, four miles in length, passed through the city. On each side of it were colonnades, so that the throngs of people could walk under the covered ways of the beautiful avenue from one end of the city to the other. A palace for the Syrian king or Roman governor, an ornamental arch, a temple of Jupiter on one summit of the neighboring mountain, and a citadel on another, were the other chief attractions. The whole was surrounded by a wall. " Luxurious Romans were attracted by its beautiful climate. New wants continually multiplied the business of its commerce. Its gardens and houses grew and extended on the north side of the river. Many are the allusions to the history of Antioch in the history of those times, as a place of singular pleasure and enjoyment. Here and there, an elevating thought is associated with the name. Poets have spent their young days at Antioch, great generals have died here, emperors have visited and admired it. But for the most part, its population was a worthless rabble of Greeks and Orientals. The frivolous amusements of the theatre were the occupation of their life. They had a passion for races and for party quarrels. The Oriental superstition and imposture was in full life here. The Chaldean astrologers found their most credulous disciples in Antioch. Jewish impostors, sufficiently common throughout the East, found their best opportunities here. It is probable that no populations have ever been more abandoned than those of Oriental Greek cities under the Roman Empire ; and of these cities, Antioch was the greatest and the worst." The Olympic games were celebrated at Daphne, a beautiful, most vicious village, five miles from the city ; and thither, to see the games, and to worship Apollo, in the magnificent temple, thousands of pilgrims went every year.

It was in such a rich, prosperous, thronged, and wicked city, that the Spirit of God was now manifest. Romans, Greeks, and Jews, would all oppose the sim ple, humiliating, and purifying doctrines of Jesus. Yet many were believing. Barnabas would need aid. To this place, therefore, he brought Saul to assist in the good work. We cannot tell all which they accomplished during the year. No doubt they preached in the public places ; no doubt they tried to lead the pilgrims of a false faith to the true God and to the Messiah ; and perhaps they preached the Gospel in the very village of Daphne, endeavoring to turn the worshippers from these vanities to serve the living God.' They had, however, attracted the attention of the people so much that they gave them a new name. The people saw, strangely enough, Jews and Gentiles were united in this new sect. They heard them speak much of ' the Christ,' of him who had been crucified at Jerusalem, who, they claimed, had risen from the dead and was ' the Messiah ' whom the Jews had been expecting to appear, or ' the Christ,' in the Greek language ; the preachers preached the doctrine that this ' Christ ' was God ; whenever any one prayed, he prayed in the name of ' Christ ; ' whatever they all did, they pretended to do for the sake of ' Christ ; ' and therefore the Antiochans called preachers and pray-ers together, in ridicule or in contempt, ' Christ-ians.'

The Jews called the disciples ' Nazarenes,' or ' Galileans,' and they would not call those who believed in a false Christ, ' Christians.' The disciples called themselves ' brethren ' and disciples ; and they would not probably take upon themselves a name which meant simply ' believers in the Messiah,' for all the Jews believed in a Messiah. The idle and witty people of Antioch, who ' were famous for their invention of nicknames,' were quick to see that these men were different from other Jews and from other Gentiles, and that they had in a year organized a church of their own. It was no doubt the witty Greeks and Romans and Syrians, who fastened on the disciples the contemptuous name of ' Christians.'

There had been, within a few years, earthquakes and famines in various parts of the Roman Empire ; and Judea had not escaped. " The reign of Claudius Cæsar, from bad harvests and other causes, was a period of general distress and scarcity ' over the whole world.' In the fourth year of his reign, we are told by Josephus that the famine was so severe that the price of food became enormous, and great numbers perished." One noble woman, the mother of an eastern king in the neighborhood of ancient Nineveh, who had come to Jerusalem to worship, was so touched with pity at the misery she saw among the poor, that she sent to Alexandria to buy corn, and to Cyprus to buy figs for them; and her son, the king himself, sent large sums of money to Jerusalem. It may have been this same famine, or ' great dearth,' which Agabus the prophet foretold. The Christian converts were not slow to show their love for their brethren, and their gratitude for the new religion which they had been taught. 'According to their ability,' they sent relief to the brethren in Judea, appointing Barnabas and Saul to carry their contribution to the elders in Jerusalem.

When Barnabas and Saul reached Jerusalem, they probably found what was worse than famine. James, the brother of John, had been murdered by Herod. Peter was in prison, and was soon to be executed. By a miracle Peter was delivered, and by a miracle Herod, the murderer, the proud, selfish man, displaying himself in magnificent robes which shone with silver, to the great multitude in the royal theatre of Cæsarea, was smitten with death. In the very city in which Cornelius had been so lately converted, and which probably

Saul now passed through on his return from Jerusalem
to Antioch, the impious King, wrapped in his royal apparel, but eaten with horrible disease, was carried out
of the theatre built by his grandfather (who murdered
the innocents of Bethlehem) to die.   Barnabas and Saul
had fulfilled their mission. They had relieved the brethren of Judea; and with John Mark, (nephew or cousin
to Barnabas,³) they were on their way back to Antioch,
still to labor there for their common Lord.

³ Colossians iv. 10.   The word translated 'sister's son' may mean
cousin as well as *nephew*.

QUESTIONS.

WHILE Saul was at Tarsus, what had occurred in Palestine?
  Where had Peter been, and what had he done?
  Where had other disciples been?
  Where were these places?
  To whom had they preached in Antioch?
  Why was it that the men of *Cyprus and Cyrene* preach-
    ed to 'the Grecians'?
  What was the result of their preaching?
  About what two places do the Acts of the Apostles now
    gather?
  What two great nations are now represented in the new
    converts?
What may we suppose Saul was waiting for in Tarsus?
  How long had he been in Tarsus?
  What did the disciples in Jerusalem hear about An-
    tioch?
  Why do they send *Barnabas* to Antioch?
  Will a Christian do anything more than 'be glad,' when
    he sees 'the work of God'?
  What two things must a man be 'full of,' to be in the
    highest sense 'a good man'?
  Can a man be good at all, without these things?
  What was the result of Barnabas's coming?
  What is meant by '*added*'?
  Why was it that Barnabas went for *Saul*?
What did Barnabas want Saul for?
  How long were they in Antioch?
  What country was Antioch capital of?
  In what direction and by what means did it have trade?
  Which were the first three cities of the Roman empire?
  How was the city adorned? and by whom?
  Who came to Antioch? and why?
  Poets? generals? emperors?
  What kind of population was that of Antioch?

(11)

How did Antioch compare with other Oriental Greek cities?

What famous village near Antioch?

What celebration was held there?

Who would oppose the Gospel in Antioch?

How do you know the Apostles attracted attention in Antioch?

Why do *you* think they were called Christians?

Why would not the disciples or the Jews give the name?

Must a person be willing to be singular to be a Christian?

Who came down from Jerusalem 'in these days'?

What did one of them do?

Is this man mentioned elsewhere in the Scriptures?

What had happened in parts of the Roman empire?

What is said of the reign of Claudius Cæsar?

What is meant by 'throughout all the world'?

Did any besides the disciples send 'relief' to Jerusalem?

Who went from Antioch to Jerusalem?

Does piety make men more or less generous? why?

What had happened when Barnabas and Saul reached Jerusalem?

What became of both King and prisoner?

Who built the theatre in which the King was smitten?

Had Saul ever been in Cæsarea?

Would you rather belong to such a set of Kings or such a set of Apostles?

Must you belong to one *class* or the other?

What effect did Herod's persecution have on the preaching of the word?

What is meant by 'fulfilling their ministry'?

What especial reason is there why John Mark went back with Barnabas and Saul?

(12)

THE BEGINNING OF THE JOURNEYS.

LESSON.

Acts xiii. 1–5.

THE 'church' of Antioch was an assembly of Christians, which probably met at the different houses of the Christians for prayer, for study of the Scriptures, for worship and for the celebration of the Lord's Supper. And now there were among them, at the close of the year, or rather at the return of Barnabas and Saul from Jerusalem, 'certain prophets and teachers.' These were not prophets like those of the Old Testament. In those days a 'prophet' need not have any knowledge of things to come, or speak of what would happen in the future. He was more than a simple teacher. and less than an apostle.[1] He was a teacher, it is supposed, who at times, if not always, taught by the unusual power of a direct inspiration. Three of these prophets and teachers are mentioned, besides Barnabas and Saul. Who are these three? Simeon Niger, Lucius of Cyrene, Manaen, Herod's foster-brother.[2] We have only one item of information in respect to each of the three. Simeon is a Hebrew name, and Niger is a Roman name; so that probably Simeon Niger was a Jew who, like Saul, had lived among the Romans when he was young, or had afterwards gained the Roman name from some acquaintance or connection with them.

[1] I. Corinth. xii. 28.
[2] See the margin in the reference Bible.

The Latin word 'niger' means 'black, dark, dusky,'
and it is easy to think the name might have been given
at first contemptuously, on account of his complexion,
and retained here to distinguish him from the other
Simeons and Simons mentioned in the New Testa-
ment.³ As the word means also 'sad, mournful,' and
then 'ill-omened, unlucky,' and then still 'bad, wicked,'
the name might have been given for his natural appearance, or for his ill-fortune in life, or he may have been
noted for his wickedness before his conversion. It has
been supposed that Lucius is the same person as Luke,
the writer of the Book of Acts, who went with the
Apostle from Troas on his journeys;⁴ but it is not probable that Luke would have mentioned himself as one
of the most honored teachers of the church; " and besides, the Latin form of the name, Lucas, does not come
from Lucius, but from Lucanus." Lucius is from Cyrene, " that African city which abounded in Jews, and
which sent to Jerusalem our Saviour's cross-bearer.'"⁵
When Paul wrote afterwards from Corinth his letter to
the Romans,⁶ there was a Lucius with him, perhaps
this same one. Who was Manaen? Herod the Te-
trarch⁷ was Herod Antipas, Tetrarch of Galilee, whose

³ They are the same name: Simeon, the Hebrew form; Simon,
the Greek form; and there are *eleven* in all, besides Simeon Niger.
Simon Peter, Simon the zealot or Canaanite, (Matt. x. 2, 4; Luke
vi. 15,) Simon the Pharisee, (Luke vii. 40,) Simon the leper, (Matt.
xxvi. 6,) Simon the Cyrenean, (Mark xv. 21,) Simon the sorcerer,
(Acts viii. 9,) Simon the tanner, (Acts ix. 43,) Simon the brother of
Jesus, (Matt. xiii. 55,) Simon the father of Judas Iscariot, (John vi.
71,) Simeon of the Temple, (Luke ii. 25,) and Simeon, Jesus' ancestor, (Luke iii. 30.)

⁴ 'We,' he says, Acts xvi. 10.   ⁵ Mark xv. 21.   ⁶ Romans xvi. 21.
⁷ *Tetrarch* is a Greek word, from *tetros*, a fourth, and *archon*,
ruler, and at the first meant the *ruler of a fourth part* of a country.
It afterwards meant a ruler of any part, the same as *ethnarch*, (*ethnos*,
country, and *archon*, ruler.)

brother, Herod Archelaus, was Tetrarch of Judea, and whose brother Herod Philip, was Tetrarch of part of the rough region between Lake Tiberias and Damascus. All three were sons of Herod the Great, the murderer of the innocents at Bethlehem. The two former sons were educated together at Rome, and in childhood were no doubt 'brought up' together; and so the Christian teacher Manaen, their foster-brother, "spent his early childhood with these two princes," and had no doubt some personal acquaintance with Herod the Great. While Manaen was teacher of the Christian church at Antioch, these two cruel sons were both exiles in Gaul, by the decree of the Roman Emperor; the very one here mentioned, (Antipas,) on the accusation of his own nephew, that other miserable Herod who was smitten by a death-angel at Cæsarea. How much more honorable is the single mention of Manaen's name here in the Scriptures, though so little is known of him, than all the glory of the Herodian line!

"The Christian community at Antioch were engaged in one united act of prayer and humiliation. That this solemnity would be accompanied by words of exhortation, and that it would be crowned and completed by the holy communion, is more than probable; that it was accompanied with fasting, we are expressly told. These religious services might have had a special reference to the means which were to be adopted for the spread of the Gospel, which was now to be given to all men; and the words, 'Separate me Barnabas and Saul for the work whereunto I have called them,' may have been an answer to their specific prayers." How the hearts of all must have been filled with sacred wonder and awe at this change from the old Jewish custom, this sending out of preachers among the Gentiles, far away, to teach them also the words of the Messiah already come, and

with a deep sense of the work they were beginning
And so they came together again at the time of departure no doubt, to fast and to pray, and to consecrate
these two brethren to their great and holy work. "A
fast is appointed; prayers are offered up; the two are
ordained by that most simple act of the 'laying on of
hands.'"[8]

Why now did the Apostles go to Cyprus first? No
doubt they were divinely guided, but still guided
through human motives. Four reasons may be given,
which may have induced them to go there. First. Cyprus is not far distant from the mainland of Syria; its
high mountains are easily seen, in clear weather, from
the coast near the mouth of the Orontes, and in the
summer season there must have been many vessels passing and repassing between Salamis and Seleucia. Secondly. "It was the native place of Barnabas. It
would be natural to suppose that the truth would be
welcomed in Cyprus, when it was brought by Barnabas and his kinsman,[9] Mark, to their own connection or
friends." Thirdly. There were many Jews in Salamis.
"By sailing to that city, they were following the track
of the synagogues. Their mission, it is true, was chiefly
to the Gentiles, but their surest way of reaching them
was through the Jewish proselytes and the Jews who
spoke Greek." Fourthly. "Some of the inhabitants
of Cyprus were already Christians. There was no
place out of Palestine, except Antioch, where the Gospel had been better received."[10] John Mark is with
his uncle and Saul, as an assistant or attendant.[11]

---

[8] Acts vi. 6; I. Tim. iv. 14; v. 22; II. Tim. i. 6; Heb. vi. 2.

[9] Coloss. iv. 10.

[10] Acts xi. 19, 20; xxi. 16; iv. 36.

[11] 'And they had also John as attendant or assistant.' The

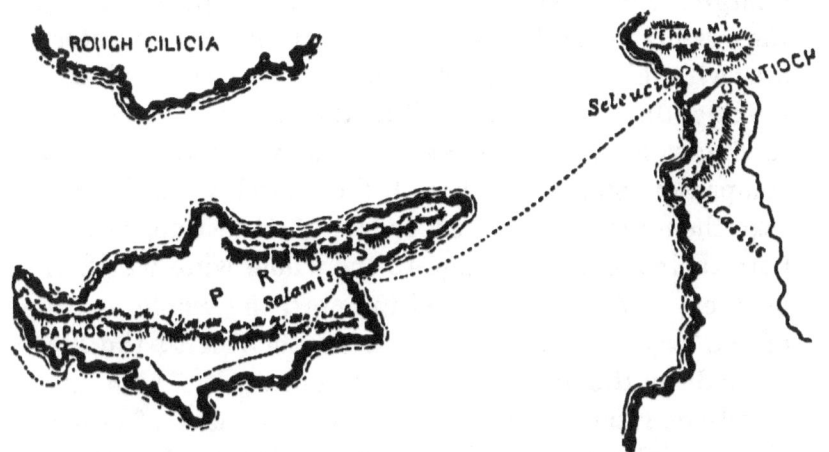

Seleucia was the port and harbor of Antioch. It was not at the mouth of the river Orontes, but six or eight miles above it. Here the disciples must come to take ship on the great sea. "If Barnabas and Saul came down by water from Antioch, they sailed on the deep and rapid, but not clear river, winding around the bases of high cliffs or by richly cultivated banks, where the vine and the fig-tree, the myrtle and the bay, are mingled with dwarf-oak and sycamore," and then turning short to the right, they crept along the coast into the harbor, protected by lofty hills. If, instead of taking this winding course of forty miles, they took the road for sixteen miles straight across, "they crossed the river on the north side of Antioch, and came along the base of the Pierian hills by a route which is now roughly covered with fragrant and picturesque shrubs, but which then doubtless was a track well worn by travellers." Here, in a sea-port, which was at the same

Greek word means literally an *under-rower*, a common sailor, who worked at the oar under the regular shipmen or seamen. And so it came to mean an attendant in the synagogue, who handed the volume or the rolls to the reader, and returned them to their place. Hence, any attendant or associate-assistant.

time a fortress and a harbor, from the piers whose "large stones, fastened by their iron cramps, protected the vessels in the harbor from the swell of the western sea, with high and craggy summits on the north-east looking down upon them," in the midst of unsympathizing sailors, the two missionaries, with their younger companion, stepped on board the vessel which was to take them from the sacred shores of Palestine, as they bore their blessed message to the whole wide world of heathen. "As they cleared the port, the whole sweep of the bay of Antioch opened on their left; the low ground by the mouth of the Orontes; the wild and woody country beyond it; and then the peak of Mount Casius, rising symmetrically from the very edge of the sea to a height of five thousand feet. On the right, in the south-west horizon, if the day was clear, they saw the island of Cyprus from the first. With a fair wind, they would run down from Seleucia to Salamis in a few hours; and the land would rapidly rise in forms well known and familiar to Barnabas." Pointing the ship to the very centre of the east end of the island, and leaving behind and far away on either side the two promontories and their mountain-headlands, the captain would steer direct for Salamis. "The ground lies low in the neighborhood of the city, and this low land is the largest plain in Cyprus. It stretches inwards between the two mountain-ranges to the very heart of the country. A large city on the sea-shore, a wide-spread plain with fields of grain and orchards, and the blue mountains beyond, composed the view on which the eyes of Barnabas and Saul and Mark rested when they came to anchor in the bay of Salamis."

Here we find many Jews, "for we learn that this city had several synagogues, while other cities had only one."[12] The unparalleled productiveness of Cyprus, and its trade in fruit, wine, flax, and honey, would naturally attract them to the commercial port. When Herod wrought the copper-mines for the Emperor Augustus Cæsar, many Jews at that time came to Cyprus. Barnabas and Saul preached here in the synagogues. 'We do not know how long they staid, or what was their success. Some stress seems to be laid on the fact that John Mark was their minister. Perhaps we are to infer from this that his hands baptized the Jews and proselytes, who were convinced by the preaching of the Apostles."[13]

[12] Compare verses 14, 15; see ix. 20, and contrast xvii. ; and xviii. 4.
[13] See I. Corinth. L 14, 16, 17.

QUESTIONS.

WHAT was the church of Antioch?
What do you mean by 'a church' now?
Where did they meet for worship?
Who were in the church at the end of the year?
How did these 'prophets' differ from those of the Old Testament?
What was the difference between 'prophet' and 'teacher'?
What was the difference between 'prophet' and 'apostle'?
Where in the Scriptures do you find this difference?
How many of these prophets and teachers are mentioned?
Whose names are the first and the last?
Was Barnabas an Apostle?
What is the meaning of Apostle?
Of what nation was Simeon Niger?
Why called Niger?
How many other Simeons are there in the New Testament?
Is Lucius the same as Luke?
Where is Cyrene, and who else was from there?
Is Lucius mentioned anywhere else in the Scriptures?
Who was Manaen?
Whose son was Herod the Tetrarch?
What does Tetrarch mean?
What notorious thing did his father do?
What notorious thing did this Herod the Tetrarch do?
What became of him and his brother?
How was Manaen connected with them?
Whom do you most honor, Herod or Manaen? Why?
What other disciple from Jerusalem was in Antioch?
In the meetings of the church at Antioch, what would be one subject they would all think of?

Do you suppose they thought themselves of sending men
 abroad to preach?

What was the Jewish custom?

What command did they receive?

Who is the source of authority?

What is meant by 'laid hands on them'?

Do you think it was at the same service in which they
 received the command, or at another, that they
 'laid hands on them'?

How many missionary journeys did Saul make?

Did his brethren send him, or who?

Where did he first go?

Do you suppose the place to which they were to go was
 revealed?

What four reasons may be given why he went to Cyprus
 first?

What does the Greek word here translated 'minister'
 mean?

Where and what was Seleucia?

How would the three go from Antioch to Seleucia?

Where was Salamis?

How long would it take to go to Salamis?

Was there more than one synagogue in Salamis?

What does this show?

What would bring the Jews there?

What did John Mark do?

Is there any way for us to preach the Gospel besides
 preaching from the pulpit?

Who are the best 'under-rowers' to pastors now?

(14)

Eighth Sunday.

THE PRO-CONSUL AT PAPHOS.

LESSON.

Acts xiii. 6–12.

BETWEEN Salamis, the commercial port at the east
end of Cyprus, and Paphos at the west end, there
must have been a well-travelled and frequented road.
The missionaries must have had several halting-places
in a journey of a hundred miles. As the history of the
Acts gives us only the important events of the journeys,
there is nothing to forbid us thinking that they preached
at settlements along the way. They travelled, no doubt,
the shortest way from one principal city to another,
between the range of mountains and the sea.

Paphos was the capital of the island. The Roman
Governor lived here. The people were mostly Greeks,
and there was a garrison of Roman troops to hold and
defend the place. While the languages of the two
nations equally mingled, the Greek religion prevailed
over the Roman, for Paphos had been for ages a place
famous for its mythological history. The temple of
Paphos, it was said, "was built on the spot where
Venus was gently wafted to the shore from her native
waves" Homer sung of Paphos: Virgil, of the temple
of Venus there, "where a hundred altars burn with
Arabian frankincense:" Horace, of the "queen of
Cnidus and of Paphos." A few years after Saul's visit,
"curiosity led Titus" (afterward Emperor of Rome,
and then on his way to conquer Judea and to destroy

Jerusalem) " to visit the temple of Venus, famous for the worship of the inhabitants and the concourse of strangers who resorted hither from all parts."

Who now was 'the Deputy'? To answer this question, we must know what the government of the Roman Empire was over Cyprus, and what office Sergius Paulus held under the government. Some years after the Empire was established on the ruins of the Republic, the Consul at Rome, who had been President of the Roman Republic, ceased to be elected by the people. The two Consuls had been for centuries chief officers of honor and of authority in the nation, (like our own President, only elected every year,) but now that the *Emperor* was supreme, the Consul was in a lower degree of honor and authority, and was elected from the *Senate*. And now that the Roman Empire had extended over so many small countries, officers were sent out to govern the *provinces;* and these officers were generally men who *had been* Consuls. These men were called *Pro-Consuls, For* Consuls, *As if* Consuls, because in the provinces they had about the same authority which the Consul had at Rome. As therefore Cicero, before the time of Saul, was Pro-Consul of the province of Cilicia, in its chief city, Tarsus; as Gallio was Pro-Consul of the province of Achaia, at its chief city, Corinth,[1] so was Sergius Paulus Pro-Consul of the province of Cyprus, at its chief city, Paphos. The word 'Deputy' stands here for Pro-Consul.[2] Sergius Paulus might have been formerly Senator at Rome. At any rate, he had in some way gained the election of the Senate, and now for a year or longer is Pro-Consul, or Governor, or 'Deputy' of Cyprus. He had under him military officers, cen-

[1] Acts xviii. 12–16.
[2] The Greek word is the same word commonly used to translate the Latin pro-consul into Greek.

turions, captains, etc., and civil officers, assessors, judges, etc.; and he himself, as a Judge, held his own court, just as Gallio, the Pro-Consul at Corinth, held his court when the people attempted to accuse Paul before him. The Pro-Consul was perhaps not unlike the Governor whom our own Congress sends out to administer the laws of the United States in a territory before it becomes a State.

Sergius Paulus, the Pro-Consul at Paphos, was a 'prudent' man: he had a candid and inquiring mind: he admitted the sorcerer to his presence, and sent for Barnabas and Saul. And now, before him as a Judge, Truth and Falsehood come in conflict in the Apostle and the Magician.

It is not strange that we find this magic-worker with this dignified and sober official, and indeed spending some time with him, as it would seem. "For many years before this time, and many years after, impostors from the East, pretending to magical powers, had great influence over the Roman mind." Even educated Romans had become superstitious. There were at Rome soothsayers from Asia Minor: there was magic medicine from Syria: there were magic tables of calculations from Babylon: there were even Jewish fortune-tellers, the gipsies of that day. Even the great generals, like Pompey and Julius Cæsar, consulted these soothsayers and astrologers as oracles. And it was not without some shade of truth that the great Latin satirist, Juvenal, describes the Emperor Tiberius Cæsar, 'sitting on the rock of Capri, with his flock of Chaldean astrologers round him.' These magic-workers, so numerous throughout the Empire, would of course gather around such places of resort as Paphos; and it is not strange, therefore, that the Pro-Consul, like more illustrious men, should have with him this 'false prophet,'

who, though a Jew, had given himself the Arabic name
of Elymas, or, The Wise. But it shows the impartial
candor of his mind that he sent for Barnabas and Saul
also, and wished to hear from them "the word of God."
Perhaps he expected to hear the declaration of an oracle
or to see some wonder wrought. Perhaps Elymas was
ready to answer wonder with wonder, as the Egyptian
magicians answered Moses' in the presence of Pharaoh.

But when Saul did nothing more than to preach the
simple faith in Jesus as the Messiah, Elymas sought to
turn away the Governor's mind. Truth was on one
side: falsehood on the other. There was a plain conflict. It was of the highest importance that the Gospel should not be overthrown by false and hypocrit-
ical arts. And when Elymas attempted to prejudice
and pervert the Pro-Consul's mind unfairly against the
faith, he was suddenly silenced in an awful manner.
Filled with that same Holy Spirit which gave Peter
power to see and to denounce the lies and hypocrisy of
Ananias and Sapphira, Saul was able to see the wicked
malice of this man, and to denounce his imposture.
Conscious of his apostolical authority, derived from
God, as was Peter when he solemnly told Simon, the
magician of Samaria, "Thy *heart is not right* in the
sight of God," Saul boldly and solemnly exposed the
wicked deception of Elymas and his hatred of righteousness. He called down a miracle upon him, as an awful
warning to all such impostors, and a rebuke to all who
trusted them, as well as a proof that what he said was
the word of God. The Roman Governor, not like many
proud men in Judea, who, when they were 'astonished,' 'marvelled' and still disbelieved, and then reviled, took the proof of Saul's doctrine with an honest
heart, and believed in Jesus of Nazareth.

' Exodus vii. 11, 22 ; viii. 7.   ' Acts viii. 21.

The conversion of such a prominent man could hardly fail to excite much attention in Cyprus; and we may believe that through his influence other Gentiles, even in dissolute Paphos, and in various parts of the island, received the simple doctrines of salvation which he had learned in his own soul.

Such is Saul's first recorded triumph among the Gentiles: the conversion of a man of authority, in one of the vilest cities of the heathen; an official under the great nation which oppressed the Jews, higher in office than the centurion Cornelius at Cæsarea; an honored, powerful governor of a province, yielding his heart to the simple " truth as it is in Jesus."

" And now, from this point in the Apostolical history, PAUL appears as the great figure in every picture. Barnabas, henceforward, is always in the background. The great Apostle now enters on his work as Preacher to the Gentiles, and at the moment of his active occupation of the field in which he is called to labor, his name is suddenly changed. As Abram was changed into Abraham, when God promised that he should be the ' father of many nations;' as Simon was changed into Peter when it was said, ' On this rock I will build my Church,' so Saul is changed into Paul at the moment of his first great victory among the Heathen." Before this, he has always been called Saul. At this point, he is " Saul who also is called Paul." After this he is always called Paul. In all his epistles written afterward, he calls himself Paul,[*] and never Saul. And Peter, in one of his epistles, calls him " our beloved brother Paul."[*] Why is it that his name is changed, and changed just at this time?

Three principal reasons have been given for the change.

[*] See the first verse of all Paul's Epistles, except Hebrews.
[*] II. Peter iii. 15.

The first reason is, "that he adopted it himself, after his conversion, as expressing his own feelings." The Roman name Paulus means *little.* As Saul, before his conversion, was like "the unbridled King Saul," the proud, self-confident persecutor of David, so Paul the convert, lowly and penitent, wished to indicate by his very name that he was "the *least* of the Apostles," and "*less than the least* of all saints."

The second reason is, that Sergius *Paulus* gave him his own name as a grateful memorial of his own conversion; "that, as Scipio was called Africanus from the conquest of Africa, and Metellus was called Creticus from the conquest of Crete, so Saul carried away his new name as a trophy of his victory over the heathenism of the Pro-Consul Paulus."

The third reason is, "that Paul used the Gentile form of his Hebrew name from this time, to show that he was a friend and teacher of the Gentiles." Gentile names were often adopted in Jewish families, as the *Greek* names Philip[1] and Alexander,[1] as the *Roman* names, Crispus, Justus, and Niger,[2] as in our own time the scattered Jews take names from the countries in which they are. Sometimes, too, there were double names, one national and the other foreign, as Belteshazzar-Daniel, Esther-Hadassa,[3] Herod-Agrippa, Simon-Peter, and so Saul-Paulus. Whichever opinion we adopt, it is natural that the name of the Roman Pro-Consul should bring the name of PAUL here to the mind of the inspired writer. It is natural, too, that henceforth among the Gentiles he should use the Roman name; and then, having used it on his travels, and

---

[1] Matt. x. 3; Acts xix. 33, 34; vi. 5; xxi. 8.
[2] Acts xviii. 8; i. 23; xiii. 1.
[3] Daniel x. 1; Esther ii. 7.

during the more important part of his life, he should write to the Gentile churches, " I, *Paul* the Apostle."

Paulus was the name of a well-known family among the Romans, one of the most distinguished members of which, Emilius Paulus, fell fighting against Hannibal at Cannæ. It is possible that when Paul's father, or the family, obtained the Roman citizenship, there was some connection or attachment of the family to the Roman Paulus family, and so the parents could gratify their Hebrew and their Roman attachments, by naming their son Saul *and* Paulus.

QUESTIONS.

WHERE was Paphos ?

> Do you think the Apostles preached at any places be-
> tween Salamis and Paphos ?
>
> What was Paphos ?
>
> What people lived there ?
>
> What religion prevailed ? and why ?
>
> What famous general afterward visited this city ?
>
> What celebrated poets wrote of this city ?
>
> Was the religion of Paphos moral ?
>
> What is the morality of heathen religions now ?
>
> What did Saul bring to Paphos ?

What was 'the Deputy' ?

> What was a Roman Consul ?
>
> What was a Roman Pro-Consul ?
>
> What famous orator had been Pro-Consul of Cilicia ?
>
> What other Pro-Consul is mentioned in 'the Acts' ?
>
> What is the name of this 'Deputy' ?
>
> How had he been elected to this office ?
>
> What office may he have held at Rome ?
>
> What officers were under him ?
>
> What officer in our own government was the Pro-Consul
> somewhat like ?

Whom did the Apostles find with the Pro-Consul ?

> What other men like him are mentioned in the Scriptures ?
>
> Is it necessary to think he tried as a prophet, to foretell
> future events ?[1]
>
> What did educated Romans think of such men ?
>
> Will education keep a man from absurd and wicked
> things in religion ?

Was the Pro-Consul doing a strange thing in having this
magician with him ?

> What is the meaning of Bar-jesus ?[2]

---

[1] See page 43.

[2] Compare Matt. xvi. 17 with John i. 42, and xxi. 15.

(15)

What language is 'Elymas,' and what does it mean?

Whom does the Pro-Consul send for?

Do you think he wished to know the truth?

What kind of a man was he?

What do you think he expected from the Apostles?

Between what two things was the conflict?

What did Elymas try to do?

What right had Saul to call down blindness on this man?

What other instances in the Scriptures of such power exercised, and by whom?

What was the miracle for?

How did Saul publicly condemn Elymas' secret motives?

Have we a right, as Saul did, to condemn the motives of another?

How did the Pro-Consul differ from the proud Jews who saw our Saviour's miracles?

What influence would the Pro-Consul's conversion be likely to have through the island?

What must we have, which Saul had, to lead men to Jesus?

What change is made in the Apostle's name here?

What other similar changes of name in the Scriptures?

What is he called before and after this time, in the Scriptures?

Did the Apostle afterward call himself Saul or Paul?

What did Peter call him?

What three ways are there of accounting for the change?

Were Gentile names ever adopted in Jewish families?

What examples have you of double names in the Scriptures?

Who is now *first* in the rest of the Book of Acts, Paul or Barnabas?

When you think of the King of Israel, is Saul a good or a bad name?

When you think of the Apostle to the Gentiles, is Saul a good or a bad name?

How can you make your name for ever a good or a bad name?

Ninth Sunday.

'PERILS OF ROBBERS' AND 'PERILS OF RIVERS.

LESSON.
Acts xiii. 13, 14; xv. 36–39. II. Corinthians xi. 26, 27.

FROM Paphos, ships would be much more frequent to the coast of Pamphylia than to Alexandria or Cyrene, on the Egyptian coast of the Mediterranean, or than to any of the flourishing cities around the Archipelago to which Paul did afterwards go. It is very probable that when the Apostles were ready to depart, a ship was just about to sail to Attalia or to Perga, and that they took advantage of the opportunity to go thither. A second reason why they went to Pamphylia next, may have been, that Paul might like to go now among those provinces near Cilicia. Pamphylia was next his native province, and the people were in some respects like the Cilicians. A third reason may have been, that the people of Pamphylia were more rough and less educated, and probably more simple-hearted " than the inhabitants of those provinces which were more completely penetrated with the corrupt civilisation of Greece and Rome;" and Paul might have thought, therefore, that they would be more likely to receive the simple truth. A fourth reason, we may suppose, was that Paul thought of the many families " in the great towns beyond the mountains of Tarsus, such as Antioch in Pisidia, and Iconium in Lycaonia," and he hoped through them to reach the Gentiles, " who flocked there, as everywhere, to the worship of the synagogue." We can hardly think that Paul had a direct vision at this time, like the trance in the temple,[1] or like the vision at Troas,[2] for these visions seem to be recorded, not as frequent but as extraordinary events. Whatever was the inducement to visit these regions rather than others, Paul and Barnabas and Mark sailed out of

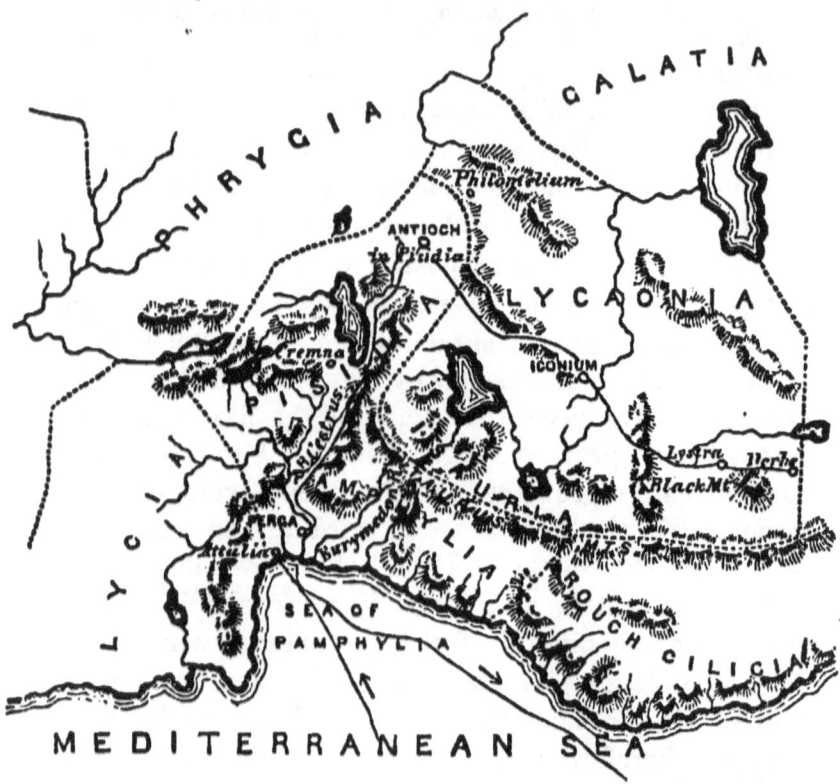

Paphos, around past the promontories at the west end of the island. Not many hours after the promontories of Cyprus, on the east, had receded in the horizon, would be seen before them, far in the north-west, the hills of Lycia, and far in the north-east, the high cliffs of Paul's native province, between which they sailed straight "to the innermost bend of the bay of Attalia."

[1] Acts xxii. 17–21   [2] xvi. 9.

As they sailed over this bay, they would see a line of "ragged mountain-summits," stretching along in a curve, like the curve of the coast, back through the interior, and enclosing a wide plain, itself like a bay hemmed in by the mountains. Back from the shore, like Tarsus, and like Tarsus, on a river, was Perga, in this large plain, with hills on the sides, a valley in front, with the river Cestrus connecting it with the sea and " with the mountains behind." We know almost nothing of this city, except that near it, on a height, was a temple of Diana, and that an annual festival was held in honor of the goddess. Just near this temple we may suppose the vessel, sailing up the river, bringing the great Apostle, came to its moorings.

The Apostles did not stay long in Perga. There is no notice of their preaching here on their outward journey, as there is on their return.[3] If they did preach at this time, the preaching does not seem attended with very marked results. Mark left them. It is clearly against their wishes; for afterwards Paul condemned Mark for "going not with them to the work." Possibly, too, it was the cause of ill-feeling between Paul and Barnabas, as "afterwards it was the cause of quarrel and separation."[4] Mark probably found a ship in the river about to sail to Palestine. He saw now the peril of the journey up through the rough country and the mountains. He thought of his pleasant early home in Jerusalem. He shrunk from the work, and wished to be with his friends; and, as there was opportunity to reach home by a ship direct to Cæsarea, or to some other point of Palestine, he "departed from them from Pamphylia." We are not to think that Mark forfeited his Christian character. Dwelling always before in Je-

[3] Acts xiv. 25.   [4] Acts xv. 37–39.

rusalem probably, and unacquainted, like Paul and
Barnabas, with these rougher provinces, he may have
had a wicked timidity; and he weakly allowed his
natural longing for home to over-balance the interests
of the great cause. He was the child of a Christian
mother; he knew the sincerity and devotion of the disciples who met to pray in his mother's house;[5] he had
felt and seen the power of their religion in persecution;
he had heard the prayers for Peter in prison; he had
been in Antioch when the Spirit of God abounded unto
the salvation of many; he had seen Paul's preaching
confirmed by a miracle at Paphos; he knew Barnabas
and Paul were on a most important mission, sent by
the Holy Ghost to carry the Gospel to unknown parts
of the earth; and yet now, just when his assistance and
company would be needed, if ever,[6] he falters and
shrinks from the work. Afterwards, however, he was
willing to go with the same Apostles on a second missionary journey,[4] and though Paul at that time would
not take him, he did go with Barnabas to Cyprus.[4] But
in later years Paul was reconciled and, indeed, attached
to him; for, when he writes to his brethren in Colosse,
he commends Mark as a fellow-worker unto the kingdom of God, and 'a comfort' to himself;[7] and he writes
Timothy to bring Mark to him, for "he is profitable to
me for the ministry."[8]

After Mark had left them, Paul and Barnabas took
their perilous way a hundred miles directly into the interior. Their journey lay up through the circle of
mountains, whose "ragged summits" they had seen
from the sea. From the broad plain beyond Perga,

[5] xii. 12.
[6] The region of the mountain-robbers was now before them.
[7] Colossians iv. 10, 11.
[8] II. Timothy iv 11.

they toiled upwards to the high table-land on the other
side of the principal mountain-range. "In all parts of
ancient history, the lawless and marauding habits of the
people of these mountains were notorious." Although
the Apostles passed a little to the one side of the district of Isauria, the name which is more than any other
in Asia Minor connected with daring robbery, yet the
people of that region carried their dashing and plunder-
ing excursions into all the surrounding country. The
Pisidians also were robbers, like their neighbors on the
east, and even the Pamphylians nearest the mountains
"had not quite given up their robber habits, and did
not always allow *their* neighbors to live in peace."
Even Alexander the Great, who once marched from Perga through this same country towards Phrygia, "found
some of the worst difficulties of his whole campaign in
penetrating through this district." One of the roughest
campaigns in the wars of Antiochus the Great, King
of Syria, was among the hill-forts near the upper waters
of the Cestrus and Eurymedon. And many years after
this time, not very far from the very route which the
Apostles must have taken, at Cremna, a robber-chief
defied the Romans, and died a desperate death in these
mountains. "No people through the midst of whom
Paul ever travelled, abounded more in those 'perils of
robbers' of which he himself speaks, than the wild and
lawless classes of the Pisidian highlanders;" and it is
no doubt to the perils of this journey in part that he
alludes when, writing to the Christians of Corinth, he
sums up the sufferings of his life. Here certainly he
was 'in weariness and painfulness,' and 'in watchings
often,' and 'in perils by the heathen,' if not 'in perils
of robbers.'

There were other perils, too, from the very nature of
the country and its climate. There were 'perils of riv

ers.'* We perhaps do not fully appreciate the danger in which an Eastern traveller is, from the crossing of streams, or even from travelling by their side, as when Paul followed the valley of the Cestrus. The dry water-courses then are often flooded with wonderful suddenness. High and steep mountains and violent rains, suddenly swell the streams until they are torrents. "All the rivers in the East are liable to these violent and sudden changes. And no district of Asia Minor has more of these 'water-floods' than the mountainous tract of Pisidia, where rivers burst out at the bases of high cliffs, or dash wildly down through narrow ravines." Probably there were bridges, but these might be swept away by the impetuous and swollen floods, tossing and tumbling on their way from the heights and precipices of Pisidia to the Pamphylian Sea. "The Apostle's course was probably never far from the channels of the Cestrus and the Eurymedon; and it is interesting to know that just in this vicinity, to this day, in the village of Paoli, (St. Paul,) his name is still retained." It is the custom of the people of Perga, at the beginning of the hot season, to move up from the plains to the cool, basin-like hollows on the mountains. The people may be seen climbing to the upper grounds, men, women, and children, flocks and herds, camels and asses, like the patriarchs of old. If, then, St. Paul was at Perga in May, as very likely he may have been, if he left Antioch when the sea was first 'open' in the spring, he would find the inhabitants going directly on the route of his own journey. He would not wish to stay in Perga. We may think of him as joining some cara-

---

* In II. Corinthians xi. 26, it is 'perils of *waters.*' The word strictly means rivers, or swollen rivers, torrents, *floods*, as in Matt. vii. 27, "the rains descended and the *rivers* came," the swollen, rapid torrent, like our *freshet.*

van of families up to the heights, as journeying along a
road with frowning cliffs on either side, with fountains
bursting out among the flowers, with dashing and dangerous floods across the path, as climbing up even in a
few hours into a colder climate, into a wilder and more
barren region, with valleys of sand between the rocky
hills, until at length he and Barnabas came out on the
central table-land of Asia Minor, and, passing the shore
of a beautiful lake, came to Antioch of Pisidia.

QUESTIONS.

WHERE do the missionaries go next ?

Who composed ' his company ' ?

Do you suppose them directed by the especial revelation of the Spirit ?

What four reasons may be given why they go there ?

How many of these reasons are like those which led them from Antioch to Cyprus ?

Do you suppose Paul had a vision ?

Where was Perga ?

How did its situation resemble that of Tarsus ?

What do we know of Perga ?

How long did they stay here ?

Do you think they preached ?   Why ?

What town on the coast had they passed when they reached Perga ?

Where is it mentioned afterwards ?

What painful event took place at Perga ?

How do you know this return was against Paul's wishes ?

What do you think led Mark to leave them ?

Was he right, or wrong, do you think ?

Do you think Mark forfeited his claim to be thought a Christian ?

What had been Mark's home-influences in religious things ?

What was there to make him timid ?

Is there any time when it is wrong for every one to be timid ?

How can a man gain courage in doing right?

Who and what will help him ?

Did Mark ever return to his work ?

Where is Mark next mentioned ?

On what occasion ?

What did Barnabas wish ?

What did Paul say, when Mark wished to go ?

Did they ever work together again?

Can you prove Paul became attached again to Mark?

Where did Paul and Barnabas now go?

What made their work now toilsome?

What famous robber-region were they near?

What was the character of many Pisidians and Pamphy
lians?

What famous generals had much trouble here?

What, in one of his letters afterwards, describes Paul's
toil and peril?

What other peril from the nature of the country?

How may 'perils of waters' be translated?

What was true of Pisidia in comparison with the rest of
Asia Minor?

How many of these perils can you suppose Paul was in
on this journey?

What other of his sufferings may have happened at this
time?

What time of the year do you suppose it was?

What time of the year did the people of Perga leave
their city? and for what?

What new reason is there, then, for not staying longer
now in Perga?   •

What changes in country and climate, in going up from
Perga to Antioch in Pisidia?

The course of what stream did they follow?

Where was Antioch in Pisidia?

Why called Antioch *in Pisidia?*

(18)

Tenth Sunday.

JESUS OF NAZARETH, THE MESSIAH.

LESSON.

Acts xiii. 15–41.

OF Antioch in Pisidia we know but little, but it was a town of sufficient consequence to be a Roman colony.[1] Romans and Roman soldiers and Roman military standards and Roman magistrates were seen here. The great road from Smyrna and Ephesus to the ' Cilician Gates,'[2] near Tarsus, led through this town; and Antioch was about half-way between the Archipelago and the ' Gates.' Here, among Romans, Greeks, Pisidians, were Jews in larger or smaller numbers; for here is a synagogue in which Jews and Gentile proselytes met to worship. If you had gone into this synagogue, you would probably have seen the women separated from the men, either in a separate gallery, or behind a lattice-work partition: the men all with hats on: the desk in the centre, where the reader ' opened the book in sight of all the people:' " the carefully closed ark on the side of the building nearest to Jerusalem," where the rolls or manuscripts of the law were kept: " the seats[3] all round the building, from

---

[1] The meaning of Roman *colony*, in connection with a town, will be seen when we come to the description of the colony of Philippi, in Twentieth Sunday. Antioch in Pisidia was a *colony*, like Philippi.

[2] See the map of Cilicia, in First Sunday.

[3] In the East, probably there would not be raised seats, as in the drawing, but rather matting without benches.

which 'the eyes of all those in the synagogue were fastened' on the one who speaks: the chief seats nearest
the ark, and the platform for the 'ruler' or 'rulers' of
the synagogue." After the opening prayer, "the sacred
roll of manuscript was handed from the ark to the
reader by the attendant or 'minister,'* and parts, first

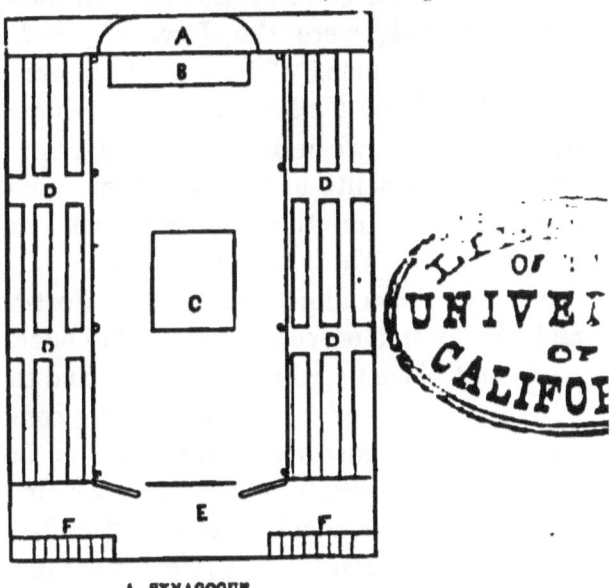

A SYNAGOGUE.

A—Sacred recess of the Ark, with doors or curtains in front. B—Platform for
chief speakers. C—Reader's desk. D—Seats, with women's gallery above them.
E—Hall or court. F—Stairs to women's gallery.

of the law and then of the prophecies, were read in
the regular order of the Sabbath-lessons. The reader
stood in the desk and all the congregation sat around.
The manuscript was rolled up and handed back to the
'minister' and returned to the ark. Then followed a
pause, during which strangers or learned men who had
'any word of consolation' or of exhortation rose and
addressed the congregation. And then, after rehears-
ing the story of the suffering of the chosen people, or
the allegorical interpretation of some dark passage of

* Luke iv. 17, 20 ; see also note 11, page 46.

Holy Writ, the worship was closed with a benediction and a solemn Amen," uttered perhaps by the congregation.[8]

On the Sabbath after Paul and Barnabas reached Antioch, the congregation came together as usual in the synagogue. There were Gentiles as well as Jews in the seats along the sides—converted proselytes from the city and the country around. In the gallery, or behind a lattice, were the Jewesses, and among them 'honorable women.' The two strangers came in; they were offered the *Tallith*, the loose, fringed, white, four-cornered scarf worn on the shoulders or head—the regalia of an Israelite in the synagogue—and receiving it, they sat down on the seats with the others. Prayer was offered. The 'minister' handed 'the book' from the ark to the reader at the desk. Portions of the law and the prophets were read. The book was handed back, and placed again in the ark. And then the 'rulers of the synagogue' "sent to the new comers, on whom many eyes had already been fixed, and invited them to address the assembly, if they had words of comfort or of instruction to speak to their fellow-Israelites." We can almost see Paul, as he rises to speak. With a face full of earnestness, and an attitude at once animated and emphatic, he stretches out his hand and commences his address.

We may not have recorded all that Paul said, but we certainly have the substance of what he said, and that substance in his very words:

ADDRESS IN THE SYNAGOGUE.

Notice now the object of this address, and its principal parts.

The Object. The one great object was to prove to

---

[8] Nehemiah viii. 6.

the native Jews and the Gentile proselytes, mingled in the synagogue, that JESUS OF NAZARETH *is the* MESSIAH *predicted in the Hebrew Scriptures.*

To prove this, he does not state his proposition at the beginning of his address, and at once proceed to prove it from the Scriptures, as perhaps we would do; but he takes the more usual form of exhortation in the synagogue.

I. THE NATIONAL HISTORY. (Introductory: 16th to 22d verse.) As it was customary to rehearse some part of the nation's history, he gives a partial account of God's dealings with the Hebrew people. Paul does here just as Peter did at the first assembly after our Lord's ascension [6] and at the Pentecost,[7] and as Stephen did before the national council,[8] when they wished to win the fixed attention of the people. He makes the history, the promises, the prophecies, to which all would be eagerly attentive, the introduction to his argument. He therefore first sketches the history of the nation from the bondage of Egypt to King David. The congregation sees, too, that Paul firmly believes their Scriptures.

II. THE PROMISE. (23d verse.) He next says that that great promise made to David,[9] (which all Jews were expecting to be fulfilled,) that some one of David's posterity should reign on his throne, as Lord and Deliverer, *is* fulfilled in Jesus of Nazareth, a 'Saviour unto Israel,' the long-expected Messiah. This is the plain statement or proposition which he then goes on to prove.

III. PROOF THAT JESUS OF NAZARETH WAS MEANT IN THE PROMISE. (24th to 37th verse.) Next comes the argument to prove, from their own Scriptures, that

---

[6] Acts i. 16.   [7] ii. 16.   [8] vii. 2.
[9] I. Chronicles xvii. 11-14; II. Samuel vii. 12, 13, 16; Psalm LXXXIX. 3, 4.

Jesus is the one person of David's posterity whom God meant in this promise: that is, to prove that the ancient Hebrew Scriptures were fulfilled in this Jesus. Three proofs are given.

First Proof. (24th and 25th verses.) Jesus of Nazareth appeared after his extraordinary forerunner had announced his coming, just as the prophets declared the Messiah would come.[10] All the people acknowledged John the Baptist a wonderful prophet, sent of God.[11] He could not and he would not lie, and yet he always said, while fulfilling his mission, ' I am not the Messiah, but one among you, who cometh after me, is the Messiah. I am the forerunner,[12] as Isaiah says.[10] HE is the ONE coming after the forerunner.'

Second Proof. (26th to 29th verse.) Jesus of Nazareth was in innocence and in ignominy slain, as the Scriptures declared the Messiah would be: the rulers did not understand that the Scriptures declare that the innocent Messiah should be condemned and slain, as they plainly do. And so they, in ' condemning ' Jesus, in finding ' no cause of death ' in him, in asking Pilate to slay him, fulfilled these very prophecies[13] which they did not understand. The death of Jesus on the cross,[14] and his burial in the sepulchre,[15] therefore, particularly fulfilled the Scripture. The Apostle, while making this second proof that Jesus is Messiah, *appeals* also to the Jews (children of the stock of Abraham) and proselytes (whoever feareth God) to receive the ' word of salvation ' sent, *because* the rulers have rejected it.

---

[10] Isaiah xl. 3 ; Malachi iv. 5, 6.   [11] Matthew xiv. 5 ; xxi. 26.

[12] John i. 23.

[13] Such prophecies especially as Isaiah liii. 3, 5–9, etc., and Daniel ix. 26, etc. The Jews understood these and others to refer to the coming of Messiah.

[14] Isaiah liii. 12.   [15] liii. 9.

Third Proof. (Verses 30 to 37.) Jesus of Nazareth rose from the dead. We know surely God raised him from the dead; for those who knew him best, who came up from Galilee to Jerusalem with him, *many* persons, bear testimony that they saw him, not *once*, but '*many* days.' This fact is therefore well established, and it is in direct fulfilment of God's promise to our ancestors. *For, just as* God foretold to David that the Messiah should be of his seed, when he said, 'Thou art my son, this day have I begotten thee,' which we have always understood as referring to the Messiah, and *just as* he said that his mercies and promises should be surely received by David and by us his posterity, *so* did he foretell to David that the HOLY ONE, the MESSIAH, '*should not see corruption*,' that is, his body should not be corrupted in the grave, but should be preserved from decay and death. This promise made to David, 'Thou shalt not suffer thine Holy One to see corruption,' cannot mean that *David* was the Holy One, for David's body saw corruption in the grave, but it meant that the MESSIAH, the HOLY ONE, should not see corruption; and that Messiah is Jesus of Nazareth therefore, for God raised Him up again, and HE *saw no corruption.*

These, then, are the three arguments: The Scriptures say that the Messiah will have a forerunner: Jesus of Nazareth had a forerunner. The Scriptures say that the Messiah will be unjustly condemned and slain: Jesus of Nazareth was unjustly condemned and slain by our very rulers, who were blindly fulfilling the Scriptures. The Scriptures say that the Messiah shall rise from the dead: Jesus of Nazareth *has* risen from the dead. Therefore,

JESUS OF NAZARETH *is* THE MESSIAH.

IV. THE PRACTICAL APPLICATION. (Verses 38, 39.)

Take this Jesus, then, the Fulfilment of the Ancient Scriptures, as your Messiah. Your sins may be forgiven, if you believe in Him ; and though you cannot be made just by that law of Moses which has this day been read in the desk of the synagogue, because you have all broken it, yet all of you, who believe in Jesus as Messiah, may become *pardoned*, and so justified, by Him.

V. THE WARNING. (Verses 40, 41.) And beware lest the dreadful prediction of the prophets to all who simply wonder at the works of God, and despise them, come upon you.

QUESTIONS.

WHAT do we know of Antioch in Pisidia?

Describe a synagogue.

What were the three principal parts of the worship?

On what day of the week did the missionaries go to the synagogue?

How were they taken notice of? By whom?

What was the custom with Israelite strangers?

What was the one great object of Paul's speech?

Does Paul state this object at first?

I. What is the first division of the speech?

What common custom does Paul follow?

What other speeches in the New Testament follow this custom?

What period of Jewish history does he describe?

How would the Jews like this story?

What would be the effect on their minds in reference to the rest of the speech?

Who were there in the synagogue that 'feared God (16th verse) besides men of Israel?

What is meant (17th verse) by 'exalted the people'?

What is meant by 'suffered their manners'?

When God 'suffers' sin, does he cause it?

Did David ever commit sin?

What is meant, then, by 'a man after mine own heart'?

II. What is the second division of the speech?

What promise is this?

Where do you find it recorded?

What is meant by David's seed reigning forever?

III. What is the third division of the speech?

What does Paul take his proofs from?

Why was it important to prove this?

1. What is the first proof that Jesus is Messiah?

Why did the Jews think the Messiah would have a remarkable forerunner?

What did the Jewish people think of John the Baptist
Why ought they to receive John's word as true?
What did John say of himself?
Whose words did he quote?

2. What is the second proof that Jesus is Messiah?
   In what respect did the 'rulers' misinterpret their own Scriptures?
   How did they fulfil the Scriptures they misunderstood?
   Why did they misunderstand them?
   To whom, then, did the promise of the prophets come? (26th verse.)
   What two classes are addressed in the twenty-sixth verse?

8. What is the third proof that Jesus is Messiah?
   How do we know God raised him from the dead?
   How many persons saw him alive after his resurrection?
   What persons were they?
   Did they see him more than once?
   What passage did Paul quote to prove again that Jesus is David's son?
   How did the Jews commonly understand this passage?
   What passage did he quote to prove whatever is promised to David's son is sure?
   What passage to prove the Messiah would rise from the dead?
   Why couldn't this passage mean David?
   Whom did it mean? Why?

State now Paul's three proofs that Jesus is Messiah.
   Which is the strongest of the three proofs?

IV. What is the fourth division of the speech?
   What is the object of preaching? (38th verse.) Through whom?
   What advantage is it to believe Jesus is Messiah more than to live by the law of Moses?
   Whom does that law condemn?
   Are we, or are we not, under Moses' law?
   Whom does Messiah save?
   V. What is the fifth division of the speech?
   To whom does this warning now come?

Eleventh Sunday.

AN EXTRAORDINARY THING IN A SYNAGOGUE.

LESSON.
ACTS xiii. 42–50.

THINK now of Paul's new position, as he stands in the synagogue of Pisidian Antioch, at the close of his address. He has been saying the same things which he had listened to with so much bitterness when Stephen made his speech before the Sanhedrim. How strange it seems, when we think of the two attitudes: Saul, with the garments of the witnesses at Jerusalem, and consenting to the death of Stephen; Paul, in the synagogue at Antioch of Pisidia, repeating the story, the prophecies which Stephen repeated, and *finishing the argument* which Stephen would no doubt have finished, had he been permitted. Here is a change which only the Spirit of God can make.

" This address made a deep and thrilling impression on the audience. While the congregation were pouring out of the synagogue, many of them crowded around the speaker, begging that ' these words,' which had moved their deepest feelings, might be repeated to them on their next occasion of assembling together." [1] And when most of the people had gone, many of the Jews and Gentiles, who had been powerfully moved by

---

[1] The words ' the next Sabbath,' are translated in the margin, ' in the week between,' and it is not quite certain whether they mean the next Saturday or some other day. The Jews were accustomed to meet in their synagogue on Monday and Thursday, as well as Saturday.

the proof that Jesus was the Messiah, still clung to Paul and Barnabas, and followed them. The Apostles urged them to hold fast their present convictions, and knowing the opposition and the persecution which this belief in Jesus everywhere excited, to ask God's grace, to keep and to help them.

It is not probable that these two good men were idle through the week. They attended, no doubt, the meetings at the synagogue, if there were any. They found opportunity for conversation with many persons: they were invited to the homes of the people: they taught and argued the Messiahship of Jesus, proving it by quotations from the Hebrew Scriptures which they had not cited on the Sabbath. They and their doctrine were soon known through all the town by both Jews and Gentiles. All this seems evident, for the next Sabbath, 'the whole city' flocked in a great multitude to hear the word of God. The crowding of the people to hear this new doctrine, especially the number of the Gentiles not proselytes, the common, profane, uncircumcised, unholy throng, touched at once the bigoted pride and envy of the Jews. They could not endure that all these were to be their equals in religious things, that 'the favored people' were to be degraded to this low level. Instead of hoping and believing that many of the multitude would become proselytes to their own faith, they selfishly feared that their own importance and dignity would be lessened, if the blessings God had given them should be shared by the multitude. Stubborn and wilful in their exclusiveness, "they who on one Sabbath had listened with breathless interest to the teachers who spoke to them of the promised Messiah, were on the next Sabbath filled with the most excited indignation when they found that this Messiah was 'a light to lighten the Gentiles,' as well as 'the glory of his people Israel.'" An uproar was made; and when Paul, who is evidently the chief speaker, again addressed them, they reviled and contradicted.

And now, right here in this synagogue of Pisidia, occurs the great change in the Apostle's whole life-course of preaching — indeed, in the whole apostolic method of preaching. He boldly turns away from the Jews to the Gentiles. We do not know that this had at any time been done before. Paul indeed understood fully that whenever the time should come when the Gentiles would hear his message and the Jews would not, he was not to hesitate to turn to 'the uncircumcised,' 'the unclean,' 'the dogs,' 'the offscouring.' He knew such a thing would violate the Jewish custom, and would meet with scorn and contempt and spiteful persecution; but the words of the vision on the road to Damascus, the command repeated at Damascus, and the words of the vision at Jerusalem, were all plain and positive. He was to offer his message always to the Jew *first*, and then to the Gentile.[2] Right here was the turning-point and test of his Apostleship to the Gentiles. Never before had there been a time when, in a mixed mass of circumcised and uncircumcised crowded together in a synagogue, the faith of the Hebrew Scriptures had been offered openly to Gentiles who *were not proselytes*, and offered to *them because* the Jews rejected it. Jesus had indeed praised the faith of *individual* Gentiles, like the Roman centurion at Capernaum,[3] and the Syrophenician woman.[4] Peter had preached to the *household* of Cornelius, the Roman officer, but it was distinctly separate from all Jews. So Sergius Paulus, the Roman Governor of Cyprus, had believed, but it is not said that there were *synagogues* in Paphos, nor does

---

[2] Romans i. 16.   [3] Luke vii. 9.   [4] Matt. xv. 28, and Mark vii. 26.

it appear that there were *Jews*, other than the 'false
prophet,' *present*. But here were both Jews and Gentiles together in great numbers. In the hearing of both,
the word of life had been spoken ; the Jews had rejected
it ; and therefore Paul, boldly breaking through all
bigotry, narrow pride, and exclusiveness, turned directly *away from* the Jews to the unproselyted Gentiles.
Here, then, he stood forth fully revealed, the *Apostle to
the Gentiles.*[*] We, in our day, can hardly feel how
much strength of character it needed to take this bold
position, nor how much especial heavenly grace and
strength even an inspired Apostle required for this most
extraordinary and most difficult duty.

The Apostles take pains to make the impression, that
this extraordinary conduct by them in the synagogue,
is not the result simply of their own judgment and wish.
They quote immediately from the Hebrew Scriptures to
show they are right in turning from Jews who reject
the Gospel, to Gentiles who receive the Gospel. From
their own sacred writings, they quoted a prophecy
which predicts the preaching of the word of God to
people outside the Hebrew nation, and they claimed
that the time of the fulfilment of the prophecy had
come. "I have set thee to be a light *to the Gentiles*,
that thou shouldest be for salvation *to the ends of the
earth.*" They still more boldly claimed, also, that they
were acting by the direct command of God ; that in
this prophecy, God directed them to perform this most
unusual duty: 'For so hath the *Lord commanded us:*'
a duty which was no longer to be unusual with them.
Wherever, afterwards, the Jews rejected their message,
they turned to the Gentiles.

Two effects were immediately produced by these bold

words of the Apostles. The Gentiles gladly hailed this most extraordinary message to them : the Jews burned with more bitter opposition, until at length they set into motion an angry persecution.

The Apostles' hearts were filled with joy, for they had great success in preaching to the Gentiles. For all the perils of robbers and of rivers, for all his weariness and watchings on the road, Paul had now an abundant reward. The good news spread through the country. Through a large region of even wild Pisidia, and perhaps of Phrygia, * the good news of salvation through Jesus Christ was 'published.'

The Jews probably shut the Apostles out of the synagogue at once, but they were not satisfied with that. They determined to drive them out of the city ; and they succeeded, by trick and by intrigue. They excited 'the devout and honorable women, and the chief men of the city.' There were many women, who were proselytes to the Jewish religion, in the towns out of Palestine ; and they had no small influence. Most of the women in Damascus, it is said, were proselytes. Here in Antioch of Pisidia, there seem to have been not only Jewish women, but other women, who attended the synagogue. As the women whom the Jews excited were called 'devout,' they held probably the Jewish faith : as they are called 'honorable' in this Gentile city, they were probably at first Gentiles. It is not likely that the Jews would go directly to Gentile women who did not accept the Jewish faith. It is not likely that strict Jewesses could have had large influence in

* "Antioch in (or near) Pisidia, being a border city, was considered at different times as belonging to different provinces. Ptolemy places it in Pamphylia, and Strabo in Phrygia." This is accounted for by supposing that Pisidia was formerly part of Phrygia, but in Paul's time, a part of Pamphylia. See the map in Ninth Sunday.

this Roman town. We suppose, therefore, that these women were proselytes rather than native Jews or open Gentiles. Exciting these women of position and .of recognised piety against the Apostles, and either by the influence of the women or in addition to them, exciting the chief men of the city, the Jews organized a systematic persecution. "Whether the supreme magistrates of the colony were induced by this unfair agitation to pass a sentence of formal banishment, we are not informed," but the Apostles were expelled out of the limits of the colony.

QUESTIONS.

WHOSE speech is Paul's speech in Antioch like?

What resemblance can you trace?

What change had taken place in Paul?

Can you account for this great cnange in Paul in more than one way?

What kind of an impression did Paul's speech make?

What did the Gentiles in the synagogue wish from Paul?

Do you think these 'Gentiles' were proselytes, or not?

What is meant by 'the next Sabbath'?

When was the next time of assembling?

Was there a 'congregation' left in the synagogue after 'the Jews were gone out'?

What is a proselyte?

What advice did Paul and Barnabas give to those who followed them? Why?

What is meant by 'the grace of God'?

What did the Apostles probably do during the week?

What proves that they were not idle?

Did the multitude who came together 'to hear the word of God,' come intending to obey it?

Is it right to induce people to come to church from other motives than to obey the word of God?

What made the Jews envious?

Why is the word 'multitudes,' and not multitude, used?

Why should the Jews have been glad to see 'almost the whole city' there?

What might they have expected or hoped?

What did they? why?

What is the extraordinary thing in this synagogue?

Had this ever been done before?

What led Paul to think that such a time would come?

How did this offer differ from former offers to Gentiles?

Did our Saviour ever preach to Gentiles?

Was this different from Peter's preaching to Cornelius?

How did it differ from Paul's preaching to Sergius Paulus?

Do you think the Gentiles to whom this offer was made were proselytes, or not?

Can you *prove* that Paul was the Apostle to the Gentiles?

What sort of boldness did it need for. the Apostle to take such a position?

Does the courage now needed to be a Christian differ from it?

How does Paul show he is right in turning to the Gentiles?

Who is 'thee,' in the forty-seventh verse?

What does 'ends of the earth' mean?

From what prophet is this quotation made?

What other bold claim did the Apostles make?

Did this conduct in the synagogue continue to be an extraordinary thing with the Apostles?

What two effects were produced by this conduct?

What is meant by 'glorified the word of the Lord'?

What is meant by 'ordained to eternal life'?

How far was the Gospel preached?

What did the Jews first against the Apostles?

What more did they determine to do?

How did they now attempt to do it?

Through what two classes of persons?

What was often true of women in Gentile towns?

What three classes were there, to one of which it is supposed these women belonged?

Which one of the three did they belong to?

What does 'devout' show?

What does 'honorable' show?

What was the result of the persecution?

Do you think there was a formal sentence of the magistrates?

What is meant by 'coasts'?

(22)

Twelfth Sunday.

FLIGHTS FROM CITY TO CITY.

LESSON.
Acts xiii. 51, 52; xiv. 1–7.

THIS was the first persecution of Paul and Barnabas since they began their missionary journey. And now, thrust out of Antioch and out of Pisidia, they did not forget the words of their divine Master to the Twelve.[1] As a testimony against the wicked persecutors of Antioch, they shook off the very dust from their feet as they took their way along the dry, barren road to the east. "It was taught by the Scribes that the dust of a heathen land defiled by the touch. Hence, the shaking of the dust off the feet implied the city was profane." And one of greater authority than the Scribes had taught that that city was profane, and exposed to condemnation in the day of judgment, which persecuted his servants and disciples.

But as the banished missionaries trod the 'sunburnt road' up the mountain-side, they left behind them, in the city, a company of men filled with the purest joy. The Gentiles who had sincerely believed were rejoicing in their new-found faith: they were full of that highest joy which the human heart is capable of receiving—the joy of the Holy Ghost. They had lost their teachers; they were in the midst of trial and persecution: but the words and the grace of Jesus had entered their trusting hearts, and they could only rejoice.

[1] Matt. x. 14. 15.

After the Apostles had climbed the mountain-range east of Antioch,[2] they looked down on a large plain— the largest, it is said, in Asia Minor. As they descended the other slope of the mountains, on the west or north-west from Iconium, they could see, in the far distance, across the elevated table-land of the plain, two bold, high mountains—Mount Argæus,[3] a hundred and fifty miles away, almost in the east, stretching itself far above the line of the horizon, and Black Mountain, a strange-looking mass of rock and earth, rising from the plain 'like a lofty island from the surface of the ocean,' a hundred or more miles distant in the southeast, in the very direction of Tarsus. Coming down the heights, they could probably see the city of Iconium for some time before they reached it, situated as it is, far out in the plain. If they struck across to the road from Philomelium, they could see the city for twelve or fourteen miles of their journey.

We know more of Iconium since the time of Paul than during his life. It has become a famous place, as the city in which the great Turkish Empire had its first beginnings. The town still remains, with its walls built of broken columns, capitals, pedestals, and other pieces of sculpture, its eighty gates, its towers with Arabic inscriptions : with its great mosque, 'the minaret reaching to the stars ;' with its colleges, churches, public baths, its fortified palace, its carpet and colored leather manufactories : with its massive Arabic architecture and famous Mohammedan tomb. How it looked in the time of Paul we do not know. We can think of the town as in the plain, surrounded almost on every side by mountains covered with snow. " The elements

[2] They may have crossed the range sooner than is indicated by the line on the map.

[3] See map of Cilicia, First Sunday.

of its population would be as follows: a large number of trifling and frivolous Greeks, whose principal places of resort would be the theatre and the market-place; some remains of a still older population, coming in occasionally from the country, or residing in a separate quarter of the town; some few Roman officials, civil or military, holding themselves proudly aloof from the inhabitants of a subjugated province; and an old settlement of Jews, who exercised their trade during the week, and met on the Sabbath to read the law in the synagogue."

Into the synagogue went the two strangers, as they did at Antioch: who, though persecuted and forced to leave their work in Pisidia, did not leave their success behind them. There also a great multitude of Jews and Greeks ('proselytes or heathen, or both') believed the Gospel. And although the bitter and proud Jews did not permit the believers of Iconium to have peace, any more than they did their 'brethren' of Antioch, they did not succeed in driving the Apostles away at once. Although they 'stirred up' the Gentiles, 'the heathen,' to prejudice and ill-feeling, yet the people believed the doctrine, and the Apostles abode there 'long time.' Here, sixty or eighty miles from their late enemies, at Antioch, they reasoned with the Jews out of their Scriptures. They gave another and more striking proof of their authority to explain the word of God. They did miracles. Who could now fail of being convinced of the right and truth of their words?

We suppose Paul and Barnabas were in Iconium some months. The time must have been much *longer* than *two weeks*, for they were in Antioch of Pisidia as long as that;[4] and their stay in Iconium is evidently

---

[4] As they went into the synagogue at Antioch on the Sabbath-day, (Saturday,) they must have reached the city on Friday at least; and

compared with their stay in preceding places. '*Long time* abode they,' it is said, just after the description of their stay in Antioch. The time must have been *shorter* than a *year ;* for the same narrative which declares that they spent 'a whole year' in Antioch in Syria,[5] and that Paul spent 'a year and six months' in Corinth,[6] and 'dwelt two whole years in his own hired house' in Rome,[7] would not have failed to note here a time so long. "There is a tradition of certain events said to have occurred while the Apostles were in Iconium ; and we may safely adopt so much of the story as to imagine Paul preaching long and late to crowded congregations, as he did afterwards at Troas ;[8] his enemies bringing him before the civil authorities, with the cry that he was disturbing their households by his sorcery, or with complaints that he was 'exceedingly troubling the city.'" No doubt, also, the Apostles preached the word from house to house, 'opening and alleging that this is the very Christ.' And notwithstanding all the opposition, they had their good reward for 'weariness' and 'perils' in the 'great multitude' of converts.

During these months the whole city became divided into two great parties, ("a common occurrence on far less important occasions, in these cities of Oriental Greeks :") one party holding that they were good and true men, preaching with sincerity and by God's command : the other, that their preaching and doctrine were pretension and falsehood, and perhaps also that their miracles were mere magic or deception, like the

they did not leave the city till after the 'next Sabbath-day'—not at least till Sunday or Monday. This would make from nine to eleven days. There was probably considerably more time consumed after the second Sabbath in 'stirring up' the women and chief men.

[5] Acts xi. 26. [6] xviii. 11. [7] xxviii. 30. [8] xx. 7–11.

works of all sorcerers. "But here, as at Antioch, the influential classes were on the side of the Jews. A determined attempt," which had no doubt been gathering force from month to month, "was at last made to crush the Apostles, by loading them with insult, and actually stoning them to death." When the actual assault was about to be made, the disciples in some way discovered it in time to flee to some of the smaller towns or villages.

We must not think that because it is said Lystra and Derbe were 'cities of Lycaonia,' it is meant that the Apostles passed now out of one province into another. Iconium was the capital of Lycaonia. The great plain on which the Apostles looked down from the mountains comprised a large part of the province of Lycaonia. "It was a bare and dreary region, unwatered by streams, though in parts liable to occasional floods." Lystra and Derbe were small and retired places, little known. The writer, in calling them 'cities of Lycaonia,' only intends to fix their situation. They were perhaps small towns, "with a rude dialect and simple superstition," off on the boundaries of the province, where the customs of the people did not change, as in the great cities, and "where Greek, though certainly understood, was not commonly spoken." The exact sites of these cities are not known, but it is supposed they were at the foot of Black Mountain. The flight from Iconium was therefore towards the south-east, towards the huge, dark pile which, standing out in the plain, looks so much like a high 'island in the midst of the sea.' Perhaps, however, they did not go directly to Lystra, for they preached also in the 'region round about.' This must have occurred before the events at Lystra took place; for when they left Lystra, they went *directly* to Derbe; and when they left Derbe, they returned at once, it would seem, to Lystra and to Iconium. It may have been that the peril was so great that they did not venture to preach at once in these cities, but were for a while in some of the still more obscure settlements under the shadow of the great mountain. Whether they first preached in " the region round about," or went out from Lystra into the surrounding country, a most important event occurred in Lystra. It is to be noticed that there is no mention of any synagogue in this city. Nothing is said of any Jews, except those who came from Iconium. We shall· see afterwards that there were in the town at least two or three Jews.

" We are now instantly brought into contact with Heathen superstition and mythology; yet not the superstition of an educated mind, as that of Sergius Paulus, nor the mythology of the refined and cultivated Athenians, but the mythology of a rude and illiterate people. Thus does the Gospel, in the person of Paul, clash with opposing powers," one after the other : with the crafty sorcerer, the Roman official, the bitter Jew, the cruel magistrate, and now with false divinities.

QUESTIONS.

WHAT does shaking the dust off the feet signify ?
What difference was there in the teaching of the Saviour
and of the Scribes in respect to this ?
Does 'the disciples' mean Paul and Barnabas ?
What can give the highest joy in the bitterest persecu-
tion ?
Are sacred and holy things gloomy or joyful ?
Does the Holy Spirit design to make men sad or gloomy ?
Is it religion or the want of it which makes many pro-
fessing Christians gloomy and doleful ?
What kind of a country did the Apostles now enter ?
How was Iconium situated ?
How has the city since become famous ?
What was the mixture of population in Paul's time ?
Where did the Apostles go in this town ?
What success did their preaching have here ?
When it is said they '*so* spake,' etc., do you think any-
thing peculiar in their preaching in this town is
meant ?
Were these Greeks 'proselytes' ?
What was the result of the persecution at first ?
How far were they from Antioch in Pisidia ?
What did they besides argue from the Scriptures ?
How long were they in Iconium ?   How do you prove it ?
How long do you think they were in Antioch of Pisidia ?
What tradition is there in respect to Paul in Iconium ?
What does 'word of his grace' mean ?
What else did they ?
What did this 'testimony' prove ?
Were all who heard and saw convinced ?
What happened during this time ?
What did the two parties probably claim in respect to
him ?
What was true of such divisions in Oriental cities ?

Were all who took Paul's side Christians ?

What is meant by the Gospel ?

What did the persecutors determine to do ?

What two parties united in this persecution ?

Whose rulers are 'their rulers' ?

Was stoning a Jewish or a Gentile punishment ?

To what kind of a place did they flee ?

In what direction ?

Did they pass out of the province in which Iconium was ?

What was Iconium in respect to the province ?

Why are these called 'cities of Lycaonia' ?

What kind of country was Lycaonia ?

Where were Lystra and Derbe ?

Did they preach the Gospel anywhere else than in these places ?

Was this preaching before or after they entered Lystra ?

In what kind of places was this preaching ?

Can you think of any other religion than one, which teaches us to go as willingly to the obscure and the poor as to the influential and the rich ?

How does true piety in the heart make men feel in respect to poor and rich ?

What sort of people were the Lystrians?

Were there Jews among them ?

How did the superstition of the Lystrians differ from that of others ?

What kinds of people had the Gospel now come in conflict with ?

What opposite effects had been produced ?

Does the Gospel always produce some effect when it is faithfully preached ?

(24)

Thirteenth Sunday.

JUPITER AND MERCURY.

LESSON.

Acts xiv. 8–20.

"IT was a common belief among the ancients that the gods visited the earth in the form of men. Such a belief with regard to Jupiter, 'the father of gods and men,' would be natural in any rural district, and nowhere more than in Lystra; for Lystra, as appears from the description given,[1] was under the especial protection of Jupiter, and the divinities were imagined to haunt the cities under their protection. The temple or the statue of Jupiter was a conspicuous object in front of the city gates: what wonder was it, therefore, if the citizens of Lystra should be prone to believe that their 'Jupiter which was before the city' would willingly visit his favorite people?" Mercury was the messenger and herald of the gods, especially of Jupiter, and hence was naturally thought to attend Jupiter on his expeditions. The Lycaonians, especially in the region of Lystra, would quickly believe any story of these two divinities appearing together, if a miracle had been wrought, such as this which Luke records.

"We suppose that Paul gathered groups of Lystrians about him, and addressed them" in the open squares of the city, or other places of public resort, as a modern

---

[1] 'Which,' in the thirteenth verse, relates to 'Jupiter,' and not to 'priest,' as the Greek clearly shows. It was Jupiter whose image or temple was before the city, and so was its protection.

missionary might address the natives of a Hindoo village. Although the 'speech of Lycaonia' was a rough, rude dialect of Greek, like some broken accent or 'brogue' in respect to our own English, or the obscure remnant of some older language, yet the people would understand Paul when he spoke to them in Greek.

As Paul was preaching one day, he saw seated on the ground a helpless cripple, weak in his feet, who had never walked, earnestly listening to his words. Paul saw at once more than his deformity and helplessness. He '*steadfastly beheld*' him. (and these words in the Greek are peculiarly forcible: they mean, he looked with a sharp, piercing gaze, as the gaze of one stretching forward to look intently.) By the power of the Holy Spirit, he was able to penetrate the very secrets of the cripple's soul: he saw that 'he had faith to be saved'' from the disease of his body, if not from the spiritual disease of his soul. As Peter, 'fastening his eyes upon' that other cripple at the Beautiful gate of the Temple,' said to him, 'In the name of Jesus Christ of Nazareth, rise up and walk,' so Paul to this heathen cripple in his idolatrous audience at Lystra: 'Stand upright on thy feet.' God's power instantly met human faith, and wrought a mighty change. "The lame man sprang up in the joyful consciousness of a power he had never felt before, and walked like one who had never been infirm." Notice the combination of results in the miracle: strength in place of weakness; soundness and straightness instead of disease and deformity; the art of walking, of balancing and moving at the same time, by one who had never learned.

'Faith to be *healed.*' The Greek word is, 'to be *saved.*' It may be in the sense of 'to be saved' from disease, that is, to be healed, or it may be to be saved from sin.

Acts iii. 1–4, etc.

"And now arose a great tumult of voices from the crowd. Such a cure of such a disease, so sudden and complete, would have confounded the most skilful physicians." The people, filled with astonishment, at once concluded that the divinities were come. They cried out in their mother-tongue that Jupiter and Mercury, n the form of men, were again in Lycaonia. Paul was the 'chief speaker.' They took him, therefore, for Mercury, the god of eloquence. Barnabas must be Jupiter, because Jupiter and Mercury always were companions in their earthly appearances, " though we may well believe that there was something majestically benignant in the appearance of Barnabas, while the personal aspect of Paul was the rather insignificant. It is also possible that Barnabas was *older*, and therefore more *venerable* in appearance than Paul."

The news of a miracle, and that the gods had done it, spread quickly through the small town. The gods had come again! They had cured the cripple, lame from birth! All the people were excited and in tumult. How should they honor the heavenly visitors! The priest of Jupiter's temple at the city gates was called to sacrifice to his god. The priest and his attendants, wearing garlands of leaves and flowers on their heads, and bearing them in their hands, brought oxen to make sacrifice ; and a " procession moved amidst crowds of people to the house in which the Apostles were." By some persons, 'gates' has been supposed to mean ' the gates of the city which the excited people hung with garlands in idolatrous honor of Paul and Barnabas within :' by others, the gates or doors of the house, opening from the street into the hall which led to the inner court, the reception-room or sitting-room of the house.

The Apostles were horror-stricken, when they knew

what the people were doing. Rending their clothes and rushing out among the people, they opposed the people, and expressed their abhorrence of what they were going to do. It may be that Luke has preserved only the short outline of Paul's speech.

Notice the argument :

I. We are not gods, but men with feelings like yours.

II. Worship of such gods is wrong, as we have preached to you : these gods are mere vanities, mere nothings : we declare to you one Living God.

III. This one God, and not your 'vanities,' made all things : the heavens above, the earth beneath, all things

IV. In ancient times some excuse might possibly have been offered ; for having no such light as the Jews, the Gentiles everywhere walked in their own ways.

V. But there is no excuse now, as there was really no excuse then ; for rain from heaven, and the seasons which bring us fruit, and all the wonderful manner in which the earth and the heavens are made, show one God Alone, whom alone we ought to worship.

How coldly this address of Paul fell on that ignorant, superstitious people, eager to offer oxen and garlands in sacrifice to men like themselves. The natural religion of poetry and of imagination they liked, but the worship of One Jehovah only, they did not like. The crowd were ' scarce restrained' from worshipping mortals like themselves. They slowly led away the victims.

But instead of gratitude that the lame man had been healed in their city, we now find a very great and surprising change of feeling. Excited in one direction, they were soon excited in another, as were the Jews at Jerusalem, when one day they cried, 'Hosanna,' and the next day, 'Crucify him.' " The Lycaonians were

proverbially fickle and faithless." Some of the hostile
Jews from Iconium had come to Lystra on some errand ; perhaps on purpose to persecute the Apostles.
" When they heard of the miracles worked on the lame
man, and found how great an effect it had produced on
the people of Lystra, they would be ready with a new
interpretation of the occurrence." And just as at
Jerusalem the Jews said that Jesus 'cast out devils
by Beelzebub, the prince of devils,' so might they say
that this miracle was "not by Divine agency, but by
some diabolical magic. This is probably the true interpretation of that sudden change of feeling among
the Lystrians, which at first sight seems very surprising." They first declared these miracle-workers gods :
the miracle-workers themselves denied that they were
gods : the Jews said that it was sorcery, magic, the
work of devils and of Beelzebub : excited and ignorant
and easily duped, they not only believed it, but suffered
themselves to be led on to persecution and to murder.
In the very streets the mob stoned Paul, then bar-
barously dragged him out of the gate, and cast him out
as dead. Their superstitious change was as sudden as
that of the 'barbarous people' afterwards at Malta,
who first thought Paul a murderer, and then a god.[4]
The Apostle mentions this stoning in his catalogue of
his sufferings.[5] Both at Lystra and when he wrote to
the Corinthians he must have thought of the stoning of
Stephen. And as Stephen's death only increased the
number of disciples, so does the stoning of Paul only
bring into sight others who believed on Jesus, and one
who was afterwards fellow-apostle and fellow-missionary with Paul. 'Disciples stood round about him,'
when he lay as dead, when he recovered from the swoon
and rose up.

[4] Acts xxviii. 4–6.   [5] II. Corinth. xi. 25.

Among these disciples of Lystra, we have reason to believe, was Timothy. His mother was a Jewess, his father a Greek; and about two years later, when Paul came to Lystra again, he found Timothy *already* a Christian, and ' well reported of by the brethren." In one of his letters afterwards to Timothy, Paul reminds Timothy of his knowledge of his own persecution ' at *Antioch, at Iconium, at Lystra*." " We have thus the strongest reasons for believing that Timothy was witness of Paul's injurious treatment, and this too at a time of life when the mind receives its deepest impressions from the spectacle of innocent suffering and undaunted courage. And it is far from impossible that the generous and warm-hearted youth was standing in that group of disciples, who surrounded the apparently lifeless body of the Apostle, outside the walls of Lystra." His mother Eunice, and his grandmother Lois, probably dwelt there,' so that there were in Lystra at least three Jews when Paul came. Educated in the study of the sacred Scriptures by his mother and grandmother,[10] he was ready to receive the Gospel when it came to him. It was not without a divine purpose, therefore, that Paul was permitted to be persecuted at Iconium, and that he fled to Lystra to suffer anew; for here it is that he finds a convert who is to be another faithful preacher of the Gospel.

" Derbe is somewhere not far from the Black Mountain." In a few hours he would come to that place. He probably had no persecution in this town; for when he writes to Timothy that he was witness of his suffering ' at Antioch, at Iconium, at Lystra,' he does not mention Derbe. " It may have been a quiet resting-

---

⁸ Acts xvi. 1.   ⁷ II. Tim. iii. 10, 11.
⁸ II. Tim. i. 5.   ⁹ Acts xvi. 1–3.   ¹¹ II. Tim. iii. 15.

place after a long journey full of toil and danger."
Here Paul recovered his strength after the stoning;
here he gained new vigor after his weariness; but here
also he was still preaching the Gospel, for here he
made many disciples.[11]

[11] Margin of 21st verse.

QUESTIONS.

WHAT especial reason is there why the Lystrians would expect the gods to visit them ?

What is meant by 'Jupiter which was before the city' ?

Who was Jupiter ?   Who was Mercury ?

Where did Paul speak in Lystra ?

What language did he speak ?

What was the 'speech of Lycaonia' ?

What hearer was there in one of Paul's audiences ?

What does 'impotent' mean ?

How long had he been a cripple ?

What does 'steadfastly beholding' mean ?

What, besides his lameness, did Paul see ?

How could Paul 'perceive' faith ?

What other miracle does this miracle resemble ?

How many points of resemblance can you trace ?

What two things united to make this mighty change ?

Are there any other than these two things necessary in
the conversion of a soul ?

Are they exercised differently from what they were in
this cripple's case ?

How many results of this miracle can you mention ?

What did the cripple's *leaping* show ?

What effect did this miracle have on the assembly ?

Why did they call Paul, Mercury ?

Why Barnabas, Jupiter ?   What suppositions can you
make ?

What was now proposed ?

Whom did they call for ?

What does 'gates' mean ?

Why had not the Apostles prevented this procession before ?

Why did they rend their clothes ?

How do you know that Paul, and not Barnabas, spoke ?

What was the first point in the argument ?

What does 'of like *passions*' mean ?

(25)

What was the second point?

What does 'vanities' mean?

What was the third point?

What was the fourth point?

Do you suppose 'all nations' includes the Jews?

Does God ever *excuse* sin?

What is the fifth point in the address?

What is meant by 'left not himself without witness'?

Does God wish to have us 'filled with gladness'?

What is there especially in rain and fruit and the seasons which shows this?

What is the whole argument designed to prove?

What was the effect of Paul's speech on the people? ·

What was this sacrifice intended to express?

Was it in any way a sacrifice for sin?

Do men naturally like natural religion? Why?

Do men naturally like to practise the Christian religion? Why?

What other interpretation might have been given of the miracle?

Do you think it was given by these Jews?

Had the Jews in Palestine ever so explained miracles?

What were the Lycaonians proverbial for?

Did they actually stone Paul *to death?*

Why didn't they stone Barnabas?

What change as sudden as this in the minds of two different peoples at two different times?

When Paul 'rose up,' was there a miracle?

Who were these 'disciples'? Lystrians or others?

What fellow-laborer afterwards joined Paul at Lystra?

What reason have we to believe that he was among these 'disciples'?

Do you think the evidence sufficient?

What do you know of Derbe?

What did Paul there?

What was the result?

THE JOURNEY HOME.

LESSON.

ACTS xiv. 21–27.

DERBE is the end of Paul's first missionary journey. He was now not very far from his own home at Tarsus. Derbe could not have been further from the celebrated pass through the mountains[1] down to Tarsus, than from Iconium. He was at the one foot of that mountain-range, at the other foot of which lay his native province. The journey of a day or two would have probably taken him into Cilicia. "But his thoughts did not centre in his earthly home." He thought of his converts in the different places through which he had come: how exposed they were to persecution and to doubts of the truth, and to trouble from the arguments of the Jews; how much they needed strengthening in the faith, the comfort of his presence, and his words; and especially how they needed to be formed into organized and fixed churches for their mutual strength and protection. And so, after staying in Derbe long enough perhaps to recover Paul's strength, and for the persecuting spirit in Lystra to subside, Paul and Barnabas turned their steps back upon the road which they came. At Lystra, Timothy may have been one who helped make up the church; for there, as well as

---

[1] The famous 'Cilician Gates,' a narrow mountain-pass, through which many an ancient army marched on the route from west to east, and from east to west. See the map of Cilicia, First Sunday.

in Antioch and Iconium, it would seem that a church was formed. Undaunted by danger, by their own bold example they encouraged the disciples, even when they told them that they could only be disciples of Jesus by passing through great suffering and affliction. What undoubting confidence must these good men have had in their religion, when they "ventured to .address to their earliest converts such words of encouragement as these : ' We can only enter the kingdom of God by passing through much tribulation.'" In ordaining ' elders in every church,' they followed the example of the churches in Judea, which had their elders distinct from the Jewish elders.² Jewish elders had existed since the time of Moses.³ This is the second time when the elders of the *Christian* Church are spoken of, the first being when the elders of Jerusalem are mentioned. They are frequently mentioned afterwards.⁴ Paul himself writes to Titus to ordain elders.⁵

The Apostles must have remained in each place a day or more, and very likely several days ; for there must have been in each place a time appointed for fasting, and time for its observance. On their journey home, probably they did not preach publicly in the towns, for that would only have kindled at once the fury of persecutors, and put the brethren in greater peril. The brethren themselves would now preach in their own cities ; and besides, it would be natural for Paul to think, even as soon as this, of making a second journey to these churches, as he afterwards did. The stay of

² xi. 30.
³ Numbers xi. 16, 17. Deuteronomy xix. 12; xxi. 2–6; xxxi. 9. I. Sam. xxx. 26. I. Chronicles xxi. 16. Ezra v. 5; vi. 14. Matt. xv. 2; xxviii. 12. Acts iv. 5; vi. 12.
⁴ xv. 4, 6, 23; xvi. 4; xx. 17.
⁵ Titus i. 5.

the Apostles in these cities was therefore quite different
from what it was on their way out. Then it was most
public, the whole city of Antioch flocking to the synagogue, the whole city of Iconium divided into parties
in respect to them, the whole city of Lystra hailing
them first as gods, and then mobbing them. Now the
visit must have been quite private: they gathered
around them a few disciples in some private house, and
with devout and solemn rites, organized the church of
God in the place.

How differently, too, would the Apostles approach
the various places from what they did before. As they
came across the great plain from the south towards
Iconium, they would look on the city before them, and
think sorrowfully of the wickedness and cruelty which
they had seen and felt both there and in Lystra; and
joyfully and thankfully would they think of what they
had been permitted to accomplish. As they climbed
again the mountains towards Pisidia, they would rejoice
that now in Iconium and Lystra, churches were founded
in spite of persecution. As they saw again in the distance Antioch, what pure pleasure filled their hearts in
anticipation of meeting the converts whom, months before, they left, 'filled with joy and with the Holy Ghost.'
Welcomed again by these dear converts, they soon
learned their state and the attitude of the Jews at the
synagogue. Giving them instruction in respect to any
difficult questions which might have arisen, 'confirming
their souls,' 'exhorting them to continue in the faith,'
'ordaining them elders,' and rejoicing again and again
that they had offered the Gospel to the Gentiles in the
synagogue, they took their perilous way again down
through the mountains, past lake and torrent and river
and robber-haunts, to the plain of Pamphylia. "If our
conjecture is correct, that they went up from Perga in
the spring, and returned at the close of autumn, and

spent all the hotter months of the year in the elevated districts, they would again pass in a few days through a great change of seasons, and almost from summer to winter. The people of Pamphylia would have returned from their cold residences, to the warm shelter of the plain by the sea-side; and Perga would be full of inhabitants." This may be the reason why Paul and Barnabas now stopped to preach in Perga. " We read neither of conversions nor of persecutions here. The Jews, if any Jews resided here, were less inquisitive and less tyrannical than those at Antioch and Iconium; and the votaries of ' Diana before the city' at Perga,'* were less excitable than those who worshipped ' Jupiter before the city' at Lystra. And when the time came for returning to Syria, they did not sail down the Cestrus, but travelled across the plain to Attalia, on the edge of the Pamphylian gulf." This was the city, at the innermost point of the bay, towards which they sailed on their way from Cyprus to Perga, a city which, from that time to this, has existed and flourished, and retained its name.' From this city, centuries after, the two great armies of the Crusaders, having come down to the coast, through parts of the same districts over which Paul and Barnabas travelled, embarked, like them, for Antioch in Syria. " Behind the town is the plain through which the waters of the Catarrhactes flow, perpetually constructing and destroying and reconstructing their fantastic channels. In front of it, and along the shore, are long lines of cliffs, over which the river finds its way in waterfalls to the sea, and which conceal the plain from those who look towards the land from the inner waters of the bay, and even encroach on the prospect of the mountains themselves."

* See page 59.
' On our modern maps, in the Turkish province of Anadolia, you may still see the name of *Adalia.*

The Apostles stepped into the little ship which was to bear them back to Palestine, and which was to mark the track the Crusaders followed. Passing the high cliffs of Rough Cilicia, the long coast of Cyprus, and the familiar scenery about Tarsus, they passed on to the place 'whence they had been recommended to the grace of God, for the work which they fulfilled.' Unlike the Crusaders, whose arrival was anxiously waited for by the 'Prince of Antioch,' and by a great gathering of his nobles and chief men, and who were "brought into Antioch with much pomp and circumstance, in the midst of a great assemblage of the clergy and people," the Apostles, unattended, stepped on shore at Seleucia, or on the bank of the Orontes at Antioch, and found their brethren. Quickly the assembly of the church was gathered. Gladly, eagerly they heard the story of the strange and perilous journey. Sorrowfully they grieved over the wickedness of the persecutors; thankfully, joyfully they praised God that the great mission, undertaken with trembling and with solemn awe in their hearts, had been fully accomplished, and that 'He had opened the door of faith to the Gentiles.'

The Apostles had been gone probably the greater portion of a year. We have supposed them starting, at the opening of navigation, from Seleucia, remaining in Cyprus two or three weeks, consuming a week more on the way to Pisidia in the spring, remaining two weeks or more in Pisidian Antioch, three or four months in Iconium, two weeks in Lystra and the region round about, three or four weeks in Derbe, and consuming two months or more on the returning journey in the latter part of autumn.

So ended the first missionary journey, the work of so much labor, of so much faith, of so much lofty Christian courage; a journey so successful and of such inestimable consequences to us Gentiles.

QUESTIONS.

WHAT success had the Apostles' preaching in Derbe?

What other meaning is there for the words, 'had taught many'?

How far was Derbe from Tarsus?

What were the 'Cilician Gates'?

Do you suppose Paul failed to think of Tarsus now?

What else did he think of?

Who may have helped make up the church at Lystra?

What strange kind of encouragement did the Apostles give to their new converts?

What especial reason was there why Paul should say this at Lystra?

What does this show in respect to their religion?

When religion promises happiness here, does it promise freedom from trials?

Does religion itself bring trouble?

What does 'confirming the souls' mean?

What does 'the faith' mean?

Had 'elders' been ordained at any other place?

How long had the office of 'elders' existed?

What was the difference between a Jewish and a Christian elder?

At what places are other 'elders' mentioned in the New Testament?

What is meant by 'ordained'?

How long did the Apostles remain in each place?

Do you suppose there was a separate meeting for prayer and fasting?

Did they preach publicly? Why?

What is meant by 'commended' them?

Who is meant by '*the Lord,*' on whom they believed?

In what particulars were their visits different now from their visits on the way out?

What would they think of, as they approached the different towns?

(27)

Do you think they felt any especial interest in Antioch in Pisidia ?

Do you think they preached elsewhere in Pisidia than in Antioch ?

Is there anything which may mean that they did ?

What reason might there have been for stopping to preach :ow in Perga ?

What difference in the route down from Perga to the sea, from that on the way up ?

Where was Attalia ?

Who else embarked here for Antioch ?

What is meant by 'recommended to the grace of God' ?

What is it to 'fulfil a work' ?

How does the Apostles' disembarking at Antioch compare with that of the Crusaders ?

How were they welcomed ? By whom ?

What was the one great thought in the minds of all after the Apostles had told their story ?

State the outline of the journey, giving an event in each place.

How long had the Apostles been gone ?

Can you distribute the time ?

What were the chief Christian characteristics necessary to prosecute successfully such a journey ?

Why is this journey so important to us ?

What is the 'door of faith.'

How had it been opened to Gentiles ?

What one thing only, did all the journeying, all the teaching, all the persecution mean ?

(28)

Fifteenth Sunday.

A DIFFICULT QUESTION.

LESSON.

ACTS xiv. 28; xv. 1, 2.

HOW long Paul and Barnabas remained in Antioch, we cannot determine accurately. It is supposed they were there five or six years. We may be sure, however, that they were not idle. Indeed, a new question was now arising, which would require no small thought and attention. After a time, there came down from Judea 'certain men'[1] who introduced a subject into the assembly which at once aroused all the feelings both of Jews and Gentiles. This subject was the occasion of a long and troubled controversy; it was the means of sending Paul again to Jerusalem; and it involved the most momentous consequences to all future ages of the Church and the world. It was debated with the most eager earnestness on each side, by the evil-minded and the true-hearted; and afterwards, at Antioch and at Jerusalem, by two parties, both of whom were no doubt sincere and honest. The question to be decided was this:

Whether converts from the Gentiles ought to obey the law of Moses.

The disturbers at Antioch said at first, that Gentile converts *ought to be circumcised*, but this really meant the same thing as when they said afterwards, at Jeru-

---

[1] Notice that they are not called '*brethren.*'

salem, that they ought to be circumcised *and to keep the law of Moses*. For to demand that they should be circumcised, was to demand that they should submit to the initiatory rite of Moses' law in becoming a Jew, and was therefore only a *test* of submission to all the ceremonies and rites of the whole Mosaic law—that is, to all the rules about eating clean and unclean meats, about washings, sacrifices, etc. The real question, then, was: [2]

Whether converts from the Gentiles ought to obey the law of Moses.

To understand the real perplexity and difficulty which this question would excite among the disciples at Antioch and at Jerusalem, we must think of the broad, distinct line which, in the mind of a Jew, was always drawn between a Jew and a Gentile. If we notice three things, they will help us to understand the difficulties of the question.

I. The separation between Jews and Gentiles was first *religious*. The Jews were scattered everywhere among the Gentiles, " over every part of the Roman empire. In every important city of the east and the west, were some members of that mysterious people, who had a written law, which they read and re-read, week by week and year by year, in the midst of those who surrounded them—who were bound everywhere by a secret link of affection to one city in the world, where alone their religious sacrifices could be offered—whose whole life was utterly abhorrent from the temples and images which crowded the neighborhood of the synagogues, and from the gay and impure festivities of the Greek and Roman worship. Hence the Jews in foreign nations were surrounded by an *idolatry* which shocked all their feelings, and a *shameless profligacy* which was

---

[2] See, also, in the Letter in reply, verse 24.

even associated with what the Gentiles called religion." Even the Gentile proselytes who went over to the Jewish faith, "were looked on with some suspicion by the Jews themselves, and thoroughly hated and despised by the Gentiles." With intensest hatred and contempt, the Jews hated the idolatry of the Gentiles, their *many* gods, their unclean and abominable *sacrifices*, their *many* temples, instead of one, their horrible and shameless impurity even in honor of their gods. The *religious* separation was therefore a very wide one.

II. The separation was *intellectual*. Side by side with the synagogues in strange cities, and "with the doctrines of Judaism, the speculations of Greek philosophers were taught and discussed in schools;" so that "it might be said that Plato and Aristotle, Zeno and Epicurus, as well as Moses, 'had in every city those that preached them.'" The Jews naturally suspected and hated all the philosophy and science which had formed the mythology and theology of the Gentiles. Indeed, as we have seen, many of her teachers would not allow their pupils to study the Greek language and literature. An *intellectual* separation was therefore added to a religious one.

III. More than this, the separation was *social*. Then, as now, the Jews mingled freely with Gentiles in all places of 'buying and selling, conversing and disputing,' but in their families they were entirely separate. It was 'unlawful,' in their *domestic* relations, 'for a man that was a Jew to keep company with one of another nation.'[4] The charge made against Peter by his fellow-Christians, was: 'Thou wentest in to men uncircumcised, and didst eat with them.'[5] This matter of *eating* or of *not* eating with Gentiles, had great influ-

[3] xv. 21.   [4] x. 28.   [5] xi. 3.

ence over the Jews' life. The table and the daily meal, is one place where acquaintance ripens into friendly feeling, and friendly feeling ripens into attachment. " With the man with whom I can neither eat nor drink, let our business intercourse be what it may, I shall seldom become as familiar as with him whose guest I am, and he mine. If we have, besides, an abhorrence of the food which each other eats, this forms a new obstacle to closer intimacy. Nothing better than this could possibly be devised to keep one people distinct from another. It causes the difference between them to be ever present to the mind, touching as it does upon so many points of social and every-day contact." It keeps people separate better " than any difference of doctrine or worship."

" I will buy with you, sell with you, walk with you, talk with you, and so following; but I will not eat with you, drink with you, nor pray with you,"

says Shylock the Jew in the *Merchant of Venice.*

The *social* separation therefore every day and every hour strengthened the *religious* and *intellectual* separation of Jews from Gentiles.

This wide separation was most rigidly maintained, like the separation of *caste* among the Hindoos. "A Hindoo cannot eat with a Parsee or a Mohammedan; and among the Hindoos themselves, the meals of a Brahmin are polluted by the presence of a Pariah, though they meet and have free intercourse in the ordinary transactions of business."

Now, how was it possible for a Jew, educated according to the law of Moses, even though he believed on Jesus as the Messiah, to receive a Gentile *religiously, intellectually, socially,* unless he would not only forsake idolatry and the heathen way of thinking of Christian things, but would also consent to eat only the clean meats; in short, unless he would consent to circumcision, to all the washings and sacrifices and tithes, *which the law of Moses* commanded.

We must remember that one previous point had been settled, that the *Gentiles might* receive the Gospel and *might be converted.* The conversion of Cornelius under Peter's preaching had settled that.[*] The precise point *now* to be settled was, *whether Gentiles already converted ought to obey all the particulars of Moses' law.*

Notice now how the recent missionary journey would bring up this question for decision. "Paul and Barnabas had no doubt freely joined in social intercourse with the Gentile Christians at Antioch in Pisidia, at Iconium, Lystra, and Derbe. At Antioch in Syria, too, they had lived with much 'freedom' with the Gentile brethren." The Jewish Christians, especially those who had not been out of Judea and Jerusalem—some of them, at least—thought this all wrong. They could not endure the thought of receiving directly into the church these multitudes of converts from the Gentiles without their agreement to obey the regular Jewish laws. Some of these Jewish Christians were no doubt most sincere in opposition to receiving the Gentile Christians, without coming under Moses' law. "We can well believe that the minds of many may have been perplexed by the words and conduct of our Lord himself; for he had not been sent 'save to the lost sheep of the house of Israel;' and he said that 'it was not meet to take the children's bread and give it to dogs.' To them this change "was a rebellion against all that they had been taught to hold inviolably sacred." The Jews, 'the holy people,' would soon be swallowed up, they would think, in this "universal and indiscriminating religion"

[*] Acts xi. 18.

of Christianity, if this were the way in which it was to be administered. And Saul of Tarsus, the young Pharisee, who, years before, sat 'at the feet of Gamaliel,' was the principal person who was now trying to make this change. Very likely, therefore, it was 'certain' 'of the sect of the Pharisees" who went down to Antioch to attend to this matter.

See now the precise *form* the discussion took. These men did not say, that it would be *well* to be circumcised; it would *avoid difficulty* in the church, it would *better satisfy* the minds of the Christian brethren at Jerusalem, if they would be circumcised and keep Moses' law: but very falsely they said: 'Except ye be circumcised after the manner of Moses, *ye cannot be* SAVED.' Such a doctrine must have been instantly opposed by Paul with his intensest energy. The very foundations of Christianity were in danger of being undermined. "He did not yield, 'no, not for an hour.'"

For some time the discussion was continued in Antioch; perhaps for months, or even for a year. There was anxiety and perplexity among the Syrian Christians. The minds of Gentile converts were troubled and unsettled. The Gospel of Christ was perverted. Great harm was being done. And so it was determined that Paul and Barnabas and others should go up to Jerusalem, and there, in an assembly of apostles and elders, have this difficult question settled. At Jerusalem were the principal Apostles, James and Peter and John. From Judea, the party who raised the vexed question came, and would exist at Jerusalem in its greatest strength. At Jerusalem, the other question about Peter's preaching to the Gentiles had been decided. Jerusalem was the place where all religious questions had been decided for centuries. Jerusalem was therefore the place where, once for all, this question ought to be decided; and Paul and Barnabas were the persons who ought to go and represent the side of truth and of right there.

QUESTIONS.

HOW long were Paul and Barnabas in Antioch?
>Who at length came to Antioch?
>What did they teach?
>When they required men to be circumcised, what *test* was it?
>What were some of the other observances required?

What then was the difficult question?
>What is the general reason why it was difficult?

What was the *first* characteristic of this separation?
>How did the scattered Jews' appear to Romans and Greeks in foreign cities?
>What did the Jews see connected with the Gentile religions?
>How would a proselyte be thought of both by Jews and Gentiles?
>What was the distinction between the Jews and Gentiles in respect to the doctrine of God?
>What in respect to sacrifices?
>What in respect to temples?
>What in respect to moral purity?

What was the *second* characteristic of the separation?
>What doctrines were taught in these foreign cities?
>What was the Greek and Roman mythology?
>What would the Jews think of Greek and Roman philosophy?
>What did some Jewish teachers think of the Greek language?

What was the *third* characteristic of the separation?
>In what respect did the Jews mingle freely with Gentiles?
>In what respects did they keep themselves separate?
>What was thought unlawful?
>Where do you find this rule referred to?
>How was it that the rule about *eating* kept them separate?

What separation in a modern heathen nation is something like this ?

State now the difficulties in receiving a Gentile or a Jew into
the church.

What previous point had been settled ?

When had that been settled ?

What did the Apostles say at that time ?

What was the precise point now ?

How did Paul's recent journey bring up this question ?

Do you think the Jewish Christians sincere in opposing
Paul ?

What had our Saviour said which they might quote on
their side ?

Of what sect were the men who came to Antioch from
Judea ?

In respect to the *form* of their demand, what did *not* these
men say ?   What *did* they say ?

What did Paul think of such a doctrine ?

Why was the doctrine dangerous ?

What shows that the discussion continued some time ?

What is the difference between 'dissension' and 'disputation' ?

What would naturally be the result among the Syrian Christians ?

Could they honestly be in trouble about it ?

How could the question be decided ?

What was determined at last ?

Why was it proper that it should be decided at Jerusalem ?

THE COUNCIL.

LESSON.

GALATIANS ii. 1–10; ACTS xv. 3–22.

THIS third journey of the Apostle to Jerusalem after his conversion, is supposed to be the one which Paul speaks of in the second chapter of his Letter to the Galatians.[1] There seems to be little doubt that these are the men whom Paul there calls 'false brethren,' who were 'brought in unawares,' and 'who came to spy out his liberty,' that is, to see whether he was living freely with Gentiles in Antioch, and 'to whom he did not give place, no, not for an hour.'

We are there told that Paul did not go up to Jerusalem simply by the direction of the Antioch Christians, but also 'by revelation,' by the direction of a vision, like the vision in the Temple years before, or at Troas afterwards.[2] We are told, also, that Titus was one of the 'other disciples' who went with him; for Titus was a Greek, and 'uncircumcised:' he was a specimen of the Gentile converts, that the Apostles and elders and disciples at Jerusalem might see what kind of persons they were who were now made the occasion of this controversy. It is evident that through all the 'dis-

[1] There have been various opinions in respect to which of Paul's *five* journeys to Jerusalem is meant by the passage in Galatians, in which he speaks of going up 'fourteen years after.' "The view we have adopted is that of the best critics and commentators."

[2] Acts xvi. 9.

putation' at Antioch, most if not all of the Christians held to the side of Paul, for it is said they were 'brought on their way by the Church.' If the greater part of the Church had condemned Paul's course, it is not likely that we would have had this notice of their sympathy and attachment. "The course of the Apostles was along the great Roman road which followed the Phœnician coast-line, and traces of which are still seen in the cliffs overhanging the sea, and thence through the middle of Samaria and Judea." Along the way, they saw believers already converted, some of whom, in Phenice, had been converted under the preaching of 'those scattered abroad' after the persecution of Stephen.³ The number had probably increased since that time. In Samaria, Philip the Evangelist, and Peter and John, had preached years before, and the Gospel had been received with 'great joy,' at least in one city.⁴ To whatever churches they found on the way, they told over again the story of their journey among the Gentiles, and how 'a door of faith' had been 'opened to the Gentiles.' In all these places, there was great rejoicing among the assembled believers. To the church at Jerusalem, too, they at length told the same story.

With what strange feelings must Paul have entered Jerusalem now! Twice before, since his conversion, had he been in the holy city.⁵ This third time, he came on a far more important errand, and probably was in the city much longer than at either of the other times.⁶ During the fourteen years since his conversion,⁷ there had been many changes. Death had taken away many

---

³ xi. 19.

⁴ viii. 8, 14, 25 ; ix. 32.

⁵ Acts xxii. 17; Galatians i. 18 ; and Acts xi. 30.

⁶ Galatians i. 18 ; Acts xii. 25.

⁷ 'Fourteen years *after*,' is supposed to mean '*after*' his conversion.

of his early companions, "but some must have been there who had studied with him 'at the feet of Gamaliel.'" Herod Agrippa, who killed James and would have killed Peter, had met his awful death. The Jews had far less power than then to persecute and tyrannize over the Church. Some of the Pharisees—perhaps some of Gamaliel's school—like Paul, had believed that Jesus was the Christ. But though they had believed, they had not, like Paul, altogether relinquished their rigid and intense zeal for the law; and it was with them Paul was now to discuss this most difficult question.

Think for a moment how much was involved in the settlement of that question : Whether Gentile converts ought to obey the law of Moses. The question was then to be decided for all countries outside of the land of Judea; for in all countries, Gentile converts would surely be made. It was to be decided for all ages till the end of the world. It was to be decided there in Jerusalem, whether we Gentiles of America, in these distant days, shall be required, when we believe in Jesus the Saviour, to submit to the 'washings,' and 'fasts,' and 'sacrifices,' to observe the Passover and other feasts, and the whole ceremonial of the Mosaic law.

When Paul and Barnabas, then, bringing Titus and others with them, told to the assembled church the story of their wonderful success in preaching the Gospel among the Gentiles of Cyprus and Asia Minor, the Pharisee-members of the church said at once that these Gentile converts must certainly ·be circumcised and commanded 'to keep the law of Moses.' This was an attack on the whole course of Paul, who had admitted Gentiles to the Church, and who had not left them, so far as we know, any direction in respect to the ceremonial law. It was casting a suspicion and a reproach on Barnabas. It was saying, too, that Titus, whom they had brought with them as a Christian brother, with whom they had *eaten* and kept company, must be circumcised or he could not be *saved*.

The whole subject was now opened. There was earnest conversation about it, in the homes of the disciples, wherever the brethren met, and at the meetings of the church, for some days. We know that Paul, before the great public meeting took place, at which the final decision was to be made, consulted privately the Apostles,[*] and told over his journey, his labor, and the result of it all ; and that James, Peter, and John, 'pillars' of the Church, agreed with and sympathized with Paul.[*]

At length the great meeting was appointed, that which is now called in Church history,

THE FIRST COUNCIL OF THE CHRISTIAN CHURCH.

This council may have been in session more than one day. To understand fully the deliberations of this important body, let us divide its proceedings into the different parts :

First, there was much earnest debate, (verse 7,) and perhaps, among eager-minded Jews and strong Pharisees, even violent controversy. How long this 'disputing' lasted, we do not know. The Spirit of Inspiration did not dictate that this discussion should be preserved, but only the words which divinely moved Apostles spake. It consumed, however, doubtless, no small part of the whole council.

Secondly, Peter, on the part of the Apostles, was the first who gave his opinion, (verses 7 to 11.) It was proper that he should speak first, because he first of all preached the Gospel to the Gentiles. He spoke, 1. (verse 7) of his own preaching to the Gentiles a long

---

[*] Galatians ii. 2.   [*] Galatians ii. 9.

time before, at Cæsarea; of the Gentiles' belief in the
word of God, and of God's directing him to go to
them : [10] 2. (verses 8, 9) of the decisive fact that the
Holy Spirit had been sent to these Gentiles as He had
been to the Jewish believers,[11] and *that* was God's testimony that both Gentile and Jew were alike to him
3. (verse 10) of the yoke of the Jewish law, which
bowed down their neck beneath its pressure — com
posed, as it was, of so many sacrifices, fasts, types,
carefulness in respect to eating with Gentiles and with
defiled persons ; of how no one had ever been able to
bear up under all the ceremonies it commanded, so
weighty were they; of how the Pharisees themselves
could bear testimony to the carefulness and exactness
and the labor of keeping that law ; and of how they
ought not to put this yoke on Gentiles, to whom God
had, without it, given the Holy Spirit : 4. (verse 11)
of the grace of Jesus, the Messiah, and not the law of
Moses, as the way of being saved for us who are Jews,
as well as for these Gentiles.

Peter gave his decision, therefore, in favor of Paul,
and against the sect of the Pharisees.

Thirdly, Barnabas and Paul next spoke, one following the other, (verse 12.) Probably Barnabas spoke
first.   He had been known longer among the brethren
of Judea than Paul. " There was a great silence through
all the multitude, and every eye was turned on the missionaries while they gave the narrative of their journeys."   They said that God, by *miracles* and *wonders*,
had shown that the Gentiles were to be the same as the
Jews in the Church.   At Paphos, a wilful and wicked
magic-worker had been struck blind ; at Iconium, during a long residence, 'signs and wonders' had been

---

[10] Acts x. 14, 15, 19, 20, 28.   [11] x. 44, 45; xi. 15, 17, 18.

done. These wonderful works showed that God had been with them, and that it was He who had helped them plant so many churches in the midst of perils, and robbers, and rivers, and mountains, and persecuting Jews, and wicked, cruel, superstitious Gentiles. They said, too, that on their return, they found these Gentiles faithful, and rejoicing in God in the midst of their trials. The *Holy Spirit* had given testimony to Peter's preaching to the Gentiles at Cæsarea, but both the *Holy Spirit* and *miracles* had testified to their preaching in Cyprus and Asia Minor. This we suppose is the substance of what Barnabas and Paul said, one speaking of some things and the other of others.

Fourthly, James the Apostle now spoke, (verses 13 to 21.) There were two Apostles of the name of James.[12] James, the brother of John, was killed by Herod.[13] *This* James is supposed to be he who was also called 'James the Just.' "No judgment could have more weight with the Pharisees than his." After the long narratives of Barnabas and Paul, the multitude would look with solemn silence for his opinion. James spoke, 1. (verses 13, 14) of Peter's preaching to the Gentiles, and of their conversion by the Spirit; and then, 2. (verses 15 to 18) proved, by quoting a passage from the Hebrew Scriptures, that the conversion of the Gentiles had *always* been God's purpose. Peter was right in preach ing to the Gentiles, said the Apostle James; for ir Amos, the prophet, it is written that God will build again the Jewish nation,[14] after its downfall, *in orde*

---

[12] Matthew x. 2, 3; Acts i. 13.   [13] Acts xii. 2.

[14] The tabernacle is the *tent*, or the *house* of David; and the royal house is used here as a figure of the nation. It is as if it were said, 'I will build again the Royal Throne of the Hebrew Nation.' The Royal Throne of England is used as a figure for the government or the nation of England.

that the *rest* of mankind and *all* the *Gentiles* might seek after God. It is evident, therefore, that from the beginning God meant that the Gentiles should be converted and brought into the Church, for God knows all his works from the beginning. Wherefore, 3. (verse 19) he judged that Gentiles who turn to God should not be troubled with rites and ceremonies : but yet, 4. (verses 20, 21) they ought to be taught to avoid certain things which might be the occasion of trouble and offence to their Jewish brethren ; *four* things, *especially* forbidden by that law read every Sabbath in the synagogues, four things they should be instructed to avoid— meat offered to idols,[15] sensual lusts, things strangled, and blood. If the Gentiles and the Jews were now to *eat* together, they must both agree to give up those things which were offensive to each other. The Gentiles ought to give up meat polluted by idols, and meat from animals strangled,[16] and meat with blood in it, since the very sight of these things on the table would at once arouse the horror of a Jew.[17]

Fifthly, this advice of James seemed right and good, and the council solemnly adopted it, (verses 22 and 29.) It was neither at one extreme nor at the other. It released the Gentile converts from obeying the whole Mosaic law. They need not be circumcised, nor offer sacrifice, nor observe the feasts, the fasts, the washings,

[15] 'Pollutions of idols,' that is, "the flesh of animals offered to idols, which remained over and was eaten by the worshippers, or was sometimes sold in the markets." This flesh, according to Moses' law, was polluted.

[16] A strangled animal would of course retain the blood in the flesh, while the Levitical law was that the blood should be *poured out* when the animal was killed, (Leviticus xvii. 13.) 'Strangled animals,' that is, "those animals which, like fowls, were caught in snares, and whose blood was not let."

[17] Leviticus xvii. 10--14.

etc. At the same time, it commanded them to observe certain parts of the law, the violation of which would prevent the hearty agreement of Jews with Gentiles.

The church—' the elders and the brethren '—agreed upon this wise and just arrangement: the Apostles, in their honored and dignified character, recommended and approved it: the Holy Ghost confirmed it.[18] This most difficult question was therefore answered by a clear and satisfactory decision.

[18] verse 28.

QUESTIONS.

WHAT other account of this journey to Jerusalem have we besides that in the Acts?

By whose direction then did Paul go?

Who was one of the 'certain other'? (xv. 2.) Why?

What does 'being brought on their way by the church' mean?

What are the 'certain men' in Acts called in Galatians?

What does 'spy out our liberty' mean?

When had the Gospel been preached in Phenice and Samaria? By whom?

Do you think these churches had not heard this news before?

How many times before, since his conversion, had Paul been in Jerusalem?

On what occasions?

'Fourteen years after' *what?*

What changes had taken place?

What was involved in the question?

Who now started the question again?

What was it saying in respect to Paul and Barnabas and Titus?

Whom did Paul consult privately?

What is this great meeting called in church-history?

How long did it continue?

What was the first part of the council?

Who took part in it?

How much time did it consume?

What was the second part?

Why should he speak first?

What was the first point in his speech?

Where do you find the account of this?

What was the second point?

What is the reason here why Jews and Gentiles are alike?

(31)

How does faith purify the heart?

What was the third point in his speech?

Explain the meaning of this verse.

What is the fourth point?

What is meant by 'the grace of the Lord Jesus Christ'?

How can we be saved now?

What was Peter's decision, therefore?

What was the third part of the council?

What *addition* did they make to *Peter's* argument?

At what places had miracles been wrought?

What was the fourth part of the council?

How do you distinguish from each other the two Apostles of this name?

What was this one also called?

What were the first and second points in his speech?

What prophet does he quote?

What is the meaning of 'the tabernacle of David'?

What is the meaning then of the sixteenth verse?

How does he prove that God from the beginning intended to convert the Gentiles?

What were the third and fourth points in his speech?

If the Jewish Christians and Gentile Christians were to eat together, what must the Gentiles give up?

What is meant by 'pollutions of idols'?

Why were strangled animals and 'blood' named?

How were these four things forbidden every Sabbath?

What was the fifth part of the council?

Who confirmed the decision?

(32)

Seventeenth Sunday.

THE LETTER AND THE LETTER-BEARERS.

LESSON.

ACTS XV. 22–35; GALATIANS ii. 9–14.

ONE thing only now remained; to send the decision of the church to the Gentile converts so anxiously waiting for it. That there might be no charge of misrepresentation against Paul and Barnabas, or other objection by the 'false brethren' at Antioch, Judas-Barsabas and Silas were appointed to go with the Apostles. They were to carry a letter from the church, containing the decision of the council, and were to explain ' by word' what was written within.

And so the little company take the road back to Antioch—a larger company than when they came—Judas, Silas, Paul, Barnabas, Mark,[1] Titus, and ' others.' While they are on their way with the letter, let us think of two or three things which had been decided by the council at Jerusalem, from which they were now returning.

I. Paul had been publicly recognised by the church, and by the inspired Apostles, as Apostle to the Gentiles. His first missionary journey had been approved by the council. And besides this, James, Peter, and John[2] saw that Paul was called of God to a special

---

[1] Mark, you remember, came back from Pamphylia to *Jerusalem.* We find him very soon again at Antioch. It is probable that he was in this company with his kinsman, Barnabas.

[2] This is the only time Paul and John met, so far as we know. John here disappears from the Scriptures till we see him again in the isle of Patmos.

work among Gentiles.[3] They therefore gave him and
Barnabas their ' right hand of fellowship,' appointing
them to preach the Gospel to the Gentiles, and themselves to preach to Jews.[3] Paul's apostleship to the
Gentiles had been therefore *publicly* established.

II. The three Apostles at Jerusalem had directed
Paul and Barnabas especially ' to remember the poor.'[4]
" The Jewish Christians in Jerusalem were exposed to
peculiar suffering from poverty, and we have seen Paul
and Barnabas once before the bearers of a contribution
from a foreign city to their relief." That Paul was
' forward to do' this we know from his epistles afterwards,[5] in which we see that he kept in mind the poor
' brethren' of Jerusalem in his journeys.

III. Titus, the Greek, who came up with them to
Jerusalem, had not been circumcised;[6] and so a Gentile,
without yielding to the law of Moses, had been publicly recognised as a believer. The case of Titus would
be used as an example with other Jews and Gentiles,
as Paul himself mentions the fact when he writes to the
Gentile Galatians.[6]

The company of travellers were joyfully received at
Antioch, especially the two missionaries and the two
letter-bearers from Jerusalem. " The whole body of
the church was summoned together to hear the reading
of the letter; and we can well imagine the eagerness
with which they crowded to listen to such an important communication." When it was opened they read,

---

[3] Galatians ii. 9.   [4] Galatians ii. 10.

[5] A collection at Corinth for the saints at Jerusalem is recommended in I. Corinthians xvi. 1–3 ; and the same passage shows that
Paul recommended the same thing to the Galatians. The Macedonians and the Achaians made collections for poor saints at Jerusalem. Romans xv. 26.

[6] Galatians ii. 3.

that in *four* things *only* they would be required to obey the Mosaic law. They were not obliged to be circumcised, nor to offer the many sacrifices at the temple, nor to practise the Jewish purifications, nor to make the Jewish difference between clean and unclean meats, except in respect to meat offered to idols, strangulated meat, and meat with blood in it. In a word, except these four things, which every one ought willingly to observe, the whole exact and burdensome routine of Moses' law was not binding on them. What rejoicing this glad news made among them we can best appreciate by thinking how it would be in our day. Suppose the demand was made to-day that the Gentile Christians of America must keep the law of Moses, must offer sacrifices at Jerusalem, must eat none but clean meats, must purify ourselves at every defilement according to the slow and exact processes of the Levitical law, and in all other things be governed by the ceremonial law of Moses: suppose that we had sent good men to Jerusalem, to have the decision made by authorities in the church there under the direction of the Holy Ghost: suppose we should receive on their return such a letter as this which was read in Antioch. We can imagine the pleasure and the pious thanksgiving of the Antioch Christians, on their release from the yoke of the bondage of the law.

How much, too, the words and the sympathy of Judas and of Silas added to their rejoicing. 'Being prophets,' by the especial teaching of the Holy Spirit' they exhorted and confirmed the brethren. And after some short stay, the church permitted them to depart. Silas, however, had a new and a greater work to do, although perhaps he did not know it. He was to be-

' See page 43

come the fellow-missionary of Paul. Guided by the Divine Spirit, and thinking he could do good in Antioch, he remained with the two missionaries and with many others who were there, 'teaching and preaching the word of the Lord.'

There is one other event which occurred at Antioch in connection with this subject of the council and the letter. It is supposed that while Paul and Barnabas were remaining in Antioch, that visit of Peter to Antioch took place during which Paul found it necessary to reprove Peter.* For some reason, which we do not know, Peter came from Jerusalem to Antioch, and while there, at first lived freely, eating freely with the Gentiles. This was in accordance with the decision of the council. But when other Jewish brethren came down from Jerusalem from James, who seem to have retained their old Jewish prejudices against eating with Gentiles, Peter 'withdrew and separated' himself from the Gentiles, living with the Jews only. This was not in violation of the *letter* of the decree of the council, for that said nothing about compelling the Jewish Christians to eat with the Gentile Christians; but it was plainly opposed to its *spirit*, since the decree was meant to promote the social fellowship of Jewish and Gentile Christians. Other Jewish Christians followed the example of Peter, and even Barnabas was led to do the same thing.

This inconsistent conduct of Peter, which was likely to make anxiety and perhaps controversy again in the church, Paul resisted with all his might. We find here a little of Peter's old fickle impulsiveness, but it is his only departure from his unfaltering steadfastness that we find anywhere after his bitter repentance for denial.

* Galatians ii. 11.

Paul did not spare him the rebuke he thought he deserved. 'Before all,'' he 'withstood him to the face,'' and emphatically reminded him that he was in effect going back to the old and false principle, that a man was justified by keeping the law of Moses, and not, as all Christians now believed, by believing in Jesus the Christ. The whole occurrence was no doubt some months, perhaps a year, after the council.

"This scene, though merely mentioned, is one of the most remarkable in sacred history; and the mind tries to picture to itself the appearance of the two men. It is therefore at least allowable to mention here that general notion of the forms and features of the two Apostles, which has been handed down in tradition, and was represented by the early artists. St. Paul is set before us as having the strongly marked and prominent features of a Jew, yet not without some of the ✓ finer lines of Greek thought. His stature was diminutive and his body disfigured by some lameness or distortion, which may have provoked the contemptuous expressions of his enemies."[10] His face is represented as long and oval, his nose eagle-shaped, his eyes sparkling and gray, under thick, overhanging eyebrows united at the centre, his complexion transparent, his forehead high and bald, his hair brown, and his beard long, flowing, and pointed. "St. Peter is represented to us as a man of larger and stronger form," 'with a broad forehead, rather coarse features, an open, undaunted countenance,' a quick, dark eye, a pale, sallow complexion, "and the short hair which is described as entirely gray at the time of his death, curled black and thick round his temples and chin, when the two Apostles stood together at Antioch, twenty years before their martyr-

---

* 14th verse.   [10] See II. Corinthians x. 1, 10.

dom." These traditions and pictures may have at least a partial foundation in truth.

Though the strongest indignation is expressed in Paul's rebuke, we have no reason to suppose that any actual quarrel took place between the two Apostles. Peter most likely saw at once his fault, and melted into penitence. "His mind was easily moved to quick and sudden changes; his disposition was loving and generous; and we should expect his sorrow to be at Antioch what it was at the high-priest's house in Jerusalem." How delightful it is, too, to turn to the closing words of his own second letter to Christian believers, in which, while he is thinking and writing of the pure and peaceful happiness of the future world, he touchingly alludes to ' *our beloved brother Paul.*'[11] The very fidelity of his brother-Apostle at Antioch, made deeper and broader in the great heart of the noble Peter his love and esteem for Paul to the end of his days.

[11] II. Peter iii. 15, 16.

QUESTIONS.

WHAT one thing remained to be done ?

What was the object of sending persons with Paul and Barnabas ?

How many made up the party who returned to Antioch ?

Why do we think that Mark was in the company?

What had the council decided in respect to Paul ?

What was decided in respect to his journey ?

What did James, Peter and John ?

What is meant by 'right hand of fellowship' ?

What is meant by 'the heathen' and 'the circumcision' ?

Did Paul see John at any other time ?

What direction did the three Apostles give to Paul ?

What shows that Paul did this ?

Where does he say that he did ?

What had been decided in respect to Titus ?

Why was this important ?

How would the party be received at Antioch ?

To whom was this letter addressed ?

Was it directed to *all* Christians in these places ?

What does 'troubled you with words' refer to ?

What does 'subverting your souls' mean ?

Who claim authority in the expression 'to whom *we* gave' ?

Who had hazarded their lives ?   Where ?

Who is the highest authority in respect to the necessary things ?

Why are these things called 'necessary' ?

Who are 'they,' in the thirtieth verse ?

What does the word 'multitude' show in respect to the size of the Antioch church ?

What other office than letter-bearers did Judas and Silas hold ?

What was a prophet ?

What is meant by 'confirmed them' ?

What providential purpose was there in Silas's remaining ?

How much of Silas's life did this stay at Antioch change ?

Why is it especially important to seek divine guidance
when we make changes in our homes or our business ?

What other event is supposed to have taken place at this
time at Antioch ?

How did Peter live at the first ?

What did he afterwards ? after what ?

'Withdrew and separated himself' from whom ?

What is meant by 'fearing the circumcision' ?

Did Peter violate the decree of the council ?

Who followed his example ?

Can a man confine his wrong acts to himself ?

What trait of Peter's character is shown here ?

What did Paul say and do ?

How long a time after the council might this have been ?

Was there any open quarrel between the two Apostles ?

What might be expected naturally from Peter ?

How did Peter afterwards speak of Paul ?

Where does he say this ?

What had he just been writing about ?

What was the effect therefore of Paul's reproof ?

What will be the effect of every just and kind reproof
in the heart of a good man ?

(34)

Eighteenth Sunday.

STARTING ON THE SECOND JOURNEY.

LESSON.

ACTS xv. 35–41; xvi. 1.

FOR many days, for some weeks or months, Paul and Barnabas continued to preach and teach in Antioch. The church of 'Christians' must have increased largely by this time. There must have been many in the city to listen to the doctrines of Jesus, for it was 'with many others also' that they taught. Simeon Niger and Lucius of Cyrene and Menaen were perhaps there still. Mark and Silas and Titus were there. Many strangers, among those who flocked to this city and its famous oracle, as well as the people of the city, must have listened to these numerous preachers. It was not necessary that all these 'prophets' should remain there, even after Judas and Peter had departed. Other churches, feeble and struggling, needed the aid and sympathy of strong instruction and Christian visitation. Paul could but think again and again of the pro-consul at Paphos, of the brethren and elders at the other Antioch and at Iconium and Lystra and Derbe; and he longed to see them and help them and do them good. At length Paul proposes to Barnabas a visit to all those cities of their former journey. The full purpose of the visit must have been to see what was the condition of the churches, to strengthen them in the faith, and to carry them the decision of the council at Jerusalem.

Barnabas is ready to go, but he wishes to take John

Mark with them. Paul had tried Mark once. Once before from this very city, from the very port of Seleucia, he had started with Mark; and when they came to the real hardship of the journey, Mark withdrew and came home. He remembered the painful separation at Perga; and he could not consent to risk such a failure the second time. Paul could not take Mark again.

The Scriptures are honest in their narrative. They tell us plainly that Paul and Barnabas, though missionaries and holy men, had a 'sharp contention' about this matter. It was a personal opinion and not a doctrine about which they contended. It was not some very grave question about Jews or Gentiles, but simply the fitness or unfitness of a person for a work. There were severe words no doubt between Paul and Barnabas. Placing ourselves on one side and on the other, we can see reasons why each one might think himself right in adhering to his own opinion. We can think how Paul would prize a steadfast will and undaunted courage in a work of constant danger: how he would think the whole work put in peril or disgraced by withdrawal from it: what an embarrassment and hindrance a timid or half-hearted companion would be to him: how Mark's first failure in such an important work made Mark untrustworthy in Paul's esteem for a journey through wild mountain-passes and rough enemies. We can think how Barnabas loved his kinsman: how he thought of the pleasure of taking him again to his native island: how Mark had cost him many prayers and much anxiety: how 'his dearest wish was to see him a missionary of Christ:' how Mark had repented of the wrong he had done in withdrawing from Perga: how, now won back to obedience, he had come from his home in Jerusalem, and was ready now to face all the difficulties and dangers of the enterprise: how, to reject him now, was to treat harshly his sincere and tender repentance, and to diminish his influence as a preacher and servant of Jesus. "Paul's natural disposition was impetuous and impatient and easily kindled to indignation." Barnabas was once foremost among the 'prophets' of Antioch, when Paul was last, and now Paul only was chief of all. Barnabas might possibly have thought, too, that as he had first introduced Paul to the Apostles at Jerusalem, as he had first brought him to Antioch, it was but right that Paul should listen to him in his love for his relative. Each clung to his own opinion. No doubt both were to be blamed, as other good and great and inspired men are blamed for their sins.

As they could not agree, they must separate; but we cannot suppose they parted in anger, like enemies." "Divine Providence overruled their quarrel to a good result." They divided the whole journey between them. Perhaps the agreement was made that Paul should go to the cities on the main land, and Barnabas should again go over the island. It may be that Barnabas went from Cyprus to Perga too.[1] As Perga was the place to which Mark went before, it would be natural for Barnabas and Mark to go as far as that again. So Barnabas and Mark sailed again no doubt from Seleucia to Salamis, leaving Paul in Antioch to do upon the land his part of the visitation of the churches.

Paul now went through Syria and Cilicia. Of course he did not go by sea. Taking Silas, he went therefore first to those churches in the region of Antioch and in his native province in which he had before labored.[2] Churches already existed in Cilicia. The letter of the

[1] If Barnabas went through Cyprus and then up to Perga, and Paul to Antioch in Pisidia, then both of them went to all the cities of their previous journey.

[2] Galatians i. 21.

council had been addressed to the Gentile brethren in *Cilicia* as well as in Syria and in Antioch. It was a good thing, too, that Silas, who was recommended in the letter of the council, was with Paul, on his visit to the

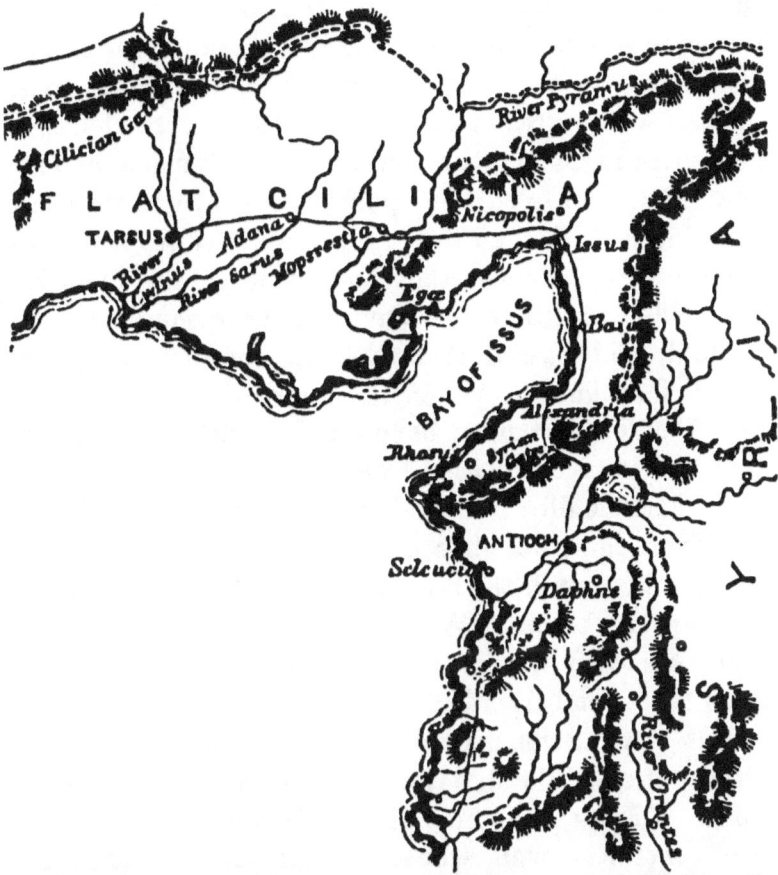

Compare this map with the map of Cilicia in the First Sunday. It will be well to compare any of the maps with the general map in the Frontispiece.

churches of Syria and Cilicia. We cannot tell the exact cities in which these churches were. Possibly Paul may have struck off first into the country east of Antioch, or into the valley of the Orontes, and may have visited some of the cities there; but more likely he and

Silas crossed the bridge over the Orontes at Antioch, and took the road towards the north. They crossed the mountain-range, the boundary between Syria and Cilicia, through the gorge called 'the Syrian Gates.' Among the cities on the road around the corner of the great sea were Alexandria, named after Alexander the Great, and Issus, at the very corner, where the same great general won a great victory. "If there were churches anywhere in Cilicia, there must have been one in Tarsus. Paul had lived there perhaps some years since his conversion." If then they took the direct Roman road from Issus to Tarsus, they now came to the plain of Flat Cilicia, with which Paul had been familiar from a child, and passed through two conspicuous cities[*] which Paul knew. When he entered his native city, how Paul's heart must have swelled with thankfulness that he had been rescued from the self-righteous deeds of a Pharisaic life: how he burned to rescue his beloved city from the vain idols and dumb statues of heathen religion he saw in the streets. Even here in Tarsus a change had begun. We may hope it penetrated the Apostle's own family, and that some of his early acquaintances and friends had been brought to Christ.

But the missionaries did not make long stay here. Other cities of the first journey lay beyond the mountains. Across 'the sunny plains of Cilicia,' beyond that great mountain-wall, whose lofty towers stretched far away to the east and to the west, lay the high tableland of Lycaonia. On the first journey, Paul had climbed through this range of Taurus, between Perga and Pisidia: now he struck straight across to Derbe first. "There is no sufficient reason to think that he went by any other than the ordinary road." There was

---

[*] Mopsuestia and Adana.

one opening in that great mountain-chain. This pass, made as if the mountains had been rudely rent apart, was the door through which peaceful travel and warring armies, from ancient times, had passed between the high central lands within and the lower sea-plains without. This was the ancient Cilician Gates. Through this gorge had marched the grand army of Cyrus on his way towards Babylon. Alexander the Great, with his army, came down through these gates to the plains of Cilicia. Cicero once rode through this craggy defile, and wrote back to his friend a description of his journey. Many an army had its fate decided in this wild mountain-gap. Towards these Gates of Cilicia, which admitted them to the interior of Asia Minor, the travellers now took their way. They followed first, no doubt, the valley of the river by the side of which Paul played in boyhood. Perhaps more than once Paul had ridden along this very track, in boyhood and youth, or even when preaching in Cilicia after his conversion. As you approach the mountain, "the hills suddenly draw together and form a narrow pass guarded by precipitous cliffs. In some places the ravine contracts to the width of ten or twelve paces, leaving room for only a chariot to pass. It is an anxious place to any one in command of a military expedition. The scene around is striking and impressive. A canopy of fir-trees is high overhead. Hundreds of feet high, on either side, rise the bare limestone cliffs." Up, and still upwards, climb the travellers, over rocks and over hills, over the confined streams which sweep the narrow road, through forest and shade, till the last height is reached, and they come out on the open country, four thousand feet above the sea. Turning to the left and the west, they take the road towards Iconium. "As Paul left the mountain-passes, and came along down the lower heights, his heart, full of affection and anxiety all through the journey, would beat more quickly at the sight of the well-known objects before him." The thought of his disciples, the recollection of his friends in these remote places, would come with new force upon his mind, for now the tender-hearted Apostle was approaching the home of his own converts of Lycaonia. In the distance was the same well-shaped form of the Black Mountain rising out of the same wide-spreading plain near which lay Derbe and Lystria, and away beyond was the more important city of Iconium. Two or three days must have been consumed already since they left Tarsus.

Derbe, the last place of the former journey, is now before them. We can imagine the joy of the converts on meeting Paul; the inquiries for Barnabas; the welcome to Silas; the questions about the 'brethren' of Cilicia and Antioch and Jerusalem; the reading of the letter of the council; the 'teaching and preaching,' the encouragement and solemn warning of Paul. This is all we know of Derbe. No wonderful or striking event occurred which seemed good to the spirit of inspiration to record, although there may have been a quiet and extensive Christian influence working in many hearts The work of God is noiseless and without observation often where it is most powerful and lasting.

QUESTIONS.

HOW long must Paul and Barnabas have been in Antioch?

What difference was there between 'teaching' and 'preaching' religious doctrines?

What shows that the church was large?

Do you think there was more than one congregation in Antioch?

Who were the teachers in Antioch?

Who had now departed?

Why might some of these teachers be spared from Antioch? ⬎

What would Paul naturally think of?

What did he propose to Barnabas?

What was the design of the visit?

Did he mean to go over the *whole* of the former journey?

What does Barnabas answer to Paul's proposal?

Did Paul agree with Barnabas? Why?

Was there anything more than calm disagreement between them?

If they sharply disputed with each other, does it show that they were not good men?

What four reasons can you give why Paul should not take Mark?

What seven reasons can you give why Barnabas should wish to take Mark?

What reasons were there also from the position of the men?

Which one should have yielded?

How was their dissension overruled?

What similar blessing comes from the division of the church into denominations?

· Do you suppose the two Apostles parted in anger?

If Christian denominations differ, how should it be?

What is there to show that the Antioch Christians took Paul's side?

How did they divide the former journey between them?

Where did Barnabas and Mark go?

How can you arrange the whole of their former journey between them?

Who went with Paul?

Where did they go first?

What additional evidence have we now that there were churches in Cilicia?

Why was it a good thing for Paul to have Silas with him?

What valley may they have first visited?

What is more likely?

What gorge would they pass through?

Through what cities near the corner of the sea?

What plain did they strike into after leaving Issus?

Is it probable that they went to Tarsus?

What was the direct road to Derbe?

Where did Paul cross this mountain range before?

For what mountain-pass did they strike?

What generals had led their armies through this pass?

What orator had described it?

What was the narrowest width of the pass?

What would be their first thoughts on reaching the high land?

What is said of Derbe?

How does the kingdom of God often make progress?

Is religion any the less strong when it is silent?

Does it speak the less forcibly to you, when it speaks silently?

(36)

A NEW COMPANION AND NEW TRAVELS.

LESSON.
ACTS xvi. 1-8.

NOW we follow the missionaries to Lystra. Perhaps others went with them from Derbe. No miracle is now performed. No excited multitude rush together to hail men like themselves as gods: no fickle, deluded crowd, with the fury of a mob, now stone the man whom they had honored as a god. Quietly and peacefully the missionaries did their work here, as they did at Derbe. Here, however, they found one who was to go with them in their work and who was to become of great service to the Church.[1] Timothy had been gradually prepared for the work he was now to do. His mother had instructed him in the holy Scriptures from childhood;[2] and his grandmother was a woman of faith and prayer. He had grown to be a young man, and had listened to the preaching of the stranger, who healed a cripple lame from his mother's womb. He was convinced that Jesus was the Messiah. He no doubt saw Paul stoned by the brutal mob. He became a faithful and earnest disciple of Jesus the Messiah. He was well known to all the brethren of the place and of Iconium; and by them all he was well spoken of, as

---

[1] Some persons have supposed that Timothy was from Derbe, but it seems more probable that he was from Lystra.

[2] II. Timothy i. 5; iii. 15.

devoted and true. Paul saw that he was just the person, in his natural ability, and in his earnest, affectionate consecration to the Master, to be of great service in preaching. He found Timothy ready to go with them, and he determined to take him. Perhaps Paul thought, too, that Timothy was fitted to teach and to attract both Jews and Gentiles, since he was the son of a Greek and a Jewess.

But Timothy himself was not legally a Jew, and therefore he might be suspected everywhere in the synagogues, and might create excitement, trouble, persecution. To prevent any difficulty of this kind, Paul 'took and circumcised him,' so that, although the son of a Jewess, he might now be a Jew according to the rite of the law.

But was not Paul violating the decree of the council? the very letter which he had brought with him to the church of Lystra? No, not at all. That decree said that the Apostles laid upon the brethren no other *burden* than four necessary things. No one *need* be circumcised, if he did not wish to be. If any one wished to be, there was nothing to prevent. If it should be thought best to gain influence with the Jews, so that they would more readily listen to the Gospel of Jesus, it was perfectly proper. At Jerusalem Paul refused to circumcise Titus, because some persons had said that circumcision was *necessary*, if a man *would be saved*—that *no one could be saved without it*. *That* he denied. Timothy was already known and well spoken of, as a Christian. Paul circumcised him, not that he *might be saved*, but that he might more directly and more effectively influence the Jews.

It is not improbable that Timothy was now ordained as a preacher of the Gospel of Jesus, at Lystra, or more likely at Iconium, since before that solemn ceremony took place, Paul seems to have learned from the brethren of Iconium their opinion of Timothy. In his letters to Timothy afterwards, the Apostle alludes to the time when he was consecrated to the work of the ministry ' by the laying on of hands.'[3] The ordination of a Christian young man to the ministry would add great interest to the visit of the Apostle to Iconium; and as it might have been in a private manner, it could have been done without exciting another such contention between two factions in the city as took place on the former visit.

We have no distinct account of a visit to Antioch in Pisidia. Yet we can hardly suppose that Paul did not in some way communicate with the church there; for Paul started with the intention of visiting ' every city where they had preached the word of the Lord.'[4] If Paul and Silas and Timothy remained some weeks at Iconium, there would have been abundant time to visit Pisidia, or to see, more than once, the elders and principal persons of the Antioch church. It is very likely that they finished the circle of the churches, which they meant at the first to visit. Possibly that was all they designed to do, at starting on the journey; but now they resolved to carry the good news of the Gospel still further. The decree of the council, which they had delivered to all the churches, would be glad news everywhere to Gentiles who might wish to obey the words of life.

We know very little of the Apostle's visit through Phrygia and Galatia. No cities are mentioned. Perhaps he visited Colosse,[5] which is supposed to have been in Phrygia, and to the people of which city Paul with Timothy afterwards wrote a letter.[6]

---

[3] I. Timothy iv. 14; II. Timothy i. 6.
[4] xv. 36.   [5] Colossians i. 1, 2.

The letter of Paul to the Galatians tells us some thing of his visit to their province. It was certainly 'in infirmity of the flesh' that he preached the Gospel to them '*at the first ;*'[6] and it has been thought that Paul was sick among this people, and that this accounts for his speaking of their great kindness to them. He say that they received him 'as an angel' or messenger 'of God,' and if it had been possible they would have 'plucked out their own eyes' for him.' Whatever was the infirmity of the flesh among the Galatians, he 'set forth' to them 'Jesus Christ, the crucified one.'[8] Some at least were converted;[9] and 'some churches of Galatia'[10] were added to the other established churches of Cilicia and Lycaonia and Phrygia, before the little band of earnest missionaries left the province.

As they journeyed westward, they were forbidden by the Holy Spirit to *preach* in *Asia*, but *not* to *enter* the province. Then they turned to the north towards Bithynia, but the Holy Spirit forbade them to *enter* that province. It is very likely that Paul's design was to reach some of the great cities on the coast of the Archipelago, the emporium of trade at or near the ends of the roads through central Asia Minor. These great cities of pro-consular Asia, which afterwards were to contain churches, were not yet to have the Gospel preached in them. Ephesus, Smyrna, Philadelphia, Sardis, Pergamos, Thyatira, Laodicea, those seven cities to which John wrote his wonderful letters,[11] were not yet to spring into existence. Leaving Bithynia on the right hand, they entered Asia, and passed along the borders of Mysia, without preaching, to Troas, one of the chief cities of Mysia.[12]

---

[6] Galatians iv. 13.   [7] iv. 14, 15.   [8] iii. 1.   [9] iii. 27.

[10] i. 2.   [11] Revelation i. 11.

[12] It is very difficult to fix the exact geographical boundaries of

WESTERN ASIA MINOR.

Now Paul strikes into a new kind of life: now he
comes into the old classic region. Along these western shores of Asia Minor, many of the earliest events
of Grecian history took place, and there, sprang up the
races which had so much to do with forming the national character of Greece. The Roman legions too
shook these same shores with the tramp of war, and
these petty kingdoms of antiquity were forced to bend
before the iron sceptre of Cæsar. As he came in sight

Galatia, Phrygia, Mysia, Bithynia, Asia, in the time of Paul. 'These
boundaries were continually changing, and these names implied a
larger or smaller territory at one time than another.' The province
of Asia (not the *continent*) probably included at least Mysia, Lydia,
and Caria.

of the waters of the Archipelago, he looked out on
the sea on which have transpired so many wonderful
events of history and poetry and song. He was near
the old battle-ground of the Trojan war. As he
came near to Troas, he struck the well-built national
road which would have led him to the very gates of
Rome. Xerxes had stood on this ground with his great
army, on his way to be conquered by the brave Greeks.
Julius Cæsar had been here with all his pomp of war.
Alexander the Great, too, gathered here new strength
for his conquest. And all around him was the scene of
Homer's great poem, Mount Ida, the Simois, and Sca-
mander. Paul was a scholar; and he could not be
without some knowledge of all these things as he entered Troas.

QUESTIONS.

WHAT is the next place to which the Apostles go ?
  Whom did they find there ?
  How had he been gradually prepared for his work ?
  Was he well known at any other place ?
  What did the 'brethren' say of him ?
  What did Paul see in him ?
  Who was Timothy's father ?
  How would this help Timothy in his work ?
Why was not Timothy legally a Jew ?
  Why did Paul circumcise him ?
Was not Paul violating the decree of the council ?
  Why did Paul refuse to circumcise Titus at Jerusalem ?
  Was there any similar reason now for refusing to cir-
    cumcise Timothy ?
  If Timothy's mother had been a Greek, would Paul
    have circumcised him ?
  If he had not circumcised Timothy, what would have
    been the effect on the Jews ?
Do you suppose Timothy was now ordained ?
  Can you prove that Paul helped ordain Timothy ?
  What is meant by 'the laying on of my hands' ?
What cities do you think are referred to, in the fourth verse ?
  What 'decrees' were delivered ?
  Why may you suppose they had some communication
    with Antioch in Pisidia ?
  Would Gentile Christians be glad to hear the decree of
    the council ?
  How would this fact have helped to increase the numbers
    daily ?
Was Phrygia nearer Antioch in Pisidia or Iconium ?
Where was Galatia ?
  What does Paul say of his preaching to the Galatians
    at first?
  What has this been thought to mean ?

(37)

How do you know churches of Galatia must have been
formed ?

What especial expressions of the Galatians' attachment
to Paul are given ?

In what direction did they go next ?

Why did they not preach in Asia ?

Why did they turn back from Mysia ?

Why did they not go into Bithynia ?

Where was Bithynia ?

What was Asia ?

What did it probably include at this time ?

What was probably Paul's object, if he wished to preach
in Asia ?

What churches were afterwards founded in Asia ?

How could they *pass by* Mysia, and yet come to Troas ?

In entering Mysia, were they not violating the command
not to preach in Asia ?

Is the Holy Spirit as really present to guide believers
now, as he was to show Paul his course ?

To what place did the Apostles come ? Why 'came
down ' ?

What region was Paul now entering ?

For what events are these shores famous ?

What road did they strike near this place ?

What old battle-ground was supposed to be near ?

What great generals had been here ?

The scene of what famous poem was here ?

Do you suppose Paul knew anything of these things ?

What greater purpose had he than any who had pre-
ceded him there ?

(38)

FROM ASIA TO EUROPE.

LESSON.

ACTS xvi. 9–15.

AT Troas, Paul looked out over the island-sea. He saw the high lands which rose from the islands of Tenedos and Imbros, in the north-west. Possibly, when the sun went down behind the distant line of the sea, broken here and there by an island, he could see, over Tenedos and Imbros, the higher hills of Samothrace, and further to the west, the lofty Mount Athos, on the very coast of Europe, the long promontory on which it is stretching miles out into the sea towards Asia.

What must have been the thought of the earnest Apostle, filled with zeal for his Master, as he looked over the waters towards another great continent! Would the Gospel be preached in that distant country? How he would long to preach it there himself. He had been forbidden to preach in 'Asia.' Perhaps there was a work for him to do, in the distant and 'miserable heathenism' of Europe. Thoughts like these would be natural to Paul. And in the night, there was a vision of a man from the distant Macedonia, urging the spiritual wants of his country. It was a vision sent of God to show him his work. The breaking morning after that eventful night, found the Apostle ready to take the suggestions of the Spirit as his rule of life. Per-

haps in the east the sun rose, as in the description of
Virgil:

"And now the day-star was rising from the summit of lofty Ida,
And was leading on the day." [1]

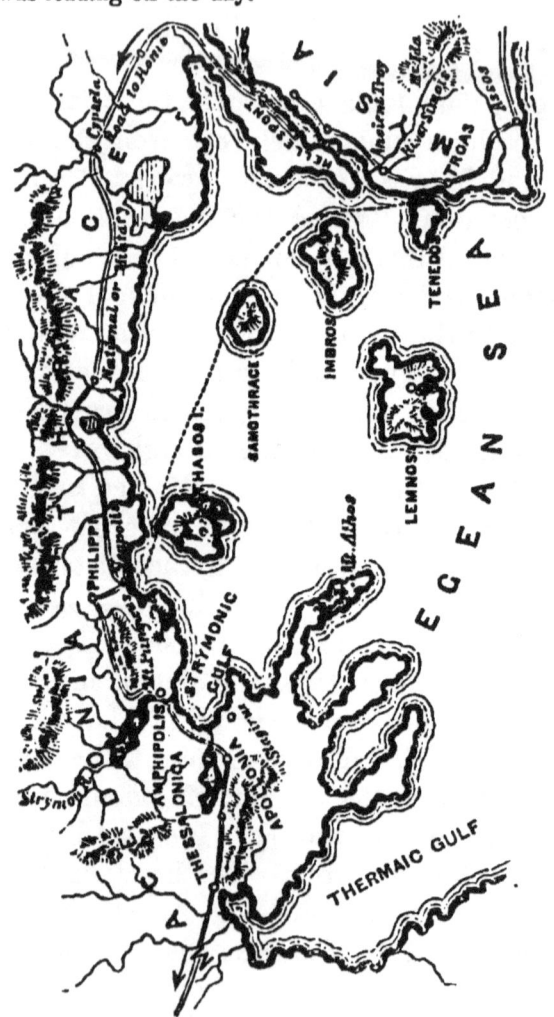

The islands of the sea were illumined, and the waters
sparkled in the light. Four travellers might have been
seen at the shipping of the harbor, seeking passage to

Æneid ii. 801.

Europe. The ship on which they embarked, 'loosed' from port and 'sailed before the wind'[2] to Samothrace. When God gives direction, all things are propitious. Once out of the harbor, Tenedos, with its fables of refuge for the Grecian fleet and of the wooden horse, in the story of the Trojan war, was on the left: the coast of Mysia on the right. On they glide, past the Hellespont, the scene of so many real and fancied exploits, while deep under the water on the opposite side, between Tenedos and Imbros, was said to be the cave of the great Sea-God, and on the high summit of the island to which they go, is Neptune's throne, overlooking all the sea. Perhaps the sailors told over these fables, as they guided the ship. To Paul they were 'vanities,' and only showed him the foolishness of the wisdom of man — the wild vagaries of mind to which Greeks and Romans bowed down to worship.

Samothrace has a high shore, and under it the ship anchored for the night. It is not probable that the Apostles went on shore here. Their work lay further on. It is well, however, to notice that this island took its name from the country near which it lay. It was Samos of Thrace, (Samo-Thrace,) to distinguish it from another Samos, famous in history, off the coast of Ephesus. The next day, a few hours brought the little company of missionaries into the channel between the island of Thasos and the shore, and then to Neapolis. The shore, unlike that of Samothrace, is low. The Apostle does not seem to stop at Neapolis. The town was the sea-port of Philippi. As, therefore, in Syria, he preached at Antioch, and not at Seleucia, so he goes directly to 'the chief city' of the region.[3] The distance from

---

[2] To sail in 'a straight course' must have been, of course, to sail *with* the wind; and the wind must have been in the south-east.

[3] Philippi was not the chief city. The margin has it, more correct

Neapolis to Philippi is about ten miles, and the road across a range of high hills. When we reach the high ground, "an extensive and magnificent sea-view is opened towards the south." We see Neptune's throne on Samothrace, in the south-east: we see the broader island of Thasos just in front, while far to the south highest of all, towers Mount Athos, on its long peninsula. Turning our backs on this delightful view, we begin the descent on the other side of the ridge; and now we see a "plain, level as an inland sea, and which, if the eye could reach it all, would be seen winding far within its mountain-enclosure, to the west and north." It is either "exuberantly green," from its famous fruit-fulness of soil, if it is summer, or "cold and dreary" if winter. This is the memorable plain of Philippi. "The whole region around is eloquent of the history of the last battle of the Roman republic. On some part of this very ridge, were the camps of Brutus and Cassius. The stream before us, is the river which passed in front of them. Below us is the marsh by which Antony crossed, as he approached his antagonist. Directly opposite is the hill of Philippi, where Cassius died. Behind us is the sea, across which Brutus sent the body of Cassius to the island of Thasos, lest his death should dishearten the army before the final struggle. The city of Philippi was itself a monument of the end of that struggle. And now a Jewish Apostle had come to the same place, to win a greater victory than that of Philippi, and to found a more durable empire than that of Augustus."

Philippi was 'a colony.' What is meant by this expression? A Roman colony was a very different thing from what we think of as an English colony in

ly, the *first* city, that is, the first city to which they came. Thessalonica was the chief city, the greatest of all in Macedonia.

our time : a company gathered in almost any loose manner, and going out to Australia, to Hudson's Bay, or to India, to settle the country ; or like the colonies of Virginia or Carolina, two centuries ago. The Romans divided the world into two classes of people, Romans and Not-Romans, or more proudly, into ' citizens ' and ' strangers.' When a colony was to be formed, a certain number of *citizens* went from Rome, in stately form, like an army, and either took possession of a town already built, or laid out a town for themselves. This town they fortified, and they themselves were the garrison. In all the pride of Roman citizens, . in the midst of a population of ' strangers,' they established the laws and customs of Rome. They aimed to make the city ' a miniature resemblance of Rome.' The banners and the ensigns of Rome were hung out ; the *fasces* and the *toga*, the *magistrates* and the *lictors* were seen. " Every traveller who passed through a colony, saw the insignia of the Imperial city. He heard the Latin language and was responsible strictly to the Roman law." The coin had Latin inscriptions, even if the city were in a Hebrew or a Greek or an Egyptian province. This was the ' colony.' It was designed to be a strong military outpost to establish and to secure the authority of the great empire. After a time, some of the native inhabitants of the conquered town would gradually be united with the Romans, and they then formed part of the colony.

Every native ' citizen,' and every adopted ' citizen,' had certain rights, among which three were esteemed perhaps the greatest of all his privileges. He was *never to be scourged :* he was *not to be arrested*, except in extreme cases : he had the *right to appeal*, when he thought he was unjustly treated in the courts, *from the magistrate to the Emperor.* ' Strangers ' possessed none of

these rights; and it was not an easy thing to become a
'citizen.' We shall soon see how Paul claimed for himself two of these rights, what advantage they were to
him, and what rebuke they were to his persecutors;
and hereafter, we shall see how he claimed the third
right.

Romans and Greeks mingled in the colony of Philippi; but there were few Jews in the city. The Jews
are a trafficking people; and this was a military, and not
a mercantile city. We find no synagogue in Philippi,
but only a place of prayer by the river-side. The Jews
in strange cities, when they could have no synagogue,
were accustomed to build a 'house of prayer,' "a slight
and temporary structure, often open to the sky." Probably for the sake of the ablutions connected with the
worship, these houses were by the sea or near a river.
In Philippi, the 'house of prayer' was outside the gate,
and by the river-side. It may be that the assembly
was composed only of women. Women only are mentioned, and these are not all native Jews. Lydia, at
least, is a proselyte. She is from Thyatira, a city of the
province of Asia. She is a seller of purple; that is, her
business is connected with the art of dyeing that particular color, which Homer mentions as produced in the
region of Thyatira, and which is known to have rendered that city famous. "In this unpretending place,
and to this congregation of pious women, the Gospel
was first preached in Europe. The missionary party
came up from Neapolis in the early part of the week,
for it would seem that there were 'certain days' before
'the Sabbath.' On that day the strangers went and
joined the little company of worshippers at their prayer
by the river-side. They 'sat down and spoke,' thus
assuming the attitude of teachers."

The simple-hearted Lydia believed that Jesus is Mes-

siah and Saviour, and was baptized. 'Her household'
also are baptized. *Family religion* quickly follows
faith in Jesus, in the simple and sincere heart. Another
effect, too, follows from genuine piety: *genuine hospitality.* The house, as well as the heart of Lydia, was
opened. With a generous and loving care for her religious benefactors, and with gratitude to the Great Master who sent them, she constrained the little band of
good men to make her house their home. What a peaceful and beautiful picture is this, of Lydia and her household, in their simplicity and purity and artless faith!
How the soft and holy influence of Christian woman-
hood sanctifies, how the sacred instruction of these
great and good men exalts, how the very atmosphere
of peace and quietness pervades the united family of
friends and guests. We can hardly help thinking of
the peace and the hospitality and the instruction of the
Palace Beautiful, in the path of Bunyan's pilgrim.
How wide the contrast between this picture and that
picture of religion which the Roman poet, Horace,
sketches for us, in this very same region, by the side of
a neighboring river: "The Edonian matrons, in frantic
excitement, wandering, under the name of religion,
with dishevelled hair and violent cries, on the banks of
the Strymon."

It may have been Lydia, so quick to show her faith
by her works, who, afterwards returning to her native
place, aided in the establishment of that church to which
the Apostle John wrote in the Revelation, and which
he commended for "works, and charity, and service,
and faith, and patience." '

' Revelation ii. 18, 19.

QUESTIONS.

WHAT could Paul see from Troas?
> What would he think of and desire?
> Was he intending to preach in Troas?

What occurred in the night?
> Where was Macedonia?
> How did Paul regard this vision?
> What does 'assuredly gathering' mean?
> What poet has given a description of sun-rise here?

Who were the four travellers?
> How do you know there were four?
> Could they sail *exactly* in a straight course to Samo-
> thrace?
> What does the expression mean?
> What story was connected with Tenedos?
> What with the sea between Tenedos and Imbros?
> Whose throne was fabled to be on Samothrace?

Why do you think that the vessel anchored at Samothrace
for the night?
> What does the name of this island mean?

Where did they land the next day?
> What was Neapolis?
> Why didn't they stop here to preach?
> What does the 'chief city' mean?
> What was the chief city?
> What is the plain of Philippi memorable for?

What was Philippi?
> How did the Romans divide the world?
> How did the Greeks divide it?
> What was the Jewish division?
> How was a Roman colony formed?
> What did the 'citizens' aim to make the city?
> What signs of Roman power were seen?
> What was the design of forming a colony?
> Could foreigners become Roman citizens? How?[1]

What were three great rights of a Roman citizen?

Were there many Jews in Philippi?

    What shows it?

    What was the 'house of prayer'?

    Why was it built by the river-side?

    Who composed this assembly?

    What would have been thought by the people of a preacher who would seek such an audience?

Who was Lydia?

    For what was her native city famous?

    At what time in the week did the Apostles reach Philippi?

    What does '*sat down* and spake' show?

    If Lydia 'worshipped God' before Paul came, was she not God's child?

    Who only can 'open the heart,' to make a person God's child?

    When a person really begins to 'attend unto religious things,' what does it show?

What is meant by 'household'?

    What is the natural result of conversion in a father or mother?

    What is another natural effect?

    What characteristics can you mention of Lydia's character?

    What characteristics of the family and guests at this time?

    What two other pictures by what two other authors?

    Where was the river Strymon?

Is Thyatira mentioned elsewhere in the Scripture?

    What may Lydia have done?

    In the Apostle John's praise of the church there, can you see anything of Lydia's character?

(40)

ROMAN LAW.

LESSON.
ACTS xvi. 16 – 39.

THE quiet of the little company in the house of Lydia was not to continue. The Apostle was soon to come into direct conflict with the power of Roman law in the 'colony;' and that strong law was soon to establish his independent rights.

It is to be carefully noticed now, that the first persecution in Europe is very different from those which Paul had endured in Asia Minor. At Antioch in Pisidia, at Iconium, at Lystra, it was the Jews who persecuted Paul; but there were no Jews in the persecution at Philippi. On the other hand, the Philippians persecuted the Apostles, in part because *they* were *Jews*. Before, the conflict had been between Christianity and Jewish prejudice; now, it was between Christianity and pure paganism—a paganism established and secured by all the cultivation and power of two great and wise nations. To understand how this conflict was brought about, we must know something of one form of pagan superstition.

" In the lively imagination of the Greeks, the whole visible and invisible world was peopled with spiritual powers." These were called *demons.* The Greeks thought them good as well as evil. Some have believed " that a wicked spiritual agency was really exerted in their prophetic sanctuaries and their prophets." The Greeks and Romans declared that the strange motions made by these prophets, and the words of their oracles, and the other indications of spiritual power, were the work of Apollo, or of *Python*, as he was sometimes called. There was a great variety of these manifestations, and they were often seen. These diviners or soothsayers or ventriloquists, therefore, were said to be possessed of *the spirit of Python.* "Sometimes those supposed to be possessed of this spirit were of the highest rank of society; sometimes they went about the streets like insane impostors of the lowest rank." As the people valued their ravings and wild mutterings enough to pay money for them, these miserable persons were sometimes used for gain. Very often they were slaves. Such a slave might be of high value to a man who cared nothing for religion nor for wicked deception nor for the misery of the poor wretches who were either lunatic or really possessed by the evil spirit. The value of such a demoniac slave was so great at times, that two or more persons were partners in owning the property. This was the case of the 'female slave' possessed with a spirit of Python[1] at Philippi. She was owned by two masters or more, who from her ravings made 'much profit.' "We all know the kind of sacredness with which the ravings of common insanity are apt to be regarded by the ignorant; and we can easily understand the notoriety which the gestures and words of this demoniac would obtain in Philippi. It was far from a matter of indifference, when she met the members of the Christian congregation on the road to the house of prayer, and began to follow Paul and to cry: (either because some words she had overheard mingled with her diseased imagination, or because the

[1] See the margin in the reference Bible.

evil spirit in her was compelled to speak the truth:)
'These men are the servants (bondmen) of the Most
High God, who are come to announce to you the way
of salvation.'" "The whole city must soon have been
familiar with her new cry," for she continued it several
days. Paul knew this, and he could not endure that
the pure religion of Jesus should be contaminated by
such unholy assistance. Their preaching, and the worship by the river-side were better without *such* testimony. While he pitied the poor demoniac, he remembered the words of the Master, 'In my name they shall
cast out devils,' (*demons*.) When "he could bear the
Satanic interruption no longer," grieved at heart, and
in the name of Jesus the Messiah, he commanded the
evil spirit to come out of her.

With the healing of the mind and of the spirit of this
poor slave, the wicked masters lost their gain. Enraged, they dragged Paul and Silas into the forum—
the open court or market-place, like the open squares
used in some of our cities for market-places. Timothy
and Luke were not taken. Paul was the man that
wrought the cure. Silas was Paul's intimate companion. Perhaps Timothy and Luke were not with Paul
and Silas on that day. Paul and Silas were quickly
dragged (as Paul himself *hauled* men and women to
prison²) "before the *Prætors*," or magistrates.

"The excited complainants must have felt some difficulty in stating their complaint. The slave that had
lately been such a lucrative possession had suddenly
become valueless, but the law had no remedy for de-✓
stroying the value of property by the casting out of
spirits. The true state of the case was therefore con-✓
cealed, and an accusation laid before the Prætors in the
following form: 'These men are throwing the whole ↳

² See note 2, page 22

city into confusion; moreover, they are Jews; and they are attempting to introduce new religious observances, which we, being Roman citizens, cannot receive and adopt.'" Dividing the accusation into the three parts, we can easily see what was true and what was false. "It was quite false that Paul and Silas were disturbing the city, for nothing could have been more calm and orderly than their worship and teaching at the house of Lydia, or at the place of prayer by the water-side." It was true that they were Jews. There was cunning and spite in accusing them of this; for "the Jews were generally hated, suspected, and despised, and had lately been driven out of Rome in consequence of an uproar." The citizens of the colony, too, would think it their duty "to copy the indignation of the mother city." · It was true, too, that Paul and Silas were indirectly violating the law. "The Roman law condemned the introduction of foreign religions, especially such changes in worship as were likely to unsettle the minds of the citizens, or to produce any tumultuous uproar. Paul and Silas had undoubtedly been doing what in some degree exposed them to legal penalties, and were beginning a change which tended to bring down, and which at length did bring down the whole weight of the Roman Law on the Christian martyrs." We can see, then, why 'the multitude rose up.' A wonderful slave had lost her spirit of prophecy · the cause of wonder and excitement and curiosity had been taken away: the hated Jews had done it: they were breaking the law of 'the colony.' The excited crowd rose into a mob. The Prætors, if they would be popular, must not hesitate. It was no time to think of further proof. The rough form of the Roman sentence was pronounced: '*Go, lictors: strip off their gar-*

ments : [3] *let them be scourged.'* "The order was promptly obeyed, and the heavy blows descended." The Roman scourging was much more severe than the Jewish, and the Apostles received 'many stripes.' "Bleeding and faint from the rod," the jailer was told 'to keep them safely.' "Not content with placing the Apostles among other common offenders in the jail, he thrust them 'into the inner prison,' and then forced their limbs, lacerated as they were and bleeding from the scourge, into a painful and constrained posture by means of an instrument used to confine and torture the bodies of the worst malefactors. We must picture to ourselves something very different from the rough comfort of an American jail. The inner prisons of the ancients were rather pestilential cells, damp and cold, from which the light was excluded, and where the chains rusted on the limbs of the prisoners."

But cruel as was the scourging, cold and hard as were the prison-walls, the spirit of joyfulness was in the hearts of these good men. Sleepless because of their pain and fatigue, with heart and voice, they sung praises to God. What they sung, we do not know, but it would be strange if, at such a time, the Psalms of David did not rise to the lips of a Jew. How comforting and how hopeful would have been such words as these, chanted in the Hebrew manner :

> " The Lord looseth the prisoners :
> The Lord raiseth them that are bowed down :
> The Lord loveth the righteous :

[3] "It is quite a mistake to suppose that the magistrates rent *their own* garments, like the high-priest at Jerusalem." That was a *Jewish,* not a Roman custom. "Some commentators think the magistrates tore off the garments of Paul and Silas with their own hands, but that is not necessary." It is more probable that they gave the customary order to the lictors, their attendants.

The Lord preserveth the strangers,
But the way of the wicked, he turneth upside down." [4]

" Let the sighing of the prisoner come before thee :
According to the greatness of thy power,
Preserve thou those appointed to die." [5]

"Attend unto my cry,
For I am brought very low
Deliver me from my persecutors,
For they are stronger than I.
Bring my soul out of prison,
That I may praise thy name." [6]

" Happy is he that hath the God of Jacob for his help.
Whose hope is in the Lord his God." [7]

The other prisoners heard them. Slaves, debtors, robbers, murderers perhaps listened to the cheerful songs of the new prisoners. These were strange criminals : these were new sounds echoing out on the night-air from the inner prison. These must be good men, too, who, bleeding from the scourge and at midnight, sing praises to God. The very songs of Paul and Silas preached their religion to their fellow-prisoners. Who can say that some of these very prisoners did not afterwards believe in the Saviour, because new hopes and new desires were awakened by what they that night heard and saw ? It may be that the earthquake occurred just as the Apostles were finishing [8] those other words of the Psalmist :

" He brought them out of darkness
And the shadow of death,
And brake their bonds in sunder.

---

[4] Psalm cxlvi. 7–9.   [5] lxxix. 11.   [6] cxlii. 6, 7.

[7] cxlvi. 5. The whole cxlvi. would have been most appropriate and comforting.

[8] The tense of the Greek verb signifies that they *continued* to sing, and the prisoners continued to listen. " The Apostles *were singing* and the prisoners *were listening*, when the earthquake came."

> Oh! that men would praise the Lord
> For his goodness and for his wonderful works
> To the children of men;
> For he hath broken the gates of brass
> And cut the bars of iron in sunder." [*]

The iron bars and the gates were broken asunder by that God to whom they sung and prayed. And they were free to go.

But there was something more dreadful than earthquake to the prison-keeper. "By the Roman law, the jailer was to undergo the same punishment which the malefactors who escaped were to have suffered." What was his consternation when, awakened out of his sleep, he saw the doors open. He at once supposed the prisoners had fled. Inevitable death must be his fate. Suicide was better than such disgrace. "Philippi is famous in the annals of suicide." The jailer would have added his name to the list of Cassius, Brutus, Titinius, and many others who rashly died by their own hand after the great battle of Philippi, had not Paul's loud voice reached him. Instead of death, he found spiritual life. Startled, trembling, remembering his crimes, his eagerness to cast the persecuted men into the inner prison, the near approach of death and his unfitness to die, and recalling, too, perhaps, that the very cause of all the persecution of these good men, was that the demoniac had said they taught a *way of salvation*, he sprang in with a light and fell down before his prisoners, to ask that all-important question: 'What must I do to be saved?' Believe on Jesus as your Lord and as the Messiah, was the faithful answer. Like Lydia, his heart was opened to hear and to believe. Like Lydia, he and his house were baptized. *Family religion* again followed piety in the head of the household.

---

[*] Psalm cvii. 14–16.

Christian hospitality followed next. 'He washed the ∟ stripes' of the wounded and bruised men. He brought them out of the wretched cell into his house; he gave them food; and there was great rejoicing that night. The Gospel had a second home in Europe.

On reflection, the magistrates became convinced of the rashness and irregularity of their proceedings; or perhaps they heard that the Jews cast out the spirit because the slave cried after them; or the earthquake may have alarmed them. At any rate, in the morning, they sent a new order by the lictors [10] to the jailer. Evidently they feared lest some authority from Rome might inquire into the accusations against the prisoners, and the regularity of yesterday's trial. '*Let those men go*,' [11] is the contemptuous expression. The jailer was full of joy.

But now it was Paul's turn. Now he claims his rights as a Roman citizen. If *he* had violated Roman law in one thing, the magistrates had violated it in two other far more important points. They had *arrested* two *Roman citizens* on the mere outcry of the people, and, with hardly the forms of a trial, had hastily passed sentence on them. They had *scourged* two *Roman citizens*. The reply of Paul is therefore the noble assertion of his just rights. The magistrates had done a great wrong: Let them come and make it right. It was the time for the magistrates to tremble. Should their crime become known at Rome, as Paul himself might make it known, they would certainly lose their power, if they would not be most severely punished;

---

[10] The word 'sergeant,' means here 'rod-holders,' *lictors*, the attendant officers of the magistrate.

[11] It might be translated, *Let those fellows go.*

for their rashness had put the whole majesty of the law in peril. With servile humiliation, quite the contrast of their yesterday's presumption, they came privately and besought their abused prisoners to go quietly from the city.

QUESTIONS.

WHAT is this lesson the account of ?

What difference is there between the Philippian persecution and those in Asia Minor ?

What two things had been in conflict before ? What two now ?

What was a *demon ?*

What is meant by 'the spirit of Python' ?

Why were demoniac slaves thought valuable property ?

What shows that this 'damsel' was held as very valuable ?

What is meant in the margin by 'of divination' ?

What harm did her outcries do ?

How do you explain the way in which she had learned what she said ?

Was this new cry known in the city ?

Whose words and what words did Paul remember ?

If this miracle was done publicly, what depended on the success of Paul's command ?

What was the effect of the cure on her masters ?

Who escaped ?

What is meant by 'market-place' ?

Who were these rulers ?

Was the accusation made in a regular form ? Why ?

What are the three parts of the charge which they made ?

Was the first part true or false ?

Was the second part true or false ?

What wicked cunning was there in this part ?

What was true in reference to the third part ?

Explain the cause of excitement.

Was the command of the magistrates the regular decision of a court ?

Whose clothes did the magistrates rend off ?

Did the magistrates themselves rend off the clothes ?

What does 'many stripes' show ?

(41)

Did the jailer do more than he was commanded ?

> Where are 'the stocks' ?
> What caused their joyfulness ?
> What would they be likely to sing ?
> How did they preach their religion without knowing it !
> What happened while they were singing ?

What was the first alarm of the jailer ?

> What did he intend to do ?
> What was true of Philippi in respect to suicides ?
> Who prevented the jailer ?
> Would a *guilty* prisoner use such words as Paul's ?
> What made the jailer ask such a question of his prisoner ?
> If there was an earthquake now, would you be led to ask this question ?
> Why isn't it better to seek 'to be saved' now ?

What did Paul tell the jailer was the way to be saved ?

> Has there been any change since that time ?
> What is it to believe on the Saviour ?
> What two results followed the jailer's conversion ?

Why did the magistrates send new orders ?

> What does the word '*sergeants*' mean ?
> Was the order of the magistrates respectful ?
> Who had broken the law more, the magistrates or Paul ?
> How did Paul assert his rights ?
> Who held the power now ?
> Who must now seek favor ?

Twenty-second Sunday.

THE FOUNDING OF THE THESSALONIAN CHURCH.

LESSON.

ACTS xvi. 40; xvii. 1–4.

THE Apostles yielded to the request of the magistrates, but they did not go in hasty flight. With the dignity and self-possession of innocent men, they went first to the house of Lydia, where they met the brethren and gave their farewell words of comfort; and then they left the city. Luke probably remained behind.[1] Perhaps Timothy did. Paul and Silas only are mentioned at Thessalonica.[2] The new church of the Philippians, in which the families of Lydia and of the jailer held a prominent place, may have needed the instruction and care of Luke and Timothy. Timothy, it will be remembered, was the son of a Greek, and it is supposed that Luke too was a Greek. They could mingle with the Greeks and Romans of Philippi without creating suspicion or excitement.

If we stop for a moment and fix in the mind the outline of three great provinces, it will help us much to gain a clear idea of the Apostle's journeys now and hereafter in all this region. In Paul's time, the country from the great Hæmus mountain-range (which runs

---

[1] Luke was with the Apostle at Philippi, as the seventeenth verse shows, 'followed Paul and *us*,' but the account of Paul's journey is continued from this point to the twentieth chapter *in the third person.* See seventeenth chapter, 'Now when *they*, etc.

[2] xvii. 10.

almost parallel with the Danube) to the southernmost
cape of Greece was divided into *Illyricum, Macedonia,*

and *Achaia.* If Paul did not *preach* in *Illyricum,* he
went to the very borders of the province. He afterwards wrote from Corinth to Rome, 'from Jerusalem
round about unto Illyricum, I have fully preached the
Gospel of Christ.'[3] Paul travelled over *Macedonia* and
Achaia several times. In his letters written later in
life, we find many allusions to *Achaia.*[4] We now see
him taking the first of his journeys into *Macedonia.*
From Philippi, his course struck off towards the centre
and the capital of that great province.

[3] Romans xv. 19.
[4] Rom. xv. 26; II. Corinth. ix. 2; xi. 10; I. Thess. i. 7, 8.

At Philippi, if not before, Paul had entered the great Roman military road. It was the great state road which led from the west to the east. It was built at enormous expense, and reached from Dyrrachium on the Illyrican coast (opposite Brundusium, from which point the road continued to Rome) to Cypsela' in Thrace, and perhaps farther. Possibly Paul trod this identical road at Troas. Philippi was the first important city in Macedonia on this state-road; and Thessalonica was about half-way between Dyrrachium and Cypsela. Along the stone pavement of this Roman road, Paul and Silas, two Roman citizens, travel, still sore from their scourging; not now fleeing for life nor by night, but holding the fate of the Philippian rulers in their own hands. As they passed the mile-stones, carefully put up all along the way, they would be reminded that every foot-pace was taking them towards the seven-hilled Monarch of the World. In later years, on the other side of the Adriatic, Paul trod the same pavement at Appii Forum and Three Taverns.° Amphipolis and Apollonia divided the distance between Philippi and Thessalonica into three nearly equal parts. We may think of Paul and Silas as lodging over-night in each of these places, since the journey from one place to another was about one day's travel. The road to Amphipolis lay across the plain north of the mountains of Pangæus' celebrated for their gold and silver-mines and for their beautiful roses. "The ancient name of Amphipolis was ' Nine-Ways,' from the great number of roads from Thrace and Macedonia which met at this point." It was afterwards called Amphipolis,' because the river flowed almost around it. Xerxes crossed this

---

' See map in Twentieth Sunday.   ° Acts xxviii. 15.

' Amphi, *about*, polis, *the city.*

river here, and offered to it a sacrifice of white horses. The river spread out into a lake above the town. The city is just in a pass of the mountains, and commands the best road from the sea up to the Macedonian plains. It was a place of consequence therefore. Demosthenes spoke of it in his famous orations to the Athenians.

Paul and Silas had come thirty-three miles. The next part of the journey was thirty miles to Apollonia. The Roman road is " along the edge of the Strymonic gulf, first between cliffs and the sea and then across a well-wooded sea-plain, where the peak of Mount Athos is seen far across the bay to the left. As we leave the sea, we have before us on the coast Stagirus, the birth-place of Aristotle the philosopher, and just where the mountains close on the roads is the tomb of Euripides, the tragic poet." Apollonia was somewhere on the road across the neck of the three-pronged peninsula, and about thirty-seven miles from Thessalonica. The country is varied and picturesque. There is a long valley in which are two lakes. Then the sea appears again. Then there is another valley, the long and fruit-ful valley of the river Axius, and right before us on its bank is Thessalonica, the largest and most important city on the great road. It was named for Thessalonica, a sister of Alexander the Great.* It was the capital of Macedonia. When Cicero was exiled from Rome, he lived here. The great Roman generals, Antony and Octavius, were here after the celebrated battle of Philippi. And from that day to this it has been one of the chief cities on the European side of the Archipelago. Before Constantinople was built, it was the capital of all that region around the head of the Ægean. It was at the head of the busy Ægean Sea and at the

* Its former name was Therma. It was re-named when re-built and adorned by Thessalonica's husband, Cassander.

outlet of the trade of thrifty and fertile Macedonia; and "there probably never was a time, from the day when it first received its name, that the city was not a busy commercial town. It ranks in our own day, in European Turkey, next to Constantinople.* We see how appropriate a place it was for one of the starting-points of the Gospel in Europe; and we can appreciate the force of the expression used by Paul a few months after leaving the Thessalonians, when he writes to them: 'From you sounded out the word of the Lord, not only in Macedonia, but in every place.'[10]

Thessalonica became in this part of Europe, like Antioch in Syria, a city where *Christians* were known and where their influence was felt.

In Thessalonica there was a synagogue; for in this busy, trafficking town were many Jews. Perhaps the reason why Paul and Silas did not stop in Amphipolis and Apollonia was that there was no synagogue.

As Paul and Silas now enter the Thessalonian synagogue, we may recall the entrance of the two strangers into the synagogue of Pisidian Antioch, and Paul's address in reply to the invitation of the chief men. Although the city was Greek, and his work was mainly among Gentiles, Paul came first, as his manner was, to the Jews; and at first all the Jews listened with patience and with curiosity. For three Sabbath-days and at any intervening meetings and in conversation from day to day, he reasoned with them. His address to the Thessalonian congregation was on the same great subject as that to the Pisidian Jews and Gentiles; but only the three chief points of his discourse are given: (1.) That the Messiah of the Scriptures must be a suffering Mes-

---

* The name of Thessalonica is not yet entirely lost. It is now Salonica. One of the modern missionary stations has been in Salonica.

[10] I. Thessalonians i. 8.

siah; (2.) That the Messiah, after death, must rise
again; (3.) That *Jesus of Nazareth* suffered, died, and
rose again, and therefore *was the Messiah foretold.*

Here, as at Antioch, were Jews and proselytes ('de-
vout *Greeks*') in the synagogue. Here, as there, some
Jews at once believed, and a multitude of Gentile-
Greeks, and of the 'chief women' also 'not a few.'

From the letter, which Paul soon afterwards wrote
back to the Thessalonian believers, we gain a glimpse
of his conduct and of his way of preaching in Thessalonica. We see him preaching with unflinching
courage[11] and without flattery.[12] We see him encouraging and correcting his converts as carefully and kindly
as a father his own children,[13] loving and cherishing
them as tenderly and gently as a nurse her own offspring,[14] watching over 'each one,'[15] and like a faithful
shepherd and friend, ready to give his own life for his
loved flock.[16] Well might the Apostle write them : "*Ye
are witnesses*, how holily and justly and unblamably we
behaved ourselves among you."[16] At Thessalonica, too,
Paul labored to support himself while he preached—
very likely at the trade of tent-maker, which he learned
when a boy. Late at night, no doubt, the Apostle
might have been seen by lamp-light working at the
rough tent-cloth, so as to be chargeable to nobody.[17] It
was the Apostle's way of teaching what he preached,
and of enforcing what he commanded in his letters·
'Study to be quiet and to work with your own hands,'

[11] "After that we had suffered and were shamefully treated at Philippi, *as ye know*, we were *bold* to speak to *you*." I. Thess. ii. 2.

[12] "Neither at any time used we flattering words, *as ye know*."
Verse 5.

[13] Verse 11.   [14] Verse 7.

[15] Verse 8. "Affectionately desirous," etc.

[16] Verse 10.   [17] Verse 9.

and 'if any man would not work, neither let him eat,'[18] and of warning men not to be 'busy-bodies,'[19] but to do their own work.[18]

The converts left at Philippi did not forget Paul's sufferings. 'Once and again' the Philippian believers, Lydia and the jailer foremost among them no doub', sent gifts to him while at Thessalonica.[20] Perhaps the jailer himself came over the road through Amphipolis and Apollonia to bring the money and the gifts contributed.

God abundantly blessed the Apostles' faithful labors in Thessalonica. A large church was gathered. Although the persecution seems to have commenced after Paul and Silas had been there only three weeks, very likely they remained there a somewhat longer time. After the Jews began to persecute, he no doubt turned to the Gentiles. The Thessalonian church, we have reason to believe, was made up in good part of Gentiles; for in the letters to these converts, "the Jewish Scriptures are not once quoted," and he addressed those who had turned from *idols*.[21]

To the pious Greek converts, what a new and blessed comfort was there in the doctrine of the resurrection of the dead. We can still read on the sepulchres of heathen Thessalonica ancient inscriptions which say that after death there is no resurrection, and after the grave no meeting of loved ones. How different from this thick darkness was the light and hope of Paul's doctrine, not to sorrow for those who sleep in Jesus as those others who have no hope.[22]

---

[18] Notice the words, I. Thessalonians iv. 11, 'as we *commanded* you.' II. Thessalonians iii. 10.

[19] II. Thessalonians iii. 11.

[20] Philippians iv. 16, 15.

[21] I. Thessalonians i. 9.

[22] iv. 13, 14.

QUESTIONS.

DID the Apostles go directly from the prison out of the city?
Who were 'the brethren'?
Who went with Paul from the city?
Who remained? How do you know?
Into what three provinces was the whole great peninsula then divided?

Where in the Scriptures is Illyricum mentioned?
Did Paul *preach* in Illyricum?
Did Paul travel into Achaia more than once?
What province was he now in?
On what road did Paul now travel?

At what point on the road was Thessalonica?
How far did this road reach?
Where did Paul travel on this same road afterwards?
Where do you find the notice of it?
What parts did Amphipolis and Apollonia divide the journey into?
What was the ancient name of Amphipolis? Why?
Why was it called Amphipolis?
What made it a place of consequence?
What did Xerxes here?
Between Amphipolis and Apollonia what birth place? what tomb?
Near what river was Thessalonica?
For whom was Thessalonica named?

What exile had lived here?
What has Thessalonica been since that time?
What before Constantinople was built?
Why was its position good?
How does it rank now?
What is its name now?
What has been there in modern times?
What sentence of the Apostle illustrates its influence then?
What resemblance between Thessalonica and Antioch?

(43)

Why did the Apostles pass through Amphipolis and Apollonia without preaching?

Why was there a synagogue in Thessalonica?

How long did Paul reason? Where? With whom?

What resemblance can you draw between his visit here and at Antioch in Pisidia?

What does 'opening and alleging' mean?

What were the three points of his discourse?

What does 'consorted' mean?

What proselytes are mentioned?

How do we know what Paul's conduct and preaching were in Thessalonica?

Why did it require courage?

How was he like a father to his converts?

How like a nurse?

What other verse shows his fond affection?

How did he support himself?

What commands did he enforce in this manner?

What was the result of Paul's labors in the city?

Were the members of the Thessalonian church Jews or Gentiles?

What shows it?

What comfort was there to them in the doctrine of resurrection?

Twenty-third Sunday.

THE MOB OF THE IDLERS.

LESSON.
ACTS xvii. 5–13.

THE Jews of Thessalonica were as envious as the Jews of Antioch in Pisidia. They did not like to see the multitude yielding so fast to Paul's teaching. Especially when they thought how the Roman Government looked on all Jews with suspicion, they did not like to see these stranger Jews, who preached strange doctrines, gaining influence with the inhabitants. They therefore quickly found means to hinder and to silence the two faithful preachers.

"A multitude of idlers about the market and the landing-places abound in every such city." These low fellows[1] the Jews got together, and, by their arts, excited them into a mob. They made an uproar through the city. Then they assaulted the house of the man[2] whose guests Paul and Silas were supposed to be. They hoped to find the two hated men; to bring them out; and then to get the excited people[3] to pronounce a

[1] 'Market-place loungers' or idlers, the phrase means.

[2] A 'Jason' is mentioned in Paul's letter from Corinth to Rome (Romans xvi. 21) as Paul's kinsman. Very likely Jason of Thessalonica went to Corinth. The name is one Greek form of Joshua or Jesus.

[3] The word translated 'people' in the fifth verse means the *people gathered in the forum to judge and try causes*, the *demus*, the public assembly; a different word from 'people' in verse 13

judgment against them. Paul and Silas were absent; and so the mob dragged Jason, and some other Christians whom they found, to the city magistrates.

It is to be noticed now that this is not Roman authority. Thessalonica was called ' a *free* city.' It was in a Roman province, but was allowed to govern itself; that is, the citizens elected their own magistrates, and were not ruled by a Roman Pro-consul and a Roman garrison.' This was a privilege and a compliment to the city, in return for its help in the wars; and the Greeks would be most careful to preserve it. The magistrates, therefore, to whom the crowd carried Jason, were not the Pro-consul of Macedonia and his attendants, like the Pro-consul of Cyprus at Paphos, but the *Greek city magistrates.* Like the people, they would be very jealous of the rights of their free city, and particularly careful to do nothing to forfeit them. The accusation against the Christians and Jason, which the Jews and the mob cried out before the magistrates, was therefore well formed to increase the excitement. It was in substance this:

"These men, who are setting the whole world in confusion, are come hither at last. And Jason hath received them into his house. And they are all acting in the face of the Emperor's decrees, for they declare there is another King, whom they call Jesus."

These Jews would be glad to put themselves on the side of the Emperor's authority, and to cast off from themselves the suspicion of the government by fastening it on this new sect against which their charges were in part true. Jason and his fellow-Christians did receive Jesus to be King, as Paul had taught; but none of them taught or believed that Jesus was an earthly king, in opposition to Cæsar.

' The Pro-consul, who ruled the *province* of Macedonia, probably lived in Thessalonica, but had no authority over the city.

If the accusation was true, there was cause for alarm
to the magistrates and to the people. The charge was
a charge of sedition. The freedom of the city might
be in peril. The people and the magistrates were therefore 'troubled.' "It is evident that the magistrates
were excited and unsettled as well as the multitude.
No doubt they were anxious to stand well with the
Roman government, and not to injure themselves or
their city by a wrong decision in this dispute between
the Christians and the Jews." Their course was a wise
one in the circumstances. It was to 'take security'
from Jason and his companions. By this expression it
is most probably meant that a sum of money was deposited with the magistrates, and that the Christian
people of the place made themselves responsible that
no attempt at sedition should be made against the government, and that the peace should be kept in Thessalonica itself. In this way the disturbance was quieted."

But though the magistrates had gained quiet in the
city, Paul and Silas were in peril. The lower classes
were still excited. The Jews were in a state of unreasonable and fanatical rage. The Apostles could not
appear in public as before, without danger to themselves and to their fellow-Christians, who were security
for their good-behavior. They must be silent, if they
remained. Silence was impossible with Paul. He *must*
preach. That was the one great command to the disciples; and to the earnest heart of Paul it was *woe* if
he did *not* preach. Under the same watchful care of
'brethren,' which let Paul down in a basket from the
walls of Damascus, the two pilgrim-preachers departed
the same evening from Thessalonica.

"Passing under the Arch of Augustus and out of the
Western Gate, the Great Road crosses the plain and
ascends the mountains." Paul and Silas, in the silence

of the night, took their way again along the paved highway. Gradually separating from the bay, they crossed the broad river whose waters flow from the distant mountains of the north and west, through nearly the whole length and breadth of Macedonia. If they had gone on as far as Edessa, they would have had from the high lands "a glorious view of all the country" which stretches leagues on leagues from the nearer mountains to the sea. To that place, however, Paul was not directed, but turning south, away from the great thoroughfare and into a smaller, they went down to Berea. "If this journey was at all what it is now, the travellers first passed the gardens in the neighborhood of Thessalonica, and then crossed a wide tract of fields of grain, and then the bed of 'the wide-flowing Axius,' near which the day must have broken upon them." Then there was another wide, long stretch of plain : then a river, with high artificial banks to guard against floods. Then the road enters a vast forest, in which were "spaces of cultivated land and villages concealed among the trees." Then, after miles of travel through the woods, the road begins to ascend, and leads up to the gate of Berea.

We know little of this city as it was. At the present day, it is one of the most pleasant towns in the region. "Plane trees spread a grateful shade over its gardens: streams of water abound in every street." There are some few remains of Greek and Roman buildings. But Berea has a more noble renown than that which springs from splendid walls and temples. The Jews here were more noble-minded than those whom Paul and Silas had left. When Paul and Silas presented, in their synagogue, the arguments to prove that Jesus was the Messiah, "they not only listened, but examined the Scriptures themselves, to see if his arguments were confirmed by prophecy." They persevered also. *Daily* they did it. '*Therefore* many of them believed,' as every one who candidly and diligently and obediently searches the Scriptures, to know and to *do* the truth, will believe. *Because* a man searches the Scriptures rightly, *therefore* will he believe. Here, too, were 'honorable women' who believed. At Antioch in Pisidia, 'honorable women' had aided to persecute Paul, but at Thessalonica 'chief women,' and at Berea 'honorable Greek women,' were his helpers and disciples. But just as persecuting Jews followed Paul from Antioch to Iconium, so they did from Thessalonica to Berea, as soon as they knew they were preaching there their doctrine of the Messiah.

How long Paul was here, it is not said. "From the fact that the Bereans were '*daily*' searching the Scriptures for arguments in favor of or against the Apostle's doctrine, we conclude that he remained in Berea several days, at least." It would be a week or two weeks, before the Thessalonian Jews would get knowledge that the preachers were at Berea, and before they could make the journey, for Berea was sixty miles from Thessalonica.

QUESTIONS.

WHAT was the cause of the Jews' persecution?

Were they envious of the same thing as the Pisidian Jews?

What especial reason in Thessalonica for their envy?

What is meant by 'lewd fellows'?

What did they accomplish with these fellows?

In what other place is there a Jason mentioned?

What did they hope to accomplish?

What does 'people,' in the fifth verse, mean?

Who were taken besides Jason?

What kind of authority is now exercised?

What is meant by a *free* city?

Who were the rulers before whom Jason was brought?

What were the people and the magistrates very jealous of?

What was the general accusation?

Against whom was it made?

What was the charge against *Jason?*

What was the definite accusation?

Against whom was this made?

Why would the Jews be glad to make such an accusation?

Was the accusation true?

What was the crime in the accusation?

Was there any reason why the people should be 'troubled'?

What course did the magistrates take?

Did they act hastily, like the magistrates at Philippi?

What is meant by 'taken security'?

Why were the Apostles still in peril?

Why did not Paul remain silent in Thessalonica?

Why did they send them by night?

What road did the Apostles take?

In what direction was Berea?

What kind of a town is it now?

Why were the Jews here more noble-minded than those of Thessalonica?

What things were 'those things'?

What proves that they persevered?

Why did many Bereans believe?

What is the reason why many persons do not believe?

How should the Scriptures be examined?

What difference between the 'chief women' of Berea and of Antioch in Pisidia?

Who followed the Apostles from Thessalonica?

Is it meant that Paul preached at this time *all* the doctrines of 'the word of God'?

How long was Paul in Berea?

What difference in the departure of Paul from Philippi, Thessalonica, and Antioch?

How does it compare with his departure from Pisidian Antioch, Iconium, and Lystra?

(46)

Twenty-fourth Sunday.

THE JOURNEY TO GREECE.

LESSON.

Acts xvii. 13-16.

THE Thessalonian Jews " came like hunters on their prey," but they could not take away the faith already in many hearts, nor prevent others still from receiving it. They made it, however, unpleasant, and no doubt unsafe, for Paul to preach in Berea. The Berean Bible-readers were his steadfast friends ; and although they thought it best to send Paul away, they kept Silas and Timothy[1] to instruct and to assist them. Perhaps the fact that Silas and Timothy might be of some service to the new church of Thessalonica was an additional reason for their remaining. It was no doubt some of the Berean converts who went with Paul on his way. Luke and Timothy and Silas had been taken from him : who else than these warm-hearted converts was there to go with him in his trials ?

Why did Paul go to Athens ? He could not, of course, go back to Thessalonica. If he had gone back to Edessa or further west, the busy thoroughfare of the Roman road would soon have brought the Thessalonians

---

[1] If Timothy was not at Thessalonica with Paul and Silas, (see beginning of Twenty-second Sunday,) the Thessalonian persecutors would not be so bitter against *him*. Besides, it might not be wise in them, in a Greek city, to attack a man whose father was a Greek, (xvi. i.) Timothy may have brought the gifts from Philippi to Thessalonica, perhaps just as Paul came away.

on his track. It would be better to pass out of the province and far beyond their reach. It seems probable, therefore, that he went directly to Athens by sea, although it is supposed by some persons that the phrase, ' to go *as it were* to the sea,'[2] shows rather that he went by land. We suppose that he took ship somewhere near Dium,[3] to which place there was a road from Berea. Here, near the lofty Mount Olympus, with its broad base, its sides dark with woods, its glittering, snowy summit rising above the clouds and on which was thought to be the throne of the gods—here, where all the associations of ancient Greece begin to suggest themselves—Paul embarks for the ancient capital. "The shepherds from the heights above the celebrated Vale of Tempe may have watched the sails of his ship that day, as it moved like a white speck from the waters of the Thermaic Gulf into the Ægean Sea."

As Paul looked back, the gigantic Olympus was close behind, with its many ridges and many vales : the mountains beyond Thessalonica grew dim : Mount Athos, away off towards the north-east, far out on its peninsula, seems ' like an island floating in the horizon.' " Gradually the nearer heights of snowy Olympus recede into the distance, as the vessel approaches nearer and nearer to the centre of all the interest of classic Greece. All the land and water in sight becomes more eloquent as we advance. Poetry and history are on every side : every rock is a monument : every current is alive with some memory of the past." The long island of Eubœa shuts them off from a distant view of the pass of Thermopylæ, where Leonidas and his three hundred Spartans defied the mighty host of Xerxes, and from the plain of Marathon, where the

---

[2] The Greek words translated ' *as it were,*' do not mean that there was any deception. [3] Map on page 146.

Athenians bravely stood against the armies of Persia. At length the island is passed, and the ship rounds the southern extremity of Attica, "Sunium's high promontory—still crowned with the white columns of that

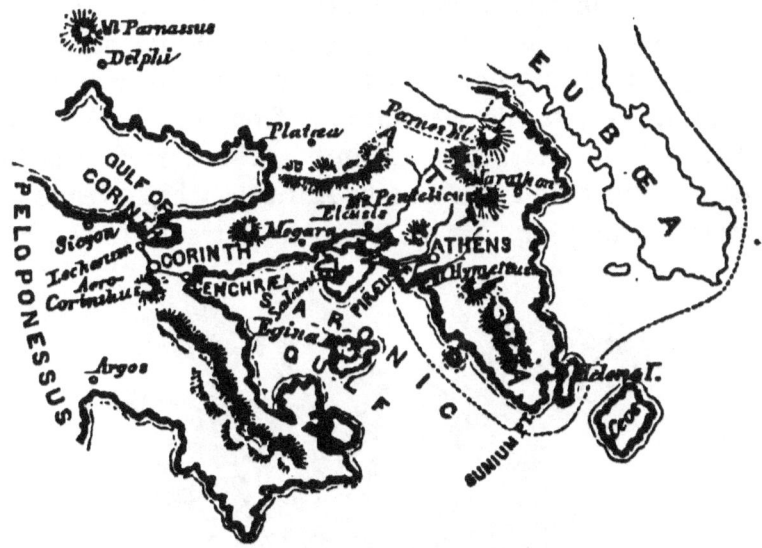

temple of Minerva which was the landmark to Greek sailors," and which showed Athens was near at hand.

"To one who travels in classic lands, no moment is more exciting than when he has left the cape of Sunium behind, and eagerly looks for the first glimpse of that city which was 'the eye of Greece, mother of arts and eloquence.'" As the ship sails slowly up the gulf, a light suddenly flashes in the distant air as from a mirror. It is the flashing of the armor of Minerva's great statue, standing with poised shield and spear on the summit of the citadel of Athens. And now from the deck of the vessel you can see Athens itself, its famous buildings, its surrounding hills. Directly before us is the illustrious island Salamis, near which Xerxes, from his high throne on the coast of Attica, saw his fleet, his last hope, destroyed. The atmosphere, famous for its

clearness, reveals even the distant mountains, which
seem nearer than they are.   And now, as we approach
the harbor, the high craggy peak which we see crowded
with temples and statues, in the centre of the city, is the
citadel,[4] from the top of which the colossal Minerva
looks over her idolatrous kingdom.   White sails are
plying in the harbor, and making their busy errands
from the *Piræus* to *Cenchræa* — from the harbor of
Athens to the harbor of Corinth.   The Piræus was to
Athens what Seleucia was to Antioch, what Neapolis
was to Philippi.[5]   As we near the entrance to the Pi-

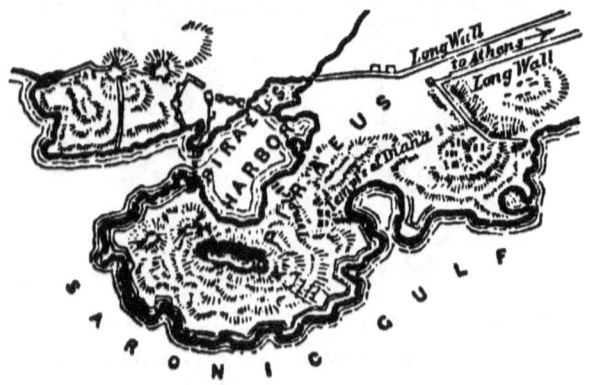

ræus, " the land seems to rise, and conceals all the
plain.   Idlers come down on the rocks to watch the
coming vessel.   The sailors are all on the alert.   Suddenly an opening is revealed ; and a sharp turn of the
helm brings the ship in between two piers, on which
towers are erected," and from one to the other of which
a chain was sometimes thrown to keep out hostile ships.
" We are in smooth water, and we cast anchor in the
basin of the Piræus.

" Had Paul come to this spot four hundred years be-

---

[4] The *Acropolis :* acro, *top* or *summit*, polis, *city*—the highest part
of the city, the *citadel*, (the *armory* and *defence*.)

[5] See pages 47 and 131.

fore, he would have been *in Athens* from the moment of his landing at the Piræus. At that time the two cities were united by a double line of walls, made famous by the name of 'the *Long Walls.*'" Between these walls a populous street five miles in length then stretched across the plain. Since that time wars had often swept over the land. The Romans now ruled here as everywhere; and " on each side of the road, as Paul went up to Athens, were broken fragments of the masonry which had once been the pride of Athens." Passing along this ruined street—this street of ruins— Paul came to the gates of Athens; and through them entered at once a city well described in those three short words of inspiration, '*full of idols.*'⁶ Here, close by the gates, is " an image of Neptune on horseback, hurling his trident." Here is a temple to Ceres, the goddess of agriculture, " on the walls of which an inscription tells us the statues within were the work of the celebrated Praxiteles." Paul goes through the gate. " Sculptured forms of Minerva, Jupiter, and Apollo, of Mercury and the muses, stand near a sanctuary of Bacchus. Temples, statues, altars abound on every side."

In every street are seen the works of art, designed to serve the purpose of idolatry. There were statues to all the mythological divinities. There were images of every god on Olympus. There were chiselled forms of fabled heroes, such as Hercules and Theseus. " Every public place and building too was a heathen sanctuary. The Record House was a temple of the mother of the gods The Council House had statues of Apollo and Jupiter, with an altar of Vesta. The theatre was consecrated to Bacchus. And as if the idolatrous imagination of the Athenians could not be satisfied, altars were

⁶ See the margin of the sixteenth verse.

erected to Fame, to Modesty, to Energy, to Persuasion, and to Pity." "One traveller tells us, 'There were more gods in Athens than in all the rest of the country;' and the Roman satirist hardly exaggerates when he says it is easier to find a god there than a man."

Here, in the midst of all this magnificent workman- ship and beauty, Paul reflected. "His path had been among the forms of great men and deified heroes, among the temples, the statues, the altars of the gods of Greece. In every form of beauty and grandeur wrought out by the sculptor and the architect, he had seen the vain fancies of the Greek mythology." And men were wor- shipping these dumb, dead, beautiful things which they themselves had made, and knew nothing of the one true God or of the true Messiah. In all that great, eager, thinking city, only one man's great heart 'was stirred in him' for the sin and folly of this worship, when he saw Athens, the pride and beauty of that land, '*full of idols.*'

The friends who came with Paul now returned. They bore with them Paul's command to Silas and Timothy to hasten to him. There was much work to be done; and there was need of help.

QUESTIONS.

WHY did the Bereans send Paul away?
  Who remained? For what reason?
  Who 'conducted' Paul?
Why did Paul go to *Athens?*
  Did he go by sea or land?
  What has 'as it were' been thought to show?
  Was there any deception?
  Where may we suppose he took ship?
  Near what mountain?
  What celebrated Vale did he pass?
  What other mountain on the other side?
  What celebrated battle-fields on the main-land?
  Who fought there?
  What was the most southern point of land?
  What would he see as he sailed up the Saronic gulf?
  What was the Piræus?
  What was Cenchræa?
  What other places similar to the Piræus and Cenchræa?
How would it have been different, if Paul had come to the
Piræus four hundred years before?
  What were the 'Long Walls'?
  What were at the gates of the city?
  What inside the gates?
  What were some of the particular objects in the streets?
  How were the public buildings idolatrous?
  To what virtues and abstractions were altars erected?
  What did one traveller say about the gods of Athens?
  What Roman sarcasm is given?
  What does 'wholly given to idolatry' mean?
What characteristics of the Athenians would a worldly-
minded man have noticed?
  What has the city of Athens always been admired for?
  What things were the pride of the people?
  What one principal thing did *Paul* notice?

Why was it not as right for Athenians to worship Jupiter
    as for the Jews to worship Jehovah?

Were they both different conceptions of the same being?

Is it right to worship God *through* images? Why?

Do you suppose the heathen worship the image simply,
    without the *idea* of a God *in* it?

Why may we not use a picture or an image to *help* our
    conception of God?

Is there any Mediator in heathen religion?

Can men be saved without a Mediator?

Is anything more meant by 'his spirit was stirred' than that
Paul *pitied* the Athenians?

When men commit sin, what ought we to think of be-
    sides their wretchedness?

When '*they* departed,' where did they go?

What message did they bear?

Why 'with all speed'?

If the Spirit of God is all-powerful to assist, why can
    not one man do the whole work as well as more?

Have we any account of Silas and Timotheus coming to
Paul?

(48)

Twenty-fifth Sunday.

THE GRECIAN CAPITAL.

LESSON.

ACTS xvii. 16 - 21.

PAUL was alone in Athens. Doubtless he went, as usual, at once to the synagogue, but we have no account of what was said or done there. While he waited for Silas and Timothy, he had time to see the beautiful city and its idolatry. Three places would attract his attention, as they did the attention of every traveller: the Market-place, (the *Forum*,) Mars' Hill, (*Areopagus*,[1]) and the Citadel, (the *Acropolis*.)

The *Forum*, or market-place, was the meeting-place of the people. It was a little valley formed by three hills on three sides. On the east of it was the citadel, "towering high above the city of which it is the glory and the crown." On the north is the craggy Mars' Hill. On the west side was "a sloping hill partially levelled, (the *Pynx*,) the famous meeting-place for political assemblies." From the Pynx and the Forum, in ancient times, the orators and the statesmen spoke to the people. Here poets recited their verses to an audience skilled in all the points of nice criticism: here the artists exhibited their statues and paintings: here goods of all descriptions were bought and sold: here

[1] A compound Greek word, from pagus, *hill*, and Areo, *of Mars*, the god of war.

the public assembly of 'the people'[2] met to discuss and to make the laws of the city, to sit as council and to decide as judge in many of the legal questions. In Paul's time, " when Athens could be proud only of her recollections of the past," the Forum was still the centre " of philosophy, of idleness, of conversation, and of business." This 'market' was far more than the open market-spaces, to be seen in many modern cities. It is " rather to be compared to the beautiful squares of such Italian cities as Verona and Florence, where historical buildings have closed in the space with narrow limits, and sculpture has peopled it with impressive images." "Among the buildings of greatest interest in the Forum, were the porticoes or porches, which were decorated with paintings and statuary." Two of these were, the Portico of the King, on the roof of which were statues of Theseus, the ancient hero, and of the God of Day; and the Portico of Jupiter, in front of which was Jupiter's image, and within which were paintings illustrating the rise of the Athenian government. Among the trees were statues of great men, such as Solon the Lawgiver, Cimon the Admiral, and Demosthenes the Orator. Here were statues to Mercury, the messenger and the orator of the gods; to Apollo, who had delivered the city from the plague; "and in the centre of all, the altar of the Twelve Gods." " If from this point we look up to Mars' Hill, we see the temple of Mars, and we know that the sanctuary of the Furies is just hidden by the projecting ridge of rock. If we look to the Citadel, we see in the distance, on the ledges of rock, a series of little temples to Bacchus and Æsculapius, to Venus, to Earth, and to Ceres.

Areopagus, or Mars' Hill, had also its decorations; but it was mainly famous for being the place where the

---

[2] See page 152, note 2.

highest and most awful court of the nation held its solemn sessions.[3]

The Acropolis,[4] or citadel was the top of the towering hill which we saw from the sea. It was in the cen-

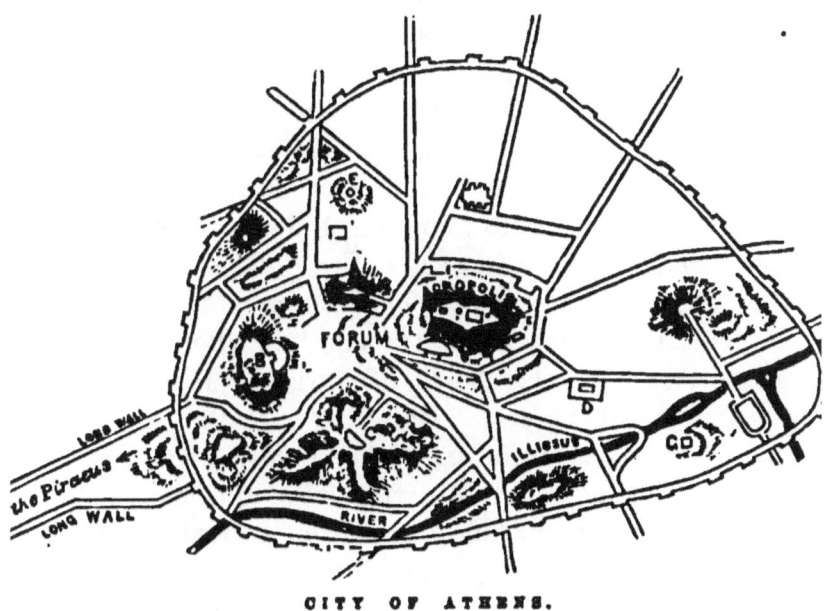

CITY OF ATHENS.

A. Areopagus. B. Pynx. C. Museum. D. Temple of Jupiter. E. Temple of Theseus. F. Lyceum. G. Temple of Fortune.

tre of Athens, as it was also the very centre of the pride and patriotism of the Athenian people. It was a steep mass of rock, and could be ascended only from one side. While therefore it was the security of the city, it was made also the polished ornament for the display of Grecian art. An orator said: "it

[3] A fuller description of Mars' Hill will be given in the next chapter.

[4] See page 160, note 4.

was the middle space of the five circles of a shield, of which the four outer circles were Athens, Attica, Greece, and the world." The top of this hill was "a museum of art, of history and of religion, of architecture and of sculpture, dedicated to the glory of the nation and to the worship of the gods." If Paul went up the flight of rocky steps which led hither, and entered the magnificent gateway, we can imagine what he saw. At the splendid entrance was a statue of Mercury, guarding the gate: then statues of Venus and the Graces: then a bronze statue of Minerva, as the goddess of Health: then the image of Diana. Then there were statues of Pericles, the orator and statesman, "to whom the glory of the Acropolis was due:" of Agrippa, and of Augustus Cæsar: of Theseus contending with the Minotaur, and of Hercules strangling the serpents. In the centre was the Parthenon of Minerva, "the glorious temple which rose in the proudest period of Athenian history, and which, through ages of war and decay," remains 'still tolerably perfect.' Within it was the great ivory and gold statue of Minerva, the work of Phidias, and unrivalled in the world except by his own statue of Jupiter. In another smaller temple, was another small statue of Minerva, which, like that of Diana at Ephesus, was believed to have fallen from heaven.[b] There was still another statue of Minerva, the largest of all in the city. It was made of brass, "from the shields and brazen spoils of the battle of Marathon, and rose in gigantic proportions above all the buildings of the Acropolis, and stood with spear and shield as the guardian deity of Athens and Attica." It was this huge but beautiful statue which Paul perhaps saw as he sailed up the gulf towards the Piræus. "Now he had landed

[b] Acts xix. 35.

and had seen the wonders of the city. Here perhaps, by this great statue, Paul looked down on the city *'full of idols.'* "

If Paul looked from the Acropolis away over the city walls into the open country, he saw in one direction the place where Aristotle, and in the opposite direction the place where Plato, both pupils of Socrates, held their famous schools. Aristotle, the teacher of Alexander the Great, once taught in another part of the surrounding groves. There were other schools *within* the city, in Paul's day. In one of the porches of the Forum the *Stoics* met: those stern, proud men, who taught " that men should be free from passion, unmoved by joy or grief, and submit without complaint to the necessity by which all things are governed." In one of the gardens, the Epicureans met—the easy, free men, who believed that pleasure was the end of life. These Stoics and Epicureans, the representatives of Pride and Pleasure, Paul was soon to meet in the Forum, in his discussions there.

How different were the thoughts of Paul from those of many men who have visited Athens, and have seen all these beautiful works of art. " He burned with zeal for that GOD whom he saw dishonored all through the city. He was melted to pity for those who, notwithstanding their intellectual greatness, were 'wholly given to idolatry.' He was not blinded to the reality of things by the appearance of art or philosophy. Earthly beauty and human wisdom were of no value, were worse than nothing, if they made falsehood good and made vice a god." Paul, therefore, could not be silent. He exhorted in the synagogue of the Jews, reasoning, as before, from their Scriptures. He disputed with those who gathered in the Forum to discuss every new and strange subject or philosophy. He would have no dull nor weak antagonists. He would be persecuted by no mob. He would be heard with respectful attention, if he had anything to say which the Athenians thought worthy their attention. There, to the mingled gathering, he preached Jesus and the resurrection; and there, while he taught these simple doctrines, he met the human philosophers, in all the pride of their worldly wisdom—the Stoics and Epicureans who came into the Forum. One man said, What does this talking-fellow [6] say? And another, He seems to be a proclaimer of strange gods.

How contrary Paul's simple doctrines were to all their philosophy. He preached simply that Jesus was the Saviour of men from sin, and that there would be a resurrection from the dead. Neither the Stoics nor Epicureans believed there was any need of being saved, or that there would be any resurrection. The Stoics were *pantheists :* they believed the world or the universe was itself God, a great living machine that rolled on from eternity to eternity. The Epicureans were *atheists :* they believed there was no God. Both said that the soul of man would expire with his body, and so that there could be no resurrection. The Stoics taught a proud indifference to all joy, grief, anger, change in life, care, thought for the future. The Epicureans taught a love for everything which could give pleasure, without thought of right or wrong; that men should not of course seek pleasure which brought pain with it, unless the pleasure would be more than the pain; but that men should do what would give them

---

[6] The Greek word rendered 'babbler' meant originally *a seed-picker*, like a bird who picks up seed, and afterwards one who picked up items or scraps of knowledge. In the light of all their ideas of eloquence, it was therefore a sharp sarcasm when the Athenians said: What does this *item-monger*, or *dealer in small-talk*, say?'

the greatest amount of pleasure in the whole life. The Stoic was therefore taught to depend on himself for everything. He scorned to receive aid from any person or thing; and so he did not *wish*, he thought he did not *need* a Saviour. The preaching of Jesus was foolishness to him. The Epicureans sought gratification only. The doctrines of Paul forbade many kinds of pleasure as wicked. The preaching of Jesus was foolishness to them.

Still there were some in the gathering who wished to know more of this new doctrine; and they, eager to know the latest kind of religion, as well as the latest news, brought Paul to Areopagus. "Demosthenes, four hundred years before, had rebuked the Athenians for their idle curiosity, telling them they were always craving after news and excitement, even when destruction itself was hanging over their liberties;" and in Paul's time, the Athenians were still as eager as ever ' to tell or to hear some new thing.'

QUESTIONS.

TO what place in the city would Paul go first?

How would a synagogue be esteemed in Athens?

What three public places would attract Paul's notice?.

What was the Market-place?

What three hills on three sides?

What was done in this market-place and at the Pynx?

What 'people' met here?

How would it compare with the open business-squares of modern cities?

What peculiar class of buildings?

What two especially noted?

What statues of great men?

What could be seen on Mars' Hill from the Forum?

What does *Areopagus* mean?

What was it mainly famous for?

What does Acropolis mean?

Where was it? What was it?

To what did an orator liken the Acropolis?

What was on the top of this hill?

Name some of the gods and some of the men whose statues were there.

What was the principal building of the Acropolis?

To whom was it dedicated? Who was she?

What three statues of her, and what were their characteristics?

Do you suppose Paul failed to visit the Acropolis?

What, outside of the city, could Paul have seen from the Acropolis?

What schools were *within* the city?

What was the difference between a Stoic and an Epicurean?

What was the chief cause of Paul's earnest zeal?

What is the significance of '*Therefore* disputed he'?

Who were 'the devout persons'?

Whom would Paul meet in the Forum?

How would he be received?

What two opinions were expressed in respect to them?

What does 'babbler' mean?

What did such a question mean in the mouth of an Athenian?

What does 'setter forth' mean?

What did Paul preach in the Forum?

Was this the doctrine of the general resurrection or of the resurrection of Jesus?

Why was this doctrine especially connected with the preaching about Jesus?

What did the Stoics and Epicureans believe?

What were the Stoics in respect to their belief in a God? the Epicureans?

What other difference was there in their teachings?

Why was the preaching of Jesus foolishness to the Stoic? Why to the Epicurean?

Why did they take Paul to Mars' Hill?

What does 'new doctrine' refer to?

What did Demosthenes rebuke the Athenians for?

Is it wrong to wish to learn 'the news'?

Is it wise to be seeking a new religion?

Were the Athenians right or wrong in seeking to learn the new religion which Paul brought?

Was Paul right in taking advantage of their curiosity?

(50)

MARS' HILL.

LESSON.
Acts xvii. 22–34.

"THE place to which the Athenians took Paul was the summit of the hill of Areopagus, where the most awful court of Athens had sat from the earliest times, to pass sentence on the greatest criminals, and to decide the most solemn questions of religion. The judges sat in the open air, on seats hewn out in the rock; and the place was reached by a flight of stone steps directly from the Forum. On this spot, a long series of awful causes connected with crime and religion had been decided." The first one of all was fabled to have been a trial of Mars, on charge of murdering a son of Neptune. Mars was acquitted, and hence the place was called Mars' Hill, (Areopagus.[1]) The temple of Mars was on the brow of the hill. The sanctuary of the Furies, the avenging goddesses, who punished the condemned by taking away peace of mind and giving misery and misfortune, was just below the judges' seat, in a broken cleft of the rock, and gave great solemnity to the place. "Even in the decay of Athens, in Paul's time, the people regarded this spot and this court with superstitious reverence. Here they thought of the dread recollections of centuries. It was the place of silent awe in the midst of the gay and frivolous city

[1] See page 163, note 1.

To come from the Forum to Areopagus, was to come into the presence of a higher power. No place in Athens was so suitable for a discourse on the doctrines and mysteries of religion;" and when the novelty-loving and religious Athenians found Paul's conversations and address to the people in the Forum were about religion, they brought him hither to hear him. "They took the Apostle from the tumult of public discussion, to the place most convenient and most appropriate. There was everything in the place to incline those who came to a reverent and thoughtful attention. It is probable that Dionysius and other Areopagites, were on the judicial seats. The dread thoughts associated with the hill of Mars, may have solemnized the minds of some of the people who crowded up the stone steps with the Apostle, to hear his announcement of new divinities."

Think now of the Apostle on the summit of Mars' Hill. Think of the intense earnestness of Paul, and of the frivolous character of his hearers. Think of the certainty, the truth, the solemn meaning of the Gospel he preached, and of the worthless religion and mythology which made Athens famous in the earth. Think of all the temples, statues, idols, altars around him, and of what he said about temples and idols. Close to him was the temple of Mars. Just below him was the abode of the Furies. Opposite, on the Acropolis, was the splendid Parthenon of Minerva. Yet here Paul boldly declares that 'GOD dwells not in TEMPLES made with hands.' "Wherever his eye turned, he saw a multitude of statues in every form and situation. Right in front of him, towering from its pedestal on the rock of the Acropolis, was the immense brazen statue of Minerva, armed with spear, shield, and helmet, as the champion of Athens. Standing almost in its very shade, he declared that the GODHEAD is *not to be likened* to that work of Phidias, or to any other image in *gold, silver or stone, graven by art or man's device.*"

Among all the altars, he had noticed one with the singular inscription, '*To the Unknown God*,' as though the superstitious people would not omit from their worship one possible god whom they might not know. This inscription Paul took for the text of his address on Mars' Hill.

THE ADDRESS ON MARS' HILL.

It is not the *object* of this address to prove that *Jesus is the Messiah*, as it was in the address at Antioch of Pisidia;[2] but to prove to *idolaters* that there is *one God*, and that Jesus, of whom he had spoken in the Forum, would be the final *Judge* of men's good and evil deeds.

I. The Introduction: *The Unknown God*, (verses 22, 23.)

Notice with what courtesy and with what carefulness Paul adapts his introduction to his Athenian audience. He was speaking to men accustomed to oratory and to eloquence. He was speaking in a place where men had been condemned for religious offences. He does not commence, therefore, by saying that it was wrong to make these statues and idols. He might have lost the attention of his audience, and the opportunity for an argument: he might even have put his life in danger, if he had attacked at once their national gods. In commencing, therefore, he only speaks of what he, as a traveller and stranger, had seen in their city. Every car would be delicately attentive: " Ye men of Athens, I perceive that in all things you are *very religious.*[3] For, passing

---

[2] See pages 66, 67.

[3] Our English translation is generally correct, but does not quite

through your city, and beholding the objects of your worship, I saw an altar on which was written : *To the* UNKNOWN *God.* This God, whom you worship ignorantly, I wish to make known to you."

II. This *unknown* god is the ONE ONLY GOD, (verses 24 to 26.)

The reasons why he only is God, are :

1. (Verse 24.) He created all things. He is Ruler, therefore, of all heaven and all earth. He is therefore infinitely greater than the human temple of any other god, or than the temples of all other gods.

2. (Verse 25.) He does not *need* worship, as other gods seem to do. He himself *gives* life, breath, all things, to the very worshippers.

3. (Verse 26.) He created all *men*. He made them all of one blood.[4] He fixed the time of their existence in the world, and the length of their stay on earth.

III. *All men* alike *ought to worship this* ONE GOD, (verses 27, 28.)

1. Because he declares that he created all things, that he created men, that he decides the length and place of every life *in order that* men should *seek him* and *find him*, that is, worship him.

2. Because, as he created us at the first, so he *now gives us life and breath*, every day and every hour. Your own poets, too, say the same thing : that *we* are the *offspring* of God : that is, that we obtain *life from him.*

express the idea of the Greek, in the words, ' too superstitious.' The Greek words rather mean, ' *more careful about religious things* ' than other people. How true it was !

4 ' *Of one blood.*' The Greeks boastfully claimed an origin for themselves, different from the rest of the world. All beside Greeks were ' Barbarians.' Romans i. 14.

IV. GOD, then, *cannot be a statue or an image*, (verse 29.)

If we are the offspring of God, he is our Father. As we are living flesh and blood and spirit, our Father cannot be a gold or silver image, carved and graven by art, or a marble statue, chiselled by man's device, like all these images and statues, like the beautiful and colossal image of Minerva yonder, formed by the art and device of the sculptor Phidias.

V. GOD *overlooks the past, provided you will now repent* and *prepare* for his *judgment-day*, (verses 30, 31, first part.)

VI. *Jesus of Nazareth is to be the Judge at that day*, (verse 31.) That Jesus of whom I spoke to you in the Forum, is God's appointed Judge for that day, when every man shall give account of himself to God. God has given us proof that Jesus is to be his Judge at that day, because he raised Jesus from the dead.

Paul was perhaps going to show why the resurrection of Jesus proved that he would be the Judge at the judgment-day, but he was suddenly interrupted. "Some of those who listened broke out into laughter and derision. The doctrine of 'resurrection' was to them ridiculous. Others said, with a polite indifference, that they would hear him again on the subject. We have no knowledge that they sought Paul to hear him again. Curiosity was gratified. For the rest, they simply did not care.

Although Paul's address was adapted to win them, the cultivated and polished Athenians politely declined to hear him, the common people derided him. In the midst of the derision of some and the indifference of others, Paul was dismissed and the assembly dispersed.

And yet the result from all his labor was successful; for a few souls heard and believed: even one of the Areopagites, and also one of the common crowd, a woman, and some others.

"It is a serious and instructive fact, that the mercantile people* received the message of God with greater readiness than the highly cultivated and polished Athenians. Two letters to Thessalonica and two to Corinth, cities on either side of Athens, show the flourishing state of those churches. But we have no letter written by Paul to the Athenians; and we do not read that Paul was ever in Athens again."

* Of Thessalonica and of Corinth.

QUESTIONS.

WHERE did the Athenians take Paul?

    How was this place reached from the Forum?

    What made this place especially sacred?

    Why was it called Areopagus?

    Why was it a suitable place to which to bring Paul?

Contrast now some of the things around Paul with Paul's spirit.

    Show the force of 'God dwells not in temples,' etc.

    Show the force of 'the Godhead is not like unto gold,' etc.

What was the text of Paul's address?

    How does the object of this address differ from his object at Antioch in Pisidia?

I. What verses contain the Introduction?

    What is the subject of the Introduction?

    Did Paul say at once that idolatry was wrong? Why?

    What kind of an audience was he speaking to?

    How does he gain their eager attention?

    What does 'too superstitious' mean?

    What does 'devotions' mean?

    Do you think any particular 'unknown god' was meant by the inscription?

    Was it right for Paul to apply this inscription to the true God?

II. What is the second head of the Address?

  What is the first reason?

  Does God never dwell in earthly temples?

  What is the second reason?

    If God does not *need* worship, why should we worship him?

    If God *gives* all things to men, why should we ask him for them?

  What is the third reason?

    What did the Greeks boast for themselves?

(51)

What does 'determined the times before appointed' mean?

What is meant by 'bounds of their habitation'?

III. What is the third head of the Address?

1. Why did God create all men and fix their times?

What does 'feel after him and find him' mean?

2. What does God besides create us?

Which requires more power, to preserve us or to create us?

What quotation does Paul make in proof?

IV. What is the fourth head?

Give the meaning of the twenty-ninth verse?

What gold and ivory image was there on the Acropolis?

What image of brass?

What kind of stone images at Athens?

V. What is the fifth head?

What is meant by 'the times of this ignorance'?

What is meant by 'winked at'?

Does God overlook ignorance of his law?

How far is ignorance an excuse for sin?

What does he now require for which we cannot offer ignorance as an excuse?

What 'day' has God appointed? For what?

What does 'in righteousness' mean?

Will there be any complaint then that our ignorance
or our weakness was not considered in the decision?

VI. What is the sixth head?

Whom does 'that man' mean?

Where had Paul spoken of Him before?

How has God given proof that He is to be the Judge?

Why did the Athenians break in upon Paul's speech at this
point?

What two kinds of conduct were shown?

What two kinds of people probably were represented?

Was Paul's address successful?

What is an Areopagite?

When is preaching successful?

(52)

"THE CITY OF THE TWO SEAS."

LESSON.

Acts xviii. 1–5.

PAUL must have gone to Corinth by one of two routes. He took either the coast-road through Eleusis and Megara or the shorter sail of a few hours in one of the many ships plying between the Piræus and Cenchrea. When he reached Corinth, he was in a place far different from Athens. Athens was a Greek free city. Corinth was a Roman colony. It was like going from Thessalonica to Philippi.[1] Athens was a university town: Corinth was a business town. It was something like going from Oxford to London. Athens had once been greater politically than Corinth; but in Paul's time Athens had lost its business character, retaining chiefly its renown for learning, while Corinth was 'a new and splendid city,' rebuilt by Julius Cæsar, after having been once destroyed, and now kept in order by a Roman Pro-consul. It was a most important town. It was situated on the isthmus between the two seas. By mounting to the summit of the hill[2] at Corinth, we gain

[1] See page 153, and 132, 133.

[2] The fortified citadel called, like the Acropolis at Athens, (see note 4, page 160,) Acro-Corinthus, summit of Corinth. It was two thousand feet high above the sea, its sides steep, and the shadow reached half-way across the isthmus. The space on the summit was large enough for a town.

a 'magnificent and extensive view.' There is a sea on the north and a sea on the south-east. The Acropolis of Athens can be seen forty-five miles away. The mountains of Attica are in the eastern horizon. On the other side "are the large masses of mountains of north-eastern Greece, with Mount Parnassus towering at Delphi." The city lies at your feet. On either side at the coast is a harbor: on the eastern sea, Cenchrea, on the western sea, Lecheum. Hence Corinth was called by the poets 'The City of the Two Seas.' It had been and still was to some extent the crossing-place of two great routes of travel: the land-travel *along* the isthmus from the continent to the Peloponessus and the travel *across* the isthmus from sea to sea. It had been therefore and still was a city of great military importance; for it controlled both routes. In ancient and in more modern times, nations have fought for the control of this town and its citadel.

Here, more than anywhere else, would you see the Greek race in all its life and activity. For hundreds of years before Paul's time the inhabitants of Corinth had gone out in companies and colonized on many of the coasts of Europe in the west and east. As the colonies grew, the people of these towns used to come back to Corinth to trade and to see their native city. Ships came from every sea to her two harbors. In this city, too, were manufactures in metals, in dyeing and in porcelain, from which wares were sold to all countries. At certain times in the year the streets were crowded by strangers who came to attend the Isthmian Games. In Paul's time there was much of the ancient activity and life, although the old city had been destroyed and a new one, years afterwards, founded by the Roman emperor. We must think of Corinth, then, when Paul landed at Cenchræa, as a colony of the Roman Empire, in which Jews and Greeks were more numerous than Romans, and as the capital[3] of the Roman province of Achaia.

We can think of three reasons why Paul came from Athens to Corinth: First. The discouragement he met at Athens. Secondly. Corinth "was a large business city, in immediate communication with Rome and the western Mediterranean, with Thessalonica and Ephesus in the Ægean Sea and with Antioch and Alexandria in the east: the Gospel, if established there, would spread everywhere." Thirdly. Jews were numerous in Corinth. There were "communities of scattered Jews in various parts of the province," more or less connected with Corinth. "A religion which was first to be planted in the synagogue, and intended thence to scatter its seeds over all parts of the earth, could nowhere find a more favorable soil than among the Hebrew families at Corinth."

"At this particular time there was a greater number of Jews than usual in the city; for they had lately been banished from Rome by command of the Emperor Claudius Cæsar." One historian says "that Claudius drove the Jews from Rome because they were incessantly raising tumults at the instigation of a certain *Chrestus.* Much has been written concerning this sentence of the historian. Some have thought that there was really a Jew called Chrestus, who excited political disturbances: others that the name is used by mistake for Christus, and that the disturbances arose from the Jewish expectations concerning the Messiah or Christ. The events at least followed the actual appearance of *Christ.*"

---

[3] Athens was the *ancient* capital, before Greece was conquered. But under the Romans Corinth was capital of Greece, and Greece was now the *province* of Achaia.

Aquila and Priscilla were among the Jews banished
and among those who came to Corinth. They were
natives of Pontus, a province on the Euxine (Black)
Sea, directly north of Antioch in Syria. When Peter
preached on the day of Pentecost at Jerusalem, there
were men from Pontus[4] in the assembly. Possibly
Aquila and Priscilla were there; or they may have heard
the Gospel at home in Pontus from those who were
in Jerusalem at the feast of Pentecost. For some reason they had gone to Rome; and they were now banished from Rome to pursue their trade in Corinth. As
they were tent-makers, Paul 'abode' with them. If
they were not already Christians, they soon became so.[5]
With them Paul labored at the trade which no doubt
his father taught him in his youth. "Those who visited
Aquila at Corinth, in the working hours found Paul
quietly occupied with the same work as his fellow-laborers. Though he knew the Gospel to be a matter of life
and death to the soul, he gave himself to an ordinary
trade with as much zest as though he had no other occupation. He 'labored working with his own hand'
among the Corinthians, as he afterwards reminded
them,"[6] so that no one could reproach him with in-
dolence or any selfish motives in preaching.

"The Sabbath was a day of rest. On that day the
Jews laid aside their tent-making and their other trades,
and amid the derision of their Gentile neighbors went
to the synagogue." There, as often as the Sabbath re
turned, Paul reasoned with both Jews and Greeks.
"His countrymen listened with incredulity or conviction, while he 'endeavored to persuade' them to believe in Jesus the promised Messiah and the Saviour of
the world." The result seems to have been that he was

---

[4] Acts ii. 9.   [5] Verse 26.   [6] I. Corinthians iv. 12.

far more successful among the Greeks than with his countrymen.

While he was thus working in the week and preaching on the Sabbath, Timothy and Silas returned. It seems they did not reach Athens before Paul left that place. Perhaps they sailed directly from Thessalonica or Dium[7] to Cenchræa; or they may have come by land to Attica, and from Athens down the isthmus. What news would they bring from Thessalonica? Good news it was indeed, as we know from the first letter of Paul to the Thessalonians: news of steadfast converts, of men of 'aith, of diligent and careful 'Christians.'

Their arrival, and the good news they brought, produced "an instant increase of zeal and energy" in Paul, especially against the opposers who now began to resist his teachings "He himself declares that he was in Corinth 'in weakness and in fear and in much trembling,"[8] but 'God, who comforteth those that are cast down, comforted him by the coming'[9] of his friends. It was not the only time that Paul derived strength, when 'he saw the brethren and thanked God and took courage.'[10] And now, with much greater emphasis than before, he preached to his fellow-Israelites and urged them to receive Jesus of Nazareth as their Messiah.

[7] See page 158. [8] I. Corinthians ii. 3. [9] II. Corinthians vii. 6.
[10] Acts xxviii. 15.

QUESTIONS.

WHAT two routes from Athens to Corinth?

How do we suppose Paul went?

What difference between Athens and Corinth?

Why was it like going from Thessalonica to Philippi?

Why was it something like going from Oxford to London?

Which was the greater city?

How had Athens changed?

What advantage was there in the situation of Corinth?

What was the Acro-Corinthus?

What could be seen from it?

Why was this citadel important?

What two harbors had Corinth?

What two lines of travel passed through Corinth?

Would Paul see more of the real Greek people in Athens or in Corinth?

Why did the people come back to the city?

What manufactures in Corinth?

Why were the streets crowded at certain times of the year?

What was the capital of Greece in Paul's time?

What was the name of the province then?

What three reasons may be given why Paul came to Corinth?

Why were there more Jews than usual in the city?

Who was 'Claudius'?

What reason is given why he drove the Jews from Rome?

What is that historian supposed to mean?

What two banished Jews came to Corinth?

What country were they natives of?

Where was that province?

Where had men from that province heard the Gospel?

Do you suppose they were Christians?

How could they have heard the Gospel?

What was their trade?

(53)

Was it necessary for Paul to labor?

Was it degrading to his Apostolic authority to labor?

Is it honorable to be unwilling to labor? Is it right?

Where does he remind the Corinthians of his labor among them?

What reason may be given for his labor?

On what day of *the week* did the Jews go to their synagogue?

What especial doctrine would Paul 'reason' about?

In respect to what did he 'persuade' them?

Who came during this time?

Had Paul been in Corinth over more than one Sabbath?

From what place had Paul sent word to Timothy and Silas?

How did they come from Macedonia? From what place?

What news did they bring?

What is meant by 'pressed in the Spirit'?

Was this the effect of the good news or of the immediate influence of the Spirit?

Why is it a good thing to have news from earnest churches and of revivals, told in other churches?

Is it right to rely on human sympathy for our religious earnestness?

What other time was Paul strengthened by the coming of friends? Where?

What did Paul's earnestness lead him to do?

What is meant by '*testified* that Jesus is the Christ'?

What is the test of genuine religious labor?

(54)

THE FIRST EPISTLE.

LESSON.

Acts xviii. 5–7; I. Thessalonians i. 1.

PAUL'S increase of zeal and energy "was not the only result of the arrival of Timothy and Silas. Timothy had been sent while Paul was at Athens to revisit and strengthen the church of Thessalonica.[1] And now the news he brought on his return led Paul to write to his beloved Thessalonian converts. Paul wrote this letter partly to show his affection for these converts and to encourage them in the midst of their persecutions, and in part to correct some errors into which they had fallen." No doubt the Jews who excited the idle rabble of Thessalonica against Paul and Silas and Jason would continue to molest the Thessalonian church whenever they had opportunity. And it was perhaps but natural that these believers, who had had so little instruction, should fall into some mistakes. "Many of the new converts were uneasy about the state of their relatives or friends who had died since their conversion. Others, thinking Christ was soon to appear at his second coming, were persuading themselves that they need no longer continue their usual labor. Others were despising the gift of prophesying." To assist them in these troubles, and to correct their error, Paul writes them a most affectionate letter, in which he most kindly

---

[1] I. Thessalonians iii. 1, 2.

praises and encourages them. This letter is the *First Epistle to the Thessalonians.*

As we suppose this is the first epistle[2] which Paul wrote to a church of believers, and his other epistles are more or less like it, it is well for us to stop and think a moment of the general subject of the epistles before we go on. By settling two or three questions in respect to one, we settle them in respect to all.

I. First, then, How do we know the epistles of Paul were written on his journeys? They *must* have been written in towns on his journeys; for the churches to which they are addressed were established on his second and third journeys, and he journeyed all his life afterwards, till he was prisoner at Rome. Paul first preached the Gospel in Galatia and Philippi and Thessalonica and Corinth and Ephesus; and it is not likely that he wrote his letters to Galatians, Philippians, Thessalonians, Corinthians, Ephesians, during the very short time between his second and third journeys, when he was in Jerusalem, nor during that turbulent time when he was taken prisoner and sent off under a Roman guard to Cæsarea. It is more likely that he wrote them in places where he remained a much longer time, such as Corinth. It would be unnatural to suppose that they were all written from Jerusalem; for while there are many allusions to Greek and Roman names and places and events, there are few allusions to indicate that the writer was in Judea. The ancient inscriptions added at the end of the Epistles,[3] though uninspired, and though it is thought they are not all correct, yet *all* show they were written in the towns along his journeys.

II. How can we tell where each epistle was written? We cannot *certainly* decide. We can only judge of

[2] See note 12 page 184.

[3] See the end of the various Epistles.

the place and the circumstances in which the Apostolic writer is by what the Apostle says of places and persons and circumstances. For example, in this first epistle to the Thessalonians, (1.) Paul speaks as if he had but *recently* come from Thessalonica, and as if the Thessalonian believers had but *recently been converted.* He writes: 'And ye became *followers of us,*[4] having received the word in much affliction:' 'Ye were *ensamples* to *all that believe* in Macedonia and Achaia; for *they* show what manner of *entering in* we had unto you, and how ye *turned to God* from *idols:*[5] 'Ye know, brethren, our entrance unto you that it was not in vain, but after that we *suffered at Philippi, as ye know:*[6] 'We, brethren, having been taken from you *for a short time in person.*[7] In these things, Paul certainly writes as if to new converts, and as if he had lately been among them. (2.) Paul says that he has lately been in Athens.[8] (3.) He declares that Timothy had just come from Thessalonica.[9] This letter to the Thessalonians must have been written, then, after Timothy reached Paul, and after Paul left Athens; and as Timothy reached Paul at Corinth, after Paul had left Athens and after Paul had just come, a few weeks before, from Thessalonica, and as ships were often sailing too from Cenchræa to Thessalonica, there can be little doubt that Paul wrote this first letter to the Thessalonians from Corinth.[10] In the same manner, we are to decide where each epistle was written.

[4] I. Thess. i. 6.   [5] i. 7.   [6] ii. 1, 2.
[7] ii. 17. The Greek participle is past, not present.
[8] iii. 1.   [9] iii. 6.
[10] You will notice the uninspired inscription at the end of the epistle, added by another writer, says the epistle was written from *Athens.* This is generally thought by scholars to be a mistake. They agree that the Thessalonian epistles were written from *Corinth.*

III. If these epistles are simply letters written by a Christian traveller to Christian churches, how is it that they are inspired Scripture to us? Some persons may think the dignity and authority of these sacred epistles are lessened by the thought that they were written in journeying; but we must remember that the journeys were *missionary* journeys, and the missionary *divinely inspired.* Some of the most solemn and most forcible appeals to Christian churches in modern times have been the *letters of missionaries.* If they had been inspired, they would have been binding on us, like the Scriptures. If what an inspired missionary Apostle *spoke* to the people of Thessalonica when he was in their city is the word of God to us,[11] then surely what an inspired missionary Apostle *wrote* to the *believers* of that same place, from a city a few hundred miles away, is the word of God to us.

It is well for us also to take up one of these epistles, and by dividing it into parts to see how full it is of personal kindness and affection. We will see in this epistle the largeness of Paul's affectionate nature.

THE FIRST EPISTLE TO THE THESSALONIANS.[12]

I. Paul thanks God for their conversion.

Remembering their faith, love, and hope while he was in Thessalonica,[13] and how earnestly they received the Gospel in those solemn meetings,[14] he gives thanks that, in affliction or persecution, they followed his own example, and *became* examples to all believers in Macedonia and Achaia.[15] Recalling to their minds his im-

[11] Acts xvii. 2, 3.

[12] This First Epistle to the Thessalonians, it is agreed, is the first of all Paul's Epistles. There is difference of opinion in respect to the order of time in which all the Epistles were written; but in the future lessons we will follow that which Conybeare and Howson have adopted.

[13] I. Thess. i. 3.   [14] i. 5.   [15] i. 6-9.

prisonment in Philippi, and the boldness necessary to preach afterwards in their city,[16] he calls them to witness the faithfulness of his preaching,[17] his affectionate treatment of them, as a nurse[18] and a father[19] their own children, his daily labor to support himself,[20] and gives thanks to God the more earnestly, because in persecution they did not hesitate to follow him, a persecuted Apostle, as the churches in Judea had followed others.[21] (Chapters i. ii. 1–16.)

II. After he left them, he longed greatly to see them.

Though he had been absent from them only a little while, he wished more than once to return, but was hindered. He calls them his 'glory and joy.' (ii. 17–20.)

III. As he could not then come himself, he sent Timothy to them.

Timothy was sent to strengthen them in the faith and to comfort them in the persecution which Paul himself had foretold would come upon them. (iii. 1–5.)

IV. He is full of joy at the good news Timothy has brought. (iii. 6–13.)

V. He advises them in respect to their temptations and in respect to Christian virtues:

In respect to impurity and defrauding,[22] brotherly love, quiet, and good order:[23] in respect to those who have died and the Lord's second coming. He comforts them in respect to the dead by declaring those asleep in Jesus shall live with Jesus. He comforts them in respect to the second coming by saying they 'are not in darkness, and hence not likely to be overtaken by the day of the Lord' as by a thief in the night. "Wherefore comfort one another with these words."[24] He

[16] ii. 1, 2.   [17] ii. 3–6.   [18] ii. 7.   [19] ii. 11.   [20] ii. 9.
[21] ii. 14.   [22] iv. 1–7.   [23] iv. 9–12.   [24] iv. 13, 14–18 ; v. 11.

gives them directions in respect to their teachers or pastors,[25] the 'unruly,' the 'feeble-minded,' and the 'weak;'[26] and in respect to the practical virtues of forgiveness, joyfulness, prayer, thankfulness, treatment of the Holy Spirit, and of prophesying.[27]   (Chapters iv. v. 1–22.)

VI. In concluding, he asks God's blessings on them, requests their prayers for himself, and commands that this letter be read to all the brethren.   (v. 23–28.)

Such was the first inspired epistle, written by the especial influence of the Holy Spirit, and adapted to the wants of the Thessalonians: from which we, taking into account our changed circumstances, may learn the 'mind of the Spirit.'

In Corinth again the Jews resisted Paul; and again Paul turned to the Gentiles. "A proselyte named Justus, concerning whom we know nothing more, opened his door to the rejected Apostle." He probably '*entered into*' Justus's house to meet his flock there. He was shut out of the synagogue, and he must have some place to teach and preach. "He doubtless continued to lodge with Aquila and Priscilla.[28] "He *abode* there, as afterwards at Rome in 'his own hired lodging.' "[29] "It may readily be supposed that there was no convenient place for teaching in the manufactory of Aquila ·and Priscilla." Greeks would not be likely to come there and mingle with Jews lately exiled from Rome. "Justus, being a proselyte, was exactly in the position to receive under his roof both Greeks and Hebrews."

[25] v. 12, 13.   [26] v. 14.   [27] v. 16–22.   [28] Luke x. 5-7.
[29] Acts xxviii. 30.

QUESTIONS.

WHAT other result of the arrival of Timothy and Silas was there?

Where had Timothy been sent?

What had probably continued to trouble the Thessalonian church?

What three mistakes does this especially show they had evidently fallen into?

What is the object of this letter?

How do we know Paul's epistles were written on his journeys?

Where was Paul between the third journey and his journey as prisoner to Rome?[1]

Might not some of these epistles have been written from Cæsarea?

Why may we not think some of them were written from Jerusalem?

Will the same reason apply to Cæsarea?

Are the inscriptions at the end of the epistles a part of the epistles?

Are they all thought to be correct?

What do they all show?

Can we certainly decide where each epistle was written?

What is the first reason why we suppose the first epistle to the Thessalonians was written at Corinth?

Which one of these passages shows most clearly that Paul had lately been in Thessalonica?

What is the second reason?

What is the third reason?

Do these facts agree with the account in the Acts?

At what place does the inscription at the end of this epistle say it was written?

What two persons were with Paul when he wrote it?[2]

---

[1] Acts xxi. 33; xxiii. 31, 33, 35; xxiv. 27.

[2] In I. Thess. i. 1, Silvanus is the same name as Silas. Silas is the short or contracted form.

From the reasons given, does Athens or Corinth seem to you the more probable place?

How is the dignity and authority of all his epistles affected by the fact that they were written on Paul's journeys?

What is this First Epistle full of?

I. What is the first subject of the epistle?

How far does it extend?

Turn to the first chapters of the epistle and show how Paul alludes to their Christian virtues at the first.

Show how he alludes to his imprisonment at Philippi.

Show the allusion to the faithfulness of his preaching and to his kind care for them.

Show the allusion to his daily labor, and their own faithfulness in persecution.

II. What is the second subject of the epistle?

Show the passage in the epistle.

What affectionate titles does he call them by?

III. What is the third subject of the epistle?

At what place was he when he sent word to Timothy to go to them?

What did he send Timothy for?

IV. What is the fourth subject of the epistle?

How far does it extend?

V. What is the fifth part of the epistle?

How far does it extend?

Point out the passages in respect to brotherly-love, quiet and good order.

Show the passages in respect to believers who have died and 'the second coming.'

What other kind directions can you show?

VI. What is the conclusion of the epistle?

Why is this epistle adapted to us?

Did all the Jews of Corinth obey Paul's preaching?

Where did Paul teach afterwards?

What reason is there for supposing that he still lodged at Aquila's house?

Twenty-ninth Sunday.

A PERSECUTOR PERSECUTED.

LESSON.
Acts xviii. 8–17.

THE opposition of the Jews at Corinth did not prevent the real success of Paul's preaching. A church was soon formed, and rapidly increased. Many heard, believed, and were baptized. We have the name of the first convert in Achaia. When Paul afterwards wrote from Corinth his letter to Rome, he mentioned Epenetus[1] as the 'first fruits of Achaia.' But when, after he left the Corinthians, he wrote a letter back to them, he said 'the household of Stephanas' were the 'first fruits of Achaia.'[2] Perhaps Epenetus was a member of Stephanas' household. Another convert's name was Gaius,[3] in whose house Paul staid during his next visit at Corinth.[4] Not many philosophers, not many wise men, not many mighty, not many noble,[5] but many of the degraded and the profligate[6] were called into the kingdom of God. Yet one man of eminence received the Gospel as a little child; Crispus,[7] the ruler of the synagogue, probably a "man of learning and of high character."

[1] Romans xvi. 5.   [2] I. Corinthians xvi. 15.

[3] In I. Corinthians i. 14, Crispus *and Gaius* are mentioned together. It seems likely that both were converted at the same time.

[4] Romans xvi 23.   [5] I. Cor. i. 26.   [6] I. Cor. vi. 10, 11.

Paul was not to be driven away by opposition. God spoke to him in a vision, directing him to speak boldly and his success would be great. For the long period of a year and six months, he continued to teach and to preach. The promise of God was abundantly fulfilled. The Corinthian church became large and flourishing.

Two important events, we suppose, occurred while Paul labored and preached in Corinth, during the year and a half. One was the writing of a second letter to the Thessalonian Christians. The other was the coming of a new Pro-Consul to the capital of the province.

Paul had no doubt heard again from Thessalonica. There seems to have been much excitement among these Christians in respect to the second coming of the Lord. What he had written in his first letter about that subject[7] had been either misunderstood or perverted. Their wrong notions of that great and mysterious event—'the day and the hour,' of which 'no man nor angel knows, but the Father only'—was creating much trouble and needless anxiety. And therefore, to comfort and to correct them again, Paul writes

THE SECOND EPISTLE TO THE THESSALONIANS.[8]

First, he praises their 'growing faith' and 'abounding charity,'[9] their patience and faith in persecution and trouble,[10] and speaks of his prayers for them.[11]

Secondly, he tells them not to be 'shaken in mind nor troubled' about the second coming of the Lord;[12] that there would be a 'falling away from the faith first;' that they ought to be steadfast and hold firm what they had been taught by preaching and by letter,[13] and prays the Saviour and God to comfort their hearts.[14]

---

[7] I. Thessalonians iv. 13 to v. 11. See, too, pages 181, 186.
[8] See note 10, page 183.   [9] II. Thess. i. 3.   [10] i. 4.
[11] i. 11.   [12] ii. 3–11.   [13] ii. 15.   [14] ii. 16, 17.

Thirdly, he asks their prayers,[15] and commands them to be 'orderly' and 'industrious,'[16] to 'note' and 'admonish' the man who does not obey his letter.[17]

Such was the second inspired epistle written by divine direction, adapted to the present wants of the Thessalonians, and containing the doctrines which were to govern and to comfort the children of God for all time.

We need not suppose that Paul's preaching in the city and his writing to the Thessalonians occupied all his time during his long residence in Corinth. It is said he '*continued* there' a year and a half. It need not bo meant at all that he did not sometimes go out of the city to preach. "The expression may only denote that it was his head-quarters or general place of residence. Communication was easy and frequent by land and water with other parts of the province. Two short days' journey to the south were the Jews of Argos. About the same distance to the east was the city of Athens, which had been imperfectly evangelized. Within a walk of a few hours, along a road busy with traffic, was the sea-port of Cenchræa." We know there was a church established at Cenchræa,[18] and there were at other places many 'churches of God,'[19] among which Paul praised 'the patience and faith' of the Thessalonian disciples.

While Paul was thus busy in his work from month to month, a new Pro-Consul of the province was announced. His arrival from Rome was an event of great and grave importance. An exacting, rigorous, cruel man might make the people of the province wretched. A just, candid, and well-disposed man might make them contented and happy. We know little of Gallio,

.⁵ iii. 1, 2.   ¹⁶ iii. 7–13.   ¹⁷ iii. 14, 15.

¹⁵ Romans xvi. 1.   ¹⁹ II. Thess. i. 4.

except that he was the brother of the philosopher Sen
eca, and that Seneca speaks of him with much affection,
saying that he was "not only an honest man, but also
one who won general favor from his amiable temper
and popular manners." This coïncides with the description given in the Acts.

The Jews took advantage of the change of government to assault Paul, and get a decision against him
from their new officer. "It is quite evident that the
act was preconcerted and the occasion chosen. The
Jews, making use of the privileges they enjoyed as a
separate community, and well aware that their worship
was protected by the Roman state, accused Paul of
violating their own religious law. They seem to have
thought that if this violation of Jewish law could be
proved, that Paul must be held responsible to the law
of the empire ; or perhaps they hoped that he would
be given up to them for punishment." They hoped,
perhaps, too, that Gallio would be glad to please them,
or would not notice the difference between *their own*
law and the *Roman* law.

We must see, then, Gallio seated as judge in the
pro-consular court, with his military and civil officers
around him, with the robes and emblems of Roman
authority. "Before this heathen ruler, the Jews are
making their accusation with eager clamor. Their chief
speaker is Sosthenes, the successor of Crispus, or, it
may be, the ruler of another synagogue. The Greeks
stand around to hear the result, and to learn something
of the new Governor's character : *they* hated the Jews,
and were ready rather to take Paul's side than that of
the Jews. The Jews of Corinth were not so crafty in
the statement of their accusation as the Jews of Thessalonica had been : the exact charge was that Paul
taught men to worship '*contrary to law.*' What law ?

The Jewish law, or Roman law? Perhaps the persecutors meant to leave that point undecided, hoping Gallio would condemn Paul for teaching another God than the Roman gods. Gallio showed by his reply that he knew the duties of his office. He did not permit Paul to make a defence. If the case had been one of wrong or of crime against *Roman* law, he would have given it investigation, but as it was only one of *Jewish* law and superstition, they must look to that themselves. They might excommunicate Paul from their church, if they liked. He would be no judge of such questions.

The persecutors were completely baffled. But this was not all. Now their wicked artifice recoiled on themselves. The *Greeks* were gratified by Gallio's decision. Excited and glad, and enraged at the Jews, they caught the chief persecutor and beat him right before the Pro-Consul. With easy negligence, Gallio left the persecutor to *his* persecutors. He thought, perhaps, that a bitter and cruel man, like Sosthenes, did not deserve the interference of a Judge, even though law was on his side, when others, bitter and cruel, assaulted *him*. When it is said, therefore, that 'Gallio cared for none of these things,' it is not meant that he was indifferent to religious things, (although that might be true,) but that he would not meddle with what did not belong to his office and duties. It may be doubted, however, whether he ought not to have prevented the public beating of any man, even a bitter and malignant persecutor.

The result was, that the accusers were disgraced; Gallio was popular among the Greeks; and Paul was respected as an injured man. How wonderfully had the words of the vision been fulfilled! The enemies who had 'set on' Paul, had not 'hurt' him.

QUESTIONS.

DID the Jews succeed in their opposition?

How do you know a church was formed?

Who was the first convert?

How do you reconcile the two passages in Romans and in I. Corinthians?

What other person was probably converted at this time?

How is he especially connected with Paul?

From what classes were the converts taken? Prove it.

What eminent man was converted? Eminent how?

What result followed as in the case of Lydia and of the jailer?

How was Paul's duty now made known to him?

Was this more than a dream?

Has God ever given directions by dreams?

Is it right for us to rely on any such direction?

What was Paul told *not* to do?

What was Paul told to do?

If Paul had not obeyed the direction, what would have been the result to the 'much people'?

When is it wrong for us to be silent?

How did Paul know when to flee and when to stay, in time of persecution?

When is it wrong to fear receiving injury?

How long did Paul remain in Corinth?

Had he been in Corinth more than two or three weeks *before* the vision?

What two important events do we suppose occurred during this residence?

Could Paul have lived in Corinth so long without hearing from Thessalonica? Why?

What especial subject gave anxiety to the Thessalonian Christians?

Do you suppose *all* were excited about this subject?

What had Paul written about? Where?

What is the object of Paul in writing this inspired letter?

(57)

Turn to the Epistle, and point out some of the subjects of the first part.

What is the second part? Show the subject and the recommendation.

Point out the subjects of the third part.

What is meant by 'continued there'? Read the margin.

What else may Paul have done?

If the games at the Isthmus were celebrated during this time, would Paul have visited them?

To what places may he have gone?

Who arrived about this time?

What is meant by 'deputy'?

Why was this event of great importance?

Whose brother was Gallio?

What kind of a man did his brother say that he was?

What advantage did the Jews try to gain?

What did they charge upon Paul?

What would they probably hope?

What three parties made up the court?

Who is evidently the Jews' chief-speaker?

What was the exact form of the accusation? What law?

Why did not Gallio permit Paul to defend himself?

Was there any recognised violation of Roman law?

Was 'your law' civil or religious law?

Was it right for Gallio to refuse to decide?

What did the Greeks now?

What did Gallio probably think?

Does 'cared for none of these things' mean 'indifferent to religious things'?

What was the result?

What words had been fulfilled?

THE SECOND RETURN HOME.

LESSON.

ACTS xviii. 18-22.

AT length the time came when Paul thought best to leave Corinth, and to return to Judea. It had been a long time since he and Silas left Antioch in Syria. The journey had been long and wearisome, but it had been even more successful than Paul's first journey with Barnabas. In Corinth, Paul had at last found a place in which he could preach and rest without fear of successful persecution. If the Greeks of Corinth did not all welcome his preaching, neither would they permit the malignant Jews to persecute publicly a man who they well knew had committed no offence against the laws of the province. His work there, as the founder of churches, had now been accomplished. He wished to be at the coming national festival at Jerusalem.[1] It may be that Aquila and Priscilla were about to remove to Ephesus; and if so, the removal may have had something to do with Paul's return. His home in Corinth would be broken up, and he could go with them part of the way.

After giving farewell to the Corinthian church, the three went down to Cenchræa. "Descending from the table-land on which Corinth was situated, the road

---

[1] ' This feast that cometh,' in the 21st verse, means probably the Feast of Pentecost.

stretched eight or nine miles across the Isthmus," to this harbor. Here, at different times, might be seen ships from Egypt and from Syria, from 'Asia' and from Macedonia, and smaller craft from Crete and the islands of the Ægean Sea. All the sea-commerce of Corinth from the east came through this harbor. It was therefore a town of considerable size. Whether Phœbe was a convert, and the church was already formed at this place,[2] we are not yet told. If Paul had not preached here before, he may have remained here a day or more now. But here, where he landed from Antioch, the three step on board the ship which was to carry them to Ephesus.

Before the vessel sailed, however, or more likely before they embarked, a religious ceremony was performed which we must stop to notice. Either Paul or Aquila had previously taken a vow. The time of this vow had expired. "Such vows the Jews, even when in foreign countries, often took on themselves, in consequence of some mercy received or some deliverance from danger, or some other occurrence which had produced a deep, solemn impression on the mind." The obligations such persons took were: to abstain from wine and all strong drinks, not to enter any house in which was a dead body, not to attend any funeral nor to allow themselves to be made unclean according to the Mosaic law, and not to cut the hair till the end of a fixed length of time.

There is a difference of opinion about the *person* who took this vow. The words of the Scripture may mean either Paul or Aquila. Some persons think that Paul could not have made such a vow, because it would have been in violation of his own principles—the principles

---

[2] Romans xvi. 1.

frequently made than that between Corinth and Ephesus. These two places were the capitals of the two powerful and flourishing provinces of Achaia and Asia: the two great business towns on the opposite sides of the sea. We may say that the relation of these cities of the eastern and western Greeks to each other, was like that between New-York and Liverpool. Even the time of the voyage between the opposite sides of the sea, (from ten to fifteen days,) was alike. Cicero says that his passage from Corinth to Ephesus, which was a long

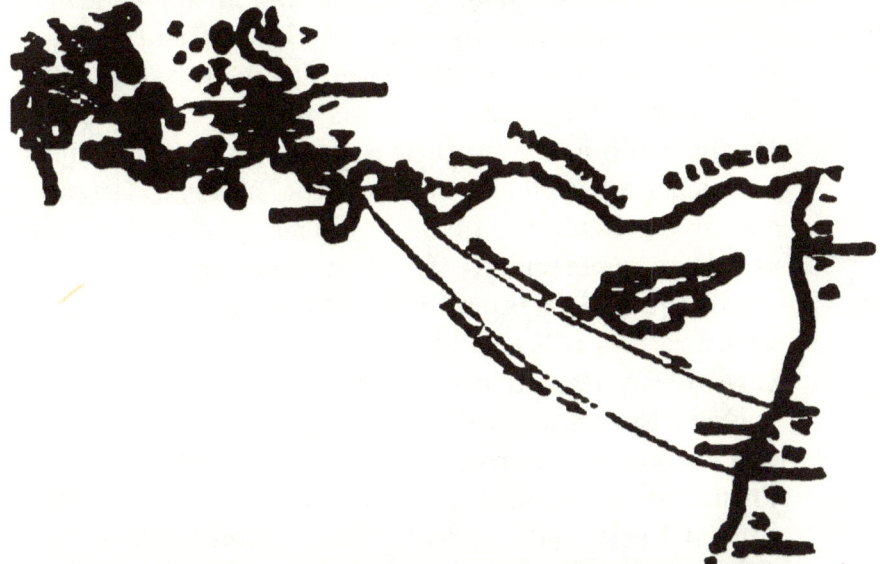

one, was in fifteen days, and that his return from Ephesus to Corinth was thirteen days in length."

The spear of Minerva's image on the Acropolis of Athens was again visible to Paul, if he sailed down the Saronic Gulf in a clear day. Off the cape of Sunium the ship would have the bank on which he came from Berea. As he wound his way among the thousand islands, he would think of the voyage 'in a straight course,' far, far to the north, from Troas to Neapolis, two or three years before. Passing, rounding, now and night, some beautiful island or some cluster o. islets, at length the long Icarus and the long Samos (reminding him of the Thracian Samos[5]) passed slowly by; and if the wind was fair, the coast off the city of Ephesus is soon before them. "It seems that the vessel was bound for Syria, and staid only a short time in harbor at Ephesus. But even during the short interval of his stay, Paul made a visit to his Jewish fellow-countrymen, and (the Sabbath being probably one of the days during which he remained) he held a discussion with them in the synagogue about the Messiah. Their curiosity was excited by what they heard; and perhaps if he had staid longer, the curiosity would soon have been followed by persecution, as at Antioch in Pisidia. But he could not grant their request." He was anxious to reach Jerusalem in time for the national festival; and, if he should not go on in the ship, he might have no other opportunity. He saw, however, enough to encourage him to promise the Ephesian Jews that he would return, if it should be God's will. We shall see how exactly Paul kept his promise.

From Ephesus, the ship sailed past Cos and Rhodes, two islands afterwards mentioned in Paul's voyages[6]. Then Paul was almost in familiar waters. Possibly the cliffs of Lycia could be seen. The previous sail of Paul and Barnabas from Paphos to Perga was in the neighboring seas. Far away to the left lay the shores of Pamphylia. Rough Cilicia lay hid behind the watery horizon in the north-east. A little further on their course, and Cyprus rose into sight, and for a day or more lay in the sea, a high, black line of land off on the left. Then came another long sail, and finally the distant outline of Palestine appears, and then the familiar

---

[5] See page 131.　　　　[6] Acts xxi. 1.

coast about Cæsarea. Here Paul, after a long, tiresome ride on the water, stepped ashore: in this *Roman* capital of the Roman *province* of Judea, although he was on his way to the *ancient Hebrew* capital of the Land of Promise.

"The journey from Cæsarea to Jerusalem is related in a single word." [1] Nothing is said of what occurred at Jerusalem: nothing of meetings with other Apostles, of controversies about disputed points of doctrine: nothing of Paul's recitals of 'all that God had done with them,' [2] nor even of the festival, if indeed Paul arrived in time. He simply made a short visit of sympathy and of courtesy to the church, and then he went down to Antioch. It is likely the journey to Antioch was made by land; and if it was, he passed over the same coast road which we have supposed he travelled when he went up from Antioch to the council of Jerusalem with the 'difficult question.'

With Paul, Antioch, more than Jerusalem, was the point of starting and of return. This visit to Antioch was probably his last; and he was to make but one more visit to Jerusalem, and that one of persecution, of suffering and of final separation.

[1] The two words, 'gone up,' are one word in the Greek. Some persons think that Paul did not go to Jerusalem at all, but he certainly intended to, when he was at Ephesus, (verse 21;) and why did he come to Cæsarea, if not to go to Jerusalem?

[2] Acts xiv. 27. The reason why nothing is said about Paul's visit at Jerusalem, doubtless is, that nothing occurred in respect to his great work *among the Gentiles.*

QUESTIONS.

HOW does this second journey compare with the first?
What kind of a place had Paul found Corinth?
Why did he now wish to return?
What was the 'feast that cometh'?
What else may have led Paul to return?
To what town did the three go first?
What person mentioned afterwards by Paul lived in this place?
Is it probable that Paul preached here at any time?
What took place before they sailed?
When were such vows taken?
What obligations were taken?
Who may 'having shorn his head' refer to?
Was that vow in violation of Paul's principles?
What reason for supposing that it was Aquila who took the vow?
Which one do *you* think took the vow?
If it was Paul, what additional reason for hastening to Jerusalem?
Through what waters did the voyage lie?
What made journeys frequent between Corinth and Ephesus?
The connection between the two cities was like what in our own day?
Where would Paul leave the course of his journey *to* Greece?
What 'straight course' would he think of?
What two islands, among others, did he pass?
What did one of them remind him of?
Where was the vessel bound for?
What did Paul in Ephesus?
What did the Jews wish?
Why did not Paul consent?
What was this visit the first beginnings of?
What did Paul promise?

(59)

Did Paul observe the Jewish feasts?

Was not this keeping Moses' law?

Did he it from obligation or from choice?

Who remained at Ephesus?

Why could they not teach the Ephesians as well as Paul?

What two islands did Paul sail past? Where are they mentioned?

The track of what previous voyage were they near? cliffs? shores? horizon?

What island on the left?

What distinction between Cæsarea and Jerusalem?

What does 'gone up' mean? What 'church'?

Did Paul go to Jerusalem?

Why have we no account of Paul's visit in Jerusalem?

What is meant by 'saluted the church'?

How was the journey made to Antioch?

When had he been over the road before?

What was Antioch in relation to Paul's missionary journeys?

What visits were there to the two cities?

(60)

THE THIRD JOURNEY.—APOLLOS OF ALEXANDRIA.

LESSON.

Acts xviii. 23–28.

PAUL must have been gone from Antioch, on his second journey, two years or more. To make the journey through Syria and Cilicia,[1] Derbe and Lystra, and other 'cities,'[2] remaining long enough in each to ascertain the condition of the 'churches,'[3] to go 'throughout Phrygia and the region of Galatia,'[4] travelling all the way on foot to Troas, must have taken from one to two months : from Troas to Philippi, Thessalonica,[5] and Berea, six or eight weeks : from Berea to Athens and Corinth, three or four weeks. He was at Corinth probably *more* than 'a year and a half ;'[6] and he must have been nearly two months from Corinth to Cæsarea by the way of Ephesus, and from Cæsarea to Antioch by way of Jerusalem. It seems likely that he was in some of these places much longer than we have supposed in this reckoning ; and therefore that the time of absence from Antioch had been from two to two and a half years.

He was now among the 'Christians' of Antioch 'a good while.' He related to them the story of his long and successful journey. He had found the churches in Lycaonia steadfast : he had explored Phrygia and

[1] xv. 41.
[2] xvi. 4.
[3] xvi. 5.
[4] xvi. 6.
[5] xvi. 12, 13 ; xvii. 1, 2, 10.
[6] xviii. 11.

Galatia and preached the Gospel there. Flourishing
churches had been planted in the far-distant lands of Macedonia and Achaia. No 'difficult question' was now
raised, by envious or narrow-minded Pharisees, when
Paul told how he had lived with the Gentiles all along
his journey. Neither famine nor controversy sent him
now on an errand to Jerusalem. With other 'prophets and teachers,' he continued to instruct publicly
and privately the believers of the city, until his desire
to know the condition of the Phrygian and Galatian
converts, and his promise to the Jews of Ephesus, led
him to plan his third missionary journey.

Barnabas and Mark are no longer spoken of. Even
Silas is not mentioned. It is probable that Silas remained at Jerusalem, where he had already been 'a
chief man'' in the church. We shall find afterwards
that Timothy was one of his companions. Perhaps he
was from the time of leaving Antioch.

It is evident that this was a *systematic* visit of churches
and places. He went over 'all the country of Galatia
and Phrygia *in order.*' He must have visited some of
the Syrian and Cilician churches, if he travelled in the
track of his former journey to Tarsus and through the
Cilician Gates. In Galatia and Phrygia Paul may have
visited other places than those he visited before. He
seems to have gone through the principal towns of
these two provinces without persecution or interruption,
making more thorough the incomplete visit of two years
before. Two things Paul designed to accomplish: first
to encourage and strengthen the converts in their trials
and against error, and secondly to make collections for
the poor Christians in Judea. When James, Peter and
John, at the council of Jerusalem, declared that Paul

' xv. 22.

was the Apostle to the Heathen or Gentiles, they directed him to remember the poor.[8] It is to these very Galatians that Paul writes when he mentions this direction of the three Apostles, and when he says : ' I was forward to do the same.'[8] We know, too, what the order was which he gave to the churches of Galatia. It was the same which he afterwards gave to the church of Corinth :[9] ' that each one, on the first day of the week, should save a certain portion of his earnings as God had prospered him, and have it ready to send, when an opportunity offered, to Jerusalem.'[9]

With this twofold object in view, we think of the beginning of this third journey. Nothing is said of Paul's exact route, till he arrived at Ephesus.[10] He no doubt passed over again the sunny Cilician plain ; looked up again at the frowning cliffs at the Great Mountain Gate ; and again trod the high table-land of Lycaonia.

After Derbe, Lystra, Iconium, and Antioch in Pisidia, we cannot fix on any cities which he visited. We only know that in the Scripture account Galatia is mentioned first, while in the account of the former journey Phrygia is first mentioned.[11] "We are at liberty to suppose, therefore, that he travelled first from Lycaonia through Cappadocia into Galatia, and then by Phrygia to the coast of the Ægean. The great road from Iconium to Ephesus passed along the valley of the river Meander and near the cities of Laodicea and Colosse ; and we naturally suppose that the Apostle approached the capital of 'Asia' along this well-travelled line." While the Apostle is making this long journey from Phrygia

[8] Galatians ii. 9, 10.
[8] I. Corinthians xvi. 1, 2.
[10] See frontispiece map for the supposed route.
[11] Compare xvii'. 23 with xvi. 6.

to Ephesus, the route of which and the incidents of which we know nothing about, our attention is directed to another great and good man, who arrived at the capital of Asia before him.

Aquila and Priscilla had remained at Ephesus some time after Paul sailed for Cæsarea, when there came a man who was destined to do the church great service. This man was a Jew and an orator. He was skilled in the Scriptures, having been taught no doubt, as Paul himself had been, by earnest and faithful parents. Besides being thoroughly acquainted with the Jewish Scriptures, he possessed, doubtless, like Paul, the knowledge of the best schools of his age. He was born in Alexandria in Egypt, " the emporium of Greek commerce, where literature, philosophy, and criticism excited the utmost intellectual activity," and where were famous schools for the training of orators. In this city, which had been " the most wealthy and splendid city of the known world," and which in Paul's time " exercised, next after Athens, the strongest intellectual influence over the age," Apollos was trained up. In this city, where Jewish learning mingled with Gentile cultivation, and which is now as famous for its translation of the Hebrew Scriptures into Greek and for its Jewish theology as for its Museum and Library,[12] he had had better opportunities to become an orator than even Paul at Tarsus; for the Jews abounded in Alexandria and possessed learned schools of their own. " With the eloquence of a Greek orator, the subject of his study and teaching was the Scriptures of his forefathers. His reputation in the synagogue was that of a man ' mighty in the Scriptures.' " Whether he came to

---

[12] The Museum was " an establishment in which men devoted to literary pursuits were maintained at the public cost." The Library contained at one time 400,000 volumes.

Ephesus directly from Alexandria or from other cities whither his earnest spirit led him to advocate his religion, is an undecided question.

But Apollos was yet only a disciple of John the Baptist. Apollos may himself have listened to the bold teaching of that honest reformer, ' clothed with camels' hair and a leathern girdle.' The sturdy doctrines of the great forerunner had seized fast hold of his earnest mind. Filled with zeal to spread John's doctrines of repentance, reformation, and the new coming of the Messiah, he taught that ' *way of the Lord* '[13] which his accepted Master taught. " We may conceive of him as travelling, like a second John the Baptist, outside of Judea, expounding the prophecies of the Old Testament, announcing that the time of the Messiah had come, and calling unholy Jews to repentance in the very spirit of Elias."

" Thus burning with zeal and confident of the truth of what he had learned, he spoke out boldly in the synagogue of Ephesus, where an intense interest must have been excited about this time concerning the Messiah. Paul had recently been there and departed with the promise of return. Aquila and Priscilla, though taking no forward part as public teachers, would keep what Paul had said before the minds of the Israelites. And now an Alexandrian Jew had introduced himself in the synagogue, bearing testimony to the same Messiah with singular eloquence and with great power in the interpretation of Scripture. Thus an unconscious preparation was made for the arrival of Paul, who was already approaching Ephesus through the up-lands of Asia Minor."

" The teaching of Apollos, though eloquent, learned,

---

[13] Matthew iii 1-3; Luke iii. 4; John i 23; Isaiah xl. 3

and zealous, had a very grave defect in it. But God had provided among his listeners" those who could teach even this learned and earnest orator his deficiency. Two humble tent-makers knew the Messiah *had* come. The prophecies which Apollos expounded so convincingly in favor of the near approach of the Messiah, Aquila and Priscilla showed to mean Jesus of Nazareth. The faithful arguments of Aquila and Priscilla convinced the great-hearted and humble-minded Apollos that Jesus was the One who was to follow John the forerunner.

Apollos soon embarked for Corinth. News from Corinth may have led him to think he could assist the church there. The Ephesian Christians gave him letters of introduction and commendation to their Corinthian brethren. To the Corinthian Christians he proved a most valuable help; for even the Jews, it would seem, who had rejected Paul, were 'mightily convinced' by the eloquent arguments of Apollos that the Jesus crucified at Jerusalem was the Messiah. "And yet evil grew up side by side with good. For while Apollos was honestly coöperating with Paul, he was unwillingly held up as a rival of the Apostle himself. In this city of critics and orators, the learning and eloquent speaking of Apollos were contrasted with the unlearned simplicity with which Paul had purposely preached the Gospel to his Corinthian audience." Some held to the new teacher, and some to the old. And this was no doubt the origin of those divisions of Paul and of Apollos which afterwards gave so much anxiety to the Apostle.[14] "We cannot imagine that Apollos himself wished or tolerated such unchristian divisions."

[14] I. Corinthians i. 12.

QUESTIONS.

HOW long had Paul been gone on the second journey?
Can you distribute the time?
How long did he remain in Antioch?
What did he there?
What two things led him to plan a third journey?
Where were Barnabas and Mark?
Where was Silas?
Who was his companion?
What kind of a visit was this?
What two things did Paul design to accomplish?
What especial direction of the Apostles did he wish to
carry out? What Apostles?
To whom does he mention this direction?
What order did Paul give in respect to this? to whom?
What is the first city named on this journey?
Did Paul go through Syria and Cilicia to reach Galatia?
What cities can you say he visited?
How are Galatia and Phrygia named differently in the
previous journey?
What may you suppose, then, in respect to the route?
Whom had Paul left at Ephesus?
Who came to Ephesus during Paul's absence?
What was he? From what place?
How did this city compare with Athens and Tarsus?
What had it to do with orators?
What four things was it famous for?
What was the subject of this orator's eloquence?
Whose disciple was Apollos?
How did he become his disciple?
What is meant by 'way of the Lord'?
What had John the Baptist preached?
What is meant by 'present in the Spirit'?
Did Apollos teach the immediate coming of the Mes-
siah?
What else did he teach?

What does 'knowing only the *baptism* of John' mean?
Where did Apollos speak?

> What combined to increase the interest concerning the Messiah?
>
> What effect would this have on Paul's coming?

Who instructed Apollos?

> What was the one particular point in their instructions?
>
> Should believers in humble station despair of convincing the most learned or eloquent?
>
> What previous preparation had Aquila and Priscilla for approaching Apollos?
>
> Is it right at all times to inform a man in error that he is wrong?
>
> How should it be done?

Where did Apollos go? Why?

> What did the Ephesian Christians for him?
>
> Whom did Apollos help in Achaia?
>
> What does 'believed through grace' mean?
>
> Why did Apollos accomplish what Paul did not?
>
> How did the subject of Apollos' preaching at Corinth compare with Paul's at Antioch in Pisidia?
>
> *How* did he show that Jesus was the Messiah?

What evil mingled with the good?

> What led to this?
>
> How do you know there were these divisions?
>
> Is it not right to prefer one preacher to another?
>
> Why were these divisions wrong?

MIRACLES AND MAGIC-WORKERS.

LESSON.

Acts xix. 1-20.

" EPHESUS was the greatest city of Asia Minor as well as the metropolis of the *province* of Asia ; and as it was constantly visited by ships from all parts of the Mediterranean, and united by great roads with the markets of the interior, it was the common meeting-place of various characters and classes of men." Among these various classes who had gathered in this stirring city were a few disciples of John the Baptist. There were 'about twelve men' who had learned John's doctrines in different places or had been converts to Apollos' preaching in Ephesus. If they had heard of Jesus as the Messiah, they did not fully understand the doctrine. Apollos must have been gone some time before Paul arrived; and it may be these disciples came to Ephesus after Apollos had departed. If they had received instruction from Aquila and Priscilla, that instruction was not sufficient. "They had only received John's baptism, and were ignorant of the great out-pouring of the Holy Ghost."

Paul had now come down from the upper country[1] and on one of the great roads from the east entered Ephesus. He found out the Jews to whom he had given his pro-

---

[1] 'Upper coasts.' Coasts does not mean, of course, coasts of the sea, but the upper *parts* or *provinces*.

mise of return ;² and he now met this small company
of John's disciples. Paul's simple, earnest question
seemed to perplex them. Though they sincerely wished
to do right, they were ignorant of the Holy Spirit's especial appearance at the day of Pentecost and since
that time. Though baptized by John, they had not
been baptized with that outpoured Spirit which the
Saviour promised. They were therefore reminded that
John himself told the people to believe on him who
should come after him, that is, on Jesus of Nazareth,
the Messiah. Convinced of the Messiahship of Jesus,
they received the baptism which he commanded his disciples to administer ; and then, on them, as on the gathered multitude at Pentecost, the gift of tongues and the
gift of prophecy descended.

Paul now took up his residence in the city. Aquila
and Priscilla were still there without doubt, as they are
mentioned both before and after this time.³ It is very
likely that Paul again worked at his trade with these
tent-makers ; for he afterwards told the Ephesian Christians that ' his own hands had ministered to his neces-
sities and to those who were with him.'⁴ Sabbath by
Sabbath he went to the synagogue to reason with the
Jews. He was present at many other meetings, or
whenever opportunity offered, to argue with his coun
trymen, with proselytes or with Gentiles. For three
months he was permitted to preach the Messiahship of
Jesus of Nazareth. Those who had invited him to return to Ephesus did not persecute him ; and although
some of them would not be convinced, and even ' spake
evil' of the spiritual truth Paul preached, opposing him

---

² xviii. 21.

³ xviii. 26 ; I. Corinthians xvi. 19   This Epistle, as will soon be
seen, was written soon after this time from Ephesus.

⁴ xx. 34.

publicly, yet they do not seem to have attempted to injure Paul himself.

Paul, however, separated himself and his disciples from the synagogue. As at Corinth, when he was compelled to leave the synagogue, so in Ephesus, God provided him a friend and opportunity to continue his work. "Tyrannus was probably a teacher of philosophy or rhetoric, converted by the Apostle." He opened his 'school' to Paul, and most likely assisted Paul in his 'daily' discussions. The converts were now therefore formed into a distinct organization; and thus the Ephesian church to which Paul wrote his Epistle was founded.

During the two years while Paul taught and preached in the school of Tyrannus much more good was done than simply within the city. Jews and Greeks throughout the whole province of Asia heard of the Christian doctrine. No doubt other churches in other places were founded. If Paul himself did not go out of the city, Timothy and Erastus,[5] Epaphras[6] and Archippus,[7] may have gone out to Colosse,[6] Hierapolis,[7] Laodicea,[7] and other neighboring towns.

We know indeed how faithful Paul was in his Christian work : that he not only taught publicly in the school of Tyrannus, but went about 'from house to house :'[8] that affectionately and 'with tears'[9] he warned them all, ceasing not, 'night and day,'[9] when opportunity offered : that he most earnestly enforced that one great lesson of the Christian preacher, '*repentance and faith*,'[10] and while, for example's sake, supporting himself by labor, he 'shunned not to declare all the counsel of God.'[11] Such faithful labor God always blesses. The Ephesian church became large and flourishing ; the Gospel became known through all the province ; and *special* miracles, beside the miraculous gifts of tongues and of prophecy, confirmed the divine doctrine earnestly preached.

The city of Ephesus was famous through all the ancient world for two especial things : the worship of Diana and the practice of magic. We shall soon see how Paul's preaching came in conflict with the worship of Diana. At present, we are called to notice how the unusual miracles which Paul wrought came in conflict with the practice of magic. The practice of magic, indeed, was closely connected with the worship of Diana. It was said that certain "mysterious symbols, called 'Ephesian Letters,' were engraved on the crown, the girdle, and the feet of the goddess." When these mystic words were pronounced, they were considered a charm, especially against evil spirits. When they were written, they were carried about as amulets or worn on some part of the body. " Curious stories are

---

[5] xix. 22.   [6] Colossians i. 2, 7.   [7] Colossians iv. 12, 13, 15–17.
[8] xx. 17, 18, 20.   [9] xx. 31.   [10] xx. 21.   [11] xx. 27.

told of their influence. The rich Crœsus is said to have repeated them on his funeral-pile; and an Ephesian wrestler is said to have been always successful against his antagonist from Miletus till he lost the parchment on which they were written. The study of these symbols was an elaborate science; and books both numerous and costly were written by learned professors" of the science. Magicians naturally flocked to Ephesus even more than they did to Paphos in Cyprus.[12] "Among those who were in the city during Paul's residence there, were several wandering Jewish magic-workers." The Jews had from the earliest times a strange fondness for these practices; and sorcery was sternly forbidden by the law.[13] And now even more than ever, in an evil age of superstition and imposture, worthless men of the chosen nation wandered from city to city, even among the Gentiles, disregarding their God and disgracing alike the law and the religion of their fathers. Seven brothers, who were magicians, soon became notorious from their conduct towards Paul in Ephesus. Their father's name was Sceva. He " is called a chief-priest, either because he had really been high-priest at Jerusalem or because he was chief of one of the twenty-four courses of priests." There must have been a negligence indeed in the father, like that of Eli of old,[14] to permit his sons, so many of them, to go so far astray from the very worship and ordinances of Moses.

The 'especial miracles,' or, as the words mean, the 'not ordinary miracles,' wrought by Paul, consisted in the communication of healing power to the diseased and the demoniac by means of garments, handkerchiefs,

---

[12] See page 52 in Eighth Sunday.

[13] Deuteronomy xviii. 10, 11; Leviticus xx. 27; Exodus xxii. 18; I. Samuel xxviii. 3, 9.

[14] I. Samuel ii. 12, 17.

and aprons. Here was a far greater effect, openly observed, than anything ever known to be produced by
the charms and amulets of the 'Ephesian Letters.' It
was publicly known that real cures had been effected by
Paul. Persons known to have been possessed of demons had been made sound in mind. A strong impression must have been made " on the minds of those who
practised curious arts in Ephesus." The wandering Jews
thought there must be some peculiar magic charm in the
name which Paul used. Especially Sceva's sons, consid-
ering nothing sacred which would add to their arts of deception, did not scruple at once to profane the name of
Jesus by pronouncing it over a demoniac. The demons
were subject neither to them nor indeed to Paul, but
only to Jesus. The authority of Jesus, used by Paul the
appointed servant of Jesus, they were forced to obey ;
but they scorned and defied the authority of wicked
men, who profanely tried to use even the holy name of
Jesus for their own purposes. In maddened frenzy,
the demoniac sprang upon the apostate priests, over-
powered and wounded them, and in violent rage drove
them naked from the house.

"The fearful result of the profane use of the holy
name of the Saviour soon became notorious throughout
Ephesus. Consternation and alarm took possession of
the minds of many : the name of the Lord Jesus began
to be reverenced and honored. The conscience of
' many that believed "[15] was moved by this testimony
against their magic arts ; and they came and made full
confession to the Apostle, and publicly acknowledged
and forsook their sorcery.

"The fear and conviction seems to have extended
beyond those who made a profession of Christianity.

[15] Or the words may mean, ' those who had previously believed.'

A large number of the sorcerers themselves openly re-nounced their practice; and they brought together the books that contained the mystic symbols and burnt them before all the people. When the volumes were consumed, they proceeded to reckon their price. Such books, from their very nature, would be costly; and all books of that age were vastly more expensive than the dearest books of our day. Hence we must not be sur-prised that the whole cost thus surrendered and sacri-ficed amounted to as much as nine thousand dollars.[16] This scene must have been long remembered at Ephe-sus. It was a strong proof of honest conviction on the part of the sorcerers and a striking witness of the triumph of Jesus Christ over the powers of darkness."

[16] The 'piece of silver' was doubtless the *drachma*, the Greek coin of the time: its value was about eighteen cents.

QUESTIONS.

WHY was Ephesus the meeting-place of many classes of men?

What was one class now in Ephesus?

How many men were there of this class?

Do you suppose they had seen Apollos?

What promise did Paul now fulfil?

What does 'upper coasts' mean?

What was Paul's question to these disciples?

Can men believe without receiving the Holy Spirit?

What answer did these disciples make?

Is the Holy Spirit a person or an influence?

Was it possible that these men could not have heard of *Divine influence?*

In whose name did the Apostle baptize?

What connection has the question about baptism with the former question?

How did John's baptism differ from this baptism?

Did John preach faith as well as penitence?

What two effects followed Paul's baptism?

What other manifestations were these effects like?

Why may we think Paul worked at his trade?

How many Sabbaths did Paul speak in the synagogue?

What was the result?

What friend received Paul? What was he?

Did Paul preach more or less often than before?

How long was he teaching in Tyrannus's school?

Who else heard the Gospel besides the Ephesians?

What other persons might have gone out of Ephesus?

Where are their names mentioned?

To what places may they have gone?

What description have we of Paul's life while residing in Ephesus?

Point out as many particulars of it as you can.

What was the one great lesson he taught?

(63)

Are repentance and faith to be exercised towards the same person (xx. 21) ?

What was the success of Paul's work in Ephesus ?

What confirmed the doctrines he preached ?

What two things was Ephesus famous for ?

How was magic connected with Diana?

What stories are told of these symbols ?

What books were written ? By whom ?

What magic-workers were at that time in Ephesus ?

What does 'vagabond' mean ?

What had been the tendency of the Jews ? for how long ?

What seven brothers ? Who was Sceva ?

What does '*special* miracles' mean ? What were these miracles ?

How did these miracles come into connection with the magic-workers ?

What did the magicians think the power of Paul consisted in ?

What is the meaning of 'adjuro' ?

What did the demoniac answer ?

What was the result throughout Ephesus ?

Is the 'many' in the eighteenth, the same as that in the nineteenth verse ?

What was the cost of the books burned ?

How do you account for this large cost ?

What did the whole occurrence prove ?

THE TEMPLE OF DIANA.

LESSON.
Acts xix. 21–34.

PAUL was never satisfied with one success in his Master's cause. When the Gospel was received by multitudes in one place, or when opposers, like Elymas the sorcerer of Paphos, or like the sons of Sceva at Ephesus, were overcome by some triumphant demonstration of God's power, Paul, confident and unwearied, pressed on to new journeys and new labors. The success of his first missionary journey with Barnabas only caused another and longer and more laborious journey to be planned. The greater success of the second journey with Silas, only led him to plan a third and more particular journey over all the same broad region. And now, here at Ephesus, on his third journey, we find him already thinking of a fourth missionary journey. The outline of Paul's plan of such a journey is given us. After again going over Macedonia and Achaia, and returning to Jerusalem with the collections for the poor, the great Apostle intends to make a fourth and still more extended journey, to Rome itself. What a different journey did he make to Rome when that time came! as a prisoner; and yet an Apostle and a preacher, though a prisoner! At present, however, Paul remained in Ephesus, to finish his work there, only sending forward Timothy and Erastus to visit the churches

of Macedonia. And while he remained, a remarkable
tumult took place in the city, connected with the worship of Diana. We need to know something more of
Ephesus and of Diana to understand it.

Ephesus had become "the chief city of Asia Minor,"
"the metropolis of the *province* of Asia," because it
was situated where it naturally received the trade of
the interior provinces, and because its admirable harbor
brought to it ships from all countries. To the north-
east, a road led through mountain defiles to Sardis and
to Phrygia. To the east, through a gorge, and then up
the valley of the crooked river Meander, went a branch
road of the great thoroughfare to the distant Euphrates,
through Iconium. Along these roads, and many smaller,
the slow and stately caravan of merchants wound, or
the petty traffickers of petty towns and villages brought
their goods for sale. From the north, from the west,
from the south and the east, from Smyrna and Troas,
from Philippi and Thessalonica, from Corinth and
Athens, from Miletus and Crete and Alexandria and
Antioch and Tarsus, came ships laden with merchandise to anchor in her harbors. Partly on a mountain-
slope, partly on a smaller, round-shaped hill, and partly
in the plain between these heights and the sea, were
the buildings of the city. The river Cayster flowed
through the plain in its winding channel to the sea. A
lake near its mouth made the inner harbor. Within
the walls, which stretched along the plain and up and
down the uneven surface of the mountain-slope, were
the principal public buildings. There was a forum with
its public buildings around the open space through which
the excited multitude "rushed up to the well-known
place of meeting." There was a gymnasium, between
the hill and the mountain, where wrestlers and racers
were trained for their contests. There were temples to

Jupiter and to Julius Cæsar. There was a vast theatre, with marble seats, one of the largest in the world, not far from the foot of the mountain. There were buildings for bathing.

But outside the walls, "one building surpassed all the rest in magnificence and in fame. This was the Temple of Diana, which glittered in brilliant beauty at the head of the harbor, and was reckoned by the ancients as one of the wonders of the world. The sun, it was said, saw nothing in its course more magnificent than Diana's Temple. Its immense foundations were carefully laid in the marshy ground," to prevent its being shaken by earthquake, it is said. Its walls were built of marble, from neighboring quarries. "All the Greek cities of Asia contributed to the building." Crœsus himself, the rich King of Lydia, helped to rear the idolatrous temple. The most distinguished architects directed the work. After many years, it reached its completion, and was then set on fire on the night in which Alexander was born. "It was rebuilt, with new and more sumptuous magnificence. The ladies of Ephesus gave their jewelry. Alexander the Great offered all the spoils of his triumphant eastern campaign, if he might inscribe his name on the walls. The Ephesians continually added new decorations and side buildings, with statues and pictures by the most famous artists." It was the Temple of Diana which gave fame to the city. "Oxford in England is not more Oxford on account of its University, than Ephesus was Ephesus on account of the Temple of Diana."[1] This temple was very different from what we now conceive a temple to be. Like other temples of the ancients, it was not roofed over, so as to receive an assembly of worship-

[1] Dr. Hodge.

pers, but consisted of several colonnades round the chamber in which the idol was. A great part of the space
was open to the sky. The graceful beauty of these columns was superior to anything the world had before
seen. Each column was the gift of a king, and the
number of them was one hundred and twenty-seven, of
which thirty-six were enriched with ornament and color.
The long rows of these graceful and beautiful columns,
sixty feet high, enclosed a space two or three times
larger than the largest churches of our cities, for the
temple was four hundred and twenty-five feet long, and
two hundred and twenty feet broad. "The folding-
doors were of cypress-wood; the part which was not
open to the sky was roofed over with cedar; and the
stair-case was formed of the wood of one single vine
from the island of Cyprus. The value and fame of the
temple were increased by the fact that it was the treas-
ury, in which a large portion of the wealth of western
Asia was laid up.[2] It is probable that there was no
religious building in the world, in which was centred
a greater amount of admiration, enthusiasm, and superstition."

It would naturally be supposed that the image within
this splendid temple would be a beautiful statue of the
goddess, like the statues of the Athenian Acropolis. It
was not so. The image of Diana was a rude figure
carved from wood, resembling more the ugly idols of
India, than the graceful statues of Greece. A woman's
form above, "terminated below in a shapeless block.
In each hand was a bar of metal. The dress was covered with mystic symbols, and the small chamber where
it stood, within the temple, was concealed by a curtain

---

[2] One modern writer says, "that the temple of the Ephesian Diana
was what the Bank of England is in the modern world."

in front." Such was the rude image which was worshipped with devout veneration at Ephesus. Like one of the statues of Minerva on the Acropolis at Athens, it was believed to have 'fallen from the sky.' And this belief added to the blind idolatry of the superstitious Ephesians.

The idolatrous pilgrims who came to the Temple of Diana, would like some memorial of their visit, some image of the goddess or model of her temple; and hence at Ephesus, as at other like idolatrous cities, another heathen custom grew up. Little images, either of the chamber in which the goddess dwelt, or of her magnificent temple, were made and sold to the changing crowd which thronged the streets. These were called 'shrines.' "They were carried in processions, on journeys and military expeditions, and sometimes set up as household gods in private houses. The material might be wood or gold or silver." Those mentioned in the Acts were made of silver. These had become scattered over the province, and borne up the roads into the interior, and carried away on ships sailing to almost every part of the known world.

We see now the cause of the excitement which Demetrius raised. The three years[3] of Paul's ministry in Ephesus were drawing to a close without any disturbance from the idolaters. Paul was too discreet a man to attack any person's occupation directly in this heathen city, although he preached as boldly as at Athens that the 'Godhead is not like to gold or silver or stone, graven with art and man's device.' "Paul's character had risen so high as to obtain influence over the wealthiest and most powerful persons in the place, and the interest of one of the prevalent trades was seriously

[3] xx. 31.

threatened." Demetrius gathered together his fellow silversmiths, and excited them against Paul. "He appealed first to their interest and then to their fanaticism." He told them their profitable business was in danger; and more than this, the temple of the great goddess Diana, (to which we can imagine him pointing as he spoke,) was in danger of being despised, and her honor and her worship, extending throughout their province of Asia and the civilized world, would soon be destroyed. His speech was like flame among straw. The crowd was instantly in a fury. In boisterous rage, they burst into a cry in honor of their goddess : 'Great is Diana of the Ephesians !' They soon filled the city with a tumult. Citizens and strangers were quickly excited by the violent outcries of this influential class of artisans. A general rush was made towards the theatre. Paul in some way escaped. But his travelling companions, Gaius and Aristarchus, were hurried off with the mob. As soon as Paul knew it, "a sense of the danger of his companions and a fearless zeal for the truth, urged him to hasten to the theatre and present himself before the people." His converts knew too well the violence of such a mob to permit him to run this hazard. Perhaps they would not have succeeded in preventing him, had not other influential friends interfered also. "And now is seen the advantage which is secured to a righteous cause by the upright character and unflinching zeal of its champion." Some of the leading men, who held the office of 'Presidents of the Games,'[4] at certain times of the year, had learned to respect Paul's character. "Whether converted or not,

---

[4] 'The chief of Asia' were ten men of wealth, who were annually elected to preside over the games, to provide the necessary expenses, and to maintain order. "They were men of high distinction and extensive influence."

they had a friendly feeling towards the Apostle; and well knowing the passions of an Ephesian mob when excited, they sent an urgent message to him to prevent him from venturing into the scene of disorder and danger. Then Paul reluctantly consented to remain in privacy, while the mob crowded violently into the theatre, filling the stone seats, tier above tier, and rending the air with their confused and fanatical cries." Never was a mob better described than when it is said 'the greater part knew not why they were come together.'

Why was *Alexander* 'put forward' to address the assembly? "It is most natural to suppose that the Jews were alarmed by the tumult, and anxious to clear themselves from blame, and to show they had nothing to do with Paul." The Jews, however, were enemies of idolatry, and the idolatrous crowd would not hear Alexander, but broke out into a wild, uproarious clamor, shouting and crying, especially around Gaius and Aristarchus, for two long hours, the name and the **praise** of their goddess.

QUESTIONS.

WHAT did the success of Paul's first journey lead him to do?
To what did the second journey lead?
What journey does Paul plan while on his third journey?
Did he accomplish what he designed?
Whom did he send on before him? Where?
What is the significance of '*so* he sent'?
What natural advantage had Ephesus in its location?
What routes by land? What by sea?
When was the city built?
What were the principal buildings within the city?
What are outside the walls?
What was thought and said of Diana's Temple?
How were its foundations laid? It was built of what?
Who helped build it? When burned?
How was it decorated?
How is Ephesus compared to Oxford?
Describe the form of the Temple.
How was its value increased?
With what great modern institution has it been compared?
What was the image of Diana?
Where was it placed?
Where did this image come from?
What other image had the same thing said of it?
What models of Diana's Temple were made at Ephesus?
Who bought them? For what?
What were they used for?
What were they made from? Carried where?
How long had Paul been in Ephesus?
Had he had any persecution?
Had he preached against idols?
What created the 'no small stir'?
What does the interference with this sale show in respect to Paul's character?
Whom did Demetrius gather?

What two things does he appeal to?
What did he tell them first?
What did he next refer to?
What is meant by 'almost throughout all Asia'?
What does the twenty-sixth verse show in respect to
    Paul's success in Ephesus?
What is meant by 'all the world'?
What was the effect of Demetrius' speech?
What was the meaning of their cry?
Why would the city soon become excited?
What building was filled?
Who were carried off by the crowd? Why?
Do you think Paul knew of the disturbance at the first?
Would Paul have withdrawn?
What did he now wish to do? Why?
Who prevented him? Why?
Who now proved Paul's friends?
Who were these men?
· By what name are they called in the Acts?
What message did they send? Why?
What few words describe this mob?
Why was Alexander 'put forward'?
Why wouldn't the crowd hear him?
What especially provoked their outcry?
Around whom would the clamor be loudest?

Thirty-fourth Sunday.

THE TOWN-CLERK OF EPHESUS.

LESSON.
Acts xix. 35–41.

ANOTHER person now appears among the excited multitude. We can see him making his way through the clamorous crowd to the stage of the theatre. And either because the excitement of the mob had worn itself out, or because the character and office of the man inspired respect, the uproar gradually died away at his appearance. It was the 'Town-Clerk' of the city. Whether we think of his official position or his character as shown by his speech, we have reason to say: "No one in the city was so well suited to calm this Ephesian mob."

Ephesus was a *free city*, like Thessalonica;[1] only the Romans were willing to pay *more* respect and honor to Ephesus than to Thessalonica. "Asia was always a favored province" with the Romans, and Ephesus was among the most favored of the Greek cities. The city had therefore its own magistrates, elected by the people. One of these magistrates was the 'Town-Clerk.' Perhaps the title of 'Chancellor' or of 'Recorder' or of 'Chief Magistrate' would have described better his office and duties. There is little doubt "that he was a magistrate of great authority in a high and very public position. He was the keeper of the state papers and of the city records; he read what was of public

---

[1] See page 153 in Twenty-third Sunday.

importance before the senate and assembly; he was present when money was deposited in the Temple of Diana; and when letters were sent to the people of Ephesus, they were officially addressed to him. Hence no magistrate was more before the public at Ephesus His very looks were familiar to all the citizens, and no one was so likely to calm and disperse an angry, excited multitude." When the multitude had grown sufficiently quiet to hear him, the Town-Clerk made a short address to them, which is an admirable model of candor, good-judgment, tact, and argument.

SPEECH OF THE TOWN-CLERK.

He presents four short, strong arguments against this turbulent excitement, every one of which is stronger than the preceding.

First Argument. (Verses 35, 36.) What man is he who does not know that Ephesus is temple-keeper[2] of the great goddess Diana? "The contradiction of a few insignificant strangers cannot affect what is notorious in all the world." 'Ye ought therefore to be quiet and do nothing rashly.'

Second Argument. (Verse 37.) These men whom you have brought here are not guilty of robbing or profaning the temple[3] nor of outraging our feelings by blaspheming our goddess. They have committed no crime against Diana. They have not even done anything to warrant this great and prolonged outcry about our goddess.

---

[2] See the margin. The word meant at first *temple-sweeper*, and was the title of the servant who took care of the temple. "It became afterwards a title of the greatest honor, and was eagerly appropriated by the most famous cities."

[3] 'Robbers of *churches*,' that is, of temples. The Greek word means '*temple-robbers*.'

Third Argument. (Verses 38, 39.) In respect to the complaint of Demetrius and the silver-smiths, why do they not make their accusation according to the regular course of law? If these men have done them injustice, there is a remedy provided. The Court is in session. There are the city magistrates—for the very purpose of trying such offenders. Or let them appeal to the pro-consul of the province!

Fourth Argument. (Verse 40.) This is the most forcible argument. Such an uproar as this puts our city and its freedom in peril. The government may call us to an account; and we have no excuse for this tumult. And you know what the Roman law is, against riotous assemblies of this kind, and the heavy penalty on us all for disobedience.

"So having rapidly brought his arguments to a climax, he calmed down the excited multitude and at once pronounced the legal words which declared the assembly dispersed." Demetrius and the silversmiths now saw *they* were in especial danger; for they had excited the tumult. The matter had gone perhaps farther than they intended. The people saw that they might be entangled also in an accusation against Demetrius. "The stone seats were gradually emptied. The uproar ceased, and the rioters dispersed to their various occupations and amusements." Thus God used the Greek and Roman authorities to protect Paul, in his perilous work of introducing the religion of Jesus into pagan and superstitious countries. The magistrates of Philippi had been compelled to respect his rights: the candid good sense of Gallio, the Pro-Consul of Corinth, had defeated Paul's persecutors: the eloquence of the Ephesian Town-Clerk had forced a riot against him and his fellow-travellers to disperse.

It would seem that this was one of the last occur-

rences of Paul's three year's residence. But before we
see him take his farewell, we must notice one other
important thing which no doubt occurred some time
during his stay in Ephesus. This was the writing of
The First Epistle to the Corinthians. Among other
reasons why we suppose this letter was written while
Paul was in Ephesus are four :

First. Paul spoke of *remaining* at Ephesus when he
wrote the letter.[4] The letter could not have been written *after* he left Ephesus.

Secondly. Apollos had been in *Corinth.*[5] Paul could
not have well known this *before* he reached Ephesus :
so that the letter must have been written after he came
down from the ' upper coasts ' and found that Apollos
had gone over to Corinth.[6]

Thirdly. Aquila and Priscilla were with him when
he wrote it.[7] It is clear that they resided in Ephesus.[8]

Fourthly. There was constant communication across
the sea from Ephesus to Corinth. And Paul was in
Ephesus about three years. Paul must have heard
often from Corinth. It seems therefore most natural
to suppose that he wrote at this time to the Corinthians.[9]

Indeed it is not only probable that Paul *wrote* this
letter to the Corinthian Church, but that he *visited*
Corinth while at Ephesus ; for when he wrote his
second letter to the Corinthians, shortly after he left
Ephesus, he said that he was now coming a *third* time

---

[4] I. Corinth. xvi. 8.
[5] Acts xix. 1.
[6] Acts xviii. 18, 19, 26.

[5] i. 12 ; iii. 4, 22.
[7] I. Corinth. xvi. 19.

[9] The ancient inscription (see the end of the Epistle) says this letter was written at Philippi. Apply the above reasons, and see what
you think

to them.[10]   If he was on his way to a *third* visit, when
he left Ephesus, then there must have been a *second*,
before he left Ephesus.   No doubt Apollos or some other
Christian had come across to Ephesus from Corinth
and told Paul of the state of things among the Corinthian Christians.   He had much to tell which was joyful
and hopeful; but much also which was painful; for
shameful sins had crept into the church.   There were
tares among the wheat.   Corinth was a most corrupt
and vicious city; and Corinthian Christians had become defiled like Christian unbelievers.   If Paul made
them a visit at this time, it was to correct and to admonish the Corinthian believers for their sins.

After his return to Ephesus from this *second* journey,
(if the supposition is right,) we suppose he sent Timothy and Erastus on before him to Macedonia; and
then after some time had passed, 'some members of the
household of Chloe, a distinguished family at Corinth,
arrived;' and from them Paul learned more fully what
was the state of things in the church of Corinth.[11]   Another evil had sprung up.   The church had become divided into parties.   There was a Paul-party, an Apollos-
party, a Peter-party, and even a Christ-party.[11]   Some
professed believers had become vilely and shamelessly
impure in their life.   Some were showing their want of
brotherly love by prosecuting their brethren in the heathen courts of law.   Some, who had gone back into open
immorality, had even begun to doubt the resurrection
of the dead.

And therefore Paul writes to them

THE FIRST EPISTLE TO THE CORINTHIANS.

And therefore do we find, among other subjects, that
four of the great subjects about which Paul writes are:

---

[10] II. Corinth. xii. 14; xiii. 1.   [11] I. Corinth. i. 11–13.

1. Their divisions into parties. He wishes and tries to have them do away with these. (Chapter i. 10–13; iii. 3–9, 21–23; iv. 6.)

II. Their permission of shameless immorality. (Chapter v. 11.)

III. Their legal prosecutions of each other, (chapter vi. 1, 5–7,) while they ought to exercise brotherly love (or *charity*) towards each other. (Chapter xiii.)

IV. The resurrection of the dead. (Chapter xv.)

In the conclusion of the letter, he directed the Corinthians to make collections for their poor Christian brethren in Judea, and to have these collections ready for him when he came, so that he might take them to Jerusalem.[12] He tells them also that he is expecting to visit Macedonia,[13] and that perhaps he will spend the winter in Corinth,[14] that he has sent the youthful Timothy on before him, and if he came to Corinth to give him no cause of fear,[15] that Aquila and Priscilla and the believers who assemble in their house, as at Corinth, send their salutations and Christian love,[16] and that he sends his own salutations and love.[17]

[12] xvi. 1–3. [13] xvi. 5. [14] xvi. 6.
[15] xvi. 10; iv. 17. [16] xvi. 19. [17] xvi. 21, 24.

QUESTIONS.

WHAT person now makes his appearance ?

What place would he take to speak ?

Why would the uproar die away ?

How was Ephesus like Thessalonica ?

Which city did the Romans respect the more ?

Did the Romans appoint the magistrates in Ephesus ?

What other name might be substituted for 'Town-Clerk' ?

What were the duties of his office ?

Would the multitude know him when they saw him ?

How many arguments does the Town-Clerk present ?

What was the object of his arguments ?

What was the first argument ?

What is the meaning of 'worshipper' or 'temple-keeper' ?

Explain the meaning of the thirty-sixth verse.

What was the second argument ?

What is the meaning of 'robbers of churches' ?

What was the third argument ?

What is meant by 'the law is open' ?

Who were the deputies ?

What is the fourth argument ?

Who might 'call them in question' ?

What were they in danger of ?

Who would be responsible for the riotous assembly ?

Which of these arguments is the strongest ? Which the weakest ?

What was done by the Town-Clerk after he finished his speech ?

What did Demetrius now see ?

Compare Paul's escapes at Philippi, at Corinth, at Ephesus.

What other thing probably occurred while Paul resided in Ephesus ?

How many reasons were given for this supposition?

What is the first reason?

Before what time must it have been written?

What is the second reason?

How do you know he had been there?

After what time must it have been written then?

What is the third reason?

How do you know they were living in Ephesus?

What is the fourth reason?

What makes it probable that Paul *visited* Corinth during these three years?

What persons brought news to Paul from Corinth?

What evils had sprung up in the Corinthian church?

What is the first of four great subjects in this Epistle? the second? the third? the fourth?

What is the subject of the thirteenth chapter of this Epistle?

What is the subject of the fifteenth?

What direction does Paul give in the conclusion?

To what other church had he given this order?

When was it to be made?

How was it to be sent?

What does Paul write in respect to his visiting them?

What about Timothy? Aquila and Priscilla?

(68)

TITUS, THE MESSENGER.

LESSON.

ACTS xx. 1, 2; II. CORINTHIANS ii. 12, 13; vii. 5–7.

PAUL'S work was now finished in Ephesus. At least
he thought it best to remain no longer. His presence
might be the cause of new excitement and perhaps of
trouble or of persecution to others than himself; and
as there were now many who could teach and preach
the doctrines of Jesus, the good work could be carried
on without him. He therefore called the disciples together, and affectionately bade them farewell. How
much had been accomplished during the three years!
There had been many converts : a large church had been
established : enemies had been convinced : many had
ceased to worship Diana : the sale of shrines had de-
creased : the whole province of Asia had heard the
word of God : perhaps it was at this very time that
the other six of the seven churches of Asia[1] were
founded. (See map on page 127.)

After the affectionate parting between Paul and the
Christians of Ephesus, we are told very little of Paul's
labors during nine or ten months. All the notice we
have of this period in the Acts is in the first two verses
of the twentieth chapter. We have, however, many
hints given us in his letters in regard to his journey,
his visits, and his labors. We shall soon see that the
second epistle to the Corinthian Christians was written

[1] Revelation i. 11.

from Philippi, and therefore from that epistle we are able to learn about Paul's second journey from Asia into Macedonia.

Who were Paul's fellow-travellers now from Ephesus to Macedonia? Timothy we have supposed was with him from Antioch to Ephesus. But he had sent Timothy on before him.[2] Two disciples from Asia are mentioned when he returns from Corinth,[3] and one of them was an Ephesian.[4] They both continued faithful friends of Paul in his journeys and labors afterwards.[5] Even when Paul was prisoner in Rome he mentions these two natives of Asia as his ready helpers and followers.[6] These are Tychicus and Trophimus. It is not unlikely that they were with Paul on the way from Ephesus to Macedonia and Greece.

Paul stopped at Troas[7] on his way. If he went by ship, he sailed again among the islands of the Archipelago, and at length anchored in that harbor from which he went before, 'in a straight course' to Samothrace.[8] Before, he had been forbidden by the Holy Spirit to preach here,[9] but now his preaching was successful. The way was open for him to do great good. He evidently intended to remain longer in Troas, but he was greatly troubled in spirit because *Titus* did not meet him there as he expected. Titus, it will be remembered, was the Greek who was not circumcised at the council of Jerusalem; and it is supposed that Paul sent him from Ephesus to Corinth[9] on an errand to the church, in part if not wholly to make ready the collec-

---

[2] Acts xix. 22.   [3] xx. 4.   [4] xxi. 29.
[5] xxi. 29; Ephesians vi. 21; Colossians iv. 7; Titus iii. 12.
[6] He mentions them in II. Timothy iv. 12, 20; and that Paul was in Rome when he wrote that epistle, see chapter i. verse 17.
[7] II. Corinthians ii. 12, 13.   [8] Acts xvi. 6, 8, 11.
[9] II. Corinthians xii 18; vii. 13.

tions for the poor in Judea. Paul, before he left Ephesus, had no doubt expected to hear from Titus an account of the condition of the Corinthian church, but as
the uproar in the theatre led him to depart sooner than
he had anticipated, and before Titus returned, he left
word for Titus to join him on his journey. Paul grew
most anxious at Troas to see Titus, and to learn how the
Corinthian Christians had received his advice and his
rebukes. " He had resolved to wait for Titus at Troas,
expecting he would come soon. He was disappointed:
week after week passed, but Titus did not come. It
was to be hoped that he would bring news of the triumph of good over evil at Corinth; yet it might not
be so. The Corinthians might have forsaken the faith
of their first teacher, and have rejected his messenger.
Paul appears to have suffered all the sickness of hope
deferred. 'My spirit had no rest, because I found not
Titus my brother.'" His anxiety did not prevent his
preaching. In the synagogue as usual, and first to the
Jews no doubt, he preached 'Christ's Gospel'—the glad
news of the Messiah. Some, if not many, were ready
to hear. "And the foundation of a church was laid
which we shall find him revisiting not long afterwards."
But now his anxiety about the more important Corinthian church and the importance of meeting Titus urged
him on. Embarking, therefore, and 'loosing from Troas,'
and sailing over the waters of the upper Archipelago,
past the familiar islands and jutting points and moun-
tain-heights, he came again to Neapolis, and from thence
to Philippi.[10]

Here were warm friends for the Apostle: the simple-
hearted Lydia with her open house, only too glad to

---

[10] As one of the objects of Paul's visit was to make collections for
the poor Christians of Judea, he would not pass by a church so important as that of Philippi.

receive him: the brethren who had assembled in Lydia's house to bid Paul farewell: the jailer and his family. Some or all of these, and others who had since believed, were full of joy and of cordial affection. "For of all the churches which he founded, the Philippians seem to have been the most free from fault and most attached to Paul." When Paul wrote his epistle to them afterwards, he finds no fault, but highly praises them; and so ardent was their love for Paul that they had sent to him gifts to cheer and to support him.[11] But even all their warmth of affection and tender kindness did not take away the gloom from Paul's mind. He himself says, that when he 'came into Macedonia,' he 'had no rest,' he was 'troubled on every side,' he had 'fightings without' and 'fears within.' It was the time perhaps, more than any other in his life, when Paul seemed to be weighed down by his afflictions, and more than all, by anxiety from the 'daily care of all the churches.'[12] But how nobly and bravely he triumphed over all his afflictions and anxieties!

"At length the long-expected Titus arrived at Philippi and relieved Paul's anxiety by better news than he had hoped to hear. The most of the Corinthian Christians had yielded to Paul's advice and rebuke, and shown the deepest sorrow for the sins into which they had fallen." They had ceased to permit the gross, open immoralities. They had already made in part at least their collections for the poor believers of Palestine.

But there were a few who did not submit with the rest of the church. They were louder and more bitter than ever in their tone against the Apostle. They were even ready to charge that he was selfish in making the collections, insinuating most probably that he had some

---

[11] Philippians iv. 15, 16.   [12] II. Corinthians xi. 28.

selfish interest in this plan of raising money and gifts
for others. "The same opponents accused him also of
vanity and of cowardly weakness: they declared that he
was continually threatening without striking and promising without performing; always on his way to Co
rinth, but never venturing to come; and that he was
as fickle in his teaching as in his practice; refusing to
circumcise Titus, yet circumcising Timothy; a Jew
among the Jews and a Gentile among the Gentiles."
It would seem, also, that there were unkind compari-
sons made between Paul and other religious teachers in
Corinth.

Having received this information from Titus, Paul
directed Titus to return and to continue the collections
in the churches of Achaia. And he sends by him another letter, not addressed as the first epistle had been,
simply to Corinth, but to all the churches in the province of Achaia; perhaps in Athens and Cenchræa, in
Argos and Sicyon and Megara. The object of the
Apostle was to encourage and calm the larger number
of the believers; and, at the same time, to warn and
denounce those who despised his Apostolic authority
and the commands of the Messiah.

SECOND EPISTLE TO THE CORINTHIANS.

Among the many subjects in respect to which this
epistle was written, we may notice,

I. Thanksgiving for deliverance from great danger in
'Asia,' probably in Ephesus. (Chapter i. 3, 4, 8–10.)

II. The reason for postponing his visit to Corinth.
(Chapter i. 15, 16, 23.)

III. Forgiveness to those who grieve for their immorality. (Chapter ii. 10.)

IV. His distress at not hearing from them by Titus.
(Chapter ii. 12, 13; vii. 5.)

V. His joy at the good news Titus brought. (Chapter vii. 6–9, 13, 16.)

VI. Directions for the collections. The example of the Macedonians ought to teach them how to give. (Chapter viii. 1–4, 6 ; ix. 6, 7.)

VII. Answer to those who were bitter against him, (chapter x. 1, 2, 10, 11 ; xi. 18, 22–31,) and to those who denied his Apostleship. (Chapter xii. 11, 12.)

VIII. Warning of punishment to those who were not penitent for sin. (Chapter xii. 20, 21 ; xiii. 1, 2.)

Any·one who reads this Epistle carefully through, will find two whole chapters (viii. ix.) devoted to the subject of the collection. It was a thing of great importance in Paul's mind, not only because he wished all believers to be generous, but because he saw that generosity exercised by the Gentiles abroad towards the Jews at Jerusalem would bind both Jews and Gentiles together in Christian love, and so prevent that foolish and wicked division in the church to which they were so liable.

Titus, the earnest-minded Greek disciple, bore this epistle to his Corinthian countrymen. When the Apostle 'exhorted' him to do it, he 'went of his own accord.' Some brother whose name we do not know, but whose praise was 'throughout all the churches,'[1] went with Titus to Corinth,

---

[1] II. Corinthians viii. 16–18.

QUESTIONS.

WHY was it best for Paul to leave Ephesus?

   State as many things as you can which were accomplished during the three years.

How long a time is passed over in these two verses of the twentieth chapter?[1]

   Where have we any particulars given in respect to this period?

   Where was the second letter to the Corinthians written?

Who were fellow-travellers of Paul into Macedonia?

   What had become of Timothy?

   Where were Tychicus and Trophimus, Paul's faithful friends afterwards?

What place did Paul stop at?

   What had he been forbidden to do, when at Troas before?

   What was the prospect in his preaching now?

   What is meant by 'a door was opened unto me,' etc.?

   What troubled Paul?

Who was Titus? Where mentioned first before?

   Where is it supposed that Paul had sent him?

   On what errand had he sent him?

   What word had Paul probably left at Ephesus for Titus?

Why was Paul so anxious to see Titus?

   What is meant by '*Christ's* Gospel'?

   How was it right for Paul to leave Troas, when there were such prospects of good from preaching?

Why is it probable that Paul now went directly to Philippi?

   Whom did he see there?

   How did the Philippian church compare with other churches?

   What was the state of Paul's mind?

   What especially weighed him down?

   Had Paul good reason to be downcast?

[1] A note in the next lesson will show how this time is reckoned.

Did he yield to it, so as to give way before it?
What was the effect of the arrival of Titus?

What news did he bring from Corinth?
What was the state of a few in Corinth?
What direction did Paul give immediately to Titus?
What letter did he send by him?
To whom is this letter directed?
What other churches were there besides that in Corinth?
What were the two objects of this letter?

Turn to this Epistle and point out his thanks for escape from peril.

Show the reason for putting off his visit to Corinth, (twenty-third verse especially.)
Show his forgiveness towards his enemies.
Point out his distress at the absence of Titus.
Show his joy at the coming of Titus.
What are his directions for the collections?
What was the example of Macedonia?
What did he say to his opposers?
What answer to the deniers of his Apostleship?
What were the 'signs of an Apostle'?
What warning against the impenitent church members, (xiii. 2 especially)?

What was one thing of great importance in Paul's mind?
How many chapters are given to the subject?
Why was it of so much importance?
Who went with Titus?

(70)

Thirty-sixth Sunday.

SIX MONTHS IN MACEDONIA AND ILLYRICUM.

LESSON.

ACTS xx. 2, 3.

AFTER Titus had gone, Paul still continued in the regions to the north of Greece. As he must have been ten months at least in going from Ephesus to Corinth and back to Philippi, and as only three months of this time were spent in Corinth, seven months at least[1] must have been spent on the journey to and from Corinth, and the greater part of the seven months must have been passed in Macedonia or Illyricum. Paul might have wished that the Corinthians should have full time to consider his letter before he reached Corinth. He might have desired to avoid any further bitterness or excitement in his opposers, till they should have considered his warnings and should have had space for repentance. He had more than time, therefore, to visit the churches of Philippi, Thessalonica, and Berea. As a Roman citizen with established rights, he could quietly instruct the Philippian believers. Perhaps he preached now in Amphipolis and Apollonia. No mob of idlers forced him again to leave Jason's

---

[1] From Pentecost (I. Corinthians xvi. 8) in May till 'the days of un-leavened bread,' (Acts xx. 6,) that is, the Passover in the next March, was ten months. Three months in Corinth leaves seven months on the road. If Paul left Ephesus before Pentecost in May, on account of the uproar in the theatre, the time must have been longer

house in Thessalonica. When he reached Corinth, he wrote to Rome that he had ' fully preached the Gospel of Christ round about unto Illyricum.'[2] It is most likely, therefore, that this was the time when he went to the prominent cities of Macedonia, as far as the very boundaries of Illyricum, or when he even preached in the towns of Illyricum. All this may reasonably be included in the words, ' when he had gone over those parts and given them much exhortation.' If this is true, then he would naturally follow the great road west from Thessalonica. And this time he must have climbed the mountains towards Edessa, from which he looked down on the broad and beautiful valley of the Axius. In Edessa he may have preached, and in other cities, till he came even to Dyrrachium, from which place he might have been ferried across to Italy.[3] On the west side, as on the east side of the Adriatic Sea, it was the same road which led to Rome. Whether Paul went into those distant regions, or never passed over the mountain boundary of Macedonia, there was enough to occupy his time till he deemed it best to turn his footsteps southward towards Greece.

" During his stay at Ephesus, and in all parts of his journey in Troas and Macedonia, his heart had been continually at Corinth. He had been in frequent communication with his inconsistent and rebellious converts." He had written them letters. He had sent messengers and messages. He had probably made them a visit. Now there were even more than ever urgent reasons why he should be in Corinth. His second letter had reached them some time before. His presence would be of great service in aiding the well-disposed and in restraining the evil-minded. He wished to receive the collections for the poor Christians of

---

[2] Romans xv. 19.   [3] See map on page 146.

Judea, so that he could take them with him on his return to Jerusalem.

If the calculation which has been made in respect to the length of time during which Paul was on the way from Ephesus to Corinth is correct, then it must now have been near the winter season. It was in November or December that Paul and his fellow-travellers turned southward, taking no doubt Berea in their course; "and this makes it likely that he went by land rather than by sea." (See the frontispiece map.) We know the ancient ship-masters did not like to venture out on the boisterous winter seas.[4] "A good road to the south had long been formed from the neighborhood of Berea, connecting the chief towns of Macedonia with those of Achaia. Opportunities would not be wanting for preaching the Gospel at every stage of his journey; and we may infer either that churches were formed in every chief city between Thessalonica and Corinth, or that the glad tidings had been unsuccessfully proclaimed."

"It was probably already winter when Paul once more beheld in the distance the lofty citadel, towering above the isthmus which it commands. The gloomy season must have harmonized with his feelings as he approached. The clouds which hung round the summit of the Acro-Corinthus and cast their shadow upon the city below, typified the mists of vice and error which darkened the minds even of its Christian citizens. Paul knew that, for some of them, he had labored in vain. He was returning to converts who had become immoral: to friends who had forgotten his love: to enemies who denied his apostolic authority. It is true the most of the Corinthian Christians had repented of their worst sins; yet even towards the penitent he could not feel all the con-

---

[4] Acts xxvii. 9.

fidence of earlier affection. And there were still left a few obstinate ones, who would not give up their habits of impurity, and who, when he spoke to them of righteousness and judgment to come, replied by openly defending their sins or by denying his authority. He now came prepared to put down this opposition with the utmost decision. He was resolved to cast out of the church these opposers of truth and goodness, just as, in the exercise of his apostolic authority, he had warned them a few months before, ' when I come again, I will not spare.'[8] His weapons are not now carnal, as when he went with horsemen and spearmen to Damascus, but spiritual, ' mighty through God to pull down the strongholds ' of his wicked enemies.

As Paul came along the isthmus road, looking out now on one sea, now on the other, and perhaps from some height catching a view of Athens, his thoughts must have gone back to happier times : when after landing at Cenchræa, discouraged from his ill-success at Athens, in a few short months a large church had been gathered in Corinth : when God visited him in a vision and promised him ' much people in this city :' when no persecutors nor opposers succeeded against him. From this busy, wicked, polluted city God had gathered a great number to be his children. " Hundreds of believers now called on the name of Jesus, who, when he first came to Corinth, worshipped nothing but gods like their own ambition and anger and lust. It was painful to think their conversion so incomplete that they were still defiled by heathen pollutions, but the most of them had repented ; the obstinate ones were few ; and if the older ones were tied by chains of habit, the children might be trained up in the service of the Lord. Such

---

[8] II. Corinthians xiii. 2.

may have been some of Paul's thoughts, as his little
company drew near the city walls and entered the well-
known gates. And what thoughts of the faithful brethren thronged their minds, of Erastus the Treasurer,[6] of
Stephanas and Epenetus,[7] of Fortunatus and Achaicus,[8]
of Gaius,[6] as they threaded their way amid the noise
and bustle of the crowded streets. Aquila and Priscilla
were not there to open their doors to Paul, (we shall
soon find they had returned to Rome,) but the hospitable Gaius, who was ever ready to entertain his believing brethren,[9] received the Apostle into his house.

It is supposed that at Corinth Paul received news
from the churches in Galatia : that painful tidings had
come across the Ægean from Ephesus concerning the
condition of the Galatian Christians which aroused his
astonishment and his indignation. "His converts there
were forsaking his teaching in respect to obeying the
customs and rites of Moses' law,[10] and were listening to
false missionaries from Palestine, who, like those who
had once come down to Antioch, said that they could
not be saved unless they were circumcised and kept the
law of Moses.[11]   They said, too, like the party hostile to
Paul in Corinth, that Paul was not an Apostle, "for he
had not, like the twelve Apostles, been a follower of
Jesus on earth : that he was only a teacher sent out by
authority of the Twelve, and his teaching was to be received only so far as it agreed with theirs."   And so
the Galatian Christians, more simple-minded than the
Christians of Corinth or of Ephesus, were being troubled
about that 'difficult question'[12] which had been care-

---

[6] Romans xvi. 23.   [7] Romans xvi. 5 ; I. Corinthians xvi. 15.
[8] I. Corinthians xvi. 17.
[9] Romans xvi. 23.   'Gaius mine host and *of the whole church.*'
[10] Circumcision, washings, unclean meats, etc.   [11] Acts xv. 1, 5
[12] See Fifteenth Sunday.

fully and emphatically decided by all the Apostles at the council of Jerusalem.[13] Some of them were even being circumcised, and were trying to keep the law of Moses.

Paul therefore wrote a most earnest letter to the Galatians, in which sadness and severity mingle, the sadness of a warm-hearted man who finds his friends leaving him, and the severity of a faithful Apostle who finds his converts leaving the truth.

THE EPISTLE TO THE GALATIANS.

Notice two of the principal subjects in this letter:

I. Paul proves that he is an Apostle independent of the Twelve.

1. Because he received his authority to preach by revelation from Jesus the Messiah. (i. 1, 11, 12.)

2. Because he was made an Apostle without consulting at all with the other Apostles. After his conversion he did not go to Jerusalem to be taught, but into Arabia. (i. 15–17.)

3. Because he saw only the two Apostles, James and Peter, for fifteen days, when he was in Jerusalem the first time after his conversion, and could not therefore have been made an Apostle by the assembly of *all* the other Apostles. (i. 18, 19.)

4. Because when he went up to the council at Jerusalem, James, Peter, and John recognized him as the Apostle to the Gentiles. (ii. 1, 7–10.)

5. Because he himself by Apostolical authority had rebuked the Apostle Peter at Antioch. (ii. 11–14.)

II. Paul shows that obedience to Jesus and faith in him, and not obedience to the law of Moses, is to save a man. (iii. 1, 2, 10, 26.) He who goes back to the law of Moses is a *slave:* he who believes in Jesus is a *son.* (iv. 1–7.)

---

* See Sixteenth Sunday.

QUESTIONS.

SHOW how Paul must have been ten months on the way from Ephesus to Corinth, and from Corinth back to Philippi.

> How long, then, must he have been in Macedonia and Illyricum?
>
> Why might Paul have delayed his visit to Corinth?
>
> What was there to occupy his time so long?
>
> Why may we suppose this is the time when he preached 'round about unto Illyricum'?
>
> What is meant by 'those parts'?
>
> Show where Paul may have gone.
>
> To what country did Titus afterwards go?

What shows that Corinth had been much in his thoughts?

> What two especial reasons why he should now press on to Corinth?
>
> Why is it likely that he now went by land to Corinth?
>
> What opportunities to preach on the way?

What sad thoughts would be natural for Paul as he approached Corinth?

> Converts? friends? enemies?
>
> The penitent? the obstinate?
>
> What was he prepared to do?
>
> How does this journey compare with Saul's journey to Damascus?

What happy thoughts would be natural also?

> Church? vision? 'much people'?
>
> The imperfect? the obstinate? the children?
>
> Of whom did Paul and his friends think, when they entered the streets?
>
> To whose house did Paul go?

What news did Paul probably receive at Corinth?

> What were these converts doing?
>
> To whom were they listening?
>
> What did they say about Paul's Apostleship?
>
> What 'difficult question' was giving them trouble?

What epistle did Paul now write ?

What two things mingle in it ?

Sadness of whom ? severity of whom ?

What is the first of two principal subjects in this Epistle ?

Could a man become an Apostle who was not one of the twelve Apostles ?

Turn to the Epistle and show where Paul declares his authority came directly from the Saviour.

What is the second reason why he was an independent Apostle ?

How does he prove that he was not made an Apostle by the election of all the Apostles ?

What is the fourth reason ?

What is meant by 'perceived the grace that was given unto me' ?

What is meant by 'the right hand of fellowship' ?

What is the fifth reason why he is an independent Apostle ?

What is the second of two principal subjects in this Epistle ?

Is *all* of the law of Moses done away ?

Can a man have faith in Jesus who does not keep the Ten Commandments ?

If a man lives a strictly moral life, by these laws of Moses, can he not be saved without faith ?

Is there any power in faith itself to save a man ?

Is there any power in works to save a man ?

Why is a man a *slave* who lives according to *all* the law of Moses ?

How is he a *son* who lives by faith on Jesus ?

Thirty-seventh Sunday.

PHŒBE CARRIES A LETTER TO ROME.

LESSON.

Acts xx. 3; xix. 21. Romans i. 8, 11, 13, 15; xv. 19, 20, 23-26, 28; xvi.

WHEN the messenger who bore the letter to the Galatians had gone, Paul resolutely set himself to work to accomplish the objects for which he came. It has been supposed that he established his authority as an Apostle beyond all dispute, and to the dismay of those who denied it, by showing 'the signs of an Apostle,'[1] that is, by working miracles. But it is hardly necessary to suppose miracles were wrought. The solemn presence of the Spirit of God could overpower all opposition, and demonstrate to the conviction even of enemies, Paul's claim, nay, his absolute duty to be an Apostle. The wilful and stubborn and immoral members of the church were no doubt brought before the solemn assembly of the church for trial: the presence of the Holy Spirit and the power of the Lord Jesus, were sought in prayer: the worst offenders, those whose open and shameless sins required so heavy a punishment, were publicly cast out of the church, as Paul had directed when he wrote them.[2]

Paul was three months in Corinth. The writing of the letter to the Galatians, and the discipline of immoral church-members, must have consumed some little time. When these were done, he visited, doubt-

---

[1] II. Corinth. xii. 12.   [2] I. Corinth. v. 3-5

less, the neighboring churches. As his letter from Philippi was addressed to the Christians of Achaia as well as of Corinth,[3] it seems that the churches throughout the province had the same faults as that at Corinth. While therefore he went from church to church, in Argos, in Sicyon, in Megara, in Cenchræa or in other places, he encouraged the good and corrected the bad. Some of the Corinthian brethren went with him perhaps; Gaius, or Stephanas, or Fortunatus, on some of these excursions. At the same time, the collections for the Christians in Judea were gathered from these places. Considerable money must have been gathered, for they had been laying by their gifts a year or more.[4] The whole sum collected was now intrusted to Paul, or else to certain persons appointed, as Paul had directed,[5] to carry their donation to Jerusalem.

We suppose that it was sometime during this three months that a Christian lady of Cenchræa left Corinth to go to Rome. She was a lady of position and of some wealth, for she was a patron or helper[6] of many Christians, Paul among the number. She was also a deaconess in the church of Cenchræa.[7] Her name was Phœbe, and she was about to sail to Rome upon some private busi-

[3] II. Corinth. i. 1.
[4] II. Corinth. ix. 2; I. Corinth. xvi. 2.
[5] I. Corinth. xvi. 3.
[6] In Romans xvi. 2, the word 'succorer' means in the Greek, a *chief* person, a *patron*, one who stands before another: when applied to men, a *front-rank* man. The fact that she had business at Rome also shows that she must have possessed some little property.
[7] In Romans xvi. 1, the word 'servant' is the same which in other places is translated *deacon*. It here means *deaconess*, an office which the separation of women from men in the East made necessary. The deaconess was an experienced and respected woman, who had charge of the sick and poor women, as the deacons did of the poor and sick men.

ness. We know Paul was intending to visit Rome in his next journey.[8] We know that he was already acquainted with some of the Christians of Rome. He therefore took this opportunity to send a letter to these Roman Christians. Paul may have been on one of his visits to Cenchræa, when he delivered his letter, ready prepared, to Phœbé, or Phœbe may have come over from the eastern sea-port of Corinth, Cenchræa, to the western sea-port, Lecheum, which was much nearer to Rome. She then passed through Corinth, and took in charge

PAUL'S EPISTLE TO THE ROMANS.[9]

Although Paul had not been in Rome, he had reason to think very highly of the Christians there.[10] The church at Rome seems already to have grown large and flourishing. Rome was so constantly in communication with all parts of the empire, especially towards the east, that it would have been strange if some believers had not found their way there. There were 'strangers of Rome' at Jerusalem some years before, when Peter preached at the Pentecost.[11] Some of these Romans may have been among the 'three thousand' converts that day, and on their return may have preached the doctrines of Jesus.

There is no reason to suppose an Apostle had been in Rome. We know Paul had not, and we know too that Paul was very careful not to interfere unasked with work which another man, especially another Apostle, had begun.[12] Certainly Peter could not have been in Rome at this time, or even before this, without Paul

---

[8] Acts xix. 21.

[9] It is generally agreed that the inscription at the end of the Epistle to the Romans is correct. See it.

[10] 'Your faith is spoken of throughout the whole world.' Romans i. 8.

[11] Acts ii. 10, 41.   [1] Romans xv. 20.

taking some notice of it in this letter. Paul was too
earnest and too warm in his feelings not to make some
allusion to his fellow-Apostle, if he was there; but,
among the many names mentioned in this epistle, the
name of Peter does not once occur.

Were these Roman Christians Jews or Gentiles?
From many of Paul's expressions in this letter, it seems
that the most of them were Gentiles. Yet as the Jews
were in all large cities, and would be in unusual numbers in the capital of the empire, and as there are Jewish names among those to whom Paul sends his greeting in Rome, we must suppose that there was a goodly
number of Jews also in the Roman church.

To this church of mingled Jews and Greeks and
Romans, Paul wrote his epistle. Unlike his letters to
the Thessalonians, to the Corinthians, and to the Galatians, this letter to the Romans is a long and careful
and learned discussion of the great doctrines of the new
religion which Jesus the Messiah had introduced. Paul
had not been in Rome, as he had been in Galatia, Thessalonica, and Corinth; and therefore he was not so well
acquainted with the Romans as he was with the Galatians and Thessalonians and Corinthians. He himself
had not founded the church in Rome, as he had these
others. And for these reasons, the epistle has few allusions to himself, and has less of that warm affectionate-
ness which breathes and throbs all through these other
loving letters. Still, although he is not acquainted
with the great majority of the Roman Christians, he
tells them that 'he longs to see them,' that 'he had
often intended to visit them, but had been prevented,'
that 'he wanted to preach in Rome,' as well as in Corinth and Ephesus.

He then discusses the one great subject, in which
both the Jews and Gentiles of the Roman church would

be deeply interested: *That Jews and Gentiles are both
equal* in the kingdom of God, *through faith in Jesus
the Messiah:* that *both are sinners: both need a Saviour:* that JESUS OF NAZARETH, THE MESSIAH, *is equally a* SAVIOUR *for both, if they both have faith in him.*

Near the end of this letter, he told them that although
they were strangers, he had 'written boldly, because
God had made him the Apostle to the Gentiles.' [13]

And now we see that the great heart of the Apostle
was not to be satisfied with making Rome the end of
his next journey, but that he had already extended his
plan to the very distant end of the Roman empire. His
plan now was, after he had returned to Jerusalem, to
make his fourth journey reach to *Spain.* And therefore
he promised to the Romans that ' when he should take
his journey to Spain, he would make them that visit
which for many years he had longed to make.' As he
was just about to start with his collections for Jerusalem, he said nothing to the Romans about making collections. He probably hoped to teach them Christian
liberality, as he had the other churches, when he should
make his visit.

And then, at the end of the epistle, there is a chapter
of kind remembrances sent to his friends, which shows
that Paul was not only the Christian Apostle, but the
Christian gentleman. How kindly he recommends
Phœbe, the deaconess of Cenchræa, to their attention
and assistance. How affectionately and gratefully he
sends his greetings to Priscilla and Aquila. · Wherever
these good people were, at Corinth, at Ephesus, or at
Rome,[14] their house was always open for the assembly
of Christians; and once at least, probably at Ephesus,

[13] xv. 15, 16.
[14] Acts xviii. 2, 3 ; I. Corinth. xvi. 19 ; Romans xvi. 3.

they were willing to put their own life in danger to
protect Paul. All the churches had heard of Aquila
and Priscilla, and were thankful to them. Paul wished
to be remembered, too, to Epenetus, one of his first
converts in Achaia, who was now in Rome. The most
of the other names in the chapter are Greek, which
seems to show that they were from Greece, and that
they were converted in the regions of Greece. Some
of the persons were Jews, and were kinsmen of Paul.

Other persons than Paul send their good wishes to
the brethren of Rome : Timothy, his youthful and faithful 'work-fellow :' Lucius, perhaps the very Lucius who
was at Antioch when he started on his first journey :[15]
Jason, the very Jason of Thessalonica it may be, Sosipater, another kinsman, (who was perhaps the same person
who soon afterwards went with Paul back to Corinth:[16])
Gaius, the hospitable friend of the whole Church, and
at whose house Paul is now writing ; and Erastus, the
Treasurer of the city of Corinth.[17]

[15] Acts xiii. 1. See page 44.

[16] xx. 4.

[17] In Romans xvi. 23, the word chamberlain means in the Greek,
when applied to a household officer, a *steward*, or *overseer :* when applied to a city, a *financial* officer, a *treasurer*.

QUESTIONS.

WHAT did the Apostle resolutely do after the letter to the Galatians had gone ?

How has it been supposed that he established his Apostolic authority ?

Is this supposition necessary ?

What was probably done with wilful, immoral church-members ?

When had Paul directed this course before ?

How long was Paul in Corinth ?

Why may we suppose other neighboring churches had the same faults as the Corinthian church ?

Where were these churches ?

Who perhaps went with him ?

What was gathered ?

To whom was it entrusted ?

What direction had Paul given in respect to opposing such persons ?

Who left Cenchræa about this time ?

What shows she was a person of position ?

What does the word 'succorer' mean ?

What does the fact that she had business at Rome show ?

What does the word 'servant' mean ?

What was a 'deaconess' ?

What was Paul intending to do after this journey ?

What did Paul send by her ?

Where did Paul deliver it to her ?

How do you know Paul thought highly of the Roman Christians ?

How is it probable the Christians first went to Rome ?

Where did 'strangers of Rome' hear Peter preach ?

Had Peter ever been in Rome ?

Why would Paul have mentioned him, if he had been there ?

What was Paul's rule about preaching where another Apostle had been ?

Were the Roman Christians Jews or Gentiles?

How does this Epistle differ from those Paul had written before?

What reason is there for not alluding to himself?

What does he say about wishing to see them?

What is the one great subject of the Epistle?

Who are equal? How are they equal?

Who are sinners? Are they equally sinners?

What is a sinner?

What is the Saviour a Saviour from?

How can we have him for our Saviour?

What is faith?

What reason does Paul give for writing boldly to strangers?

How far does the great Apostle now purpose to make his next journey reach?

After what did he hope to do this?

What was he going to Jerusalem for?

Why doesn't Paul speak of the collection in this Epistle?

What is the last chapter of the Epistle to the Romans?

Turn to the chapter, and point out there Paul's kind care for Phœbe.

Point out his attention to Priscilla and Aquila.

Where had they perilled their life for Paul?

In what places have these Christians been mentioned before?

Why were the churches thankful to them?

What is meant by 'church in their house'?

Point out the name of another convert of Paul's.

What does 'first fruits' mean?

Of what nation were the most of these persons mentioned in the chapter?

Point out the names of those with Paul at Corinth who sent their good wishes to their Roman brethren.

Who perhaps was Lucius? Jason? Sosipater?

At whose house was Paul living?

What does 'chamberlain' mean?

THE GAMES AT THE ISTHMUS.

LESSON.

Acts xx. 3, 4, 5 ; I. Corinthians ix. 24–27 ; Galatians v. 7 ; Philippians iii. 13, 14 ; I. Thessalonians ii. 19.; II. Timothy ii. 5, iv. 6–8 ; Hebrews xii. 1–4.

ONE thought which very naturally arises, as we think over all that Paul had seen in Greece, is in respect to the Grecian Festivals. Did Paul see the famous games which have helped to make Greece so celebrated? We know that there are many vivid figures of speech in his epistles, which are taken from the various feats of strength and of agility performed in these places of amusement. To be sure there was the separate and peculiar building for the race-course in almost every city which he had visited. He had been familiar with the phrases and customs of the athletic sports from early years, for at Tarsus itself was the race-building, and when a boy, he might have witnessed the contests. And especially at Ephesus, these contests of strength and of speed, and the training for them, were subjects of absorbing interest to all the people. But on the very Isthmus of Corinth, which he so often trod, was held one of the four great festivals of Greece. And in Paul's time, these 'Isthmian Games' were in their most successful operation. They were celebrated every third year, and in the spring or summer. While, therefore, it is not likely that Paul witnessed these games during this 'three months' of his last visit to Corinth, since he reached Philippi by March,[1] yet it is likely, from careful calculation, that the games were celebrated during the two years which he spent in Corinth the first time. It is proper, therefore, for us to stop and look in upon this great national festival.

Just at the narrowest part of the Isthmus was a temple to Neptune, and near it a theatre and a race-course. These buildings were about eight miles from Corinth, and Paul would pass the very spot, if he went at any time by land from Athens to Corinth, or from Corinth to Athens. The entrance to the temple was through an avenue of statues of the victors, and through groves of pine-trees, from the leaves of which the victor's chaplet was woven. The games celebrated near this temple were made sacred to Neptune. The people came pouring in from all parts of the country, to the celebration. In early times, the Athenians were especially honored at the games; they came across the gulf from Athens in a sacred vessel, and seats in a space as large as the sail of their vessel were reserved for them. The crowds of men came not only to see the games, but to buy and to sell, to visit, and to learn of the latest productions in literature and music and art. The best way to make known a newly-written book or poem, a painting or a statue, was to read it or exhibit it at these jubilant celebrations, when people from all Greece were present. Musical and poetical contests sometimes formed a part of the games; but the reading of a book or exhibition of a painting was not a part of the regular celebration.

Both the theatre and the building for foot-races at the Isthmus, were built of white marble. The building

---

[1] See page 230, note 1.

for the foot-races was called the *Stadium*, (a measure of length, equal to our furlong,) because the race-course in it was just a *stadium* long. It was a long, open edifice, with a circular end. In the circular space at the end, the various feats of wrestling, boxing, etc., took

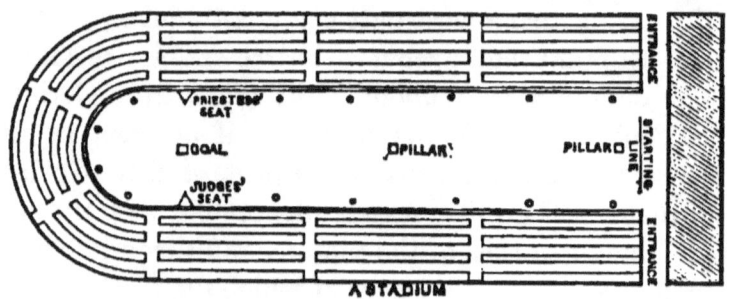

place. The race-course itself was straight. The marble seats rose on each side. The judges sat on one side, opposite the goal. Directly across from them was the priestess' altar and seat. The open space for the racers was adorned with altars and statues. At the starting-place was a square pillar, with the motto, BE THE BEST. Half-way down the course was another square pillar, with the word HASTEN. On the square pillar which was the goal, was the word TURN. The runners *turned* around the goal, when the race was twice or more times the length of the stadium.

The prize in the foot-race of the stadium was the most ancient and the most honorable of all the prizes at the games. In the time of Paul it was simply a garland of pine leaves. The simplicity of the reward was designed to heighten the value of the honor.

The men who entered their names as competitors for the prize were required to be examined, to show they were freemen, that they were Greeks by birth, and that they were not guilty of great and infamous crimes.

Then for ten months before the day of the race, they were trained by regular teachers, who had the care of such candidates. Strict rules were enforced in respect to food and sleep and exercise. The rules in respect to the manner of running were also carefully taught. The violation of any one of these, forfeited the crown. No unfair pushing or pulling or other advantage was allowed to be taken.

The games at the Isthmus were much the same as the Olympic games, and the description of one will answer in general for that of the other. We must imagine the whole Isthmus alive with people, as the day approached. We must see tents spread on the turf, beneath the clear and sunny sky of Greece. We must see traffickers bringing their wares of all kinds to this great fair; and the whole space around Neptune's temple and the theatre and the stadium filled with an eager, gay, lively, and witty people. The slow and tedious training of the candidates for the high honors of the Isthmian games, is done. The morning of the first day has arrived. The sacrifices to Neptune have been performed: the athletes have taken their solemn vows at the altar, that they have passed through the regular ten months' training, and that they will use no unfair means in the combats. The people pour into the seats, filling tier above tier, till a great multitude hover over the narrow race-course. Relations and friends of the racers are in the crowds: shouting and laughter and a great hum of voices fill the air: the judges, clad in their official robes, take their seats. A herald steps forth into the area, and the busy hum of voices dies into silence, while he makes proclamation: *'Let the runners in the stadium advance.'* The runners enter and take their places by lot. The herald calls out their names and their country one by one. If any one had taken the prize before, the an-

nouncement by the herald is received with the loudest
applause. All is silent again, while the herald calls:
"Can any one here present reproach these athletes with
having been slaves or with leading an immoral life?"
The universal silence proclaims them all the noble freemen of Greece, and every heart throbs with the sense
of the mere honor of *admission* to the area of the stadium. Many an eye of the eager racers has fallen on
the motto of the pillar at the starting-line; many a high
resolve echoes in the heart the words, BE THE BEST.
The hope of friends, the glory of success, the garlands
on the ivory table in plain sight, the disgrace of defeat,
the cheering cries of the great multitude, all unite to
swell the high thought of every man as he is placed in
position. The attendants leave them: the herald puts
his trumpet to his mouth. The signal sounds, and every
man bounds for the goal. The crowds of spectators
cheer and shout. Their cries of derision drive those
who fall behind quickly from sight, while redoubled
applause fills the air, as the two or three who are foremost pass the pillar HASTEN. The wild confusion and
clamor cease for a moment, as the rival racers bound
past the goal into the open space beyond; and sharp
and loud debate, mingled with the still louder and redoubled war of voices, almost overpower the blast of
the herald's trumpet, as he proclaims silence, and announces from the judges the name and the city of the
victor.

Other and more difficult races follow: races twice the
length of the course, with the exciting turn at the goal:
then other races, up to six and twelve times across the
track. Some racers bear off more than one prize, running again and again. Some, unsuccessful at the first,
in the first trial of the stadium, at last gain the praise
of the multitude, and the honor of the prize. Other

gymnastic feats of boxing, wrestling, leaping, quoiting, fill out the later part of the day.

The victor did not receive his prizes till the games were all over; but friends and relations crowded to him, congratulated and embraced him, " and lifting him on their shoulders, held him up to the applause of the spectators, who strewed handfuls of flowers over him." On the last day of the festival, the conquerors in all the games of foot-racing, horse and chariot-riding, etc., were summoned by proclamation to the place where the honors were awarded. " The victors, dressed in rich garments, bearing palm branches in their hands, and almost intoxicated with joy, proceeded in grand procession to the theatre, marching to the sound of flutes and surrounded by an immense multitude, who made the air ring with their acclamations. When they reached the theatre, the chorus of singers saluted them with the ancient hymn, composed by the poet Archilochus to exalt the glory of the victors, the surrounding multitude joining their voices to those of the musicians. Then the trumpet sounded, the herald proclaimed the name and country of the victor, and the nature of his prize, the acclamations of the people within and without the building were redoubled, and flowers and garlands were showered from all sides upon the happy conqueror, who at this moment was thought to have gained the loftiest pinnacle of human glory and felicity." The victors' names were inscribed in the archives of the Isthmian Games; and with all the pomp of triumph they were escorted by proud friends and relations and neighbors to their native city.

Such were the games to which Paul alluded in the imagery of his letters. It may be that he mingled with the busy crowds of the Isthmus, and gathered a knot of Greeks around him to hear of Jesus. Whatever we may think in respect to the probability of Paul's attending games where sacrifices were offered to a heathen god, we see plainly how Paul alluded to all parts of the stadium contests : both to the race and to the boxing,[2] to the *herald*[3] and to the *judge*,[4] to the eager running of the racer,[5] to the *rules of the race*,[6] and to the fading *prize* of leaves,[7] compared with the unfading crown which Jesus gives his followers.

During Paul's three months in Corinth, the Jews began again to persecute him. He had formed his plan to sail from Cenchræa, as he did before, to Judea. As soon as the sea was safe, he was ready to depart. The old and bitter hatred which in other places had put his life in peril, now rankled in the hearts of the Corinthian Jews. A plot against his life, when he should embark, was discovered. "The Jews generally settled in great numbers at sea-ports, for the sake of commerce, and their occupation would give them peculiar influence over the captains and owners of merchant-vessels, in one of which Paul must have sailed. They might, therefore, form the project of seizing or murdering him at Cenchræa with great probability of success." Paul therefore changed his plan. He determined to return on the route by which he came. By the time he reached Philippi, quite a little company was gathered to cross with him into Asia. These may have been the persons appointed by the different churches to carry their collections. Sopater may have joined him at Berea : Aristarchus and Secundus, at Thessalonica. Timothy

---

[2] I. Corinthians ix. 26.

[3] In I. Corinthians ix. 27, the figure is carried out in the Greek as it is not in our translation. The meaning of the original is, ' When I have *been a herald* to others, I myself should be rejected.'

[4] II. Timothy iv. 8.   [6] II. Timothy ii. 5.

[5] Philippians iii. 14.   [7] I. Corinthians ix. 25.

had either been with him all the way from Macedonia
to Corinth, or joined him in Macedonia.   Gaius and
Tychicus and Trophimus came all the way from Corinth.
Luke became one of the company at Philippi, or earlier
in the route.   Paul and Luke remained a little time at
Philippi, while the rest of the company sailed for Troas.

QUESTIONS.

WHAT striking figures of speech in Paul's Epistles ?
What peculiar building in almost every city ?
Why had Paul been familiar from youth with these games?
What was true of Ephesus ?
What one of the great festivals was held near Corinth ?
How often were they celebrated ?
Did Paul see these games during the three months at Corinth ? Why ?
Was Paul ever in Corinth at the time of one of these celebrations ?
What buildings on the Isthmus ? Where ?
Did Paul ever pass them ?
Describe the entrance to the temple.
To whom were the games consecrated ?
How had the Athenians been honored at the Isthmian games ?
What besides these games did people come to see ?
What was the name of the building for foot-races ?
Why was this name given ?
What kind of a building was it ?
Circular space ? race-course ? seats ? judges ? pillars ?
How did the prize of the foot-race compare with other prizes ?
What was the prize ? Why so simple ?
What was first required of men who wished to become competitors ?
How long were they required to make preparation ?
What other strict rules ?
What rules on the race-course ?
What was the appearance of the Isthmus on the morning of the contest ?
What sacrifices ? What vows ?
Describe the appearance of the stadium.

(75)

What was the herald's proclamation?

When the runners enter, what does the herald announce?

What is the next proclamation of the herald?

What effect has this on the multitude?

Who decides the race? Who announces it?

What besides the *name* of the rider is announced?

What other races and games followed?

When did the victor receive his prize?

What were the ceremonies?

In what were the victors' names written?

Who accompanied them home?

Do you think Paul would attend such games? Why?

What parts of the games are referred to in the passage from I. Corinthians?

What is meant by 'is temperate in all things'?

What is meant by '*corruptible* crown'?

What is alluded to in 'So fight I,' etc.?

What does 'keep under my body,' etc., mean?

What is meant by 'when I have preached,' etc.?

What is referred to in the passage from Philippians?

What in I. Thessalonians?

What in II. Timothy?

What three things in the eighth verse of the fourth chapter?

What allusion in Hebrews?

What does the 'great cloud of witnesses' refer to?

What allusion to the games may there be in the fourth verse?

What did the Jews begin to do again in Corinth?

What had been Paul's plan?

Why did he change it?

What would help the Jews in their plans?

Who composed Paul's company?

Where did each join him probably?

Who remained at Philippi?

Thirty-ninth Sunday.

'THE COASTS OF ASIA.'

LESSON.
ACTS xx. 6-16.

IT may be that Paul and Luke remained in Philippi to keep the Jewish Passover. A new and higher meaning was now given to that sacred festival. The Lamb, the blood of which, sprinkled on the hearts of men, prevented the death-angel from destroying the soul, had been slain for man's redemption. Jesus was the great Passover for all men. Paul and Luke could not fail to think of the comparison between the ancient Passover and the new. They either observed the Jewish feast of seven days, removing all leaven and all impurity from their houses, or they celebrated that simple and solemn rite which our Saviour gave to his Church in place of the burdensome ceremonies of the Hebrew Passover week. No doubt the Philippian Christians with Paul and Luke gathered around the Lord's table to commemorate the 'broken body' and 'flowing blood' of the Lamb of Calvary.

But there was another Jewish festival which had been made most sacred to Christians. It was at the Feast of *Pentecost* that the sacred Spirit first descended on the Christian Church. How hallowed was that day, especially in Jerusalem! With what praise, with what devout rejoicings did the disciples of Jerusalem celebrate its annual return! After the Passover, therefore,

Paul hastened on to be in Jerusalem at Pentecost.[1] But few and short visits could be made on the way, if he would reach the holy city in seven weeks. " The voyage seemed to begin unfavorably." Two days was sufficient time to sail from Neapolis to Troas, with a fair wind, and this was all the time taken on that first voyage across to Europe, when they passed the night at Samothrace.[2] But now five days were occupied. A calm, or a contrary wind, must have detained the ship. If it was a contrary wind, the track of the vessel was not now 'straight,'[3] but zig-zag, from 'tacking' from one point to another for the sails to catch the wind.[3]

If the " fragments of colossal masonry among the oak trees, the huge columns of granite lying in the harbor," the broken arches of a towering theatre conspicuous from the sea, if these ruins in our day indicate with any certainty what Troas was when Paul sailed towards it, " we may be certain that the city, both on the approach from the water and to those who wandered through its streets, presented an appearance of grandeur and prosperity. Like Corinth, Ephesus, or Thessalonica, it was a place where the Apostle must have wished to lay firm and strong the foundations of the Gospel."

We have a description of only one of the seven days which Paul spent in Troas, but that was an important day. And the whole passage is a most important one, because it shows the observance of the first day of the week as the Sabbath day. It gives us also a vivid picture of an evening service. The sacred services of the day were made doubly solemn and doubly precious by the celebration of the holy communion. And in the

---

[1] Pentecost, meaning fifty, was fifty days—seven weeks and one day—from Passover day.

[2] Acts xvi. 11. [3] See the map on page 206.

evening they came together again with mingled feelings of joy and of sadness. The vessel was to sail on Monday morning. "The place was an upper room, with a recess or balcony projecting over the street or court. Many lamps were burning in the room where the congregation was assembled. The place was hot and crowded. With the feeling that the next day was the day of his departure, and that souls might be lost by delay, Paul continued in earnest discourse, prolonging it even to midnight, when suddenly an accident occurred which filled the assembly with alarm, though it was afterwards changed into an occasion of joy and thanksgiving. A young listener, whose name was Eutychus, was overcome by exhaustion, heat, and weariness, and sank into deep slumber. He was seated or leaning in the balcony, and, falling down in his sleep, was dashed on the pavement below, and was taken up dead." Loud outcries of terror and confusion followed. Paul alone seems to be calm and unmoved. The power of the great Master was with his disciple. He went down and stretched himself upon the body, as Elisha did on the body of the child,[1] and calmly said: 'Do not lament; for his life is in him.'

The interruption seems to have broken up the regular order of the services. After the long labors of the day and evening, Paul took food to strengthen him. Even then the earnest, warm-hearted Apostle was not fully satisfied. Till the very breaking of the day, he continued to converse familiarly with the disciples. Then the congregation broke up, for it was time to go to the ship. Only Paul's fellow-travellers went on board. For some reason Paul chose to walk across the promontory to Assos. Possibly he might gain a few

---

[1] II. Kings iv. 34.

hours with the disciples at Troas, for the distance around
was twice as far as it was across to Assos. More likely
however, the Apostle preferred to be alone. Solitude,
communion with his own thoughts and with his Saviour,
and prayer, were precious to him. "The discomfort of
a crowded ship is unfavorable for devotion; and prayer
and meditation are necessary for maintaining the religious life even of the Apostle." Strength and peace
were surely sought and obtained by him from that
Saviour who often prayed in solitude, as Paul pursued
his lonely road that day across the neck of the peninsula. His walk was on the Roman road, and therefore
safe and easy. It was "through the oak woods, then
in full foliage, (for it was now the opening spring-time,)
which cover all that shore with greenness and shade."
He made no stop in Assos. "We may suppose that
the vessel was already *hove to* and waiting when he arrived; or that he saw it approaching from the west
through the channel between the island Lesbos and the
main shore. He went on board, and the Greek sailors
and Apostolic missionaries continued their voyage. As
to Assos itself, we must conclude, if we compare the
description of the ancients with present appearances,
that its aspect as seen from the sea was magnificent.
On a wall of rock rising out of the water, was a sloping
bank with a long portico on it. Above this was a mag
nificent gate, approached by a flight of steps. Higher
still was the theatre, which commanded a glorious view
of Lesbos and the sea. The whole was crowned by a
citadel of Greek masonry on a cliff of granite. Such
was the view which gradually faded into indistinctness
as the vessel retired from the shore, and the summit of
Mount Ida rose in the evening sky."

Southward, across the Gulf of Adramyttium, the
pilot guides the ship between the island and the conti

nent. On the right the bold, high, mountainous island rises: on the left lies the mainland: in front is the 'beautiful Mitylene,' the chief city of Lesbos. Here on this island, here in this very city, lived the famous poetess Sappho, surrounded by her literary circle. "The beauty of the capital of Sappho's island was celebrated by the architects, poets, and philosophers of Rome." Here the ship probably anchored for the night, protected from wind and waiting for daylight before they tried the difficult channel between the southern end of Lesbos and Asia.

A long sweep around an irregular projection of land, brought them sometime during Tuesday abreast the coast of Chios. "On one side were the gigantic masses of the mainland: on the other was the rich, fertile island, with its gardens of oranges, citrons, almonds, and pomegranates, its luxuriant vineyards and its white, scattered houses, overshadowed ·by evergreens." On the next day, Wednesday, the ship was in scenery familiar to Paul. They were crossing the bay in front of Ephesus. Sails in sight were set for Ephesus, vessels were coming out of the harbor of the great and busy city. If the sun was in the west, so that the rays were reflected from the city, the glittering columns of Diana's temple may have been in view. Paul thought of his Christian converts, and yearned to see them, but he 'had determined to sail by Ephesus.' If he would be at Jerusalem at Pentecost, he must not leave this ship. He might not find another which would take him to Palestine in time for the national festival. Before night, they were close by the side of Samos. Through a narrow pass, where the water is shut in between the island and a high, long ridge, lies the course to the *town* of Samos, and directly opposite, on the coast, and not more than a mile from Samos, is "the anchorage of Trogyllium." Here Paul might have gone ashore, if he had wished to visit Ephesus, which was now twenty or thirty miles to the northward. A better plan suggested itself to his mind. He found the ship was to stop some time at the next landing-place, and that place was Miletus, which was in direct communication with Ephesus. Though he could not visit the Ephesian church himself, he determined to send word to some of the principal members to meet him at Miletus.

" The sail from Trogyllium, with a fair wind, would require but a little time. If the vessel weighed anchor at daybreak on Thursday, she would be in harbor long before noon. The message was sent to Ephesus immediately on her arrival; and Paul remained at Miletus, waiting for those whom the Holy Spirit, by his hands, had made 'overseers' over the flock of Christ."

QUESTIONS.

WHAT were 'the days of unleavened bread'? Why so called?

What new meaning had been given to it?

Would Paul and Luke observe the Jewish festival?

Would they fail to observe the Christian form of the feast?

Was our Lord's Supper celebrated more or less often than now in the early Church?

What other Jewish festival had been made sacred to Christians? Why?

What is the meaning of the word?

Why did Paul hasten on?

How long was the voyage to Troas?

How long had Paul been in going from Troas to Philippi on a former journey?

What made the difference?

Would the course be 'straight'?

How long was Paul at Troas?

Which one of these days is described?

What day of the week, then, did Paul reach Troas?

Why is this description an important one?

Was there a synagogue at Troas?

When Paul went into the synagogues on 'the Sabbath,' what day was it?

What day did the disciples at Troas assemble?

How came there to be disciples in Troas?

What is meant by 'to break bread'?

Do you think there was a second assembly in the evening?

In what place was the meeting?

Why did Paul continue preaching so late?

Are there ever reasons now why preaching should sometimes be continued equally long?

Is Eutychus to be blamed for falling asleep?

Is there any excuse in this for sleeping in church?

(77)

Show how Eutychus might have fallen from an eastern
    window.

What would this accident produce in the audience?

What was the effect on Paul?

    Whom was he like, in falling on him and embracing
       him?

    Was Eutychus dead or in a swoon?

    How do you reconcile 'taken up dead,' and 'life is in
       him'?

Did Paul go on with the preaching?

    Does 'had broken bread,' in the eleventh verse, differ
       from 'to break bread,' in the seventh verse?

    How long did the conversation continue? What was it
       about?

Who went aboard the ship? Why did not Paul?

    How was it that Paul could walk to Assos as soon as
       the ship could sail there?

    What day was it when Paul walked to Assos?

    How long was Paul in Assos?

    What island was to be seen from Assos?

    How did Assos appear from the sea?

    What mountain in the north-east?

    What gulf did they cross? to what island?

What was Mitylene? What famous poetess had lived here?

    Who celebrated the praises of Mitylene? for what?

    Did the vessel stop here?

How far did they sail on Tuesday?

    What was on either hand?

Where was the ship the next day?

    What could be seen?

    Why did not Paul stop at Ephesus?

    What was Samos? Trogyllium?

Where was Thursday's sail? Was it all day?

    What message was sent?

    Might it have been sent from Cape Trogyllium?

THE ELDERS OF EPHESUS.

LESSON.
ACTS xx. 17–38.

MILETUS was a more ancient town than Ephesus. It was famed for having sent out many colonies, some to the Euxine (Black) Sea, some to Egypt, some to the distant west. But it was a town of far less importance than Ephesus; for the immense quantities of earth brought down by the river *Meander* had filled up the harbor and made the city only a second-rate sea-port. Here, however, the captain of the ship remained on business for a day or two.

What gladness and joy was there among the Christians of Ephesus when they heard that Paul was at Miletus. How eagerly they would take the journey of a few miles to see their old instructor and pastor, who taught them at the school of Tyrannus. "The elders of the church must have gathered together in all haste to obey the summons, and gone with eager steps out of the southern gate which leads to Miletus. By those who travel on such an errand, a journey of twenty or thirty miles over a good road is not thought long and tedious." Nor would they think the steep ascent over the mountain-ridge nor even the darkness of night as any obstacle. "The elders of Ephesus might easily reach Miletus on the day after Paul's message was received." A modern traveller who went over this same mountain-ridge in the same month of April, had, no

doubt, a similar journey, when he said: " The weather
was unsettled: the sky was blue and the sun shone, but
a wet, wintry north wind swept the clouds along the
mountain-range." From these heights the country,
' like a perfect and beautiful map,' can be seen far beyond Miletus and the Meander. Weariness from rapid
journeying would soon be forgotten at the sight of
Paul's face. There was Timothy, too, and other ' brethren ' more or less known or heard about. There at
Miletus the two parties mingled: Paul and his band
of steadfast converts, the missionary party; and the
delegation of intelligent Christian men from the great
metropolis of Asia Minor. Going one side to some
quiet spot on the shore, they thanked God that they
were permitted to see each other's faces again; and
there — in some such solitary spot — we can see the
Apostle speaking earnestly, in subdued and solemn
manner, to those to whom God had given the Christian oversight of the great and wicked Ephesus. What
a " singular contrast " did this little party form " with
the great crowds which used to assemble in the immense theatre of Miletus ! But that vast theatre is
now a silent ruin, while the words spoken by a common
traveller that day to a few despised strangers are still
living to teach lessons for all time, and to make known
eternal truths to all who will hear them. At the same
time they reveal to us, as though they were merely
human words, all the tenderness and affection of Paul,
the speaker."

ADDRESS TO THE ELDERS AT MILETUS.

This address is not a regular and formal argument,
like the other addresses of the Apostle which we have
noticed on his journeys, but rather a simple, short,
earnest exhortation. It is not an argument to *convince*

men, to lead them to believe what they do not believe, but an appeal to men to do faithfully what they already are trying to do. It is, therefore, simply the outpour· ing of Paul's earnest heart in a short, urgent, free talk with the responsible elders from Ephesus. We are not, therefore, to expect the regular divisions of a speech. We may, however, notice a natural division into five parts:

I. His life in. Ephesus. (Verses 18 to 21.) *You know* what my life in Ephesus was for the three years during which I lived among you, whether it enforced the doctrines of penitence and faith which I preached or not.

II. His journey to Jerusalem now is with foreboding of evil. (Verses 22 to 24.) He is going to Jerusalem, not *free in spirit*, as we would expect one to go who eagerly presses on to attend the national Festival, but *bound in spirit*. The Holy Spirit of God had revealed that ' bonds and afflictions ' were among ' the things ' which would certainly ' befall him there.' Not once or twice, but in *every city* the Spirit of God plainly told him these things, yet he pressed directly on to Jerusa- lem. Nothing moved him, not the prospect of the loss of life itself, from the path of duty. Was there ever a more heroic courage ?

III. His duty to them is done. (Verses 25 to 27.) When on my former return to Jerusalem, I promised to come again, if God would permit. But now I shall not see you again. My whole work for Ephesus is done. I am innocent. I have done it faithfully. I have spoken the whole word of God to you.

IV. His warning. (Verses 28 to 31.) You are now the overseers of the Ephesian church. Feed it. Watch it. Greedy, cruel men will enter it, like wolves into a sheep-fold. There are even men among you who will

pervert the truth to make themselves a party. Watch
without ceasing. Remember my example. For three
whole years I have watched and warned you all, day
and night, and with tears.

V. His farewell. (Verses 32 to 35.) As I now leave
you, I commit you to God. HE is able to build up
your church, and to give you all the eternal inheritance.
Remember these words and all my words. I have not
preached for silver or gold or apparel. These very
hands, which you see, have labored to support myself,
and indeed others also. And you ought to labor also
to support the helpless. Remember again my example
of unselfish labor; and remember more the words of
our Saviour, how *He* said : *It is more blessed to give
than to receive.*

Two things are worthy of notice in the address of
Paul. First, how much Paul speaks of himself in it!
In every one of these subjects on which he spoke, he
referred freely to what he himself had done and was
about to do. We must remember that he was among
warm personal friends, and that it was proper for a
faithful man like Paul to refer to himself as an example.
And yet notice, secondly, how solemnly the word of
God is made superior to all his *own* work. In every
subject of his address, God is made more prominent
than himself. Does he refer to his life at Ephesus ?
It was to preach to Jews and Greeks penitence and
faith towards Jesus our Lord and our Messiah. Does
he speak of his journey to Jerusalem ? It is to say
that the Holy Ghost has revealed to him what is to befall him and to speak of the ministry of Jesus. Does
he speak of his duty as ended ? It was his duty to
preach the kingdom of God. Does he warn them ?
The Holy Ghost has made them overseers. And when
he bids them farewell, it is to commit them to God,

and to repeat as his last words the words of the Saviour.

Paul's address at Iconium was to *Jews :* his address at Athens was to *Gentiles :* his address at Miletus was to *Christians.* At Iconium he argued from the Hebrew Scriptures : at Athens he argued from nature and from the truth which he found in heathen altars and Greek poets : in Miletus he argued from the words of Jesus and from his own Apostolic authority derived from Jesus. What boldness, what wisdom, what affection, what solemnity was there in Paul on all these occasions ; and how does he exhibit all these virtues as he now, at Miletus, leaves his missionary life, thenceforth to be more than ever a sufferer for his Master.

When Paul's warm and pungent address was ended, one impulse prompted all to seek God's blessing in prayer. What would a stranger have thought who should have seen that company in that solitary place all kneeling in prayer to an unseen God! It was indeed to an invisible but powerful God, who was establishing an invisible and powerful kingdom, that these insignificant men prayed—a kingdom which was to overturn Diana's temple at Ephesus and Minerva's statue on the Acropolis at Athens, to overpower the great Roman empire, and at length to triumph over all heathen authorities ; and these kneeling, praying men were the mighty powers on earth which were laying the foundations of this kingdom under the direction of their unseen King. "In praying with them, Paul *knelt down*—that unusual posture being a token of his fervor and of how much he was overcome by the scene. The posture for prayer was standing, both in the Jewish and in the early Christian church."[1] "And then followed an outbreak of natural

---

[1] Mark xi. 25.

grief, which even Christian faith and resignation were
not able to restrain.   They fell on the Apostle's neck
and clung to him and kissed him, sorrowing most because of his own foreboding announcement that they
should never behold that countenance again on which
they had so often gazed with reverence and love.   But
no long time could be devoted to grief.   The wind was
fair,* and the vessel must depart. The Christian brethren
were torn from the embrace of their friends." The
ship pulled off from the shore and stood out to sea.
The saddened elders of Ephesus turned at length their
eyes from the receding vessel, and took their slow and
melancholy journey home.

* See xxi. 1.   'With a straight course:' the wind must have been
fair.

QUESTIONS.

WHICH was more ancient, Miletus or Ephesus? which the more important?

What had the river Meander to do with Miletus?

Describe the journey from Ephesus to Miletus. How far was it?

Who now made up Paul's company?

How does this address to the elders differ from other addresses of Paul on his journeys?

What verses contain the first division of this address?

What is the subject?

What time is meant by 'the first day that I came into Asia'?

Had the *Jews* 'laid wait' for Paul in *Ephesus*?

What doctrines had he preached?

What kind of life must Paul have lived to have appealed to their knowledge of it?

What is the second subject of the address?

What does 'bound in the spirit' mean?

What caused his feeling that evil would come upon him?

How did this certain information affect Paul?

What is meant by 'finish my course'?

How could Paul speak of finishing it *with joy*, when he expected evil?

What is the third subject of the address?

What one thing did Paul certainly know?

How did this farewell differ from his former farewell at Ephesus?

What does 'take you to record' mean?

What is meant by 'pure from the blood'?

What does the twenty-seventh verse mean?

What is the fourth subject of the address?

Who makes pastors or elders in the church?

Can a person be pastor or elder without His appointment?

Whose blood is 'his own blood'?

Does this prove that Jesus is God?

What is meant by 'grievous wolves'?

What are 'perverse things'?

What is the last strong argument with which Paul enforces his warning?

What is the fifth subject of the address?

What is the meaning of 'commend to God'?

How can 'the word' 'build up' a person?

Had Paul labored at common work for himself alone?

Whose words does he quote?

Are these words found in the four Gospels?

What two things are especially to be noted in this address?

Why was it proper for Paul to speak of himself?

Show how, in each division of the address, God's work is made more prominent than his own.

What three classes of persons did Paul address in Iconium, Athens, and Miletus?

What three different sources of argument?

Give some of the characteristics of this address.

What does 'kneeled down' show?

What caused the greatest sorrow in parting?

Did Paul take leave of his missionary life here?

THE THIRD JOURNEY HOME.

LESSON.

ACTS xxi. 1–16.

THE difference in the description of the two voyages of Paul from Ephesus to Cæsarea is so marked that it is worthy of our careful notice. The account of the voyage on Paul's second return home passes quickly over the whole distance between the two cities. It is simply said: 'And he sailed from Ephesus. And when he had landed at Cæsarea.'[1] But in the account of the third return to Palestine, we have mentioned every stage of his voyage. The principal islands, the towns, the change of ships, and the incidents of the journey are noticed. Notice how particularly we have had Paul's journey described ever since Luke joined Paul at Philippi. It seems probable, therefore, that Luke described more minutely those things which he saw as an eye-witness, just as on the second journey at Philippi we had a full description of the demoniac slave and of Paul's imprisonment in the jail; and when Paul went on to Thessalonica, leaving Luke behind, there is only a general description given.[2]

Paul and his little company from the deck of the ship may have watched the little company of good men, from whom they had just separated, till the vessel had with-

---

[1] xviii. 21, 22.

[2] Compare chapter xvi. 12–40 with xvii. 1–10, and see note 1 Twenty-second Sunday.

drawn far from the shore and was headed down the Icarian Sea. "With a fair wind she could easily run down to Cos the same afternoon." The wind must have been in their favor, for they sailed in 'a straight course.'³ "With this wind the vessel would make her passage from Miletus to Cos in six hours, passing the shores of Caria (see map on page 127) and the high summits of Mount Latmus in the interior on the left, and groups of small islands studding the sea on the right." The rocky and barren island of Patmos, used by the Roman government as a place of banishment, where the Beloved Disciple so soon afterwards saw his wonderful visions,⁴ would be seen now and then through these smaller islets. The name of the town as well as of the island itself to which the vessel held its course was Cos. "It is described by the ancients as a beautiful and well-built city, and surrounded with fortifications; but its beauty had been injured by an earthquake." The island was renowned for its wine, silks, and beautiful cotton: the city, for its harbor, sheltered from winds, and for its medical school. Here was a temple to Æsculapius, the god of healing, which was 'crowded with models,' so as to become in effect a museum of anatomy." Hippocrates, the most celebrated physician of antiquity, was born here, and wrote, taught, and practised his profession in his early home. Luke, the physician,⁵ "who knew these coasts so well, could hardly be ignorant of the scientific and religious celebrity of Cos." How thankful would he be that he was not a victim to the vain superstitions with which idolatrous Greeks had filled the profession of medicine. Apelles, too, the most celebrated painter of Greece, who painted the portrait of Alexander the Great, and

---

³ See note 2 page 131.　　　⁴ Rev. i. 9.　　　⁵ Col. iv. 14.

whose most famous paintings were in the temple of Æsculapius at Cos, was said to be a native of the island. Opposite Cos, and on the coast of Caria, was Halicarnassus, where Herodotus, 'the Father of History' and the extensive traveller, and Dionysius, the literary critic and historian, were born.

Turning short around the corner of this island, the next morning the long promontory of Cnidus, which looked so much like an island, was in sight.[6] The northwest winds blow steadily and with violence along this coast during the good season. When, therefore, they passed the high precipice which forms the end of Cnidus, they ran swiftly down to Rhodes. The city was at the northern end of the island. Situated at the western end of the eastern Mediterranean, and at the entrance to the Ægean Sea, with a good harbor, it was the natural stopping-place of very many trading vessels. The island furnished "copious supplies of ship-timber," and the city was renowned for ship-building. Rhodes was "famed in ancient times, and is still celebrated, for its delightful climate and the fertility of its soil. The gardens are filled with delicious fruit, every gale is scented with the most powerful fragrance wafted from groves of orange and citron-trees, and the numberless aromatic herbs exhale such a profusion of the richest odors, that the whole atmosphere seems impregnated with spicy perfume." The city itself "rose in the midst of its perfumed gardens and its amphitheatre of hills, so united and so symmetrical that it appeared like one house." Statues abounded. The fragments of the immense statue to the sun, which was called 'The Colossus of Rhodes,' and one of the seven wonders of the

---

[6] Paul sailed past Cnidus afterwards when he went to Rome. Acts xxvii. 7.

world, and which had been shaken down and broken
to pieces by an earthquake, still lay on the ground at
the entrance to the harbor,[7] when Paul's vessel arrived.
Beauty and luxuriance were on every side ; and through
the clear and sunny atmosphere the islands of the Archipelago and the coasts of Asia could be seen for many
miles around. "It was a proverb, that the sun shone
every day in Rhodes." "We do not know that Paul
landed, like other great conquerors who have visited the
city. It would not be necessary even to enter the harbor, for a safe anchorage would be found for the night
outside ; and the vessel which was seen by the people
of the city to weigh anchor in the morning was probably not distinguished from the other coasting craft
with which they were daily familiar."

The course of the ship was now to the east, towards
the splendid scenery of Lycia, which is visible from the
heights of Rhodes. In front of them was "a long line
of snowy summits on the coast, and the sea between is
ruffled beneath the blue and brilliant sky." The point
towards which the helmsman now directs the prow of
the ship is near the further end of these mountains—
Patara, the harbor of Xanthus, the chief city of Lycia,
as Neapolis was the harbor of Philippi. Either the
vessel was to stop here, or was to follow the coast of
Asia Minor eastward. Whatever was its destination, it
was not going immediately to Palestine. Possibly Paul
intended to sail in it as far as he could towards Judea,
hoping to find a ship in some one of the ports at which
they should stop bound directly for Cæsarea. If this
was so, he may have made inquiry off the harbor of
Rhodes whether any ship was in port bound directly

[7] So enormous was this brazen statue, that when at length these
fragments were sold, it took nine hundred camels to carry them
away.

for any port of Judea. At any rate, he found a ship at Patara, which was to sail to Phœnicia. From Phœnicia he could reach Jerusalem by land along the road he had travelled before, provided there should be no vessel ready to depart for Cæsarea. Hastening, therefore, to be at Jerusalem at Pentecost, " they went on board without delay ; and it seems evident, from the mode of expression, that they sailed the very day of their arrival. Since the voyage lay across the open sea, with no shoals nor rocks to be dreaded, and since the northwest winds often blow steadily over these seas during the spring, there could be no reason why the vessel should not weigh anchor in the evening, and sail through the night. We think of Paul, therefore, no longer as passing through narrow channels or coasting along in the shadow of great mountains, but as sailing directly on through the midnight hours, with a prosperous breeze filling the canvass and the waves curling and sounding round the bow of the vessel." Before a strong wind, the trip across to Tyre might have been made in two days. One phrase especially indicates that the voyage was a quick one. It is said that ' when they had *discovered* Cyprus, they left it on the left hand,' " as if they had hardly more than seen it in the distance on the left hand *in front*, before they left it *behind* on the left hand. It was probably towards evening of the second day that the highest mountain of Cyprus appeared. "There would be snow on it at that season of the year." The next morning Paphos and the whole island were past: indeed fast passing into the north-west horizon. (See map on page 195.) "The first land in sight now would be the high range of Lebanon in Syria, and they would easily arrive at Tyre before evening."

Tyre from the earliest times had been a place of traf

fic. Since Hiram, King of Tyre, furnished Solomon materials for the Temple,[*] it had been a rich, busy, prosperous city; but in Paul's time the height of its prosperity was past. It still had some manufactures and some commerce. The ship which brought Paul stopped at Tyre to unload her cargo. It is not necessary at all to suppose that her whole voyage had been from Patara. She " may have brought grain from the Black Sea or wine from the Archipelago, with the purpose of taking on at Tyre a cargo of Phœnician manufactures." It seems likely that the same ship went on to Ptolemais. While the change of cargoes was being made, which required several days, Paul found out the Christian disciples of Tyre. Some of the Tyrian disciples were prophets, and they foresaw the perils of a visit by Paul to Jerusalem. But they could not prevent Paul from carrying out his purpose. He was there over one Sabbath, and then, as fathers and mothers and children affectionately accompanied him to the ship, he kneeled down as at Miletus, on the shore, and prayed to God. The ship took its course southward, and after the greater part of a day's sailing along the coast, reached Ptolemais, its destination. Across from this city, on the next point of the coast, was Mount Carmel, jutting out into the sea. A line from Ptolemais to Cape Carmel was like the string of a well-bent bow, for the sandy shore swept round from one point to the other in a regular curve. Here also Paul found out again ' the brethren ' and spent a day with them. Another day's travelling by land brought them to Cæsarea. The journey all the way from Troas had been accomplished in abundant time for him to reach Jerusa-

---

[*] II. Sam. v. 11 and I. Kings v.

lem before Pentecost; and therefore he had a few leisure days in Cæsarea.[9]

At Cæsarea Paul and his company found a home in the Christian family of Philip. As Cæsarea is the last place in which the Scripture previously mentions Philip,[10] it is likely he had his permanent residence here; and that his four daughters, by their superior devotedness and the gift of the prophetic office, assisted him in his work. It is natural to think that these inspired women foretold the sorrows to come upon Paul. Another prophet did plainly predict what the sufferings of Paul would be. In 'every city'[11] along the voyage the Holy Spirit had revealed to him bonds and afflictions awaiting him. At Tyre, the first place he landed on the Syrian coast, he met a voice of warning. At Cæsarea, four prophets in the very house in which he stays point out the future evil. And now that same prophet, who many years before at Antioch foretold the famine which came to pass,[12] came down from Jerusalem and foretold chains

[9] From Passover to Pentecost was, as we have seen, (page 251 note 1,) seven weeks and a day. How long was Paul on the journey?

From Philippi to Troas, (xx. 6,)	5 days
At Troas, ...	7 "
From Troas to Assos and to Mitylene, (xx. 13, 14,) .	1 "
Mitylene to Chios, to Samos, to Miletus, (xx. 15,) . .	3 "
At Miletus and to Cos, (about 3 days,)	3 "
From Cos to Rhodes, to Patara, (xxi. 1,) . . .	2 "
From Patara to Tyre, ...	2 "
At Tyre, (xxi. 4,)	7 "
From Tyre to Ptolemais, and at Ptolemais, (7,) . .	2 "
From Ptolemais to Cæsarea, (8,)	1 "
	33 "
Leaving for the 'many days' (10) at Cæsarea and in Jerusalem, before the day of Pentecost, . .	17
	50 "

[10] Acts viii. 40.   [11] xx. 23.   [12] xi. 28.

and imprisonment for Paul. By binding his own hands and feet, in the manner of the ancient prophets [13] he solemnly *represented* the imprisonment of Paul. Luke and Trophimus and the disciples of Cæsarea were greatly distressed at this sad prediction, and wept and besought Paul not to go where he would certainly be delivered up to wicked men. But what could ever daunt the courage of Paul? He was ready not only to be imprisoned, but to *die*, for Jesus' sake. When they saw his unfaltering purpose, and that they caused him only sorrow, they submitted to the Lord's will. Loading up their baggage,[14] they journeyed up to the holy city, comforted with the presence of one of the disciples of Cæsarea and of a disciple formerly of Cyprus, who then resided in Jerusalem—"who may indeed have been one of those Cyprian Jews who first made known the Gospel to the Greeks of Antioch."[15]

[13] Isaiah xx. 2–4; Jeremiah xiii. 1–11.

[14] 'Took up our *carriages*' means took up the packages or bundles they had to *carry*.

[15] Acts xi. 19. It has been conjectured that Mnason was called an 'old disciple' because he was one of the seventy whom Jesus sent forth. Luke x. 1, 17.

QUESTIONS.

WHAT different descriptions of Paul's second and third voyages home are there?

Who is with Paul on this voyage who was not on the other?

What other instance is there of this writer's minute description of what he himself saw?

What is meant by 'launched'?

Why must the wind have been in their favor?

What famous island did they pass on their right?

What was the first island on their course?

What city on this island? Famous for what?

What temple? What physician born here?

Why interesting to Luke?

What painter born here? What was he famous for?

What town opposite Cos? Famous for what?

What promontory did they pass the next morning?

Where is it mentioned in the Scriptures?

What winds prevail here?

Why would the voyage be swift to Rhodes?

Where was the city of Rhodes?

Why was it the natural stopping-place for vessels?

What was Rhodes renowned for?

The city? the atmosphere? the proverb?

What was 'the Colossus of Rhodes'?

In what direction was the voyage after leaving Rhodes?

Towards what country? To what city?

What was the city?

What was the destination of the vessel?

Why did Paul exchange ships?

Where was Phœnicia?

What change in the voyage now?

Why may we think the passage to Tyre a quick one?

Was Tyre in Phœnicia or in Syria?

Where is Tyre first mentioned in the Scriptures?

Was it more prosperous then or in Paul's time?

Why did the ship stop at Tyre?

Was Patara the beginning of the ship's voyage?

Was Tyre the end of her voyage?

Can you point out any passage in the Acts which indicates how there came to be disciples in Tyre?

Did the Spirit *command* that Paul should not go to Jerusalem?

What is the meaning of the verse?

Who came out of the city to the sea-shore?

Where was Ptolemais? In what country?

How was the journey probably made to Cæsarea?

Had Paul's journey from Philippi to Cæsarea been made in time to reach the feast of Pentecost?

Can you show it?

Whom did Paul find at Cæsarea?

Have we any notice of this man before?

What is meant by 'Evangelist'?

What does 'one of the seven' mean?

Why is the fact mentioned that the daughters prophesied?

What other prophet comes to Cæsarea?

Where else is he mentioned?

What did he foretell? How?

Whom did he resemble in doing this?

What was meant by 'deliver him into the hands of the Gentiles'?

Could this result be avoided?

Who besides the Christians of Cæsarea 'besought' Paul?

Would it have been right for Paul *not* to have gone to Jerusalem?

Was Paul's resolution mere wilful determination?

What is the proper manner in which to meet unwelcome providential events?

What does 'took up our carriages' mean?

Who went with Paul? Whom did they bring?

Why has it been thought he was called 'an old disciple'?

What significance in his coming from Cyprus?

A MOB IN JERUSALEM.

LESSON.
Acts xxi. 17-36.

THE 'brethren' of Jerusalem had no doubt heard by this time of Paul's return. No sooner, therefore, was Paul in Jerusalem, and settled in the house of Mnason, than he received their glad welcome. Everywhere he went, he found some warm friends, whose attachment no opposition nor persecution nor foreboding, could break. Silas might have been among them: possibly Barnabas and Mark, as it was the time of Pentecost.

Paul seems to have had three objects in mind in visiting Jerusalem: to *present the collections*[1] taken in the Gentile churches *for the poor Christians of Judea*, to *attend the Pentecost*, and to *overcome the hostile feeling* to him which existed in the minds of many of the Christians. Friendly as his Christian brethren were, there were still some of them who were 'zealous of the law,' and were far from liking Paul's manner of preaching to the Gentiles about keeping the law of Moses. The old and difficult question[2] still gave them trouble in some of its forms. Indeed, it was these persons, and the missionaries which they had sent out, whom Paul had found to be making disturbance in the churches of Galatia[3] and of Corinth.[4] Before he went to Rome,

---

[1] See chapter xxiv. 17, 18.
[2] See Fifteenth Sunday.

[3] See page 234.
See page 223.

he would wish, therefore, to have all misunderstanding and difficulty removed : "to win, by the force of Christian love and forbearance, the hearts of those whom he regarded, in spite of all their weaknesses and errors, as brethren in Christ Jesus."

We suppose Paul, therefore, to have spent the evening of the day on which he arrived with his friends, prepared on the next day to meet the church and to show 'what God had wrought by his ministry.'

In the morning, the elders of the church and the Apostle James were gathered together. The brethren who had brought up the collection from the Gentile churches, Luke[5] and Trophimus,[6] and whatever others had continued on the journey past Troas and Miletus,[7] went into the assembly, and 'Paul with them.' It is likely, therefore, that at this meeting the charities of the Gentile churches were presented to the church at Jerusalem, to be distributed to the poor of Judea.

After the salutations, either by 'the kiss of peace' or by words of Christian courtesy, or both, Paul told the story of his journey. He had been gone about four years,[8] since he left Antioch. He had been on a long and eventful journey; and every particular would be full of interest to his hearers. He therefore 'declared *particularly* what things God had wrought.' He spoke of the systematic visitation of the churches in Galatia and Phrygia, of his long and peaceful and profitable residence in Ephesus, of Apollos and the disciples of John, of Aquila and Priscilla, and 'the church in their

---

[5] 'With *us*,' verse 18.   [6] Verse 29.

[7] In xx. 4, it is only said that the seven brethren mentioned 'accompanied him into *Asia*.'

[8] From Antioch to Ephesus, from *one* to *two months*. At Ephesus, *three years*. From Ephesus to Corinth and back to Troas, *ten months*; from Troas to Jerusalem, about *seven weeks*, (fifty days.)

house,' of the school of Tyrannus, of those who had assisted him to preach the word in the towns of Asia,[9] of the seven sons of Sceva and the mighty triumph of God's cause over Ephesian magic-workers, of that other great triumph over the superstitious worship of Diana, of God's gracious protection through the Town Clerk from the Ephesian mob, of the troubles at Corinth, of Troas and Philippi and Illyricum and Corinth, of his letters and how he had tried to win back offenders and punish the obstinate, of his care to remember the poor and the collections they had now brought back with them, of the miraculous restoration of Eutychus at Troas, of the elders at Miletus, and of brethren at Tyre, and of his prosperous voyage and safe arrival.

Great results had been accomplished. Especially in the chief metropolis of Asia Minor, a large and flourishing church had been gathered, and he had assurance from the elders whom he met at Miletus, as well as from the Divine Spirit, that God would be with and bless his people at Ephesus.

" In such a discourse, Paul could scarcely avoid touching on subjects which would excite painful feelings and arouse bitter prejudice in many of his audience. He could hardly speak of Galatia without mentioning the attempts made there to turn aside his converts. He could not describe the condition of Corinth without alluding to those who came from Palestine, who had introduced confusion and strife among the Christians of that city. Yet he dwelt, no doubt, so far as he could, on topics in which all present could agree."

Whatever of personal feeling or personal prejudice there was, the whole assembly could but give devout thanks to God and glorify him for what he had done.

[9] xix. 10.

It was thought best, however, by the assembly, to represent to Paul the state of mind·in many of the Jewish believers in Jerusalem in respect to him, and to devise some means by which no open difficulties should occur. They told Paul, therefore, that many Jewish believers in the city who were 'zealous of the law,' believed that he had been teaching the Jews in foreign cities not to circumcise their children nor to keep the customs of Moses.

This was not true in respect to Paul. He had taught Gentiles that they *need* not circumcise their children, nor keep the law of Moses, *unless they preferred.* He had not said that *Jews* ought not to circumcise their children. They could if they liked. Indeed, he himself had circumcised Timothy, the son of a Jewess. Yet we can easily see how sincere men, especially prejudiced men, would think Paul had been constantly teaching Jews *not* to circumcise their children and *not* to keep the customs of Moses. It would be prudent to show these ardent advocates of Moses' customs, that Paul was quite *willing* at all appropriate times to do what the customs of Moses required, although he did not admit that he was *obliged* to do it.

What, therefore, is it proper to do?[10] was the question of the assembly. "It was of great consequence not to shock the prejudices of these brethren too rudely, lest they should be tempted to make shipwreck of their faith and renounce their Christianity altogether. Their feelings would be easily excited by any appeal to their Hebrew law. They might easily be roused to fury against one whom they were taught to regard as a despiser of the law and a reviler of the customs of their forefathers."

[10] This must be the meaning of ' What is it, therefore ?'

'What is it proper to do? It will soon be known that you have come,' the elders said. 'A multitude will gather. There may be violent and angry dispute and clamor. They may claim that you have gone far beyond the decree and the letter of the council in respect to this difficult question.' A plan was suggested which, it was thought, would take away all ill-feeling, by showing that Paul himself 'kept the law,' 'walked orderly,' and that these charges 'were nothing.' Four Jewish Christians were in the city who had a vow [11] according to the law of Moses. The time of the vow would soon expire, and then they would offer the customary sacrifices required by the law of Moses from those who take vows. If Paul would purify [11] himself with them, go with them to the temple, and pay for them the expense of the sacrifices offered at the termination of the vow, [12] it would be an open denial of the charges made against him. By doing this, he would be a sharer of their vow, and would show, by observing one of the ceremonies of the law of Moses, that he respected the law, and did not mean to treat it contemptuously. And if he should do this, he would not at all show that he wished Gentiles to do the same thing; for the decree of the council and the letter which had been sent to the churches, and which Paul himself had carried to the Gentiles, had told them they were required to 'observe no such thing.' Paul, who himself had taken a vow on his former journey abroad, [13] was quite willing to do this, if it would be the means of preventing outbreak or difficulty.

The next day Paul took the men and attended to the

---

[11] See pages 193, 194.

[12] "In the case of poor Nazarites, it was customary for others to be at the expense of the sacrifice by which their vow was terminated, who thus became partners in their vows."—DR. ROBINSON. [14]

[13] Acts xviii. 18.

customary acts of purification for himself. He then went with them to the temple: he purchased (as Paul · was not rich, the brethren no doubt helped him, or money was taken from the *poor fund* which had been established by the collections) the animals for sacrifice: he announced to the priest that the time of a vow made by four of his friends had come to an end, and that he had purchased the animals for sacrifice, and wished to share their vow with them by waiting till the sacrifice was made and their hair shorn and burned on the altar.

It was towards the end of a certain 'seven days' that the excitement occurred about Paul. These seven days may have been the period of the vow, or the time after Paul had given notice that he would pay the expense of the four men. At this time, multitudes of Jews from foreign parts were in town: worshippers from every land thronged the temple. Among them were some Jews from Asia, who had seen Paul at Ephesus. They had been perhaps among the Jews of the synagogue there, from which Paul had withdrawn when he and his disciples went to the school of Tyrannus; and with bitter hatred they had seen Paul building up a Christian church in Ephesus. Their strong feelings had drawn them home to the sacred festival and the holy temple; and they "now beheld, where they least expected to find him, the apostate Israelite, who had opposed their teaching and drawn away their converts. An opportunity of revenge had suddenly presented itself. They sprang upon their enemy and shouted, while they held him fast: 'Men of Israel, help! This is the man that teacheth all men everywhere against the people and the law and this place.'" A crowd rushed towards the spot; and the Jews of Asia added to the excitement by crying out that the man whom they held fast had brought Greeks into the holy temple. This was enough

to make a Jewish multitude frantic with anger, horror
and indignation. The exciting and awful news ran
through the city. The multitude was multiplied. The
crowd rushed upon Paul. They would not shed his
blood in the sacred temple, but they dragged him out
beyond those columns " on which inscriptions in Greek
and Latin warned all Gentiles against going beyond
them on pain of death." Pulling him down the steps
and beating him, they were on the very point of killing
him. The Levites quickly rolled together the gates of
the temple, " lest the Holy Place should be polluted
with murder." But before the more malicious of the
Jews could get at Paul to take his life, a company of
Roman soldiers, commanded by the officer of the garrison, wheeled through the crowd and rescued him.
Chaining him fast to two soldiers, and finding it impossible to get any good answer from the clamorous multitude, the officer commanded him to be taken up into
the garrison. Their strength was but barely sufficient.
The surging violence of the people was so great that
they *carried* their innocent prisoner in their arms up
the stairs, the maddened people shouting behind: 'Away
with him! away with him!'

QUESTIONS.

WHO were among the disciples at Jerusalem ?
What were Paul's three objects in visiting Jerusalem ?
Can you prove that two of these objects were his ?
Can you find any proof in respect to the third ?
Who did not like Paul's manner of preaching ?   In what respect ?
What question still gave trouble ?
Who were gathered to receive and hear Paul ?
Who probably presented the collections ?
How long had Paul been gone ?
How did Paul 'declare' the story of his journey ?
What particulars can you mention ?
What was one of the greatest results of this journey ?
Had not Paul preached in almost every place to Jews ?
Why is it then said, 'Among the Gentiles' ?
Whom did the Christians at Jerusalem recognise as
      causing all these results ?
What painful feelings would be probably excited ?
What two places especially would bring up the difficult
      points ?
How many Jews were there who were sensitive in respect to the law ?
What had they been 'informed' in respect to Paul ?
Was this true ?
What had Paul taught ?
What had Paul himself done ?
What was Paul's position in respect to this question ?
What is the meaning of 'What is it, therefore' ?
What was it best to avoid ?
What was likely to take place ?
What plan was suggested ?
What is meant by 'a vow' ?
What is the meaning of 'purify thyself with them' ?
Explain ' be at charges with them.'

What would 'the shaving of the head' openly show?

Would this be a violation of the decree of the council?

In which verse is the decree of the council referred to?

How soon did Paul go with these four men to the temple?

How might the necessary animals have been purchased?

Explain 'signify the accomplishment of the days,' etc.

What were the 'seven days'?

Who would be in the temple at this feast?

What foreign Jews saw Paul?

From what place were they probably?

What probably added to their excitement and hatred?

What did they now do and say in the temple?

Were they in the temple itself, or in one of the *courts?*

Why should the words they cried excite the people so much?

What was the most exciting thing in what they said?

Had Trophimus been *in the temple?*

What courts of the temple was Paul dragged out of?

What inscriptions were on what columns?

Who closed the doors? Why?

Do you suppose *all* the Jews would have taken Paul's life?

Would it have been right to have taken his life, according to their law?

Would the *mode* have been right?

How was Paul rescued?

How was he chained?

Why was he commanded to be carried off? Where?

What shows the power and violence of the crowd?

What other outcry was the outcry of the multitude like?

(84)

Forty-third Sunday.

THE ADDRESS FROM THE STAIRS.

LESSON.
Acts xxi. 37–40; xxii. 1–29.

THE 'castle,'[1] or garrison, from which the Roman
soldiers came, who rescued Paul, was the Fort Antonia, which was close beside the temple, and commanded the temple as the temple commanded the city. This
fortification was very large. "Within, it had the extent and appearance of a palace, being divided into
apartments of every kind, with galleries and baths and
broad halls or barracks for a thousand soldiers, so that
it seemed like a city." Its towers looked down on the
temple, and from them the sentinels could see what was
going on in the various courts; and flights of stone stairs
led down to the level spaces on the sides of the temple,
so that the soldiers could at any time enter and prevent
tumults. It was not always filled with soldiers, but at
the time of the festivals a military force was kept there
to suppress any outbreak against the Roman power.
Indeed, at this very time the soldiers of the fortress and
the people of the city were in great excitement in consequence of an Egyptian Jew "who, as a pretended
prophet, had led off a vast number of fanatic followers
into the wilderness, to be slain or captured by the
Roman troops."

[1] The Greek word translated 'castle,' means strictly an encamp
ment, or 'barracks.'

The Roman sentinels on the towers and the walls had watched the growing excitement in the courts of the temple; and as the multitude and the uproar increased, they sent word to Claudius Lysias, the officer of the garrison, that the whole city was in commotion. It might be a case of uprising against the Roman government, and not a moment was to be lost. With a few sturdy companies of soldiers, under their centurions, he

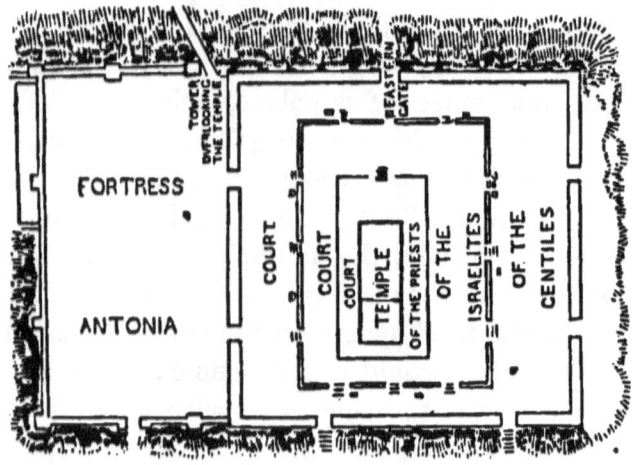

(THE TEMPLE AND FORTRESS ANTONIA.²)

rushed down the stairs into the temple-area. As he pushed directly forward to the man who was the centre of all this excitement, the crowd gave way before "the flashing arms and disciplined movements of the Imperial

---

² We must remember the difference between the *temple* and the *courts of the temple;* and also that each court of the temple was higher than the court outside of it, and that the temple was highest of all. The tower at the south-east corner of Antonia overlooked *all:* the *walls* of the fort overlooked the lower courts. We do not know exactly at what point in the wall between Antonia and the temple-area the flight of stone steps was, but the crowd of Jews were on the marble pavement of the court of the Gentiles. They accused Paul of taking Gentiles past the forbidden boundary up into the court of the Israelites.

soldiers;" and Paul was borne off up the stair-way, out
of the reach of the shouting crowd.

Once out of the reach of the mob, Paul was *led* up
towards the fortress. "At this moment, the Apostle,
with the utmost presence of mind, turned to the commanding officer who was near him, and addressing him
in Greek, said respectfully : ' May I speak with thee ? '
Claudias Lysias was startled to hear his prisoner address him in Greek, and asked him if he was not the
Egyptian ringleader of the late rebellion." Paul's calm
reply comprised much in its simple statement. He was
not an Egyptian Jew, but a Jew of Tarsus. He *could*
speak Greek, for Tarsus was a city of Greek learning.
He was no robber nor ringleader of rebels, but a re-
spectable citizen of a distinguished city. Therefore he
besought Lysias to allow him to speak to the people.
" The request was a bold one, and we are almost surprised that Lysias should have granted it ; but there
seems to have been something in Paul's aspect and
manner which from the first gained an influence over
the mind of the Roman officer, and he did not refuse
his consent. And now, in a moment, the whole scene
was changed." Paul turned about on the stairs, and
motioned with his hand to the noisy crowds below.
Something in his appearance, as of a man accustomed
to address gatherings of people, commanded their attention. The turbulent ' sea of heads ' became tranquil,
and there was ' great silence.' We can see Paul's out-
stretched wave of his hand, as he says :

**" Men, brethren, and fathers, hear now my
defence to you."** [1]

Paul's wisdom and skill and courtesy are again shown
by speaking in Hebrew. The confused multitude evi-

---

[1] The words in italics in the Bible are not in the original Greek.

dently thought some vile Gentile or Gentile Christian
had been dragged out of the inner sacred enclosure of
the temple. The sound of the Hebrew language half
disarmed them. If Paul had spoken in Greek, the most
of the people would have understood him. "But the
sound of the holy tongue in that holy place fell like a
calm on the troublous waters. The silence became universal and breathless; and the Apostle proceeded to
address his countrymen:

**"I am myself[*] an Israelite, born indeed[*] at
Tarsus in Cilicia, yet[*] brought up in this city,
and taught at the feet of Gamaliel in the strictest doctrine of the law of our fathers."**

PAUL'S DEFENCE FROM THE STAIRS.

Two charges had been made against Paul, which had
caused the uproar: *one*, that he had everywhere spoken
evil of the Jews, of their holy law, and of their holy
temple; and the *second*, that he had polluted the temple by bringing Greeks into it. It was no doubt Paul's
purpose to answer fully both these charges. The second charge, we know, was entirely false. The men in
the temple with him were Jews. Trophimus was not
in the temple, though he had been in the street with
Paul. Paul was not permitted to reach that point of
his speech where he could have defended himself from
the second accusation. His address up to the point
at which it was broken off, was in defence of himself
against the first charge. He gives three reasons to
show that he had not spoken disrespectfully of the
Jews nor of their holy law nor of the temple.

First. He was himself a Jew by birth and by educa-

---

[*] 'Verily' is meant to emphasize I. I, verily, am: I myself am.
[*] The 'yet' shows an opposite meaning in the previous clause,
'*born* indeed, yet *brought* up.'

tion, (verse 3.) He was indeed born in a distant Greek city, but was educated in Jerusalem, by Gamaliel himself, and was zealous for the law.

Secondly. There was nothing in his conversion which showed any disrespect to the law or to the temple, (verses 4 to 16.) He had indeed been converted from an enemy of Jesus and of this sect of Christians, to a preacher of the Messiahship of Jesus, but he had, during his conversion, honored both the law and the temple. 1. For the high-priest and the elders could bear witness that he persecuted these Christians because he thought they were violating the law, and that he went to Damascus to imprison them. There was no disrespect to the law in this, but eagerness to obey it. 2. On the road to Damascus he had been miraculously struck blind, by the glorious appearance of Jesus of Nazareth, and from that time he knew that Jesus was the Messiah; but in all that was said and done, there was nothing against the law or the temple. 3. In Damascus, *a man who reverenced the law* had miraculously restored him to sight and baptized him in the name of Jesus, telling him that he was to bear testimony of what he had seen and heard to all men.

Thirdly. When he came back to Jerusalem and was *praying in the temple,* he had a vision, in which Jesus appeared to him and directed him to hasten away from Jerusalem to avoid being killed. (Verses 17 to 21.) He himself had wished to remain and to convince those who knew how bitter a persecutor he had been, that this Jesus was the Messiah predicted in the law, but the voice in the temple had told him that his testimony would not be received by his acquaintances and friends, and had said: 'Depart, I will send thee far hence unto the Gentiles.'

"Up to this point, Paul had riveted their attention."

Many of them knew that he spoke the truth in respect to his early life and his persecution. "Even when he told them of his miraculous conversion, of Ananias, and of his vision in the temple, they listened still." What a solemn stillness there must have been when he accused himself of the murder of Stephen! But when the word 'Gentiles' was spoken, "one outburst of frantic indignation rose from the temple-area and silenced the speaker on the stairs. Their national pride bore down every argument which could influence their reason or their reverence. They could not bear the thought of uncircumcised heathen being made equal to the sons of Abraham. They cried out that such a wretch ought not to pollute the earth with his presence, that it was a shame to have preserved his life; and in their rage they tossed off their outer garments and threw up dust into the air with frantic violence."

If Paul had been permitted to go on with his defence, he would no doubt have tried to show, *fourthly*, that since he had been a preacher to the Gentiles, he had said nothing evil of the Jews or the law or the temple to the Gentiles: that the law and the prophecies themselves were being fulfilled by the conversion of the Gentiles: that Jesus himself was the Messiah according to the law and the prophets and according to the very ceremonies of the temple. And then he would have shown, no doubt, *fifthly*, that he had *not* taken any Greeks into the temple: that the charge of pollution was altogether a mistake. But the outcry of the people prevented him from answering farther.

Lysias, the Roman officer, seems not to have understood Paul's Hebrew speech. When he saw the people suddenly break out into such imprecations and violent actions, "he concluded his prisoner must be guilty of some enormous crime. He ordered him, therefore. to be taken immediately from the stairs into the barracks," and to be scourged till he confessed his guilt. The centurion proceeded to have Paul 'stretched out,' and bound like a criminal, 'to receive the lashes.' The rude Roman soldiers would not be very tender in their cruel work. Paul had, however, an abundant protection. A few simple words were like magic. He simply said to the centurion: "Is it lawful for you to put to the scourge a Roman citizen, uncondemned?" The centurion ordered the soldiers to stop: he went to Lysias and said significantly: "Take heed what thou doest, for this man is a Roman citizen." "Lysias was both astonished and alarmed. He knew that no man would dare to assume the right of citizenship if it did not really belong to him, and he hastened to his prisoner." He found that Paul was not only a Roman citizen, but a more honorable citizen than himself; "for while Claudias Lysias had purchased the right for 'a great sum,' Paul was 'free born.'"[*] Paul was instantly released; and the commanding officer of Fort Antonia, like the magistrates of Philippi, was 'afraid' of the innocent, unthreatening Apostle, 'because he had bound him.'

[*] See page 5.

QUESTIONS.

WHAT is the meaning of the word 'castle'?

What 'castle' was this?

Its size? its towers? its garrison?

What excitement about this time among soldiers and citizens?

How had news of the disturbance probably been brought to the chief captain?

Was his object, in sending soldiers, to rescue Paul?

What is the difference between the temple and the courts of the temple?

How was the fortress situated, with reference to the temple-courts?

In what court was the multitude?

What did they accuse Paul of?

Had not Paul been *led* all the way from the temple-court?

What did Paul now say?

Why may we suppose he spoke in Greek?

What shows the chief captain was surprised?

Could not Egyptians speak Greek?

Did not Lysias know that Paul was a Jew?

What Egyptian did the 'chief captain' refer to?

Show what points are comprised in Paul's reply.

Why did the noisy multitude grow quiet so soon?

Do you think many in the multitude knew Paul?

What were the first words Paul said?

Why are words put in italics in our translation of the Bible?

Would the multitude have understood Greek?

Why did Paul speak in Hebrew?

What is the force of 'verily'?

What is the force of 'yet'?

What two charges had been made against Paul (xxi. 28)?

Did Paul answer both of these charges? Why?

How many reasons did he give against the first charge?

What is the first reason? In what verse?

What is the second reason? In what verses?

  What is the first point in this reason?

  How had he honored the law in this?

  What is the second point in this reason?

  How does this bear on the general argument?

  What is the third point in this reason?

  What was there especially in the character of Ananias which should have led Paul to obey him?

  What did the miracle show in respect to Ananias's message?

What is the third reason? In what verses?

  What does 'prayed in the temple' show?

  Why did Paul wish to remain?

  Why was he sent away?

  What were the *words* of the divine direction to Paul?

What points in Paul's address had especially kept the attention of the people?

  What words made the outcry against him?

  Why did they 'cast off their clothes' and throw up dust?

What fourth and fifth reasons was Paul intending doubtless to give?

Why would Lysias think Paul guilty of great crime?

  Why did he order him to be scourged?

  What protection had Paul?

  What was the difference between the Roman citizenship of Lysias and of Paul?

  What does 'examined him' mean?

  What did Lysias fear?

Forty-fourth Sunday.

PAUL A PRISONER BEFORE THE SANHEDRIM.

LESSON.

Acts xxii. 30; xxiii. 1-24.

THE most natural way now for Lysias to find out
Paul's crime was to bring him down to the regular
Jewish court. He called together, therefore, the members of the Jewish Sanhedrim and the chief priests;
and then he brought Paul down the stone stairway,
no doubt with an escort of soldiers for his safe-keeping,
and 'set him before them.'

"Only a narrow space of the Great Temple court
was between the steps which led down from the tower
of Antonia and those which led up to the hall Gazith,
the Sanhedrim's accustomed place of meeting. If that
hall was used on this occasion, no heathen soldiers
would be allowed to enter it; for it was within the ba-
lustrade which separated the sanctuary from the court.
But the fear of pollution would keep the Apostle's life
safe within that enclosure. There is good reason, however, for believing that the Sanhedrim met at that period
in a place less sacred, to which the soldiers would be
admitted." The scene is no longer Roman, but Jewish.
What a change had twenty-five[1] years wrought! Then

---

[1] *Fourteen* years after his conversion Paul came with alms to Jerusalem; (see page 41;) his first journey occupied *a year* at least; his
second journey occupied about *two and a half* years; his third journey about *four* years; and the different times at Antioch (xii. 25 and
xiii. 1-2; xiv. 28; xv. 35, 36; xviii. 22, 23) must have amounted to
as much as *three* and a *half* years.

Stephen stood before the Sanhedrim, and Paul was one
who gave his 'vote.' Now Paul was a prisoner before
the same council. On the seats he may have seen some
of the very persons who then heard Stephen's speech.
Some of the elders may have been his fellow-disciples
at the school of Gamaliel. Some of them may have
been with him in his mad persecutions of the sect of
Christians. They well knew the truth of his speech on
the yesterday. But no consciousness of guilt now
flushed the cheek of Paul. The blood of Jesus had
cleansed away all which he had long ago acknowledged
to be the vilest of crimes. Now, undaunted, he could
look earnestly and steadily around on the council. Paul
spoke the first words : " Men and brethren, I have always lived a conscientious life before God up to this
very day." " That unflinching look and those confident
words so enraged the high-priest that he commanded
those near Paul to strike him on the mouth. This
brutal insult roused the Apostle's feelings, and he ex-
claimed : " God shall smite thee, thou whited wall : sit-
test thou to judge me according to the law and then,
in defiance of the law, dost thou command me to be
struck ?" These words may have been an indignant as
sertion of his rights, or Paul may have uttered " a prophetic denunciation." If they were a prophecy, they
were terribly fulfilled, when afterwards assassins, in the
Jewish war, set fire to this same high-priest's house,
drove him out of it, and, finding him in an aqueduct,
caught him and murdered him. The members of the
Sanhedrim " treated Paul's words as profane and rebellious." 'Revilest thou God's high-priest?' was now
their indignant exclamation. Paul's reply was, with all
becoming submission to that very law they had accused
him of violating, that he did not consider that Ananias
was high-priest, or he would not have violated a well-

known law. Precisely what Paul meant, it is difficult
for us to say,[1] but it seems likely that he meant that he
could not consider Ananias, who had done such an unjust and improper thing for a high-priest, really to be
the regular high-priest, though he occupied the position.

This act of cruel injustice showed Paul that he would
have no fair trial by the Sanhedrim : that they were
ready to condemn him, whatever he might say. See-
ing, then, that the council was composed both of Pharisees and of Sadducees, and knowing that the two parties were more bitter against each other than they were
even against him, and that the Pharisees did agree with
himself in the great doctrine of the Scriptures on which
the Messiahship of Jesus was founded, he wisely determined to rid himself out of the hands of these wicked
men by the division of the council. He therefore declared himself to be a Pharisee, and said that he was
really persecuted because he so earnestly advocated the
great doctrine of the Pharisees—the resurrection of the
dead. We know that this was one strong argument
which Paul had used in proving Jesus of Nazareth to
be the Messiah,[2] and that when he wrote his first letter
to the Corinthians, he occupied no small space in proving the resurrection of the dead.[4] It was probably
well known that Paul everywhere made much of this

---

[1] Five different meanings have been given to these words. (1.)
Paul confessed that he had spoken without reflection : 'I did not consider, when I spoke, that he was high-priest.' (2.) Paul spoke ironically :
'Pardon me, brethren. It did not occur to me that a man who could
do this thing could be God's high-priest.' (3.) Paul did not know the
fact that Ananias was high-priest. (4.) Paul's eyesight was poor, and
he made a mistake. (5.) Paul did not acknowledge any one but
Jesus to be high-priest.

[2] See page 60.　　　　　　　　[4] I. Corinth. xv.

argument of the resurrection of Jesus, to prove that Jesus was the Messiah. The Sadducees would hate him the more for that. When Paul was arraigned for his teaching, the doctrine of the resurrection was ' called in question.' He might rightly, therefore, put himself with the Pharisees, and say that they had a common doctrine at stake. Instantly there was a division and a dissension. The rival parties lost sight of Paul in their bitterness against each other. At length the Scribes on the Pharisees' side said they had no fault to find with Paul : that if he really had seen a vision in the Temple, or had heard a voice from God—if a spirit or angel had spoken to him—they ought not to fight against God. And now the judgment-hall was filled with contention and violence; " and soon Claudius Lysias received word of what was taking place ; and, fearing lest the Roman citizen, whom he was bound to protect, should be torn in pieces between the parties, he ordered the troops to go down instantly and bring him back into the soldiers' quarters within the fortress."

That night, when Paul was alone and sad, in his desolate condition, reflecting no doubt upon the interruption to his plan of a fourth missionary journey to Rome, another vision appeared to him. The Lord Jesus himself appeared to him and told him to be of good cheer, that he should see Rome, and that he should there bear testimony to His resurrection and Messiahship.

The next morning a conspiracy was made to assassinate Paul. More than forty Jews took a dreadful oath either themselves to perish from hunger and thirst or to slay Paul. The chief-priests and elders were wicked enough to listen to them and to help on the plot. They were no doubt more enraged than ever to think that Paul escaped from the Sanhedrim the day before. What a horrible crime was this which they agreed to do and which they concealed under the appearance of justice and religion!—to ask that Paul might be brought to a court of justice, and to murder him on the way!

"The plot was ready: the next day it was to be carried into effect; but God confounded the plans of the conspirators." One of Paul's relatives here appears. The only member of that household in Tarsus of whom we have any knowledge is mentioned: the sister of Paul's childhood. The kind and affectionate act of Paul's nephew, in the midst of so much danger to himself, shows that his mother must have had something of her apostolic brother's kind and tender and loving disposition, and that she had trained her son into the practice of her own virtues. This young man went to Fort Antonia, gained entrance into the barracks, got permission to see his uncle, and told him of the plot against his life. Paul's Roman citizenship, as well as his personal character, had already won him respect in the garrison; and the centurion promptly listened to Paul's request that the young man might be taken to the headquarters of Lysias. And the chief-officer himself either respected Paul so much, or feared him so much because he had bound him, or was of such a kind and obliging disposition, that he took the young stranger by the hand and went with him into a private place and asked him what he wished. Then Paul's nephew not only told the story of the conspiracy, but entreated Lysias not to yield to the request of the Jews. How earnestly Lysias must have listened as the young Jew went on with his story! How the resolution and patriotism of the Roman soldier rose when he knew that the Jews out of malice were plotting against the life of a Roman citizen. He promptly decided what to do, but did not tell his informant. He simply dismissed him by charging him to tell no man whatever that he had brought him this information.

Two centurions were immediately called: they were ordered to get ready two hundred of the regular soldiers, seventy of the cavalry, and two hundred spearmen: to be ready to start for Cæsarea at nine o'clock in the evening, and to take Paul the prisoner in safety to Felix the governor. And besides, as the journey was long, and they must go rapidly, they were ordered to have more than one horse for Paul. "We may be surprised that so large a force was sent to secure the safety of one man; but we must remember that this man was a Roman citizen, while the garrison in Fort Antonia, a thousand strong, could easily spare that number for one day; and that assassinations, robberies, and rebellions were quite frequent at that time in Judea." No one could tell what size the conspiracy might reach, or to what an extent the conspirators would go, if any discovery was made of Paul's departure. Everything was done, therefore, secretly as well as promptly; and an hour was fixed which would excite as little suspicion as possible. "At the time appointed, the troops, with Paul in the midst of them, marched out of the fortress, and at a rapid pace took the road to Cæsarea."

QUESTIONS.

WAS it right or wrong for Lysias to bring Paul before the council?

What was the council?

What two places were there where this 'council' met?

How many years since Stephen's trial?   Show it.

Whom may Paul have seen in the council?

How would they think of Paul?

How could he boldly face that court, when he had acknowledged himself guilty of murder?

How can the greatest criminal gain again the *feeling* of right?

Why does not Paul now say, 'Men, brethren, *and fathers*'?

What is meant by 'all good conscience'?

Can a conscience be *good* which will permit a man to persecute and murder?

Why did the high-priest give his command?

What two explanations of Paul's reply?

If a prophecy, what was the fulfilment?

Why had the high-priest done wickedly?

Were those who 'stood by' right in *their* reply?

What does 'resist not' mean?

What five meanings have been given to this answer of Paul's?

Which one do you think correct?

What did the act of the high-priest show Paul?

What two parties were there in the council?

With which party did Paul agree? on what point?

How was the doctrine of 'resurrection' called in question?

Where had Paul advocated this doctrine? for what?

Do you think Paul's position on this doctrine was well known?

What would the Sadducees think of Paul's declaration?

Was it right for Paul to make this declaration for this purpose?

In what other way can you explain this declaration?

Why did the Pharisee Scribes take Paul's part?

Why did they declare Paul innocent?

What other doctrine than resurrection did they refer to?

To what time did they refer, when an angel or a spirit might have spoken to Paul?

Why did the chief captain take Paul again from the Jews?

What would Paul be likely to think of when alone?

Why was the vision an especial comfort to him?

What conspiracy was made? By whom?

Is it at any time right to call upon ourselves such curses?

Who helped the conspiracy on?

Why is it wicked to *listen* to such proposals?

Why was their wickedness especially horrible?

How was the plan defeated?

What does this show in respect to Paul's sister?

What did Paul's nephew?

How did Lysias receive him? Why?

What was the effect on Lysias?

Why was this heathen officer more noble than the temple-councillors?

What was the plan of Lysias?

Would there be so many men and horses in this fortress?

Why were so many sent?

Was there more than one 'beast' for Paul?

What was the hour? Why?

THE CAPITAL AND THE GOVERNOR OF JUDEA.

LESSON.

Acts xxiii. 25–35; xxiv. 1–26.

THE conspirators were perhaps in session arranging the details of the plot, when the armed men tramped along the street and the striking of the horses' hoofs on the pavement rang out on the night-air. But the passing of armed companies of Roman soldiers had become too common a thing in Jerusalem to call especial attention to it, or to awaken suspicion that Paul was on the way to a place of safety.

Till about midnight the centurions would take their course directly northward, and probably along the very road which Paul took when he went to Damascus. How different the journey now! Then, an escort of soldiers at his own command : now, himself a prisoner under a Roman guard! At midnight they would be about at Gophna, (see the map on page 24,) and then would leave the Damascus road, turning to the left towards the coast. "Soon they began to descend, startling the shepherd on the hills of Ephraim and rousing the village peasant, who woke to curse his heathen oppressor as he heard the voices and the well-known tramp of the Roman soldiers." About day-break they must have been near the foot of the hilly ridges which make up the broken mountain-range. From the last hill they descended, they overlooked the plain of Sharon. "The

road then turned northwards across the rich land of the
plain of Sharon, through fields of wheat and barley, almost ready for the harvest." Some low, wooded hills
now shut off their view of the sea. Early in the forenoon
they reached the town of Antipatris. They were now out
of the mountain-passes, in an open, level country. The
foot-soldiers were no longer needed for protection, and
they might be wanted at Jerusalem. One centurion
turned back therefore with them to Fort Antonia. The
cavalry and spearmen went on, probably under the
orders of the other centurion; and in the afternoon
" their weary horses entered the streets of Cæsarea."
They went at once to the house or quarters of Felix,
delivered the prisoner, and presented the letter which
Lysias had sent. The Governor broke the seals and
read the following official despatch:

"*Claudius Lysias sends greeting to his Excellency
Felix the Governor. This man was apprehended by
the Jews and on the point of being killed by them, when
I came and rescued him with my military guard; for
I learned that he was a Roman citizen.*[1] *And when I
wished to ascertain the charge which they had against
him, I took him down to their Sanhedrim; and there I
found that the charge had reference to certain questions
of their law, and that he was accused of no offence
worthy of death or imprisonment. And now, having
received information that a plot is about to be formed
against the man's life, I send him to thee forthwith,
and I have told his accusers that they must bring their
charge before thee. Farewell.*"

" Felix raised his eyes from the paper and said: 'To
what province does he belong?' It was the first question which a Roman governor would naturally ask in

---

[1] This was false, but Lysias craftily inserted it to save himself from
disgrace. He did not rescue Paul *because* he was a Roman citizen.

such a case. The Roman law had strict rules for all legal communication between provinces. In the present case, there could be no difficulty. A Roman citizen, with certain vague charges brought against him, was placed under the protection of a governor of a province, who was bound to keep him in safe custody till the cause should be heard. Having found, therefore, that Paul was a native of the province of Cilicia, Felix simply ordered him to be kept in 'Herod's prætorium,'[2] and said to Paul himself: 'I will hear and decide thy cause when thy accusers have come.'"

The city to which Paul was now brought was one through which he had passed several times. It was built up by Herod the Great from an insignificant place to be a splendid city. In twelve years he built a wall around the town and decorated it with splendid buildings. He named it Cæsarea in honor of Augustus Cæsar the Emperor. The buildings were made of white stone. There was a theatre (from which Herod Agrippa was carried out to die[3]) and an amphitheatre. There were aqueducts for the conveyance of water. There was a temple dedicated to Cæsar. There were many other splendid buildings. There were statues and heathen sanctuaries. "The city was provided with everything that could contribute to magnificence, amusement, and health. But its great boast was its harbor." The west winds swept with great fury against this unprotected coast. At immense expense and with immense labor, Herod built a stone harbor, equal in size to the natural harbor of the Piræus of Athens.[4] "Vast stones were sunk in the sea to the depth of twenty fathoms, and thus a stupendous breakwater was formed, curving

---

[2] The palace and 'judgment-hall' (verse 35) combined.
[3] See pages 41, 42.   [4] See map page 160.

round so as to give complete protection against the south-westerly winds. It was open only on the north." "Within it a fleet might ride in perfect safety in all weathers." Into this harbor the ships which had borne Paul on his different voyages across the sea to Cæsarea had entered and here had cast anchor. When Herod's great work in the city and the harbor had been completed, Herod himself fixed his palace (or *prætorium*) there, and Cæsarea became the capital of the *Roman province* of Judea. 'Herod's prætorium' was probably the residence of Felix and other governors after Herod's death.

Although Cæsarea was the capital of Judea, it seems to have been as much a Gentile city as it was a Jewish city. Many 'heathen strangers' lived there. "The harbor was called the 'Augustan Harbor;' the city, 'Augustan Cæsarea.' Even in the Jewish synagogues the Greek translation of the Scriptures was read.

Felix, the Governor of this Roman province, was a singular example of those persons who have risen from the lowest rank to high authority. He was at first a slave. For something which he had done, we do not know what, he was made free by the emperor. When he was the freedman of the emperor he was strangely honored with military appointments, until he was made Procurator* or Governor of Judea. He was cruel, unjust, oppressive, unscrupulous and profligate. A Roman historian says: "That in the practice of all kinds of lust and cruelty, he exercised the power of a king with the temper of a slave." He had caused one high-priest to be murdered by a gang of villains at the very steps of the temple. He had enticed Drusilla, a daughter of Herod Agrippa, who was celebrated for her beauty, to

---

* The *Procurator* had much more power and dignity than the *Proconsul.* See page 51.

leave her husband and to live with him. Yet he did the Jews some good services. "He cleared various parts of the country from robbers : he pursued and drove away that Egyptian fanatic" who had attempted to raise sedition under pretence of prophetic power, and for whom Claudius Lysias mistook Paul. The story of Paul's imprisonment by him, in the Scriptures, shows, as will be seen, his servile meanness. He was now only waiting for Paul's accusers to arrive before bringing on his trial.

"The law required that causes should be heard speedily ; and the Apostle's enemies were not long in arriving. Five days either after Paul's departure from Jerusalem or after his arrival at Cæsarea, his accusers appeared. They brought with them "one of those advocates, who practised in the law-courts of the provinces where the forms of Roman law were imperfectly known and the Latin language imperfectly understood." His name, Tertullus, is Roman : perhaps he spoke in Latin. The formal accusation was made before the governor ; the prisoner was brought in ; and Tertullus made a speech in which, after flattering Felix with unmerited praise, he charged Paul with three crimes :

I. With sedition or illegal disturbances among all the Jews throughout the empire.[6]

II. With being a ringleader of 'the sect of the Nazarenes.'

III. "With an attempt to profane the temple at Jerusalem."

The first was a charge of *treason* against the Roman empire : the second was the charge of *heresy* against the law of Moses : the third was the charge of *sacri-*

---

[6] 'Throughout the world.' The Roman empire occupied almost the habitable world.

lege, an offence against the Roman law as well as the Jewish, for the Roman law protected the Jews in their worship.

Tertullus finished his speech by saying that Lysias, the Jerusalem chief-captain, had forcibly taken away Paul from the regular course of justice, when the Jews would have given him a fair trial according to their own ecclesiastical law; and that he had sent him from Jerusalem down to Cæsarea, to be tried here, when he might as well have been tried in Jerusalem. Ananias and the elders agreed to what Tertullus had said.

" The Governor now made a gesture to the prisoner to signify that he might make his defence. The Jews were silent; and the Apostle refuted Tertullus step by step."

PAUL'S REPLY TO TERTULLUS.

I. Paul expresses his satisfaction that Felix has been governor of the province for many years, because he can easily ascertain whether he himself had at any time raised sedition during those years, and also that it had been only twelve days since he came to Jerusalem at all.[7] (Verses 10, 11.)

II. In respect to *sedition,* Why does not Tertullus bring the *proof* of his charges? Why does he not prove the *time* and the *place* at which I committed these offences? Neither in the temple nor in the synagogues nor about the city have I been found disputing or exciting the people.[8] (Verses 12, 13.)

[7] Felix had been governor six or eight years; and Paul had not been in the country, during Felix's reign, before his recent return from his missionary journey, more than a very few days, if at all. What opportunity had there been for him to raise sedition?

[8] It is worthy of notice that Tertullus had accused Paul of sedition *everywhere* throughout the empire; Paul justly answers the charge only so far as respects the province of Judea. The jurisdiction of Felix was confined to his province.

III. In respect to *haresy*, Paul confessed he belonged to a 'sect,' but that he believed in the Jewish law and in the Jewish prophets. There is indeed a 'sect' of the Jews called by some the 'sect of the Nazarenes,' just as there is a sect of the Pharisees and a sect of the Sadducees. As the Roman law protected these sects of Jews in their national faith, Paul claimed protection for the sect to which he belonged. He said too that in one most important point, the doctrine of the resurrection, his own sect agreed with the sect to which his accusers belonged; and that, as for himself, in respect to all these things, he tried to live a conscientious life. (Verses 14 to 16.)

IV. In respect to *polluting the temple*, Paul declared that he was in the temple after regular purification, "not gathering a multitude nor causing a tumult:" that those very Jews of Asia[9] who first saw him there were the proper witnesses to bring against him, and they ought to state what the *act* of pollution was which he had committed.   (Verses 17 to 19.)

V. In respect to the trial before the Sanhedrim, let these members of the Sanhedrim present say whether *any* accusation was made against me there; or whether there was any disturbance there, except what arose from the doctrine of the resurrection, which both many of them and I myself believe. (Verses 20, 21.)

Paul had made a strong argument for himself, even in the mind of this wicked governor. Felix knew something of the Jews and their quarrels. He must have known something of the Christian religion too, for it had been known in Cæsarea for years. But Felix could not quite make up his mind to acquit his prisoner, as he ought to have done. He simply said he would wait till Lysias came before he would give his final decision.

[9] xxi. 27.

Even that which seemed to be kindness towards his prisoner was selfishness. He gave him all the freedom he well could, and even called Paul often into his presence; but he hoped by this means to receive from Paul's friends a bribe for his liberation. In his bold wickedness, he even had the effrontery to invite Paul to speak of the pure and holy religion of Jesus to him, while his adulterous Drusilla sat by his side. No wonder the convicted man trembled when Paul "reasoned of righteousness, temperance, and judgment to come."

QUESTIONS.

WHY would not so large a company of troops excite suspicion?

    What direction did they take? Along what road?

    Where was Antipatris? Describe the journey there.

    Why did the footmen return?

    To whom did the horsemen deliver Paul?

    What did they present him?

What was the opening sentence of Lysias's letter?

    What is not true in the second sentence?

    Why did Lysias write it?

    What is meant by 'an army'?

    Why did Lysias send Paul to Felix, if he was innocent?

    Was Lysias right or wrong in sending him?

What was the Governor's first question? Why?

    Was he doing his duty in imprisoning Paul?

    Ought Paul to have been discharged without waiting for his accusers?

    Was Paul kept in a common prison? Why?

    What is meant by 'judgment-hall'?

What was Cæsarea? Who built and adorned it?

    How many years in building? Prominent buildings?

    What was the especial pride of the city?

    Was Cæsarea a Jewish city? Why?

How had Felix risen to authority?

    How did the office of Governor in Judea differ from the same office in Cyprus?

    What kind of a man was Felix?

    What crimes had he committed?

    What favors had he done the Jews?

Why did Paul's accusers come down to Cæsarea so soon?

    Whom did they bring? Why?

    Was the opening sentence of his speech true?

    What is meant by 'providence'?

    What three crimes did he accuse Paul of?

    What does 'pestilent' mean?

What does 'throughout the world' mean?

Was the claim of Tertullus that the Jews were proceeding legally, true or not?

Who said Tertullus's speech was true?

Is Paul's speech a reply to Tertullus's speech or not?

What is the first division of Paul's speech?

How long had Felix been Governor?

Why should Paul be glad of this?

What is the second division of Paul's speech?

Did Paul in this answer one of the charges *fully*?

Temple, people, synagogues, city: why did he name these?

What is the third division of the speech?

What is heresy? How could it be charged upon Paul?

How did Paul refute this charge?

In what two things did Paul agree with other sects?

What is the fourth division of the speech?

What *proof* did Paul demand of this charge?

What is the fifth division of the speech?

What was the Governor's decision?

What is meant by 'having more perfect knowledge of that way'?

Was it right or wrong in Felix to 'defer' this matter?

Why did Felix let Paul have liberty?

With whom did Felix hear Paul preach?

What do you suppose was his motive in asking Paul to preach 'of Christ'?

Why should Felix especially tremble when Paul preached on these subjects?

Why would we tremble, if we should see clearly the meaning of these same subjects?

What is meant by 'temperance'?

Did Felix see Paul after this time?

Have *we* the power to fix 'the convenient season' when we will be converted?

(90)

Forty-sixth Sunday.

THE APPEAL TO THE EMPEROR.

LESSON.

Acts xxiv. 27; xxv. 1-22.

FOR two whole years the unscrupulous Felix kept Paul in custody at Cæsarea. "He was not bound to fix any definite time for the trial, but might defer it at his pleasure, and keep the accused in custody during the interval. The prisoner was given in charge to a soldier, who was responsible with his own life for the safe keeping of his prisoner; and the keeping of the prisoner was made sure by chaining the prisoner's right hand to the soldier's left." Paul might have been kept at the barracks of the soldiers or in a private house, under charge of his keeper. No doubt many of his Christian friends did visit him. As it was customary for the Roman troops to remain in one place a number of years, Cornelius, the centurion, may possibly have still been in Cæsarea. At least his Christian influence and that of his 'kinsmen and near friends,' may have lingered in many converts among both soldiers and people. The Apostle, who remained two years in Corinth and three years in Ephesus to instruct and direct the Corinthian and Ephesian churches, would find enough to do for two years, even though a prisoner, in teaching the church in Cæsarea. "Many messages and even letters, of which we know nothing, may have been sent from Cæsarea to brethren at a distance."

It has been supposed that Luke, during these two years, wrote his Gospel under the direction of Paul.

During these two years, the cruelty of Felix to the Jews became more and more unendurable. At last there was a terrible outbreak between the Jews and the Greeks of Cæsarea, and many Jews were slaughtered in the streets. "In the end, Felix was summoned to Rome, and the Jews followed him with their accusations." Felix, anxious to lay up favor with the Jews,[1] left Paul bound. And so it happened that "the same enmity of the world against the Gospel which set Barrabas free, left Paul a prisoner."

Festus, the new Governor, appointed by the Emperor, seems to have been an upright and honorable man. And now, just as the Jews of Corinth when Gallio was first appointed tried to get the influence of the new Pro-Consul in their favor, so the Jews of Jerusalem, when Festus, the new Governor, came to Cæsarea, tried to take advantage of the change to get Paul into their own power. On the very first visit of Festus from the modern to the ancient capital, to make himself acquainted with the people and with their favorite city, only three days after assuming authority over the province, the Jews made an accusation against Paul. They crowded around him in a multitude and declared that Paul ought not to live.[2] What their open hatred did not accomplish under Felix, they hoped by plausible arts to gain under Festus. "They asked Festus, as a favor, (and they had good reason to hope that the new governor, on his arrival, would not refuse it,) that he would allow Paul to be brought up to Jerusalem. The plea doubtless was that he ought to be tried again be-

---

[1] 'Willing to show the Jews a pleasure.' The Greek words mean very nearly the English phrase, 'wishing *to be in the good graces* of the Jews.' [2] xxv. 24.

fore the Sanhedrim. The real purpose was to assassinate him on the road." Two years had not softened
the bitterness of their hate. "The answer of Festus
was dignified and just, and worthy of his office. He
said that Paul was in custody at Cæsarea, and that he
himself was shortly to return thither: that it was not
the custom of the Romans to give up an uncondemned
man as a favor:" that his accusers must meet him face
to face, and he must have full opportunity to defend
himself. "Those therefore who were competent to the
task of accusers, should come down with him to Cæsarea, and there make the accusation."

After ten days spent in Jerusalem, Festus returned
to his capital. The very next day he ordered a session
of his court, and took his place among his councillors[2]
on the judgment-seat. The prisoner was brought in.
The accusers made many charges, but they gave no
proof of them to the fair-minded Festus. These charges
are not described by Luke in regular form, as those of
Tertullus were, but we may remember that Felix did
not acquit Paul of Tertullus' accusation, and therefore
that it still remained. Paul's reply was the same as before. He declared himself innocent of heresy, ('against
the law of Moses,') of sacrilege, ('against the temple,')
and of treason, ('against Cæsar.')

Festus soon saw that Paul had committed no crime,
especially one worthy of death.[4] He saw the difficulty
was one of religious prejudice and of Jewish law, and
was not of political character. He was therefore in
some perplexity;[5] for he did not wish to lose the
opportunity of gaining the good wishes of the Jews.[6]
"He proposed, therefore, to Paul, that he should go up
to Jerusalem and be tried *there*, in his presence, or at

---

[2] Verse 12.   [4] See verses 25, 26.   [5] Verse 20, with margin.
The words in verse 9 are the same as in xxiv. 27. See note 1.

least under his protection." Paul could, by his own
consent, if the Governor should agree to it, transfer
himself from the jurisdiction of the Governor's court to
that of the Sanhedrim. But he knew too well the danger of such a change; and he knew, too, that it was
his right as a Roman citizen to be tried by the Roman
and not by the Jewish law. He quickly declined, therefore, the proposal, and boldly claimed his rights from
Festus. At Philippi he had claimed one of the three
great privileges of Roman citizenship,[1] the *freedom
from scourging,* and now, before Festus, he claimed
another, *the right of appeal to the Emperor.* Paul's
reply to this governor of a Roman province, was full
of dignity and power:

> " I stand before Cæsar's tribunal, and there
> ought my trial to be. To the Jews I have done
> no wrong, as thou knowest full well. If I am
> guilty of breaking the law, and have done any-
> thing worthy of death, I refuse not to die; but
> if the things whereof these men accuse me are
> nought, no man can give me up to them. I
> appeal unto Cæsar."

Festus was no doubt surprised; but he had no choice.
" By the mere pronunciation of those powerful words,
'*I appeal unto Cæsar,*' Paul instantly removed his cause
from the jurisdiction of the magistrate before whom he
stood, to the supreme tribunal of the Emperor at Rome."
Only one thing was to be determined by Festus, and
he had nothing to do but to send his prisoner to Rome.
" There were a few cases in which the right of appeal
was not permitted: a bandit or a pirate, for example,
might be condemned and executed by the magistrate
of the province, notwithstanding his appeal to the Emperor. Festus therefore consulted his councillors. It

[1] See page 143.

was clear that Paul's case was not one of these, exceptions. The appeal would stand. Festus "immediately pronounced the decision of the court": 'Thou hast appealed unto Cæsar: to Cæsar thou shalt go.'

It may seem strange that Paul should have made this appeal, when he was evidently so near acquittal. There are, however, three sufficient reasons: the danger of some other attempt to take him to Jerusalem, the probability that he would be kept in prison for years in Cæsarea, and the fact that Paul wished to go to Rome. He might as well be prisoner in Rome as in Cæsarea. If he should be acquitted speedily at Rome, he would be precisely where he wanted to be; and if not, there might be many opportunities, even while a prisoner, as there had been in Cæsarea, of teaching, even among soldiers and jailers, the doctrines of Jesus.

After the appeal was decided, Festus had one other duty to perform. "He was bound to forward to Rome all the acts and documents bearing on the trial, the statements of the witnesses, and the record of his own judgment on the case. And it was his further duty to keep the accused person in safe custody, and to send him to Rome for trial at the earliest opportunity. Festus was in new perplexity. Paul had appealed; he had allowed the appeal: but no crime had been proved against the prisoner. Justly enough, it seemed absurd to him to send a prisoner to Rome without any charge of crime."

During the days while Festus was in this state of perplexity in respect to Paul, a distinguished visitor came to Cæsarea to congratulate Festus on his new position as governor of the province. This was the great-grandson of Herod the Great, (who built Cæsa-

---

* Verse 27, (xxv.)

rea,) who was at this time King of Chalcis, a small city and district east of Antioch and of the river Orontes. He was the brother of Drusilla (who lived with Felix) and of Bernice; and his sister Bernice accompanied him to this city which their great-grandfather had built. "This prince had been acquainted from his youth with all that related to the Jewish law, and was at this time superintendent of the temple, with the power of appointing the high-priest. Festus took advantage of this opportunity of consulting one better informed than himself on the points in question." He told Agrippa the story of his prisoner ' left in bonds by Felix,' and spoke especially of Paul's earnest declaration concerning a certain Jesus who had been dead but was alive again. "This cannot have been the first time that Agrippa had heard of the resurrection of Jesus, or of the Apostle Paul. His curiosity was aroused, and he expressed a wish to see the prisoner. Festus readily yielded to his-request, and fixed the next day for the interview."

QUESTIONS.

IN what kind of confinement was Paul kept?   How long?
Where might he have lived?
What Roman centurion may have still been in Cæsarea?
What was Paul doubtless doing all this time?
What has been supposed in respect to Luke?
Why did Felix cease to be Governor of Judea?
What is the meaning of 'willing to show the Jews a pleasure'?
What kind of a man was the new Governor?
What advantage did the Jews try to take?
Why would the new Governor go to Jerusalem so soon?
What three verses show how they besought Felix?
What was probably their plan? their purpose?
What kind of an answer was the Governor's?
What did he require?
How long before Felix returned?
What just Roman law did he enforce?   (Verse 16.)
Why did he return to Cæsarea?
Where was the court held?
If the 'accusers' could not 'prove' their 'complaints,' why did Paul make any answer?
What three points did Paul's reply comprise?
What did Festus see the difficulty to be?
How did Festus resemble Felix?
What proposal did he make to Paul?
What power had Paul in respect to this proposal?
Why was not this a good plan?
What does it show in respect to the honesty of Festus?
What right did Paul now claim?
What other privilege had Paul claimed before?
How was the Governor's judgment-seat Cæsar's tribunal?
What did Paul really accuse Festus of in the sentence: 'To the Jews I have done,' etc.
How did Paul sustain the Roman law?

Is it right always to sustain the law?

What must have been the effect of Paul's reply on Festus?

What was the effect on Paul's trial?

What one thing must Festus now determine?

Whom did he consult? Why?

What was the decision?

How many reasons can you give why it was best for Paul to make this appeal?

After the appeal was decided, what other duty had Festus?

What new perplexity was he in?

What came to pass in these days?

What was their object in visiting Festus?

Who was Agrippa? Bernice? Drusilla?

How were these three interested in Cæsarea?

King of what? acquainted with what? with power of what?

Why did Festus consult Agrippa about Paul?

What did he tell this king?

Which did the Jews wish first from Festus, 'judgment' or trial?

What is meant by 'their own superstition'?

Was there more than one Jesus?

Do you suppose that Festus did not understand what Paul meant by the resurrection of Jesus?

What is meant by 'doubted of such manner of questions'?

What Cæsar was Augustus?

Why was King Agrippa's curiosity excited?

THE ROYAL VISITORS.

LESSON.

Acts xxv. 23–27; xxvi.

FESTUS was determined to give his royal visitors the fullest entertainment possible from the speech of his eloquent prisoner. The occasion was therefore to be made dignified and ceremonious. He sent invitations to the principal men of Cæsarea to be present. He ordered the captains of the thousands to attend him on his entrance into the audience-chamber. And then with King Agrippa and Bernice, with his retinue of military officers and distinguished citizens, with great display he seated himself and his illustrious guests in the conspicuous part of the chamber, and ordered Paul to be brought in.

One of the times had indeed come when Paul was to bear 'the name of the Lord before kings.'[1] Here, in this royal city of Cæsarea, he was to speak before the king whose ancestor built up all this splendor, and whose father had been publicly hailed as a god by the multitude in the great theatre where he made an impious oration;[2] he was to speak before that king's beautiful, courtly and wicked sister Bernice, as he had once spoken before his other beautiful and wicked sister Dru

---

[1] ix. 15.

[2] xii. 21–23. *That* was Herod Agrippa I. *This* was his son, Herod Agrippa II.

silla; and he was to speak again before Festus, the Governor of Judea. The members of the Herodian family were well acquainted with Jewish customs and usages, but were thoroughly negligent of them and thoroughly unprincipled. The new governor of the province, though inclined to do justice, was the representative of an artful, designing, oppressive empire. On the one side was worldliness in all its dignity and authority: on the other the simple spiritual power of the Gospel.

Festus himself made an opening address to the assembly and especially to King Agrippa. It was simply the statement which he had made to Agrippa before in private, but now it was in the form of a ceremonious and stately speech. Festus, with much display, directed King Agrippa's attention to Paul. He declared that Paul was innocent of any crime punished by death. He said that Paul had appealed to the Emperor; and then he declared his own perplexity in making out a statement of Paul's case, to be sent to the Emperor. That Agrippa might hear the prisoner's own story, he had ordered this audience, and now Paul might be permitted to speak for himself.

THE ADDRESS BEFORE KING AGRIPPA.

As Paul was now invited to speak before a Jewish king, he does not try to defend himself from the charge of treason against the Roman law, but rather from the charge of heresy against the Jewish law. Indeed it had been decided that he should go to Rome and be tried before the Emperor in respect to the accusations made against him. In his speech therefore before King Agrippa Paul gives the reasons why the Jews have sought his life, and earnestly speaks of Jesus as the Messiah of the Jews.

I. Paul first declared King Agrippa's familiarity with

Jewish customs and usages a source of satisfaction to him in making his address. (Verses 2, 3.) When Paul spoke to Festus, a Roman, recently arrived from Rome, he could not of course speak so freely of customs and sects among the Jews.

II. In respect to *heresy*, or violating the law of Moses, which the Jews had accused him of, he was as far from committing that crime as any Jew. (Verses 4 to 8.) For (1.) In all his early life he had been educated and had lived as a Pharisee, keeping the law in the strictest manner, as the Jews themselves knew. (4, 5.) And now (2.) The very thing the Jews accused him of was that he believed the great promise of the Messiah made to the Jews was fulfilled. (6, 7, 8.) All the tribes of Israel claimed that the time would come when that great promise would be fulfilled. He had only claimed that it *was* already fulfilled; that Jesus of Nazareth was this Messiah; and that his resurrection from the dead proved him to be. And why should it be thought incredible among the Jews and especially among the Pharisees, who believed in the resurrection of the dead, that God should raise Jesus from the dead? By believing that Jesus of Nazareth had risen from the dead and therefore was the Messiah, he was as really keeping the law as the Jews were in expecting a Messiah at all.

III. The real 'causes' why the Jews seized him in the temple and tried to kill him in Jerusalem were not heresy, but that he had changed from a persecutor of Jesus and of his followers to their friend, and had preached to the Gentiles, in obedience to Jesus' command. (Verses 9 to 23.) This change had taken place in the following manner:

1. He had first been a most fierce persecutor of Jesus and his followers. (9–11.)

2. On his way to Damascus the evidence of a miraculous light, a miraculous voice and a miraculous appearance of Jesus himself, which he could not resist, had convinced him that Jesus was the Messiah of the Scriptures. (12–15.)

3. Jesus the Messiah, in that vision, commanded him to preach to the Gentiles, that they might be saved also. (16–18.)

4. And because he obeyed the words of the Messiah and preached to the Gentiles, the Jews tried to kill him. (19–21.)

5. But from the time of his change from an enemy to a friend of Jesus, up to that very day, there had been *no heresy;* for he had said nothing but what the Jewish Scriptures themselves taught : that the Messiah should suffer : that he should rise from the dead : that he should give the light of religion to the Gentiles as well as to the Jews. (22, 23.) And these were now the things in respect to which Paul claimed that he bore witness to small and to great. The overwhelming evidence of that miraculous vision could never be taken from his mind. Jesus of Nazareth was the Messiah of the prophets and of the law of Moses. He *knew* it; he *believed* it; and he *obeyed* the voice of the Messiah.

King Agrippa could fully comprehend all this. All the points in Paul's speech *he* could well understand. But to the Roman Festus, there was much that was strange and unmeaning. This strange vision of which Paul spoke: what was it? And the doctrine of the resurrection of the dead: "To the cold man of the world, as to the inquisitive Athenians, it was foolishness." To him, Paul "seemed like a mad enthusiast, whose head had been turned" by incessant study of the religious writings to which he referred. He broke in, therefore, upon the Apostle's speech :

"Paul, thou art beside thyself: much learning makes thee mad."

Much learning is literally 'many letters'—much study is making thee mad. It is not unlikely that in his imprisonment Paul had other manuscripts beside the Hebrew Scriptures; and that he had been diligently studying the 'rolls' of the prophets and of the law and of other religious writers. It may be that Festus referred to this when he saw the fiery earnestness of this strange prisoner before his royal guests. Paul had not been speaking to Festus, but to Agrippa; but with perfect self-possession, he calmly and earnestly replies to Festus:

"However mad I may seem to thee, most noble Festus, my words are most reasonable and sober, as King Agrippa, being a Jew, fully knows and understands. These things were not secretly done, but most openly and publicly."

"Then turning again to the Jewish voluptuary who sat beside the Governor, he made this solemn appeal to him:

"King Agrippa, dost thou believe these prophets? I know that thou believest."

The King had been educated into full belief in the inspired prophets of the Hebrews. The next natural thought therefore must have been and perhaps Paul was intending to put it into words: "Then *must* thou believe that Jesus is the Messiah spoken of in the prophets."

The King's reply prevented him, and turned the current of Paul's address: "Thou wilt soon[3] persuade me

[3] "It is universally admitted that the phrase rendered 'almost' cannot bear that translation. The name 'Christian,' of heathen coinage, in the mouth of Agrippa, does not imply any sincere or decided emo-

to be a 'Christian.'" As the word Christian cannot have been an honorary name in the mind of a Jew like Agrippa, but rather a name of contempt, "the words were doubtless spoken in irony and contempt."

But Paul was not to be put off in this way. He made a most earnest reply, as though the King's words were spoken in earnest—a reply which was as comprehensive and sublime as it was earnest—"sweeping round the bench and the audience, and ending with a touching allusion to his own captivity:"

"I would to God, that, whether soon or late, whether with little persuasion or with much persuasion, not only thou, but all that hear me this day, were such as I am, except these bonds."

"King Agrippa had no desire to hear more: he rose from his seat, with the Governor and Bernice and those that sat with them. As they retired, they discussed the case." They agreed that Paul had not only done nothing worthy of death, but nothing worthy of imprisonment. "Agrippa said positively to Festus: 'This man might have been set at liberty, if he had not appealed to the Emperor.' But the appeal had been made. There was no retreat either for Festus or for Paul." Festus had no wish to keep Paul in bonds, as Felix had done, and he only waited for a good opportunity to send his prisoner to Rome.

tion; for he was a haughty and light-minded voluptuary. The sense may be, 'really, without much ado, thou art trying to make me a Christian:' 'you would make a Christian of me, as easily and in as off-hand a way as you were made yourself.' "—Dr. Eadie.

QUESTIONS.

WHAT shows that Festus meant to make Paul's eloquence an entertainment for his guests ?

What prediction made to Paul had come to pass ?

What associations added to the force of this prediction ?

What two powers were represented here ?

Did Festus say anything in his speech which he had not already told Agrippa ?

What high testimony did he give to Paul's character ?

Who was Augustus ? Why called 'my lord' ?

Could Festus have helped doing this 'unreasonable' thing ?

What is Paul's purpose in his speech ? Why ?

What is the introductory part of Paul's speech ?

Why was Paul more glad to speak before Agrippa than before Festus ?

What is the second part of the speech ?

- What is the first point in this part of the argument ?

What circumstances can you state which show that Paul had been well known to the Jews ?

What to show that he had been one of the 'strictest sect' ?

What is the second point in this part ?

What 'promise' is referred to ?

How did 'the twelve tribes hope to come' to this promise ?

What is meant by 'instantly serving God,' etc. ?

How was Paul accused for this 'hope's sake' ?

What has the raising of the dead to do with this hope

What is the third part of the speech ?

How is this connected with the second part ?

What is the first point in this part of the argument ?

How 'many things' are here named which Paul did as a persecutor

What is the second point in this part ?

How many things united to force conviction on Paul's mind ?

What is the third point in this part of the speech ?

What was the especial 'purpose' in Paul's conversion ?

How was Paul 'delivered from the people and from the Gentiles' ?

What was God's purpose in sending him to the Gentiles ?

What is meant by 'inheritance among them,' etc. ?

What are the means by which a Gentile now can obtain this inheritance ?

What is the fourth point in this part ?

In how many cities and countries did Paul obey this command ? Why ?

Can a man 'repent of any *sin* without 'turning to God' ?

Are all 'good works' 'meet for repentance' ?

Show how the fifth point sums up this third part of the speech.

What was the one great thing which Paul felt and enforced in this part of his speech ?

What different effects did Paul's speaking produce on the two rulers' minds ?

What reason may be given why Festus thought Paul mad ?

What does 'much learning' signify ?

To whom had Paul been speaking ?

Explain the meaning of the twenty-fifth and twenty-sixth verses.

How is the twenty-eighth verse connected with the previous speech ?

What is the next natural thought ?

How was that close of the argument prevented ?

Did Agrippa mean that he was on the point of yielding to Paul's arguments ?

Explain the force of the Apostle's reply.

Why did not Agrippa listen longer ?

What was the result of the conference ?

THE PRISONER SENT TO ROME.

LESSON.
Acts xxvii. 1–13.

PAUL was sent to Rome by ship. We do not know that there were any passenger-ships in those days, sailing at regular times between the great cities of the Mediterranean; but there were large numbers of merchant-ships plying between all the towns on the coasts. Even emperors themselves were compelled to sail in these ships when they took their voyages of business, as we know that, when Titus was besieging Jerusalem, his father, the Emperor Vespasian, took a merchant-ship at least as far as Rhodes, and that, when he had ended the siege and hastened to Italy, Titus himself went by a merchant-ship which touched at Rhegium and Puteoli, places at which Paul himself touched on his voyage.[1] "If such was the mode in which even royal persons travelled from the provinces to the metropolis, we must of course conclude that those who travelled on the business of the state must have been content to go in the same manner. The sending of state-prisoners to Rome from various parts of the empire was an event of frequent occurrence. Such groups of prisoners as this which now went aboard the ship at Cæsarea must often have left Cæsarea and other eastern ports in merchant-vessels bound for the west."

It is worth while to stop a moment and think of the

[1] xxviii. 13.

busy Mediterranean, and Rome as the centre of its commerce, to help our thoughts of Paul's voyage. The
many provinces on all sides sent up to Rome their
many articles of traffic. From the province of Africa
on the south came "heavy cargoes of marble and granite" and of furniture-woods. From the coast of Asia
Minor, on the east, came the silks and spices which had
been brought "from beyond the Euphrates to the markets and wharves of Ephesus." From the Black Sea
came fish, and from the Archipelago ship-loads of wine.
From the distant west, ships with wool and other articles anchored in the harbors of Italy. Egypt especially was a country rich in the merchandise sent off
to the great metropolis. From the distant Indian
Ocean, up the Red Sea, and then down the valley of
the Nile to Alexandria, poured the constant flow of
trade in spices, dyes, jewels and perfumes. Added
to these articles of traffic, the ships of Alexandria for
Rome and for the north and west were laden with
linen, paper and glass. And still more, the great article of trade which occupied many more of its vessels
was the Egyptian wheat, which grew along the fertile
banks of the Nile and which helped to feed the multitudes of Italy. "The Egyptian grain-vessels were
usually bound for the harbor of Puteoli," and we shall
soon see the Apostle aboard one of these very ships,
and at length landing at that very port.[2] Besides the
larger vessels employed in this direct trade between the
different provinces and with Rome, we must think of
the multitude of smaller ships which were in the coasting trade, and which did not venture so boldly out on the
great deep.

It was probably on one of these coasting-vessels ther

[2] See frontispiece for illustration of this and the two following
lessons.

in port at Cæsarea, that Festus the Governor placed
Paul. It was a 'ship of Adramyttium,' a town in Mysia which Paul had himself passed when he came down
from Phrygia to Troas. It was found that the captain
intended to follow closely the coasts of 'Asia,'[3] a voyage which would be quite familiar to Paul.[4] Most
likely, however, the centurion who had charge of the
prisoners meant to sail in this coasting-vessel only till .
he could find a larger and faster vessel bound more directly for Italy.

We can see, therefore, the mingled company which
was gathered on the 'ship of Adramyttium' as she
turned her prow towards the northern entrance of the
splendid stone harbor of Cæsarea. There were the
captain and the crew: there were Julius the centurion
and his Roman soldiers: there were Paul, his two companions, Luke and Aristarchus of Thessalonica,[5] and
the other prisoners: there were the passengers bound
for longer and shorter voyages. Once out of the harbor, the vessel stood to the north. Passing Mount Carmel and Ptolemais and Tyre, the next day she "put
into Sidon." There were passengers to land, or there
was something to be added to or taken from the cargo,
or the wind made it more convenient to run into this
harbor.

In this ancient city, for so many centuries connected
with Tyre, there were undoubtedly fellow-disciples.
Christian preachers must have visited this town as one
of the chief cities of Phœnice;[6] Paul and Barnabas themselves must have stopped here, on their way up from
Antioch to Jerusalem.[7] The Sidonian Christians must

---

[3] Not Asia Minor, but the *province* of Asia.   [4] xx. 13–17; xxi. 1.

[5] Aristarchus may have been one of the prisoners. See Colossians
iv. 10, written after Paul reached Rome.

[6] xi. 19.   [7] xv. 3.

hâve heard of Paul's landing at Tyre on his last voyage
from the west to Jerusalem, two years before. Through
the courtesy of the Roman centurion, (who had no doubt
known Paul before he left Cæsarea,) these 'friends' at
Sidon were permitted to show Paul kind attentions.
Paul was permitted to go on shore to meet them.

The ship met with opposite winds after leaving Sidon.
"The direct course from Sidon to the 'coasts of Asia'
would have been to the southward of Cyprus, across
the sea over which the Apostle sailed so prosperously
two years before." But as the same strong wind which
then drove the ship swiftly towards the east now hindered his direct course to the west, the captain took
the course to the north of Cyprus, through the seas of
Cilicia and Pamphylia. There is another reason, too,
for passing Cyprus on the north. There is a current in
the great sea between Cyprus and the main shore, which
continues along the coast of Asia Minor to the Archipelago; and when they should fall into this current, the
progress of the voyage would be easier. The whole
passage must have been made by 'tacking' against the
wind. Paul was in familiar waters. Seleucia and Salamis were on either hand as they came around the
eastern end of Cyprus. The coast of his native province, the high summits of the mountains of Taurus behind Tarsus, the lofty cliffs of Pamphylia, the towns of
Attalia and Perga were slowly passed, and the ship
came to a harbor in Lycia not far from Patara.[8] This
was the harbor of Myra, a city of which little is known.
But as at Patara, on his last voyage to Judea, Paul
made a change of ships, so at Myra the centurion trans-
ferred his soldiers and prisoners to another vessel. For
here at Myra the centurion found an Egyptian grain-
ship[9] from Alexandria bound for Italy. Myra was di-

[8] xxi. 1.   [9] See verse 38.

rectly north from Alexandria; and it is not unlikely
that the powerful west wind which Paul's ship had
encountered in coming from Sidon, had forced the
heavily-laden Alexandrian ship out of her direct course.
To escape the fury of a head-wind in the open sea,
and to gain the advantage of the shore-current, she had
come over to the opposite coast of the Mediterranean.
Even in our own day it is no uncommon thing for ships
from Alexandria coming westward to sail to the north
for the sake of the current. The Apostle was now no
doubt in a much larger ship. This vessel we know was
able to accommodate two hundred and seventy six persons,[10] passengers and crew. But in this heavy-laden
ship, and with an adverse wind, the voyage was very
slow. Patara and Rhodes were slowly passed, and it was
' many days' before Cnidus was reached. Cnidus had
a good harbor; and when they should pass this promontory, they could have no longer the protection of
the coast nor the advantage of the current, but would
meet the full fury of the north-west wind. It was impossible to take the regular course straight across the
Ægean, past the island of Cythera. Instead, however,
of getting into shelter in this excellent harbor of Cnidus, the seamen hoped to run down to the southern side
of Crete, and then, with this long island as a protection, to make their way across the mouth of the Archipelago.

Here therefore the course of Paul's voyage left the
scenes of his former journeys. When once exposed to
the full force of the wind, the seamen found it a difficult task to bring the ship around the end of the island.
Having passed Cape Salmone, they were able to get on
slowly, as they had done from Myra to Cnidus, until

---

[10] Verse 37.

they reached a place called Fair Havens. "There seems to have been no town at Fair Havens," but only an anchorage sheltered from the winds, near Lasea. Very likely the passengers and sailors visited Lasea, and so the name came to be mentioned. Much time had now been spent since they left Cæsarea, enough probably for the ship in an ordinary voyage to have reached Rome, for the time of year had come when it was thought dangerous to try the open sea. The Fast of the Atonement was already past, which occurred near the end of September, after which time the ancients thought the seas especially dangerous, from the storms which occurred about that time. It was, as we would say, past the equinox, or about the time of the equinoctial storm, the time when the severer storms set in. Paul warned those who had control of the ship of the danger of going on. His good judgment taught him the risk of further exposure: he had had no little experience, too, on the sea: perhaps there was also prophetic foresight of what was to happen. It is not surprising, however, that the centurion thought more of the opinions of the helmsman and of the captain[u] than of his prisoner. Fair Havens was not well situated to pass the winter in. Farther on was Phenice, which the sailors described as a good harbor and as having a coast lying towards the south-west and north-west; and which would therefore give protection against the violent winds from those quarters. Waiting then till the furious north-west wind had ceased, and a gentle south wind had sprung up, the sailors pushed on close along the shore, not doubting but that they would soon reach Phenice.

[u] In verse 11 the word 'master' means the *governor, pilot, helmsman ;* and ' owner,' the ship-owner, or ship-master, master and owner often being one.

QUESTIONS.

HOW did passengers sail from one country to another in Paul's time?

What illustrious examples are given?

Did the sending of state-prisoners to Rome often occur?

How was Rome the centre of commerce?

What was sent from Africa? Is the *continent* of Africa meant?

What came from Asia Minor? Through what harbor especially?

The Black Sea? the Ægean? the West?

Why did Egypt send so much to Italy?

What other articles from Alexandria?

What was the Egyptians' great article of traffic with Italy?

In what Italian harbor did these ships usually discharge their cargo?

What other vessels on the Mediterranean besides these larger ones?

Into whose care did the Governor of Judea deliver Paul?

How many men had a centurion under him?

What is meant by Augustus's band?

Into what kind of a ship was Paul taken?

Where was Adramyttium?

Do you think Julius meant to sail in this ship to Italy?

What does 'coasts of Asia' mean?

When had Paul seen these coasts?

What four classes of persons were on the ship?

Who was Aristarchus?

Why did they touch at Sidon? What places had they passed?

With what city was Sidon connected?

Why must we think there were Christians here?

What respect for Paul did Julius show?

What is meant by 'sailed under Cyprus'?

On which side of Cyprus was the sea of Cilicia?

Was this the direct course?

What two reasons are there for taking this course?

What is meant by 'tacking'? Why must they have 'tacked'?

What familiar objects between Sidon and Myra?

Where was Myra? near what city?

What one event connected with Paul's travels occurred in both these cities?

Why was a change of ships now made?

What kind of a ship was the new one?

Was it larger or smaller than the one Paul left?

Where bound? From what port? Its cargo?

Were there other passengers than those on the Adramyttium ship?

In what direction was Alexandria from Myra?

Why should an Egyptian ship sailing to Italy come so much out of its way?

What is true of the sailing of such ships now?

Why was the sailing now so slow?

What two places did they pass where Paul had been before?

Where was Cnidus? What was it?

Why did not the ship stop at Cnidus?

What is meant by 'sailed *under* Crete'?

Why did they try to do this?

Why was it difficult to pass Cape Salmone?

What was Fair Havens? Why is Lasea named?

Why was sailing now dangerous?

What time of the year was it?

What reason had Paul for warning sailors in respect to sailing?

Do you think Paul meant this as a *prophecy*, or as his opinion?

What does 'master and owner' mean?

Why were they determined to push on?

Did they mean to leave Crete during the winter?

What is meant by 'lieth towards the south-west and north-west'?

What induced them to leave Fair Havens?

Forty-ninth Sunday.

STORM AND SHIPWRECK.

LESSON.

Acts xxvii. 13–44.

ALL on board seem now to have given up reaching
Rome till the next spring, but they thought they
were certain of a good harbor to winter in. The light
south wind was bearing the ship along the coast of
Crete ; the sailors were in good spirits ; the passengers
were filled with hope of rest and safety ; the very land
about Phenice may have been in sight : when in a moment all was changed. A swift, fierce storm, one of
those unforeseen eastern hurricanes, struck the vessel,
and catching it in its awful grasp, made it completely
unmanageable. It was a *typhoon,* or *euroclydon,* (a
word meaning 'east wind and waves,') rushing down
the mountainous sides of the island.[1] The sea was instantly in a foam : the sails had been 'trimmed' for a
favoring breeze from another direction : the ship would
not obey the helm, or, in the expressive words of the
Greek, 'would not look the wind in the face,'[2] and the
best the sailors could do, was to let her 'scud before
the gale.' The vessel was of course driven '*off' the
island,'* and so swiftly that the sailors feared they

---

[1] Our translation, 'arose against it,' does not fully express the *sud-
aenness* and *fury* which are expressed in the Greek words : the Greek
words mean, the tempest '*cast itself down* or *along* it (the island.)'

[2] Our translation, 'could not *bear up into* the wind,' has the same
meaning.

would be carried into the dreadful quicksands[3] on the coast of Africa. What was now to be done in such danger? Four things were done. First, the sailors took advantage of the direction of the storm to get under the protection of the little island, Clauda. "Here they would have the advantage of a temporary lull and of less boisterous water for a few miles." Taking this temporary advantage, secondly, '*the boat was hoisted on board.*'[4] It would be the height of folly, with such a load of passengers, to let go this boat, the only hope, if the ship should spring a bad leak; but to get a boat, half filled with water, over the sides of the ship in a gale of wind, was '*much work.*' Thirdly, they '*undergirded*' the ship. This was a precaution against the starting of the planks in the hull of the ship. 'Helps,' that is, ropes or cables, were passed around the frame of the ship to strengthen it and to prevent a leak. Fourthly, they '*lowered the gear.*'[5] They either took in the sails or pulled down the ropes and yards. These different preparations were made so that they might '*weather out* the storm.'

To one unacquainted with the sea it might appear that they were now beaten in all directions by the wind and waves; and on some maps the track of the ship laid down changes towards all points of the compass; but it has been shown, with no little reason, that the course was nearly straight till they reached the island on which they were wrecked. Sailors know quite well

[3] The word 'quicksands,' in Greek, is 'Syrtis,' the name of the famous quicksands on the African coast, directly towards which the ship was driving. See the frontispiece map.

[4] 'To come by the boat,' is to get mastery of it, so as to hoist it into the ship. It must have been towing behind.

[5] 'Strake sail,' verse 17. Literally, 'they *lowered the gearing.*' The sails, or only the ropes and yards, may be meant.

that sometimes it is far more dangerous to let the ship roll at the mercy of the storm, or to 'scud under bare poles,' than it is to head the ship nearly towards the wind and to spread a sail. Any one who knows what the seamen's phrase 'to tack' means, knows that a ship can be made to sail in good weather in a direction nearly *contrary* to the wind; and although this could not well be done in a storm, yet by keeping the head of the ship *nearly* towards the wind, and a small sail set, the vessel would be steadier, and would be driven slowly backward. This is called '*lying to*,' (that is, lying to the wind,) and the vessel is allowed to '*drift*,' " a plan constantly resorted to, when the object is not so much to make progress as to outride the gale." For Paul's ship " to have scudded before the gale under bare poles, or under storm-sails, would infallibly have stranded them in the Syrtis." But if the vessel was *laid to*, and was allowed to *drift* in a straight course, in fourteen[6] days she must have been very near the island Malta.

The second day of the storm, they 'lightened the ship.' The vessel had probably sprung a leak; and the crew cast overboard the things which they could afford to lose best. It was not enough, however. The leak continued; and the third day, the passengers helped the sailors' throw out all the 'tackling '—the heavy ropes, spars and yards—which could be spared. Then for many days and nights there was great distress, such as no one who had never been out on the sea in a long and furious storm and in a leaking ship, can know. The constant work of passengers and crew by day and by night, the anxious watching against leak in all parts of the ship, the violent dashing of the waves over the ves

[6] Verse 27.

Notice that in verse 18, 'they' is used, and in verse 19, 'we.'

sel and the pumping out of the water, the throwing
over of one heavy article after another, the ceaseless
plunging and rolling of the vessel, the creaking and
straining of the ship's frame and rigging, the terror of
frightened passengers and the sickness of others, the
benumbing cold and wet, the wearisome strain of mind
and body, all united to increase their helpless suffering.
And besides all this, the sky was entirely overcast.
There was neither sun nor stars to steer by.[8] "It was
impossible to know how near they might be to the
most dangerous coast. Yet the worst danger was from
the leaky state of the vessel, and this was so bad that
at length they gave up all hope of being saved," and
thought the ship must go down. Besides all this distress, there could have been no regular meals. Much
of the provisions might have been spoiled by the sea-
water; and the food which they had, must have been
taken only between their labors. Despair was in every
heart but one.

Paul, the prisoner, is hopeful and confident. While
the heathen sailors had been trying in vain to save the
ship, praying no doubt to their gods, God, who holds
the winds, had spoken to his Apostle and had answered
his prayers. Paul had another vision, like the one at
Troas,[9] in which God directed his course. In the midst
of the despairing sailors, Paul reminded them of his
warning at Fair Havens, not to reproach them, but to
show that his words were worthy of their respect and
confidence. And now he declares that *not one* of all
the crew and passengers should be lost. Only the ship
would go down. God's angel had told him the destiny
of the ship and those on board. God's purpose that his

---

[8] They had no compass, of course; and the sun and stars were the
reliance of the ancient helmsman, when out of sight of land or at
night.   [9] xvi. 9.

Apostle should stand in the presence of the Emperor should not be defeated. And for Paul's sake, God would preserve all his fellow-voyagers. We are not told whether the sailors believed that God whom Paul believed, and took heart as Paul urged them to do. Paul's high hope could but have made them more hopeful.

Still the storm continued. Day and night followed, perhaps more than once. The danger did not cease. At length, it was fourteen long days since they had been driven out into the lower Adriatic Sea.[10] About midnight of the fourteenth night, as they were tossed up and down, "the sailors suspected that they were nearing land." As they could not see, they must have heard the breaking of waves on the shore. "The roar of breakers is a peculiar sound, which can be detected by a practised ear," although persons not sailors might not distinguish it from other sounds of a storm. On sounding, they found they were rapidly running into shallower water. The anchors were quickly cleared and cast *out of the stern*, which would prevent the vessel from swinging around.[11] How anxiously they must have waited for daylight! Who could tell what might occur from the breaking of an anchor-cable? A cold rain was falling;[12] the wind was rattling the rigging, if indeed there was rigging left; and no one could yet see the rocks or what kind of shore was right before them. The ship itself might go down before morning. This the sailors knew better than the passengers; and in the darkness, and without knowing whither they would be carried, they selfishly attempted to get away

[10] Adria was the Adriatic Sea, including *then* the Ionian Sea.

[11] If they had anchored like modern vessels, *from the bow*, the vessel might have swung around on to rocks, since the wind was from behind. [12] xxviii. 2.

from the ship in the boat. Pretending to lower anchors *from the bow,* (which no doubt would have steadied the ship,) they got the boat down to the water's edge. Paul saw the sailors were intending to flee and to leave the rest to their fate, and his appeal to the centurion stopped their selfish plan. The soldiers instantly cut the lowering-ropes; the boat fell, instantly filled with water and went to the bottom, or drifted off into the darkness.

Paul the prisoner now is the chief and commanding person in all that large number. He persuades them to take food to strengthen them, himself setting the example, reverently giving thanks to God, when all others were on the point of despairing. From such a heroic courage, they also took heart. Instead of giving up to despair, they now went to work to make the ship as light as possible, so as to run her far up on the land and from her to get to shore. The cargo of wheat in the hold, which while tossing on the open sea they probably could not well get at, they now poured out into the sea. When this work of some hours was done, the day had dawned, and the land could be seen. No one could tell what land it was; but they saw a small inlet [13] with a beach, into which they resolved to thrust the ship. But to do this would require the greatest care. The rudders (of which there were two in ancient vessels, and which were large, strong oars, at the *sides* of the stern) seem to have been bound up out of the way of the cables, when the anchors were cast out of the stern. The rudder-bands were now unlashed, the anchor-cables cut, the sail hoisted, and the ship was run aground. "It does not appear quite certain whether they exactly hit

---

[13] The word 'creek,' in verse 39, is used in the maritime sense. See the Dictionary.

the point at which they aimed." But the bow stuck fast on a spot where two opposing seas had thrown up a hidden bank of earth or sand, and the waves dashing against each other just there, the stern was soon broken to pieces.

Another incident is given at this point, quite characteristic of Roman soldiers. " The soldiers were answerable with their own lives for their prisoners, and were afraid some of them should swim out and escape ; and therefore, in the spirit of true Roman cruelty, they proposed to kill them at once. Paul's influence over the centurion was again the means of saving his own life and the life of his fellow-prisoners. The centurion might care little for the rest, but he was determined to save Paul. He therefore prevented the soldiers from accomplishing their heartless purpose, and directed those who could swim "—soldiers and prisoners together, no doubt — to cast themselves into the sea first, " while the rest made use of spars and broken pieces of the wreck." Most wonderfully, not one of the whole two hundred and seventy-six failed to reach the shore through the breakers.

QUESTIONS.

WHEN did the ship's crew now expect to reach Italy ?
What was the Euroclydon ?
What is the meaning of the word ?
What is meant by 'arose against it' ?
'The ship was caught' ? 'could not bear up into the
 wind' ? 'let her drive' ?
Where was the vessel driven ?
What was the first thing the sailors did ?
What was the second thing done ? Why 'much work' ?
What was the third thing done ? Why ?
What was the fourth thing ? 'Strake sail' ? Why ?
Is it likely that the wind now beat them in all directions ?
 What three ways are there of managing a ship at such
  a time ? Which is the safest ?
 What is '*lying to*' in a storm ? '*drifting*' ?
 What is the object of permitting a vessel to drift ?
 Why would it have been unsafe for this ship to run be-
  fore the gale ?
 How long did the ship drift ? Where would they have
  been by this time, if they drifted ?
What was done the second day of the storm ? Why ?
 What the third day ?
 How do you know the passengers helped ?
 What is the 'tackling' ?
 What circumstances must have united to increase their
  suffering ?
 How long did this continue ?
 Why did the overcast sky add to their danger ?
 What was the danger worst of all ?
Did every one yield to despair of saving life ?
 Why did not Paul yield ?
 Is there anything in religion to produce hope in great
  dangers and trials ?
 Why is 'long abstinence' mentioned in the twenty-first
  verse ?

(97)

. Does it mean that Paul, or all, abstained?

Why did Paul allude to his warning at Crete?

How did Paul know without this vision that his own life would not be lost?

Can you mention any other instance of wicked men preserved for the righteous' sake?

What *especial* prediction did Paul make?

'The fourteenth night had come': fourteenth after what?

What is meant by 'driven up and down'?

What was 'Adria'?

How could the sailors tell they were near land?

What did the 'sounding' show?

Would they be likely to continue drifting backwards, after they thought land near?

Why did they cast the anchors '*out of the stern*'?

Were these anchors like our anchors?

What does the sailors' attempt to get out of the ship show in respect to their opinion of saving the ship?

What effect would casting anchors *from the bow* have had?

Do you suppose Paul meant that they had eaten nothing for fourteen days?

Was not this a time when thanks to God before a meal might have been omitted, if ever?

What do the thirty-sixth and thirty-eighth verses show in respect to the influence of Paul's hope upon the ship's company?

Why didn't they cast out the wheat before? Why now?

What does 'creek' mean? What were the 'rudder-bands'?

Why should the ship run aground 'where two seas met'?

Why would the waves be violent there?

What characteristic of the Roman soldier is here seen?

Why were the prisoners saved?

How many persons escaped to land? How?

Fiftieth Sunday.

SICILY AND ITALY.

LESSON.

ACTS xxviii. 1-16.

THE whole large number of passengers and crew was at length safe on shore. 'Not a hair' had 'fallen from the head of any' of them. The wreck lay off on the sunken sand-bar. The loss had been only 'of the ship.' Paul's predictions had been fulfilled. They were the words of God given to him to utter to his fellow-men.

People were soon found. The island was declared to be Melita. Perhaps the sailors themselves soon recognised some prominent feature of the island, by which they knew it. There were anciently two islands of this name, one of which is now called *Malta* and the other *Meleda*. Malta is no doubt the one on which Paul was wrecked, although there are those who have thought it was Meleda. Meleda was far up in the Adriatic Sea, on the coast of Illyricum. It would be very strange indeed if a vessel could have been driven so far up the gulf, without coming in conflict with any island or coast. Why, too, should not Paul have gone to Rome directly across Italy, instead of going away around by Sicily, as we shall see he did? It is by far more natural to suppose that Malta is the island; and there are some strong reasons for believing that the bay to this day called St. Paul's Bay, was, as the tradition declared it to be, the place of Paul's shipwreck.

The people are said to have been 'barbarous,' but it is not meant that they were savage, uncultivated and cruel. They did not speak the Greek language; and therefore to one who, like Paul or Luke, made use of the ordinary division of all mankind into Greeks and barbarians,[1] they were 'barbarous people.' Still they were as superstitious as they were kind. They kindled a blazing fire in the cold October rain. It was not surprising that Paul, in gathering hastily a bundle of brushwood from the wet ground, should not have noticed a viper in it. And when the heat revived the reptile from the stupor which the cold rain had produced, it clung to Paul's hand. It is not said that Paul was *bitten*, but the superstitious people thought, from the nature of the reptile, that he must be bitten, and that he would fall dead. And just as the people of Lystra first said Paul was a god and then stoned him as a magic-worker, so the people of Malta suddenly changed from calling Paul a murderer to calling him a god. Paul of course did not permit them to give him any such title, but preached to them the same doctrine which he did to the Lystrians, that he was a man of like passions with them, and that there was only one God, who made heaven and the earth and the *sea*. Very soon, too, miracles were wrought to confirm the truth of his words. The father of 'the chief man of the island,' at whose house Paul and Luke and others no doubt were hospitably entertained, was restored from an aggravated disease. Publius may have been the Roman governor, for his name is Roman. Malta belonged to Rome, and Publius was the 'chief man' of the island. But the cure was wrought by prayer to that one God whom Paul preached, and in the name of that Jesus through whom only, Paul everywhere taught men could be saved. The

[1] See Romans i. 14 · I. Corinthians xiv. 11.

healing of the governor's father, or of the father of so well known a man as Publius, was quickly known throughout the little island, and many other sufferers, brought to Paul, were healed. Every one who was healed, heard also of Jesus the Messiah, for Paul wrought no cures in any other name or power. The kindness of the people was returned to them therefore: health for hospitality.

All honor and attention were paid to Paul and his companions during his stay of three months. Julius no doubt gave him his liberty. The inhabitants, soldiers, passengers, sailors, must have heard Paul's earnest preaching during this providential delay. Perhaps many a convert thanked God for the blessing of the shipwreck.

It was soon known that another Alexandrian ship was in a harbor of Malta, passing the winter. At the prow of the vessel were sculptured images or painted figures of the twin gods, the sons of Jupiter, which were the sign or the badge of the vessel. Castor and Pollux were the patron gods of sailors. The centurion put his sailors and prisoners aboard this ship, (for it was bound for Italy,) and in the month of January[2] they were on their way towards Rome. Sicily must have been visible soon after they set sail, the distant blue mountains rising above the black line of the shore. The two promontories on the south-east corner of the island once passed, the burning Mount Etna was seen, fifty or sixty miles to the north, lifting its cone-like form, with its plume of smoke, far up into the air; and the city of Syracuse, partly on a little island in its harbor and partly on the shore, was directly before them. Syracuse was the wealthiest and largest town of Sicily; and Sicily, from its abundant fruits and its immense harvests of wheat,

[2] See xxvii. 9, (with page 315;) xxvii. 27; and xxviii. 11

was called by the Romans, 'the store-house of Italy.' In the harbor and in the town many a battle had been fought with revolutionary parties and with foreign invaders. In Syracuse, Plato and Cicero had lived; in this city, the poet Theocritus and the philosopher Archimedes were born; and here Archimedes, at work on a mathematical problem, was killed by Roman soldiers, when the Roman army captured the city. The beautiful bay swept around a circumference of five miles, and the little island on which the city had been first built had become gradually united by buildings to the shore. Here the ship remained three days. Julius, the centurion, who had been so kind at Sidon, and who had learned to respect Paul still more in the storm and shipwreck, would not refuse to let Paul go ashore. In such a busy, trafficking city as this, Paul would find hundreds of Jews; and if there was an opportunity for Paul to meet them in their synagogue, Jesus the Messiah was certainly proclaimed: so that the tradition may be true which says that Paul was "the first founder of the Sicilian church."

Sailing out of this splendid harbor, the ship turned her painted head to the north, towards the straits of Sicily. The wind does not seem to have been favorable, for they were obliged to make a circuit. If the wind was in the west and they were close to the shore and the high mountains, "they were obliged to stand out to sea to fill their sails, and so they came to Rhegium by a circuitous sweep."[3] The ship, which had for its protecting divinities Castor and Pollux, had come to a city over which 'the Great Twin Brothers' were supposed to be protectors. The Rhegians worshipped

[3] A traveller says that "when he made a voyage from Syracuse to Rhegium, the vessel in which he sailed took a similar circuit for this reason."

Castor and Pollux as their divinity. At Rhegium and at the Rhegian Pillars, twelve miles north, was the regular crossing-place from Italy to Sicily. In this ancient port, the first port of Italy at which Paul touched, the ship staid one day, waiting for a favorable wind to carry them through the difficult straits. The south wind bore them safely through the channel between Scylla and Charybdis, and in one day to Puteoli.

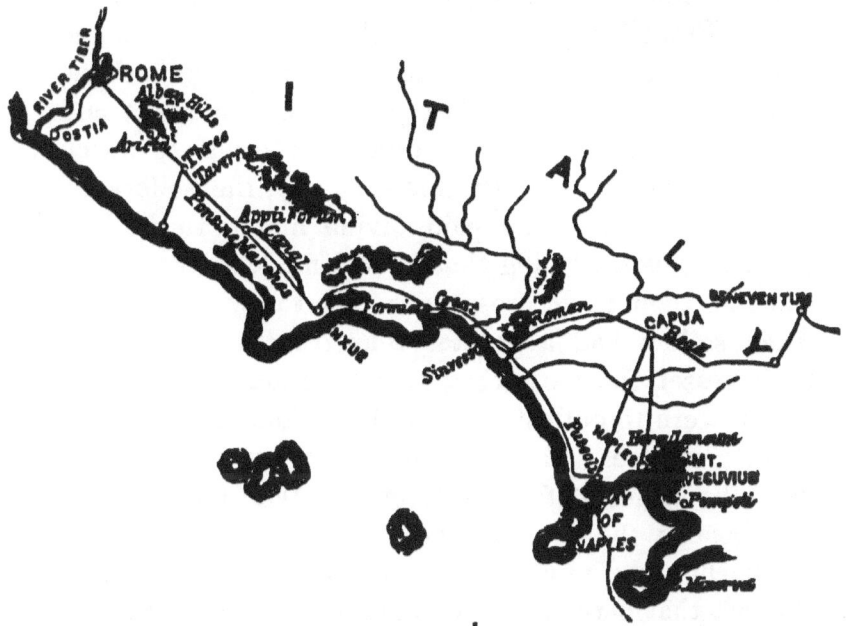

As they drew near the point of land which shut off from their view the bay on which Puteoli is situated, they could see more clearly the rich fields and vine-clad mountain sides of lower Italy. Passing Cape Minerva, the magnificent bay of Naples, celebrated for its wonderful beauty by all travellers, ancient and modern, burst upon them. Back of the middle point of the curve was Mount Vesuvius, not then a fiery volcano, but 'green and sunny,' 'with its westward slope covered with vines.' "Little did the Apostle dream, when he

looked from the vessel's deck to the right, that a ruin.
like that of Sodom and Gomorrah, hung over the fair
cities at the base of the mountain, and that the Jewish
princess Drusilla," before whom he preached at Cæsarea, "and her child, would find their tomb in that ruin."
The coast curves in most graceful forms; and at the
opposite end of this magnificent bay is the little recess
in front of Puteoli. "In all this wide and sunny ex-
panse of blue waters, no part was calmer or more beautiful. Puteoli was the Liverpool of Italy." In its fine
harbor and at its piers lay the Alexandrian grain-ships,
at the end of their long, heavy voyages; and it is said
that crowds of idlers came down to the pier to watch
these ships come in. In this very bay, the sailors of
one of these ships had paid divine honors to the Emperor Augustus, saying that he had made their voyages
safe and their trade prosperous. But now the Alexandrian sailors had a greater than Augustus on board
their vessel, the messenger of a kingdom and a King
which were to outlast the crumbling foundations of his
mighty empire. The Scripture story says nothing to
us of the business of the city, the beauty of its surrounding scenery, the strength and size of the great piers in
the harbor, the mineral springs not far off, nothing of
the fact that here armies embarked for Spain, and here
ambassadors landed from Carthage, but only that Paul
found 'brethren' who wished him to stay in Puteoli 'seven days.' Here too Christ had been preached: here in the distant West, disciples of Jesus were
found, 'brethren' of the one great household of faith:
here the famous Apostle, who had written his instructive letter from Corinth to Rome, was well known. He
was now a prisoner in chains, escaped from shipwreck.
Julius permitted Paul to remain. Why should he not
favor the man who had saved his life?

To go up from Puteoli to Rome was something like going from Liverpool to London. At a little distance from Puteoli, the great southern Roman state road passed, connecting at Brundusium with the road across Macedonia to the east, by a ferry. After a short journey from Puteoli up to Capua, the Roman soldiers and their prisoners would strike the very road which Paul and Luke had before trodden from Philippi to Thessalonica. Leaving the important town of Capua, the soldiers took up the last stage of their journey: the first mile-stone told them it was 'one hundred and twenty-five miles to Rome.' Along the stone pavement, so perfectly fixed in its place that after hundreds of years much of it still remains perfect without repairing, over arched bridges, they came down to Sinuessa, on the sea. Here the hills shut off the view of Mount Vesuvius. Then around the shore of another beautiful bay, they pass through the "long street of Formiœ, with its villas on the sea-side and above it," where Cicero had "one of his favorite retreats from the turmoil of the political world," and where, in a palanquin, he was at last assassinated. Thence, the next principal town is Anxur, on a bold coast of precipices, "with its houses and temples high above the sea." Then the road passes through miles of marshes, and for twenty miles there is a canal by its side, on which the party may have rode, as the poet Horace once did, in a boat drawn by mules. At Appii Forum, "full of low tavern-keepers and boatmen, the mules were unfastened;" and there, a few Christian men, who had heard that the Apostle had landed at Puteoli, and who had hastened to meet him, recognized the Apostle in the crowd and greeted him with holy joy and thanksgiving. Ten miles further on, at Three Taverns, more Christians met him. The weary and worn Apostle took heart and strength when he saw

his friends, (perhaps Aquila and Priscilla were among
them,[4]) and devoutly thanked God for their comfort and
friendship. With this pleasant company, the rest of
the journey quickly passed. Horsemen and carriages,
vehicles of all descriptions, and people of all classes,
increase rapidly. The villas and gardens of wealthy
citizens are all along the slope of the Alban hills. On
the upper side of the road now lies Aricia, the last town
before Rome comes into sight; "and on the hill-side
swarms of beggars beset travellers as they passed. On
the summit of the next rise, Paul of Tarsus would obtain his first view of Rome. No conspicuous building,
rising above the rest, attracted the eye." Ancient
Rome had no dome nor tower, no cupola nor spire.
From where Paul was, it was one wide-spread mass of
buildings, the dwellings of poor and rich mingled together, and the temples and palaces, theatres, colonnades and baths, were not distinguishable. After
descending to the plain, the road is in a straight line,
" with the sepulchres of illustrious families on either
hand. The old pavement then lay through gardens
and new-built houses; and throngs of people, in various
costumes and on various errands, vehicles, horsemen
and foot-passengers, soldiers and laborers, Romans and
foreigners, became more crowded and confusing. The
houses grew closer. They were already in Rome."
Julius and his prisoners had but to move on under the
arch of the gateway, " which was perpetually dripping
with the water of the aqueduct that went over it," and
they were within the walls of the Imperial city.

[4] Romans xvi. 3, 4.

QUESTIONS.

WHAT prediction had been fulfilled ?

What two islands were there called Melita ?

Which one of the two do you think this was ?

What is meant by 'barbarous people' ?

What added to the cold and wet?

What time of the year was it ?

What shows the superstition of the people ?

Did the viper come out of the *fire ?*

Did it *bite* or *sting* Paul?

What did the superstitious people think ?

Why did they change their minds ?   Like what other people ?

What promise of our Saviour was here fulfilled ?

What did Paul probably say when they gave him this name ?

Who lived in these 'quarters' ?   Who was he ?

To whom did the island belong ?

While Paul was guest at his house what did he ?

How long did Paul stay at the house of Publius ?

How do we know that many on the island heard Jesus ?

How long was Paul in Malta ?

What attention was shown while he staid ?   What when he departed ?

What ship was in port on the island ?

Was this harbor at the place of shipwreck ?

What is meant by 'whose sign' ?

Who were Castor and Pollux ?

How do you know what time of year it was when they again set sail ?

What three things were seen after they left Malta ?

What was Syracuse?   What was Sicily called ?

What historical events had taken place in Syracuse and its harbor ?

What celebrated death occurred here ?

The bay ? the island ?   How long in port ?

Did Paul probably go ashore ?   What opportunities ?   What tradition?

In what direction did the ship sail from Syracuse?
> Where was Rhegium?
> What does 'fetched a compass' mean?
> Why did they fetch a circuit? What does a modern
> > traveller say?
> What gods were the supposed protectors of Rhegium?
> Rhegium and Rhegian Pillars?
> How long was the ship at Rhegium? Why?

What celebrated strait? What celebrated dangers?
> How long was the voyage to Puteoli?
> What was to be seen as they neared Cape Minerva?
> > What after passing it?
> What mountain was visible? What was it then?
> Who perished in an eruption? What cities?

Where was Puteoli in respect to Naples and its bay?
> Puteoli? its ships? idlers? divine honors?
> What facts in respect to Puteoli does the Scripture say
> > nothing of?
> How came these brethren at Puteoli?
> Did Paul tarry or did he not?

What road did Paul strike after leaving Puteoli?
> At what point have we supposed? In what direction
> > from Puteoli?
> What other point on the road was as near as this?
> How far was Capua from Rome?
> What is there remarkable about this road?
> What was the first place on the coast?
> What was there of interest at Formiæ? Anxur?
> What marshes further on? What else?
> How did the poet Horace once travel these twenty
> > miles?

What did the poet say Apii Forum was 'full of'?
> Whom did Paul find there?
> How far on was Three Taverns?
> Who may have been among the brethren here?
> How was Paul affected at seeing the Roman brethren?
> The Alban Hills? Aricia? the view of Rome?
> Sepulchres? throngs? horses? gateway?

PAUL'S RESIDENCE IN ROME.

LESSON.

ACTS xxviii. 16–31; PHILIPPIANS i. 13; iv. 22.

WE cannot tell whether the centurion Julius ordered his soldiers with their prisoners through the narrow streets to the Forum, and then to the palace of the Emperor and that part of it called the *prætorium*, or to the great *prætorian camp* outside the city wall. The *prætorium* was the quarters of the Emperor's body-guard; and as it is likely that the Emperor would wish his guard near him, we may reasonably think that the prætorium of which Paul writes from Rome to his Christian friends at Philippi[1] was the barracks of the Imperial guard which were attached to the Emperor's palace. Julius delivered up his prisoners to the *Prefect* of the *Prætorian Guard*, as the Greek word means, or to the Captain of the (Imperial or Emperor's) Guard, as this word is properly translated into English. It was the duty of this *Prefect* "to keep in custody all accused persons who were to be tried before the Emperor." Here, on the Palatine Hill, close by the Forum, surrounded by all the illustrious buildings of Rome, by all the places where the most stirring scenes of Roman history occurred, Paul the prisoner is given up to the

---

[1] The words, 'in the *palace*,' in Philippians i. 13, are in the Greek, 'in the *prætorium*.' It is the same word which we saw was translated 'judgment-hall' in chapter xxiii. 35.

keeping of the Emperor Nero's[2] chief captain. What
a prisoner was he to be in the power of such an Emperor! We may well believe that Julius was reluctant
to give up his prisoner, from very attachment to him.
Nero had not yet arrived at that degree of cruelty which
has made his name a perpetual scorn and terror; and
his *prætorian prefect* at this time was probably Burrus,
who was a good man. We suppose that the statement
which Julius made in reference to Paul's heroic conduct
on the voyage from Judea, and the letter of Festus, obtained for Paul from the captain of the guard, favors
which other prisoners did not enjoy. Burrus soon permitted Paul to dwell by himself: probably in some
other part of the city, only the soldier to whose arm he
was chained must be with him as his guard.

Perhaps Paul went at first to lodge again with Aquila
and Priscilla. Afterwards he had a hired lodging[3] of
his own. He at once inquired what was the state of
the church in the city. As the Emperor Claudius was
dead, who some years before had driven the Jews from
Rome,[4] no doubt many other Jews besides Aquila and
Priscilla returned to Rome. The friends to whom he
sent his greetings from Corinth may have been Jews
expelled from Rome and converted by Paul's preaching while absent. There was Epenetus, one of the first
converted in Achaia, and many others with Greek
names, who may have been converted while away from
Italy.[5] And there were women, too. There were the
kind-hearted Mary, the beloved Persis, the working
Tryphena and Tryphosa, and the respected mother of

[2] Claudius, who was Emperor when Paul was at Corinth the first
time (xviii. 2,) was now dead. Nero was Emperor.

[3] Notice the difference between 'lodging,' in verse 23, and 'own
hired house,' in verse 30.   [4] xviii. 2.

[5] See for all these names Rom. xvi. 5–15.

Rufus. Many others now, we may believe, had been gathered into the church of Christ. And all of them had received much instruction and help from Paul, either directly from his preaching in other cities or from his epistle to the Roman Christians. They must have heard of his seizure at Jerusalem and of his imprisonment at Cæsarea, and must have watched with eagerness when the new Governor Festus was sent to the province of Judea, to see what would become of Paul. They were expecting that he would make that visit which he had promised them,[*] if he should be released. Perhaps they had heard of his appeal to the Emperor. Perhaps they were expecting him as a prisoner, although they may not have known that he was a prisoner till the news came that he was at Puteoli.

But although there was already a Christian church in Rome, there were also multitudes of unconverted Jews. They all lived in a separate part of the city, across the river Tiber. They were not now cruelly treated, but had returned from the exile of Claudius, to live for a while in peace; for " in the early years of Nero, which were distinguished for a mild and lenient government of the empire, the Jews in Rome seem to have enjoyed complete toleration, and to have been a numerous, wealthy and influential community." In Rome, therefore, as everywhere else, Paul spoke to his own countrymen first. He had been in Rome only three days, when he sent for the principal men among the Jews, to tell them why he, their fellow-countryman, was a prisoner, and waiting a trial before the Emperor. These Roman Jews might already have prejudices against the Preacher to the *Gentiles*. Or they might think that, as he had appealed from the Jewish law to the Roman, had refused to go to Jerusalem to be tried and had

[*] Rom. xv. 24.

preferred to come to Rome, that Paul was false to his own country and nation. Paul sets the whole matter right at once, by declaring that he was *forced* to appeal to the Emperor. In his address to them, Paul declares, (1.) His *innocence* of the charges made against him. (Verse 17.)   (2.) That he would have been *acquitted* at Cæsarea, if the Jews had not opposed him contrary to all law. (Verse 18.)   (3.) That he had no complaint to make of a just trial by the laws of his own nation, but that the *unlawful* opposition of the Jews had *forced* him to protect himself by appealing to the Roman law and to Cæsar. (Verse 19.)   (4.) That so far was he from disrespecting the laws and customs of his nation, that his only crime was believing that God would deliver his people by the Messiah, the Hope of Israel. "And therefore he said, 'Men and brethren, *for the Hope of Israel I am bound with this chain.*'"

Their answer was comforting and encouraging to Paul. "They had received no written communication from Judea concerning him;" and none of the Jewish brethren who had arrived at Rome had spoken any evil of him.   They had therefore no *accusation* to make against Paul; but they wished to hear him speak of the *doctrines* which he taught.   They said that these doctrines of Jesus were unpopular everywhere among the Jews, but as Paul was the one great preacher of these doctrines, they would be glad to hear from him the truth in respect to them.   A day was therefore appointed for this purpose, and a meeting, to be held at Paul's lodgings.

On that day Paul spoke long and earnestly to the assembled audience.   His subject was the same great subject which he had preached about at Antioch in Pisidia and at all other places: Jesus of Nazareth, the Messiah   The *proofs* were shown in the prophets and in the law of Moses. All the day long the earnest discussion between Paul and the Jews continued. Some were convinced. Some would not believe, but it was because they were not willing to be convinced. Towards evening those who disbelieved were just about to withdraw, when Paul solemnly warned them of the awful sin of closing their eyes to the light and their ears to the truth. He earnestly warned them with those awful words which Jesus himself had quoted[7] from Isaiah in respect to the stubborn and wilful; and warned them also that the salvation which was intended for them would, if they rejected it, be given to the Gentiles. And so the separation of the Apostle from the Roman Jews took place, they withdrawing to dispute among themselves about this new 'sect,' and Paul remaining to preach Jesus and his salvation to all who would hear.

Burrus permitted Paul now to hire a house of his own, and to preach in it to all who chose to come. How strangely God had ordered Paul's career and answered his prayers! The desire of his heart for years had been to visit Rome, and to preach the Gospel there. He had come to Rome—how differently from what he expected! He was permitted to preach in Rome for two whole years, as freely as at Corinth or at Ephesus. No man could harm him; no enemy could persecute him; for he was under the protection of the Roman Government, the strong arm of the Prætorian Prefect supporting and sustaining him. "We must not forget, however, that he was still a prisoner under military custody, chained by the arm, both day and night, to one of the Imperial body-guard, and thus subjected to the rudeness and caprice of an insolent soldiery." Who can say that even the soldiers chained to his side

---

[7] Matthew xiii. 14, 15; Isaiah vi. 9, 10.

were not subdued by the Gospel of Jesus exemplified in the preaching and in the life of the Great Apostle ?

But though Paul was permitted to preach for so long a time, yet his trial was delayed. Two years seem a long time for a prisoner to wait at the very door of the Emperor for a decision on the charges against him. Four reasons may be given for this delay. First. The *Emperor* might postpone the trial at his own pleasure. Secondly. The *prosecutors* might not have reached Rome. "The Roman courts required the personal presence of the prosecutor." If the prosecuting Jews from Syria did not set sail till spring or summer, they would not reach Rome till the summer or autumn afterwards. If the prosecutor did not appear, the law at this time did not bring the prisoner to the bar and acquit him, but was very indifferent about the time during which he was kept in prison. Thirdly. The *witnesses* might have been delayed. The evidence which failed at Cæsarea would be likely to fail at Rome; and the Jews might demand time to bring more witnesses. The charge of sedition brought against Paul was that he had excited sedition, not in one place only, but throughout the world,[*] that is, everywhere throughout the empire, and time might be required to collect witnesses from Judea, from Syria, from Cilicia, from Pisidia, from Macedonia, from Achaia, from "all the cities from Damascus to Ephesus." This would take a year or more. Fourthly. The *official notice* of *the case,* sent by Festus, might have been lost in the shipwreck at Malta. No case of appeal to the Emperor could be tried without such a notice. It would take no little time to send to Festus for a new notice.

Paul was not only preaching during all this time, but caring personally for his converted friends in Rome,

[*] xxiv. 5.

and instructing his converts in distant countries and cities. Letters and messengers were sent from the ' hired house' in Rome to the churches over which he watched with such tender care. During these two years were undoubtedly written

THE EPISTLE TO THE COLOSSIANS; and by the messenger who carried it to Colosse was sent also

THE EPISTLE TO PHILEMON, who is thought to have lived in Colosse ;

THE EPISTLE TO THE EPHESIANS ; and

THE EPISTLE TO THE PHILIPPIANS.

Paul was not without his near and intimate friends at this time. Near him in the city must have resided some of those faithful companions who were true to him in adversity. Timothy was with him perhaps in his own house.[9] Luke, his fellow-traveller through the long and fearful voyage, was there also and was remembered to the brethren of Colosse[10] in the letter. Tychicus, who five years before had travelled with him from Corinth through Troas to Ephesus,[11] was his messenger to carry his letters to Ephesus and to Colosse.[12] Mark, whom Paul would not take with him on his second journey, was again with him.[13] Demas, who afterwards forsook him for his love for the world, was there.[14] Aristarchus,[15] who, when at Ephesus, had been carried by the mob into the theatre, and who came with Paul from Cæsarea,[15] and Epaphras,[16] were his fellow-prisoners. His imprisonment was cheered, too, by an occasional visit of a Christian brother from some one of the many places in which he preached, as when the

---

[9] Col. i. 1, 2; Philemon 1; Philip. i. 1.

[10] Col. iv. 14; Philemon 24.   [11] Acts xx. 4.

[12] Eph. vi. 21, 22; Col. iv. 7, 8.   [13] Col. iv. 10; Philemon 24.

[14] Phil. 24; Col. iv. 14; II. Tim. iv. 10.

[15] Acts xix. 29; xxvii. 2.   [16] Col. i. 7; Philemon 23.

warm-hearted Epaphroditus of Philippi came to Paul, bringing him a present of contributions for his support,[17] and bearing back with him, when he had recovered from sickness, the Letter to his steadfast and much praised Christian friends in Philippi.[18]

[17] Philip. iv. 18. See the margin.

[18] Philip. ii. 25–30. The Epistle to Philippi is full of praise, and has hardly any censure. The simple-hearted faith of Lydia and of the jailer was enduring in its effects.

QUESTIONS.

To what place in Rome was Paul taken?

What does the verse in Philippians mean?

What two places were there with this name?

Who was the Captain of the Guard? What was his duty?

Who was Emperor at this time?

Who was 'Captain of the Guard' during these years?

Why was Paul permitted to dwell by himself? Who was with him?

What difference between the Apostle's dwelling at first and afterwards?

Why had many Jews no doubt returned to Rome?

What converts perhaps? What women?

What instruction had all the Roman Christians received from Paul?

What other Jews were there in Rome? Where did they live? Why were they not persecuted?

Why did Paul send for them? What persons among them?

What is the first point in Paul's address to them?

What is the second point?

What is the third point? 'Spake against *it*:' against what?

What does 'had aught to accuse my nation of' mean?

What is the fourth point?

What is meant by the Hope of Israel?

How was it that Paul was a prisoner 'for this cause'?

What kind of answer did the Jews make to Paul?

Do you think they had heard nothing at all of Paul's arrest and trial?

What kind of communication may 'letters' mean?

What did they wish to hear from Paul? Why?

What arrangement was made?

Was there no synagogue in Rome?

Show how the argument of Paul's address was the same as at Antioch in Pisidia.

How long did the discussion continue?

What was the result?

What warning did the Apostle give? To whom?

Who used this warning before Paul? From what prophet is it taken?

What does 'hearing, ye shall hear,' mean?

What is the meaning of 'waxed gross'?

Did God mean to *prevent* their being converted?

What prediction is there in the last words of this warning?

What especial force was there in such a prediction in Rome?

Has the prediction of this warning been fulfilled in respect to both Jews and Gentiles?

To what Gentiles now does this warning apply as well as to those Jews?

What division took place after this time?

Where did Paul dwell? Why must Roman soldiers have heard him preach?

What especial advantage for preaching had Paul now?

What three reasons may be given why Paul's trial was delayed so long?

What else besides preaching was Paul doing during this time?

What two Epistles were probably sent together? Why?

What other two Epistles are thought to have been written there?

How do you show that Timothy was with Paul?

What other fellow-traveller?

Who carried the letters to Ephesus and Colosse? Show it.

What early companion was in Rome? What 'fellow-prisoners'?

Who visited Paul in his imprisonment?

To what place did he carry an Epistle?

Prove that he had been sick.

What is a pleasant peculiarity of this Epistle?

From what persons in Rome did Paul send salutations to these Christian brethren?

Fifty-second Sunday.

THE TRIAL AND THE EXECUTION.

LESSON.

Acts xxviii. 30, 31; Philippians i. 12–14, iv. 22; Philemon 9
II. Timothy iv. 6–8, 16, 17.

WHEREVER Paul's residence was in the city, there
was a Roman soldier always with him. Of course
it could not always be the same soldier; and in the
course of two years, many changes were made. In this
way many soldiers saw Paul and knew him. Sometimes too he went perhaps to the barracks of the Prætorian Guard, whether the *Prætorium* was near the
palace of the Emperor or was a camp without the city.
So remarkable a prisoner must have excited great attention and great talk among the soldiers. At length
Paul could write what he did to his Christian friends
at Philippi : that his troubles had helped the preaching
of the Gospel, for his imprisonment for Christ's sake
was well known in all the *prætorium :* [1] that his Christian brethren were more bold to speak out for Christ,
on account of the well-known fact of his imprisonment
and the *cause* of it. God's wise and mysterious purpose was now seen in sending Paul *as a prisoner* to
Rome. How could he in any other way have gotten
into the Emperor's very household ? But now converts
were made even among the Emperor's guard or the
Emperor's servants. Cruel soldiers, under their still
more cruel master, Nero, sent by him perhaps to do

---

[1] 'In all the palace ;' in the Greek, 'in all the *prætorium.*'

some heartless murder or barbarous injustice, must have been surprised at the uniform goodness of such a man, and tenderly touched by the Christian love which bound Paul and his converts together. Servants of the royal family, familiar with the crime and the shame of the Emperor's palace, and disgusted with all the horrible vice they saw, may have heard the words of the aged and venerable Paul, telling of another and a better life, of sins forgiven and real happiness received through Jesus the Messiah. Whoever these converts ' of Cæsar's household ' were, they sent their Christian salutations to their brethren of Philippi in the letter Paul sent by Epaphroditus.

Nero was already growing more public in his acts of cruelty. He had divorced and murdered one wife to marry another. The wicked woman who was now his Empress, professed to be a proselyte to the Jewish religion ; and any man of less courage than Paul might have trembled when he thought that he was soon to be tried by an unprincipled Emperor, whose unscrupulous wife might eagerly listen to the accusations of his enemies.

———

We have now come to the end of the Acts of the Apostles. It did not seem best to the spirit of inspiration that the last years of Paul's life and his death should be described in the sacred Scriptures. Yet how eagerly we desire to know how the last hours of the great Apostle's life were spent, what kind of a death he died and in what manner he met death. It is surely not wrong for us to gather together what testimony we can about these things, and so complete the biography of this great man.[2]

---

[2] This testimony is gathered from those writers in the first centuries, called the early Christian Fathers. There have been two opin-

" It was universally believed by the ancient Church that Paul's appeal to Cæsar ended successfully; that he was acquitted; and that he spent some years in freedom ' before he was again imprisoned and condemned.' Though there is not very much evidence on this subject, " it is *all one way.*" ' According to this supposition, the story of the rest of his life will be given, dividing it into three parts: his *first trial:* his *absence* from *Rome:* his *arrest* and *second trial,* and *condemnation.*

After the long delay of two years, it is supposed Paul's trial was at length ordered by the Emperor. The Emperors Tiberius and Claudius usually heard appeals made to them in the Forum; but Nero held his great tribunal in the Imperial Palace, on the Palatine Hill. There, " at one end of a splendid hall, lined with the precious marbles of Egypt and of Lybia, we must imagine the Cæsar seated." Around him, we see twenty counsellors, men of the highest rank. Two are Consuls, others are high magistrates of Rome and the rest are Senators. " Over this distinguished bench of judges, presided the Absolute Ruler of the whole civilized world," Cæsar Nero, whose terrible power made men tremble with fear and horror, whose vices made them despise him, whose murder of his wife and mother and adopted brother was only the beginning of more general cruelty throughout Italy, and whose pitiable love of

ions among learned men in respect to the *time* of Paul's death, one class holding that Paul was executed at the end of his first imprisonment, the other that he lived some years after his first trial, and was executed after a second trial. There is a general and substantial agreement in respect to the *fact* and the *method* of Paul's execution, and no contradiction; and we have given the opinion of those who believe there was a second imprisonment, so as to give the fuller account of the two. The lesson would be made too long by giving quotations from the fathers. The principal names are, Clement, Tertullian, Eusebius, Chrysostom and Jerome.

vulgar applause led him to degrade himself by " publicly performing as a musician on the stage and as a
charioteer in the races."

" Before the tribunal of this blood-stained adulterer,
Paul the Apostle was now brought in fetters, by his
military guard." Paul did not quail. God, who guarded his life, was greater than Nero ; and in God was his
trust. The prosecutor was called to bring forward his
witnesses. Proof of the charges was required : that he
had disturbed the worship of the Jews, secured to them
by law ; that he had polluted their temple ; that he
had broken the peace of the empire by stirring up sedition in many cities, as the ringleader of the Nazarene
sect. The last charge would be considered a solemn
crime by the body of counsellors and by the Emperor.
Perhaps there were witnesses from Jerusalem, from
Ephesus, from Corinth, to give testimony against him.
Perhaps another orator, like Tertullus, complimented
and flattered the Emperor, while he painted in dark
colors the great offences of Paul. From his previous
speeches, we can think how Paul would reply. The
testimony of those present with him in the temple,
would show that he did not profane the temple. He
would show that he had reverenced and had not violated the law of the Jewish religion ; that he belonged
to one of several sects of the Jews. He would prove
that his teachings everywhere, in his letters as well as
in his preaching, had been to submit to the law of the
empire. The very letter he had sent to Rome to his
friends, (and which may have been shown in the court,)
instead of stirring up sedition against the government,
had taught them to submit to the '*powers that be.*' [3] It
may be that he spoke again of the doctrines of his sect,

---

[3] Romans xiii. 1.

and reasoned of resurrection, righteousness, temperance and judgment to come. Nero was too much hardened in crime and shame to tremble, like Felix, at these awful realities.

" When both sides had been heard, and the witnesses all examined and cross-examined, (a process which perhaps lasted several days,) the judgment of the court was taken. Each of the counsellors gave his opinion in writing to the Emperor, who never discussed the judgment with his counsellors, as better Emperors had done, but after reading their opinions, gave sentence according to his own pleasure." When we think what the Emperor was and that his wicked wife sympathized with the Jews, we might expect that Paul would have been condemned. But God so ordered it that the Emperor, from mere caprice, or from contempt of the petty quarrels of Jews, or for some other reason, acquitted Paul, ordered his chains to be struck off and that he should be set at liberty.[4]

With what profound thanksgiving to God did the Christians of Rome, and indeed everywhere, where Paul had been, receive the news of the Emperor's decree. The great Apostle was now free to go, and to preach again for his divine Master.

Paul's *absence from Rome* is thought to have been about five years. These five years are supposed to have been spent in the following manner. First, he went through Macedonia to Asia Minor. Just before his trial, in his letter to the Philippians, he wrote that he hoped to visit Philippi soon,[5] and in his letter to Philemon in Colosse, he told Philemon to *prepare him a lodging*, for he trusted his prayers for his deliverance

---

[4] We may suppose, however, that either the prosecutor or the witnesses did not appear, and that Paul was dismissed from lack of evidence.
[5] Philippians ii. 24, 23.

would be answered.[6] If he went to Philippi and to 'Asia,' his journey would be down the great road, through Italy, to Brundusium, across the Adriatic to Dyrrachium, through Illyricum on the great road to Thessalonica and then through familiar places to Philippi. Then after a happy, glad time with his Philippian children, he went on to Ephesus[7] and to the surrounding towns, among which was Colosse, and enjoyed the friendship of Philemon and the ' brethren,' staying at the ' lodgings ' prepared. The next year, it is supposed, he took his long thought of[8] journey into Spain. It is not likely that he would go by Rome, for the fury of Nero had now broken out in persecution.

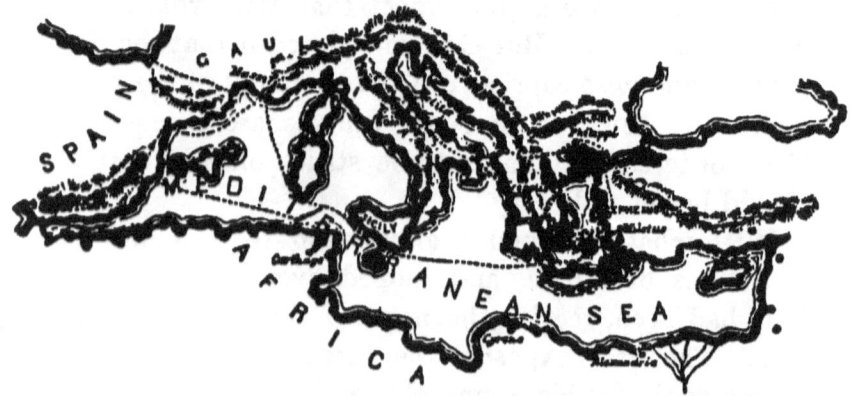

SUPPOSED JOURNEYS OF PAUL AFTER THE FIRST TRIAL.

If he went at all, he probably went by sea from Ephesus to Massilia, from which city he could, on any day, reach towns in Spain. In Spain, he is thought to have labored two years, founding churches along the coast in the principal cities. It was just about the time that he took this voyage that the great fire in Rome occurred which was the occasion of Nero's violent perse-

[6] Philemon 22.
[7] Can you reconcile this supposition with Acts xx. 25?
[8] Romans xv. 24, 28.

cution of the Christians. Paul would not of course go back to Rome at this time. He more likely sailed back to Ephesus. He had now become an aged man, between sixty and seventy years old.[9]

Timothy was now at Ephesus as the preacher and pastor of the Ephesian church. From Ephesus Paul went to Macedonia[10] for a while, where he wrote

THE FIRST EPISTLE TO TIMOTHY,

in which he gave Timothy instructions about the sacred office of the ministry, about worship and about the character of deacons.[11] The aged Apostle is about now to leave his mantle on his beloved son in the ministry. Soon after, Paul returned to Ephesus.[12] And afterwards he made, it would seem, a short visit with Titus to the island of Crete. Titus he left in Crete,[13] and soon after his return to Ephesus wrote to him

THE EPISTLE TO TITUS,

in which he gives Titus instruction in respect to the churches which Christians had already founded in Crete. If this letter to Titus was written at Ephesus,

---

[9] At his conversion he was thirty years old or over, (see page 16.)

	30 years.
'Fourteen years after,' (Gal. ii. 1, Acts xv. 2,) he went from Antioch to Jerusalem with the 'difficult question,'	14 years.
His second journey and stay at Antioch was about	3 years.
His third journey was about	4 "
At Cæsarea,	2 "
Journey to Rome and in Rome, nearly	8 "
From his acquittal to Ephesus, were about	4 "
	60 years old or over.

[10] I. Timothy i. 3. [11] I. Timothy iii. 1–6, 14, 15, 8–10.
[12] iii. 14. [13] Titus i. 5.

it shows where Paul was intending to spend the next
winter, for he directs Titus to come to him before the
next winter at Nicopolis,[14] a town of considerable importance in Illyricum; and if the second letter to Timothy was written afterwards at Rome, it seems to show
that Paul went from Ephesus to Miletus and to Corinth,[15] on the way to Nicopolis and on his way to
Rome; for he says that one of his fellow-travellers was
left at Miletus sick, and that Erastus, the former Treasurer of Corinth, had staid behind in that city. From
Nicopolis, perhaps Paul hoped to visit and to preach in
many of the towns of Illyricum.

Paul was now not very far from Rome. The Christians of Rome had been accused of setting fire to the
city. Nero had persecuted them with savage fury.
The first great slaughter of Christian martyrs had
begun. Paul was the very chief of the Christians. He
would soon be known, wherever he was, and everywhere he would have enemies. Perhaps for this reason he
had not remained long in one place except in distant
Spain. "There is nothing improbable in supposing
that, upon the testimony of some informer, he was arrested by the magistrates of Nicopolis and forwarded
to Rome for trial. The second imprisonment was severer than the first. It was now dangerous for Christians
to make themselves known publicly as friends of the
Apostle. The horrible wickedness of Nero had been
fully and publicly seen. The people were greatly excited and indignant on account of the tremendous con-
flagration which had burnt to ashes half their city. Nero
himself was accused of setting the city on fire. The
unprincipled and murderous Emperor tried to turn suspicion from himself, by accusing the Christians of the
crime and by persecuting them. "Some were cruci-

[14] iii. 12.   [15] II. Tim. iv. 20.

fied : some were disguised in the skins of beasts and
hunted to death by dogs : some were wrapped in robes
impregnated with inflammable materials and set on
fire at night to illuminate the circus and the gardens of
Nero. 'A very great multitude' perished, the whole
body of Christians being considered as involved in the
crime of firing the city." This was in the first excitement, and the first excitement was past when Paul
reached Rome. But the city had in it many *informers*,
who were ready to accuse any unhappy Christian of
this great crime. It could not have been long before
Paul was brought up to the court. His case was not
now tried by the Emperor, but by the single judge
whom the wicked Emperor had appointed over the
city. At the first hearing he escaped, although his
friends all deserted him.[16] 'Nevertheless,' he wrote to
his dear son Timothy, 'the Lord stood by me and
strengthened me ; and I was delivered out of the mouth
of the lion."[17] What the charge at this first hearing
was is not told us : perhaps the charge of firing the
city. Paul perhaps was able to make it appear to his
judge that he was innocent of that charge ; for he was
absent from the city at the time. While in prison
again, waiting a hearing probably on another charge,
the venerable Apostle wrote his last letter. His heart
yearned over Timothy, and he longed to have him a
faithful minister of the Messiah. He wrote therefore
to urge upon Timothy his solemn duties,

THE SECOND EPISTLE TO TIMOTHY.

He did not expect to escape condemnation and execution ; but he wrote like one whose spirit was lifted far

---

[16] II. Timothy iv. 16, 17.

[17] It may be that Paul actually saved himself from being thrown to
the wild beasts by declaring himself a *Roman citizen.*

above all human suffering. Almost alone in that great and wicked city, Luke the only one of his constant friends who was with him,[18] with an unjust sentence, the bench and the sword of the executioner plainly in the path before him, Paul is a *triumphing conqueror.* Hear the Christian hero: "I AM NOW READY TO BE OFFERED, AND THE TIME OF MY DEPARTURE IS AT HAND. I HAVE FOUGHT A GOOD FIGHT, I HAVE FINISHED MY COURSE, I HAVE KEPT THE FAITH: HENCEFORTH THERE IS LAID UP FOR ME A CROWN OF RIGHTEOUSNESS, WHICH THE LORD, THE RIGHTEOUS JUDGE, SHALL GIVE ME AT THAT DAY."

In these, his last days, he cannot forget those dear friends who had been his comfort in so many hours of trial, Aquila and Priscilla, who had fled, we may suppose, from the persecution to Ephesus,[19] and he could but wish for the kind sympathy and presence of some of his faithful fellow-laborers. He urges Timothy to come to him.[20] He had no longer any reproach for Mark, but wishes him to come to him in his old age.[20] If Timothy and Mark reached Rome, to cheer their great teacher's last days, there could have been but a very little time before his condemnation. We do not know what crime Paul was accused of, nor what was the reason for the sudden end of his trial; but we know that he was condemned.

The privileges of a Roman citizen saved Paul no doubt from the wild beasts, from torture, or from crucifixion. He was sentenced to be beheaded, according to general tradition; and tradition says too that the place was outside the gate, on the road to Ostia, the harbor of Rome. (See map on page 327.) The throngs of people, merchants, sailors, travellers, letter-bearers,

---

[18] II. Tim. iv. 11, 10, 12. [19] Verse 19. [20] Verse 11, see page 60.

messengers, priests, citizens from all provinces, strangers from all countries, who hastened that day from the harbor to Rome and from Rome to the harbor, little knew that a greater hero than Roman historian or Roman poet ever praised was being led out to execution. "Through the dust and tumult of those busy crowds the small troop of soldiers silently threaded their way, under the bright sky of an Italian midsummer." There, not far distant from the city, the axe of the lictor or the sword of a military executioner severed the head of Paul the Apostle from his body; and the heroic and enraptured spirit took its eager flight to the presence of Jesus. "Weeping friends took up the corpse and carried it for burial to those subterranean labyrinths where, through many ages of oppression, the persecuted church found refuge for the living and sepulchres for the dead."

The Roman emperors are dead: the great Augustus could not preserve his empire from destruction after he was gone: the detestable Nero is remembered only to be execrated. But Paul of Tarsus is not dead. He lives in all the churches of Christendom to-day. He is revered by thousands and by millions as a great teacher. The kingdom he helped to establish is stronger now than when he was on earth, a *kingdom which cannot be moved.* Multitudes of Gentiles thank the great Apostle to the Gentiles for his sufferings and courage and martyrdom. And in the Last Great Day myriads of souls will thank him for that life and those words which taught them the forgiveness of sin through JESUS OF NAZARETH, THE MESSIAH OF THE WORLD.

QUESTIONS.

WHAT wise providence is now seen in sending Paul to Rome?

How were Paul's 'bonds manifest in all the prætorium'?

What was the effect of Paul's imprisonment in Rome on the Christians there?

How was Nero changing about this time?

Who was the Empress?

Have we *any* account of Paul's last days in the Scriptures?

From what authorities is the remaining narrative of Paul's life gathered?

What two opinions have there been in respect to the *time* of the Apostle's death?[1]

In what respect do the opinions agree?

Which one of the two general opinions is here adopted?

Into what three parts is the remainder of his life divided?

Where did Tiberius and Claudius hear their appeals? Nero?

Who sat with him? Three classes?

Nero's power? vices? murders? love of applause?

What proof would be required at the trial?

Which charge would be thought to contain the greatest crime?

How can we tell what Paul would answer?

What especial evidence could be produced in court against the principal charge?

How was the decision given?

What reasons may be given for Nero's acquittal?

How long is it thought that Paul was absent from Rome?

What reason is there for supposing he went to Philippi?

What for thinking he went to Colosse?

Over what route would he go to these places?

Can you reconcile his visiting Ephesus with Acts xx. 25?

Where did he go the next year?

What is the probable route?

How long is it supposed that he was in Spain?

[1] On either supposition the passages in the lesson refer to the closing scenes of his life.

To what place did he return?

Show what Paul's age must have been at this time.

In what passage does Paul allude to his age?

Who was at Ephesus? What Epistle did Paul write?

Point out the passages which show the object of his letter.

What Epistle was next written?

Where was Titus? Show what the instructions to him were about.

What indication do you get from this Epistle in respect to other places where Paul lived?

On the supposition made, where did Paul go next?

What would he do there?

Where was Paul arrested? For what reason?

How did the second imprisonment differ from the first?

Why was it dangerous for a Christian to be in Rome?

Would Paul be tried by the Emperor?

What happened at his 'first answer'?

Who 'stood by him'? What does the rest of that verse mean?

What was Paul's last Epistle?[2]

Who only was with him?

What was plainly before him?

Who conquers, Paul or Nero?

What is the figure in the words written to Timothy? Show the points of comparison.

What especial kind wishes and requests of affection does he express?

What advantage would Paul's Roman citizenship be to him now?

Where does tradition say Paul was executed?

How was he executed?

What is the result of Paul's whole life?

What was the one great lesson which he everywhere taught?

If the evidence of Paul's arguments and life do not lead you to believe in Jesus as your Messiah and Saviour, can you be less guilty than the Jews who rejected the Messiahship of Jesus?

[2] The Epistle to the Hebrews has not been included in these lessons.

www.ingramcontent.com/pod-product-compliance
Lightning Source LLC
Chambersburg PA
CBHW022015110726
47901CB00006B/1531